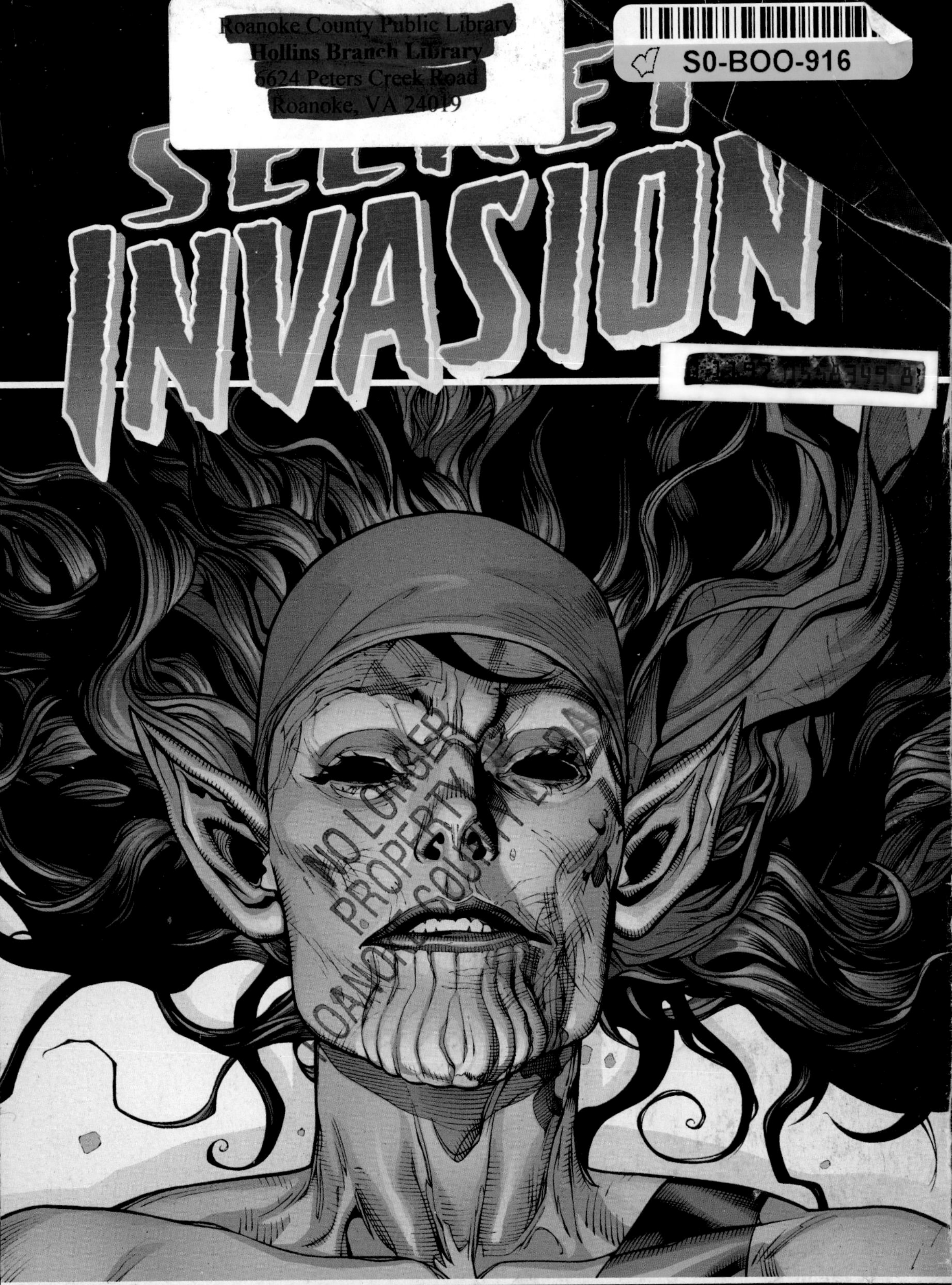
SECRET
INVASION

SECRET INVASION

WRITER
Brian Michael Bendis

PENCILER
Leinil Yu

INKER
Mark Morales

COLORIST
Laura Martin
with Emily Warren & Christina Strain

LETTERER
Chris Eliopoulos

COVER ART
Gabriele Dell'Otto

ASSISTANT EDITOR
Thomas Brennan

ASSOCIATE EDITORS
Molly Lazer & Jeanine Schaefer

EDITOR
Tom Brevoort

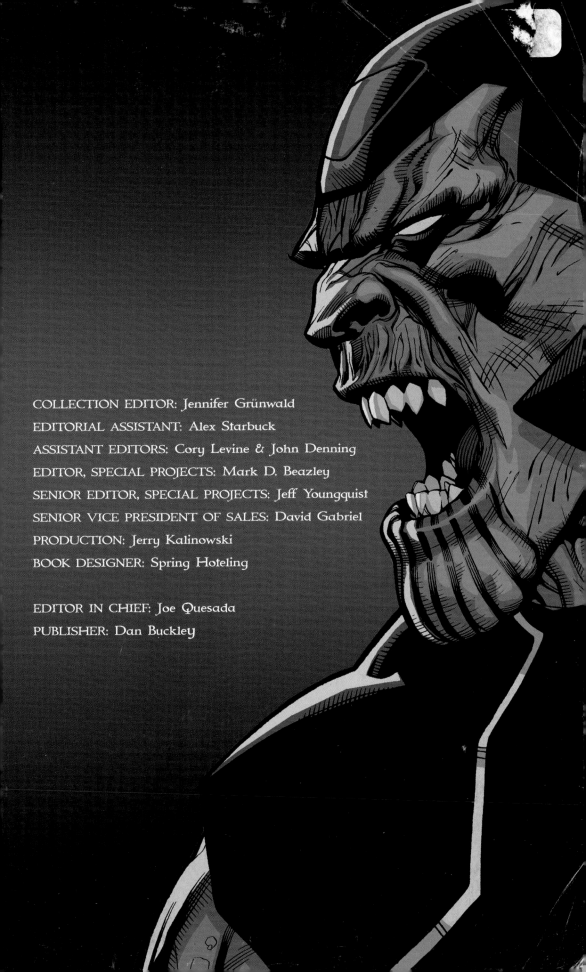

COLLECTION EDITOR: Jennifer Grünwald

EDITORIAL ASSISTANT: Alex Starbuck

ASSISTANT EDITORS: Cory Levine & John Denning

EDITOR, SPECIAL PROJECTS: Mark D. Beazley

SENIOR EDITOR, SPECIAL PROJECTS: Jeff Youngquist

SENIOR VICE PRESIDENT OF SALES: David Gabriel

PRODUCTION: Jerry Kalinowski

BOOK DESIGNER: Spring Hoteling

EDITOR IN CHIEF: Joe Quesada

PUBLISHER: Dan Buckley

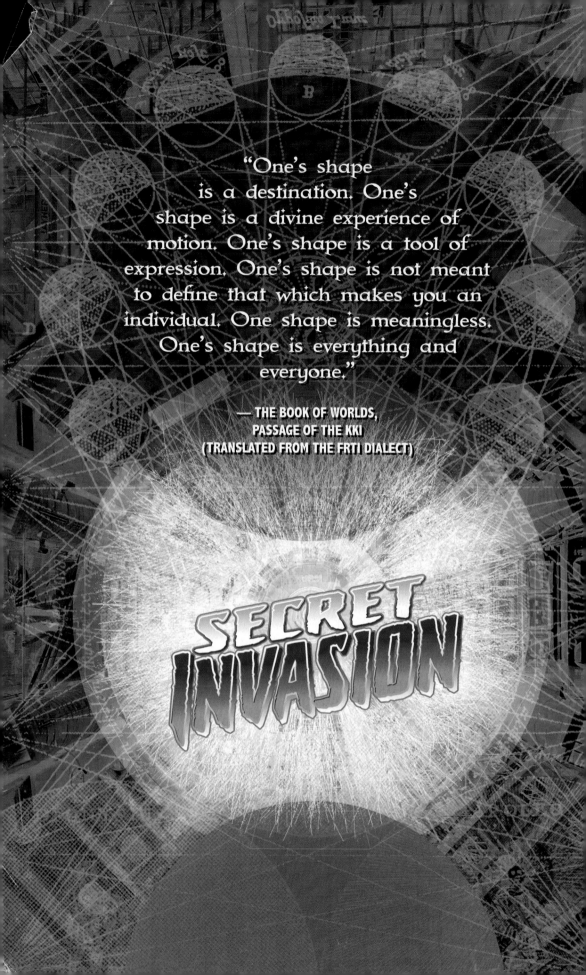

"One's shape
is a destination. One's
shape is a divine experience of
motion. One's shape is a tool of
expression. One's shape is not meant
to define that which makes you an
individual. One shape is meaningless.
One's shape is everything and
everyone."

— THE BOOK OF WORLDS,
PASSAGE OF THE KKI
(TRANSLATED FROM THE FRTI DIALECT)

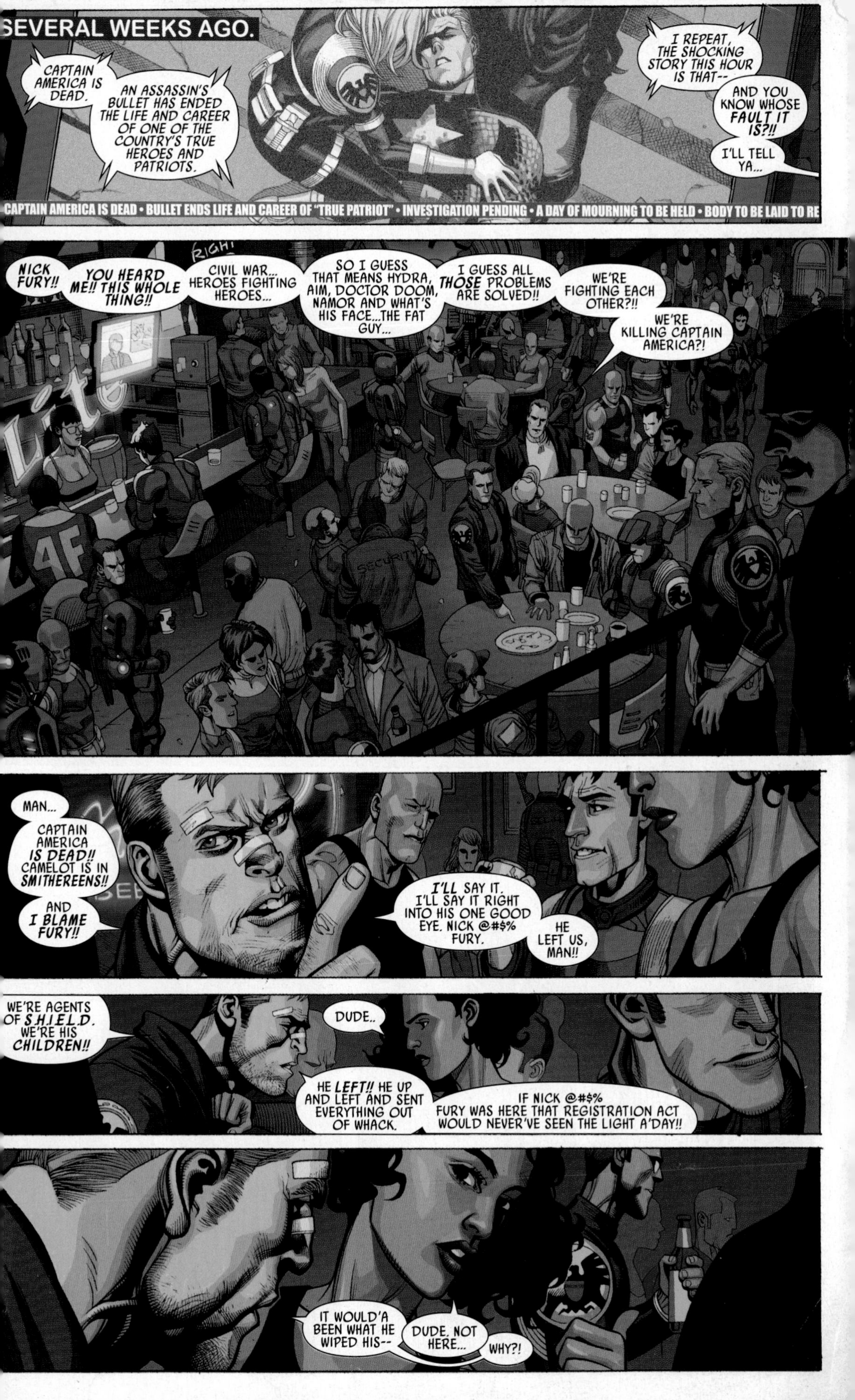

SEVERAL WEEKS AGO.
CAPTAIN AMERICA IS DEAD.
AN ASSASSIN'S BULLET HAS ENDED THE LIFE AND CAREER OF ONE OF THE COUNTRY'S TRUE HEROES AND PATRIOTS.
I REPEAT, THE SHOCKING STORY THIS HOUR IS THAT--
AND YOU KNOW WHOSE FAULT IT IS?!!
I'LL TELL YA...
CAPTAIN AMERICA IS DEAD • BULLET ENDS LIFE AND CAREER OF "TRUE PATRIOT" • INVESTIGATION PENDING • A DAY OF MOURNING TO BE HELD • BODY TO BE LAID TO RE
NICK FURY!!
YOU HEARD ME!! THIS WHOLE THING!!
RIGHT
CIVIL WAR... HEROES FIGHTING HEROES...
SO I GUESS THAT MEANS HYDRA, AIM, DOCTOR DOOM, NAMOR AND WHAT'S HIS FACE...THE FAT GUY...
I GUESS ALL THOSE PROBLEMS ARE SOLVED!!
WE'RE FIGHTING EACH OTHER?!!
WE'RE KILLING CAPTAIN AMERICA?!
4F
SECURITY
MAN...
CAPTAIN AMERICA IS DEAD!! CAMELOT IS IN SMITHEREENS!!
AND I BLAME FURY!!
I'LL SAY IT. I'LL SAY IT RIGHT INTO HIS ONE GOOD EYE. NICK @#$% FURY.
HE LEFT US, MAN!!
WE'RE AGENTS OF S.H.I.E.L.D. WE'RE HIS CHILDREN!!
DUDE..
HE LEFT!! HE UP AND LEFT AND SENT EVERYTHING OUT OF WHACK.
IF NICK @#$% FURY WAS HERE THAT REGISTRATION ACT WOULD NEVER'VE SEEN THE LIGHT A'DAY!!
IT WOULD'A BEEN WHAT HE WIPED HIS--
DUDE. NOT HERE...
WHY?!

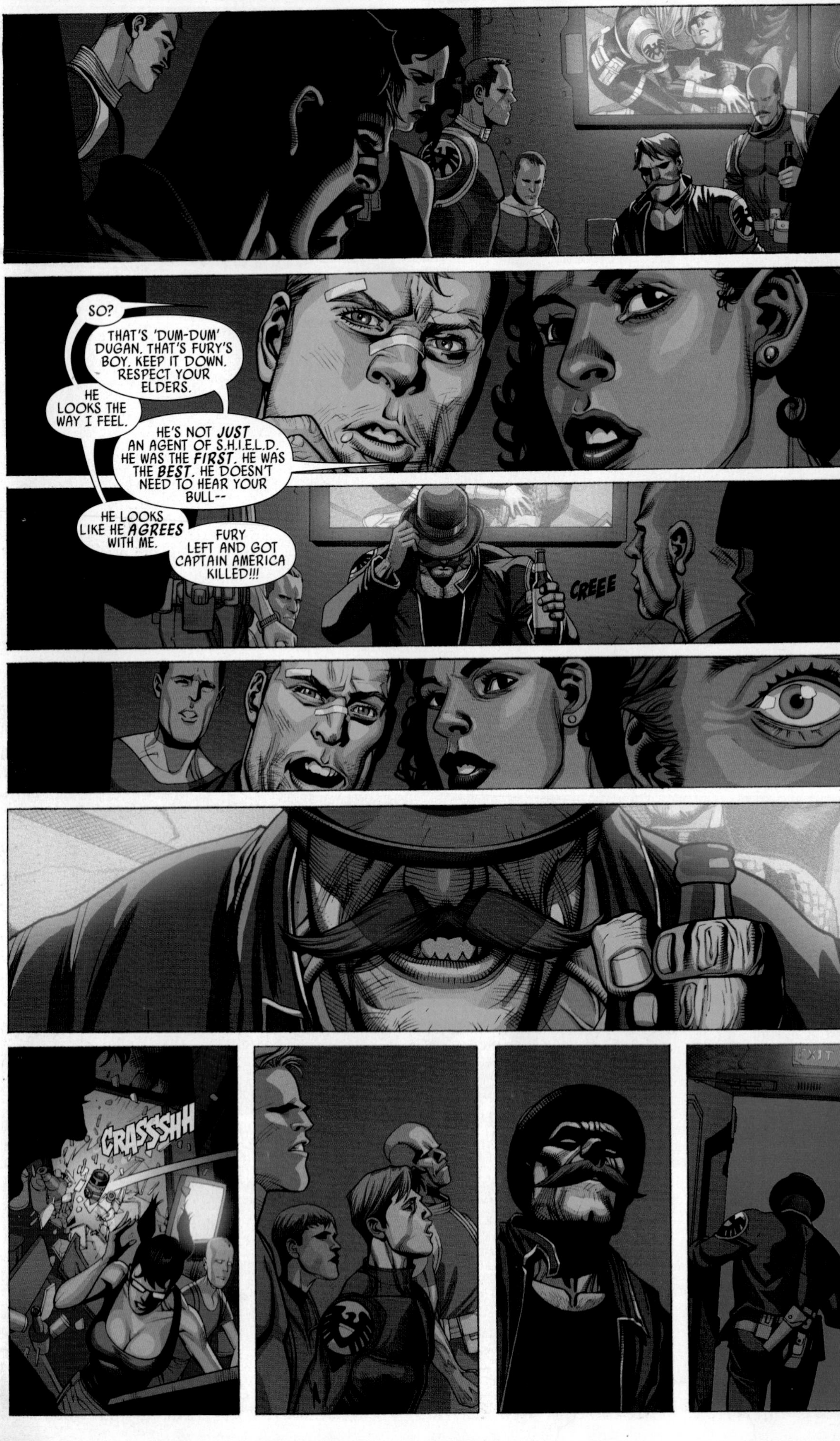

SO?
THAT'S 'DUM-DUM' DUGAN. THAT'S FURY'S BOY. KEEP IT DOWN. RESPECT YOUR ELDERS.
HE LOOKS THE WAY I FEEL.
HE'S NOT JUST AN AGENT OF S.H.I.E.L.D. HE WAS THE FIRST. HE WAS THE BEST. HE DOESN'T NEED TO HEAR YOUR BULL--
HE LOOKS LIKE HE AGREES WITH ME.
FURY LEFT AND GOT CAPTAIN AMERICA KILLED!!!
CREEE
CRASSSHH
EXIT

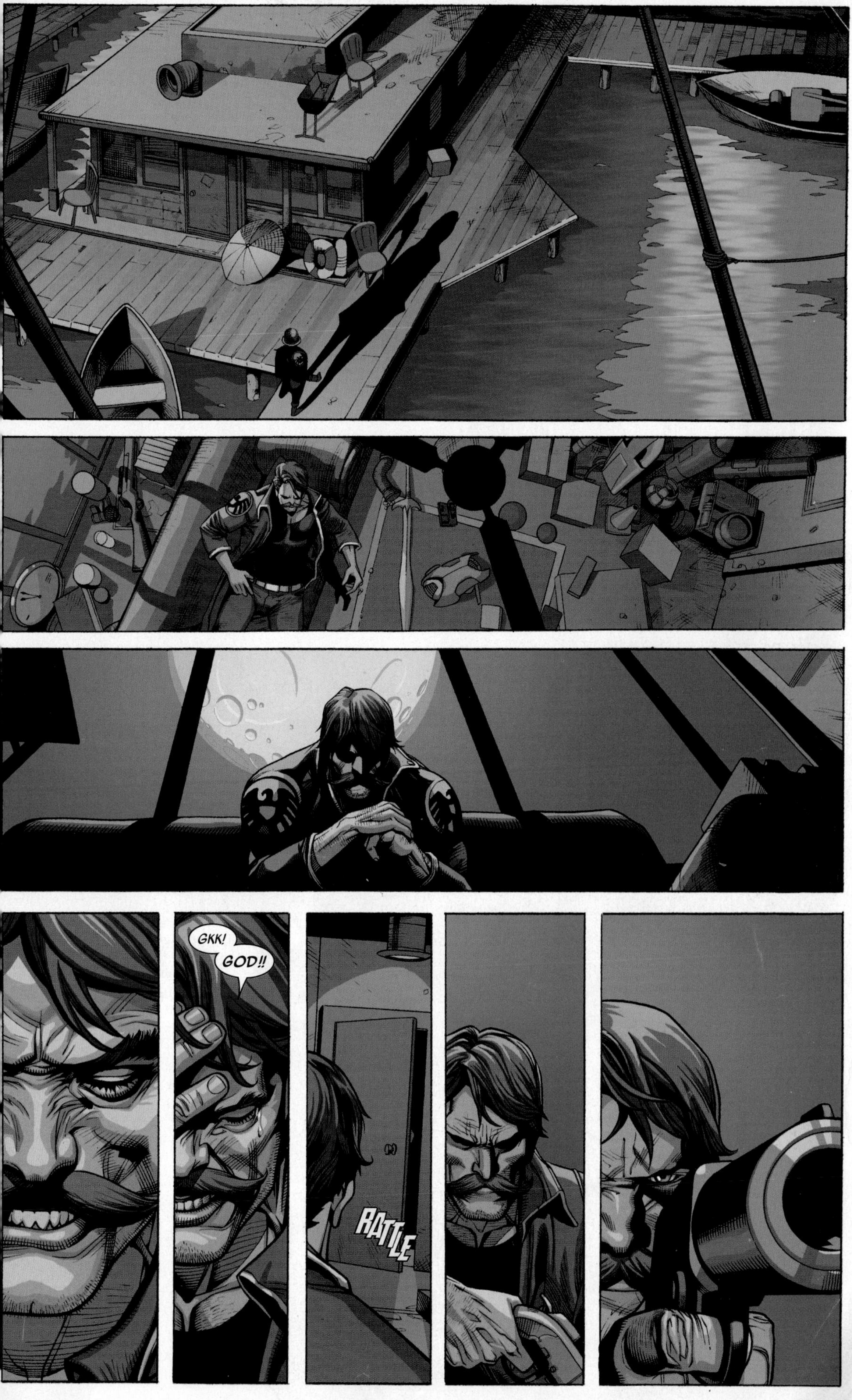
GKK!
GOD!!
RATTLE

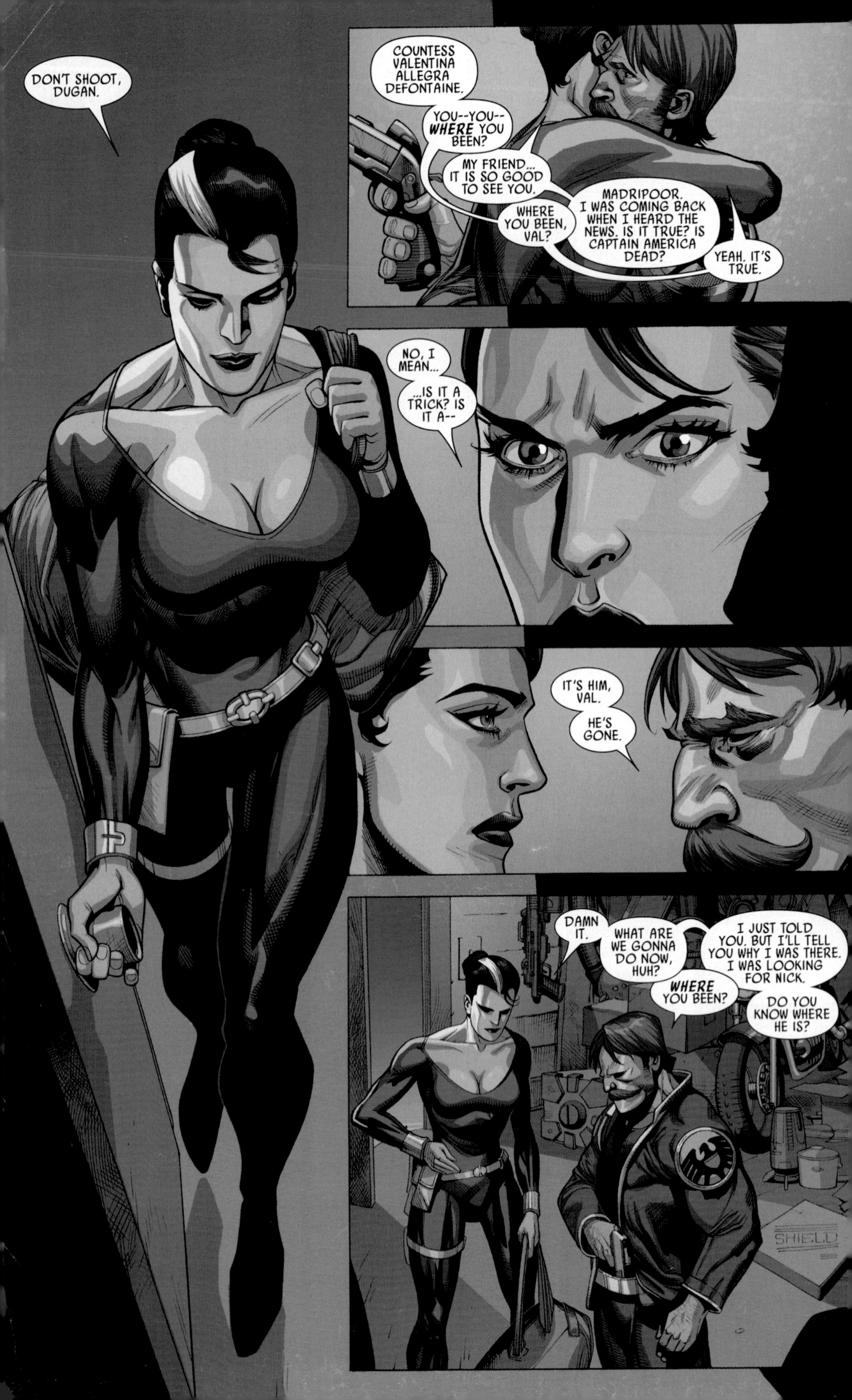
DON'T SHOOT, DUGAN.
COUNTESS VALENTINA ALLEGRA DEFONTAINE.
YOU--YOU--WHERE YOU BEEN?
MY FRIEND... IT IS SO GOOD TO SEE YOU.
WHERE YOU BEEN, VAL?
MADRIPOOR. I WAS COMING BACK WHEN I HEARD THE NEWS. IS IT TRUE? IS CAPTAIN AMERICA DEAD?
YEAH. IT'S TRUE.
NO, I MEAN...
...IS IT A TRICK? IS IT A--
IT'S HIM, VAL.
HE'S GONE.
DAMN IT.
WHAT ARE WE GONNA DO NOW, HUH?
WHERE YOU BEEN?
I JUST TOLD YOU. BUT I'LL TELL YOU WHY I WAS THERE. I WAS LOOKING FOR NICK.
DO YOU KNOW WHERE HE IS?
SHIELD

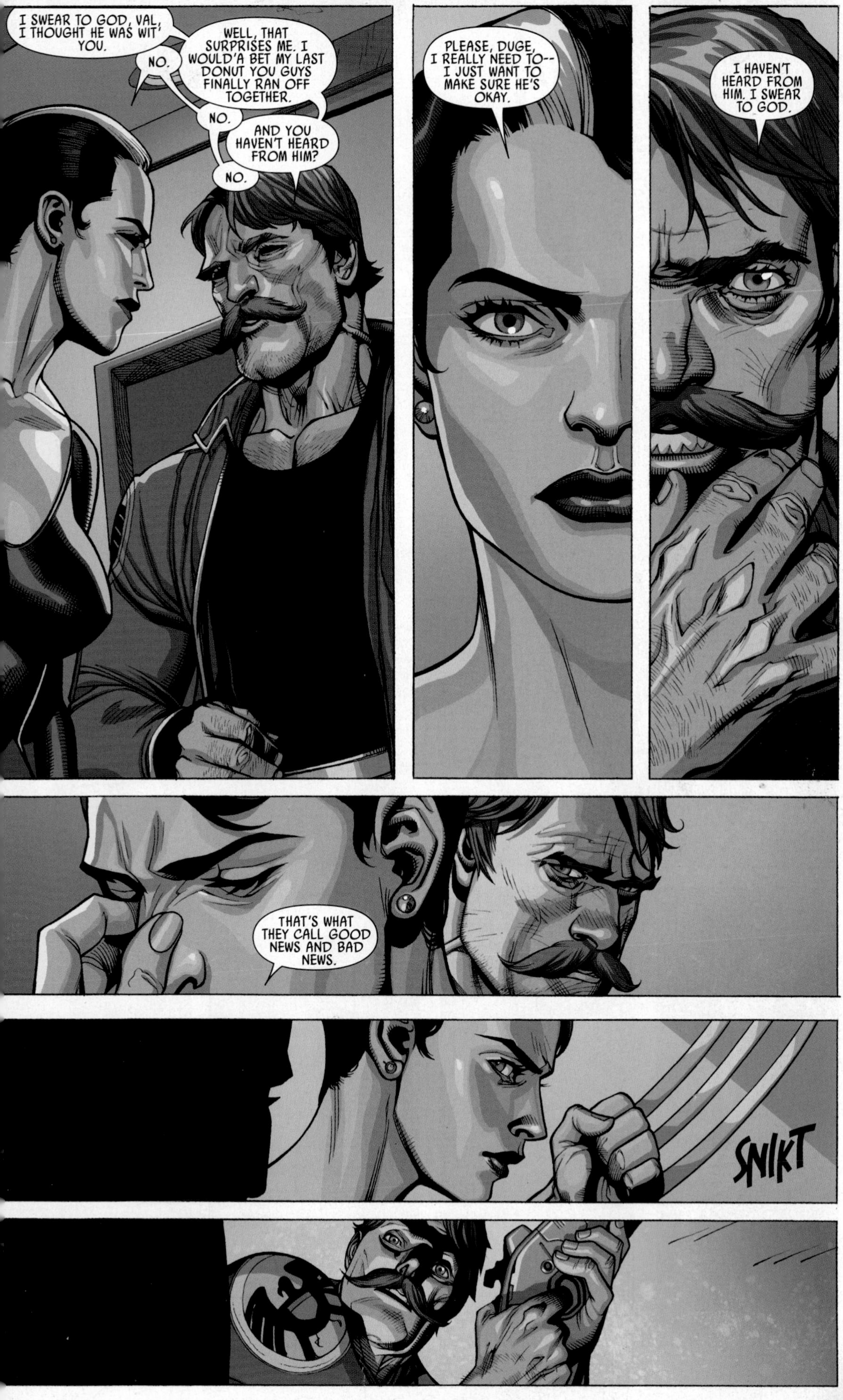
I SWEAR TO GOD, VAL, I THOUGHT HE WAS WIT' YOU.
NO.
WELL, THAT SURPRISES ME. I WOULD'A BET MY LAST DONUT YOU GUYS FINALLY RAN OFF TOGETHER.
NO.
AND YOU HAVEN'T HEARD FROM HIM?
NO.
PLEASE, DUGE, I REALLY NEED TO-- I JUST WANT TO MAKE SURE HE'S OKAY.
I HAVEN'T HEARD FROM HIM. I SWEAR TO GOD.
THAT'S WHAT THEY CALL GOOD NEWS AND BAD NEWS.
SNIKT

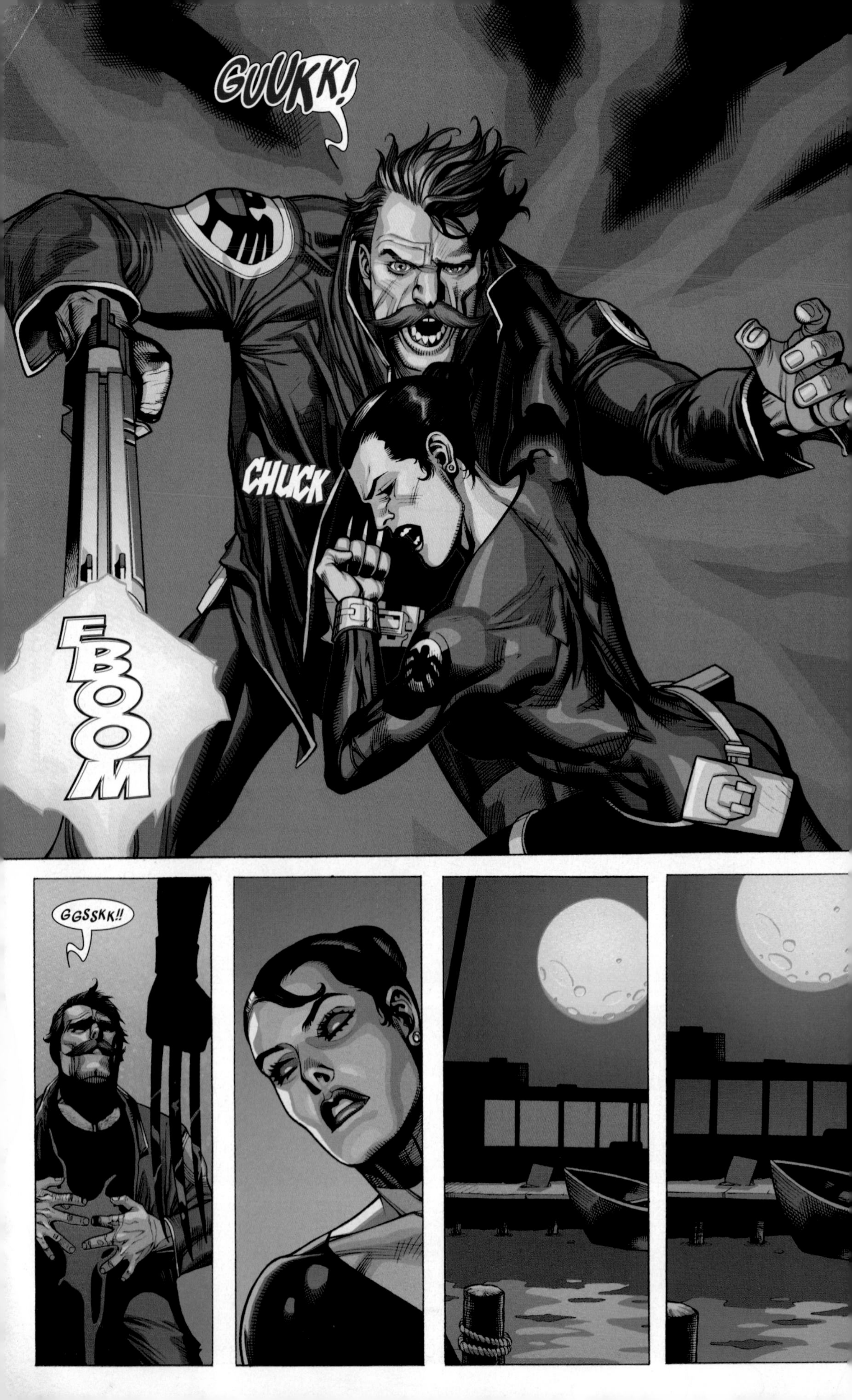
GUUKK!
CHUCK
EBOOM
GGSSKK!!

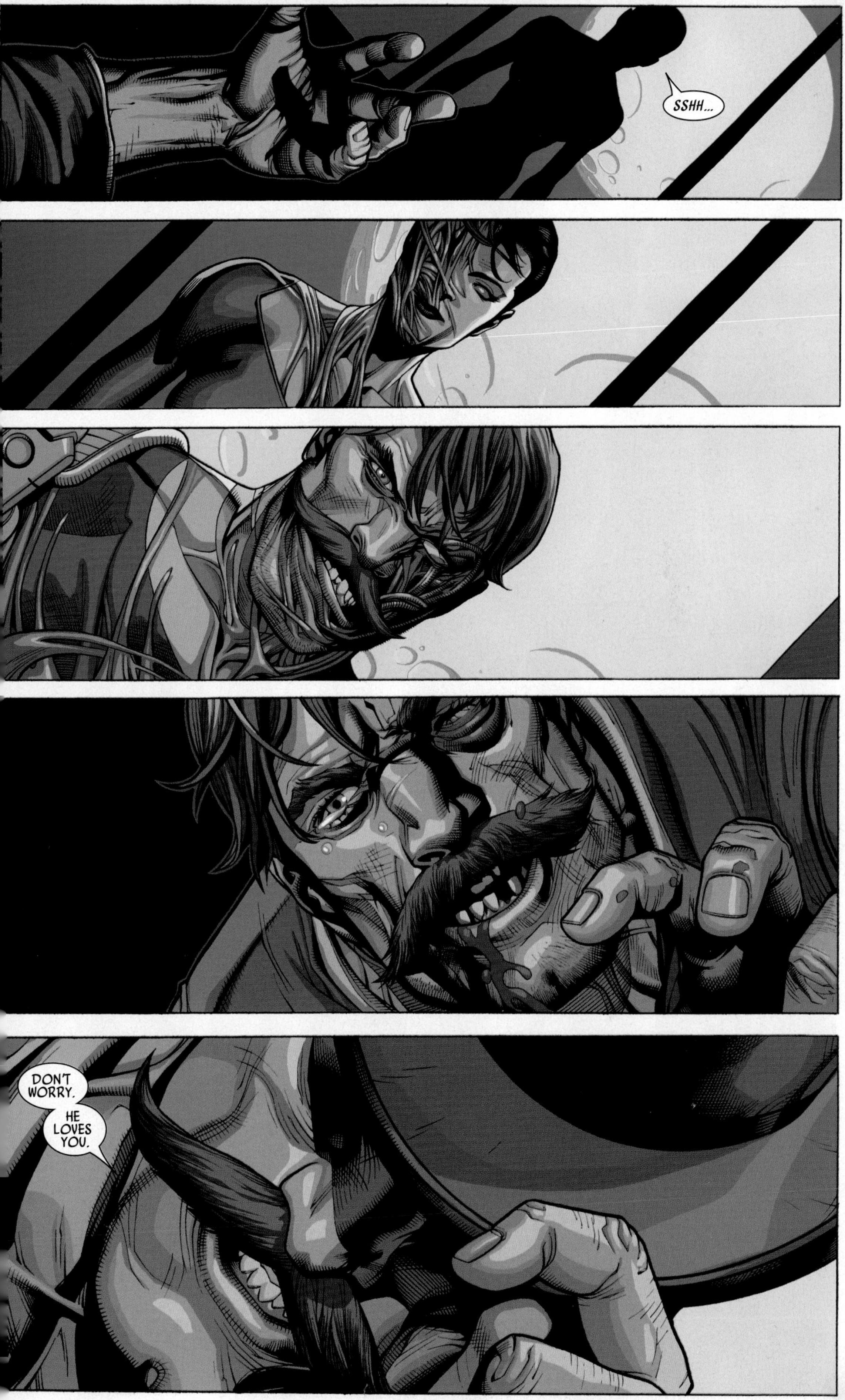
SSHH...
DON'T WORRY.
HE LOVES YOU.

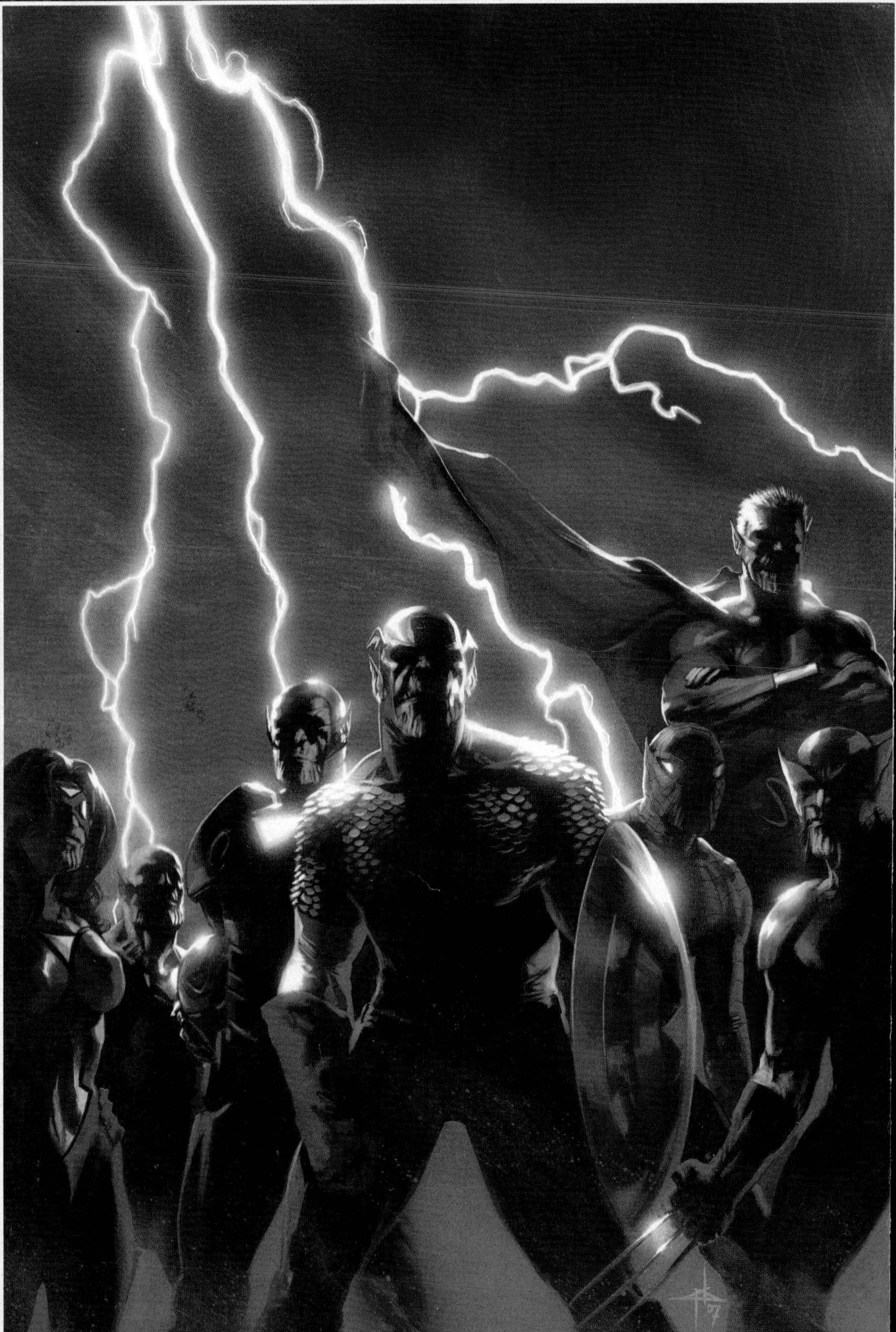

[1]

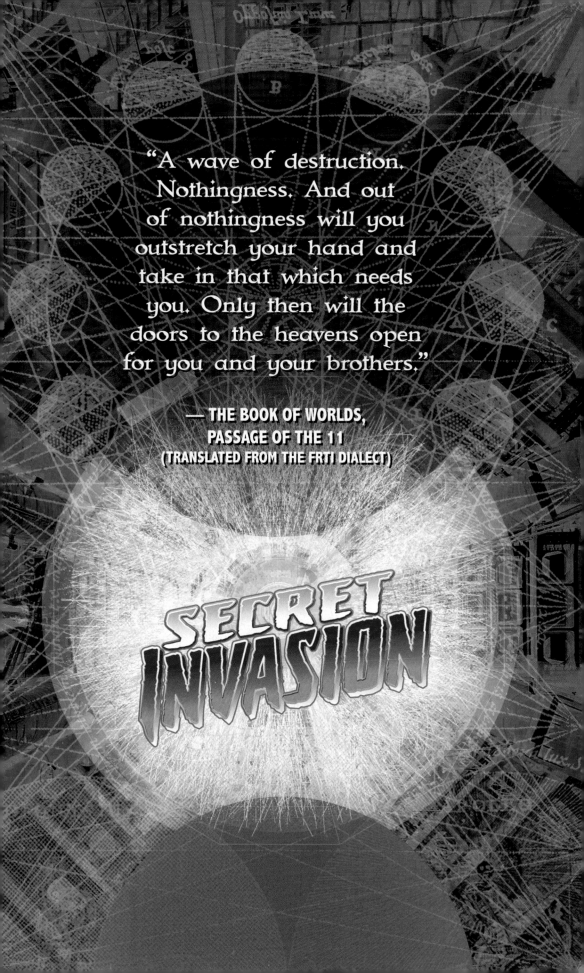

"A wave of destruction.
Nothingness. And out
of nothingness will you
outstretch your hand and
take in that which needs
you. Only then will the
doors to the heavens open
for you and your brothers."

— THE BOOK OF WORLDS,
PASSAGE OF THE 11
(TRANSLATED FROM THE FRTI DIALECT)

SECRET INVASION

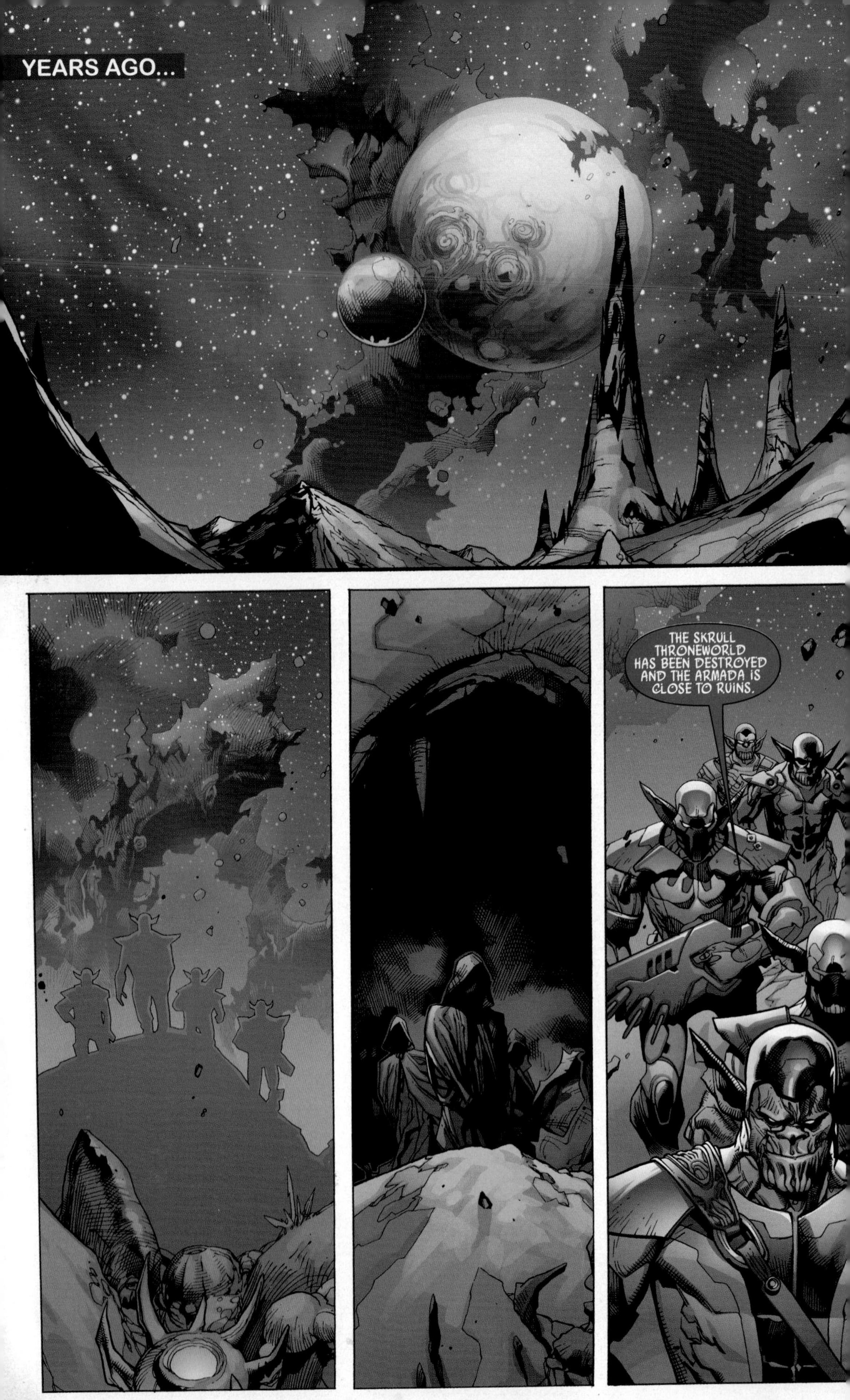
YEARS AGO...
THE SKRULL THRONEWORLD HAS BEEN DESTROYED AND THE ARMADA IS CLOSE TO RUINS.

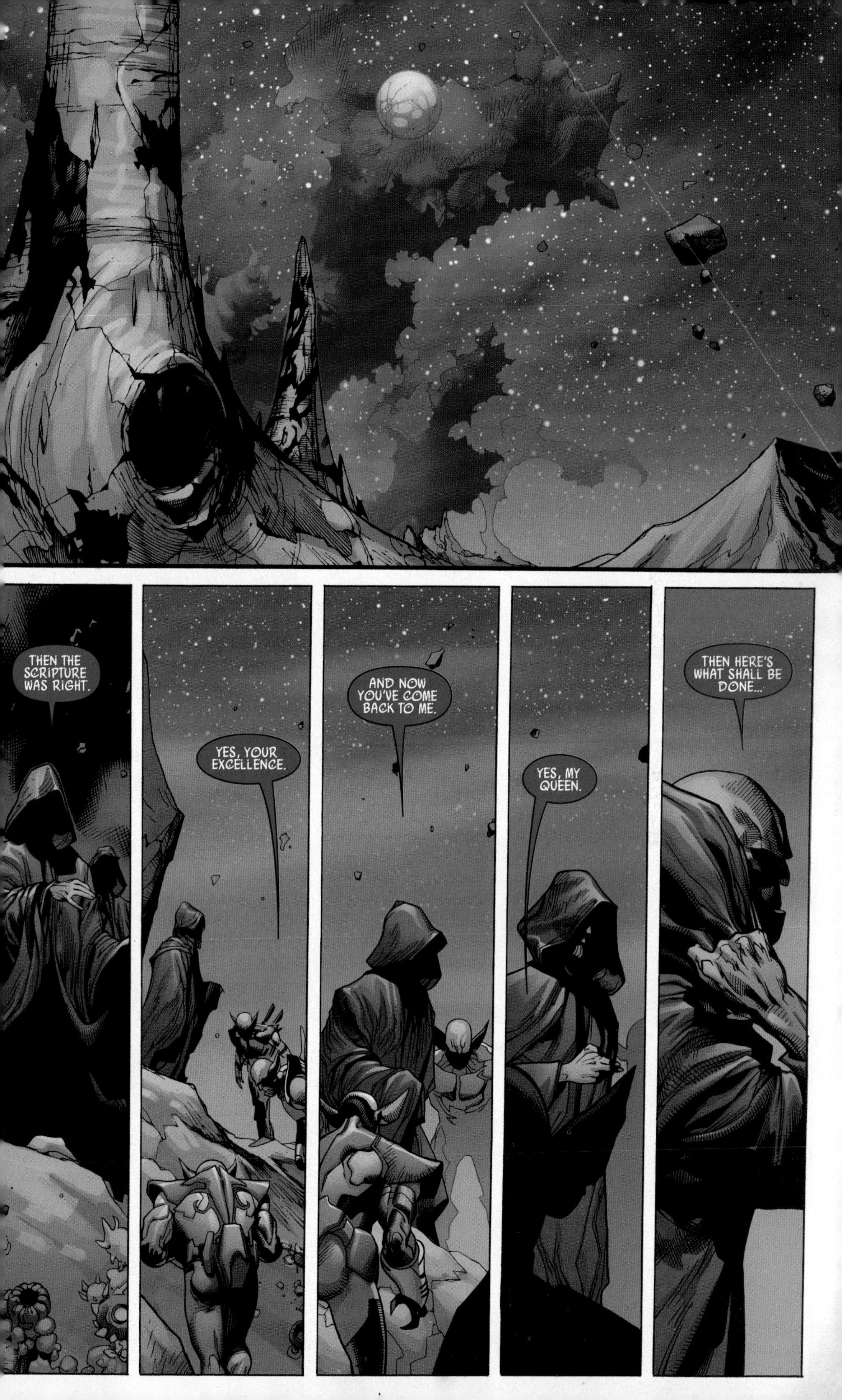
THEN THE SCRIPTURE WAS RIGHT.
YES, YOUR EXCELLENCE.
AND NOW YOU'VE COME BACK TO ME.
YES, MY QUEEN.
THEN HERE'S WHAT SHALL BE DONE...

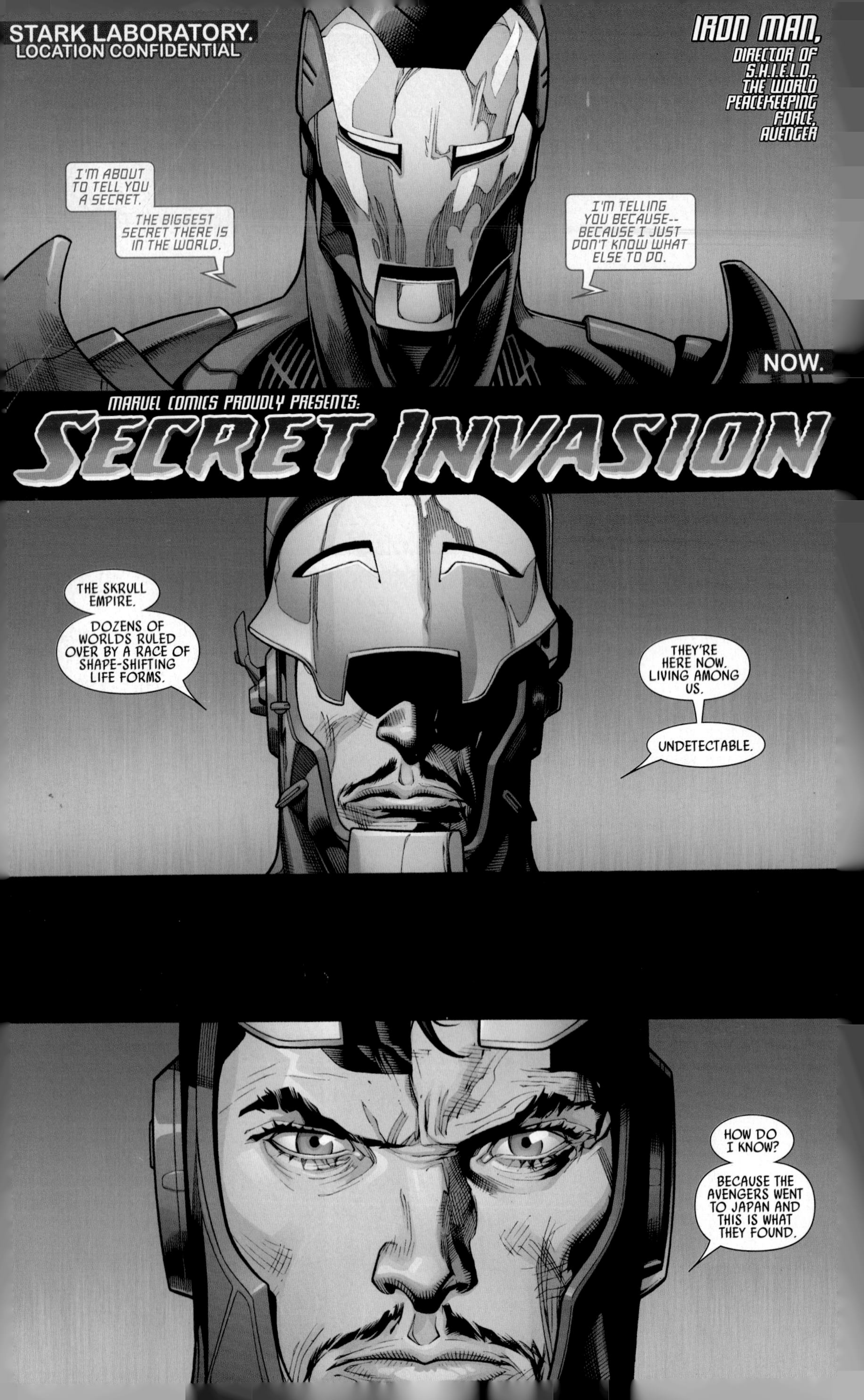

STARK LABORATORY.
LOCATION CONFIDENTIAL
IRON MAN,
DIRECTOR OF S.H.I.E.L.D., THE WORLD PEACEKEEPING FORCE, AVENGER
I'M ABOUT TO TELL YOU A SECRET.
THE BIGGEST SECRET THERE IS IN THE WORLD.
I'M TELLING YOU BECAUSE-- BECAUSE I JUST DON'T KNOW WHAT ELSE TO DO.
NOW.
MARVEL COMICS PROUDLY PRESENTS:
SECRET INVASION
THE SKRULL EMPIRE.
DOZENS OF WORLDS RULED OVER BY A RACE OF SHAPE-SHIFTING LIFE FORMS.
THEY'RE HERE NOW. LIVING AMONG US.
UNDETECTABLE.
HOW DO I KNOW?
BECAUSE THE AVENGERS WENT TO JAPAN AND THIS IS WHAT THEY FOUND.

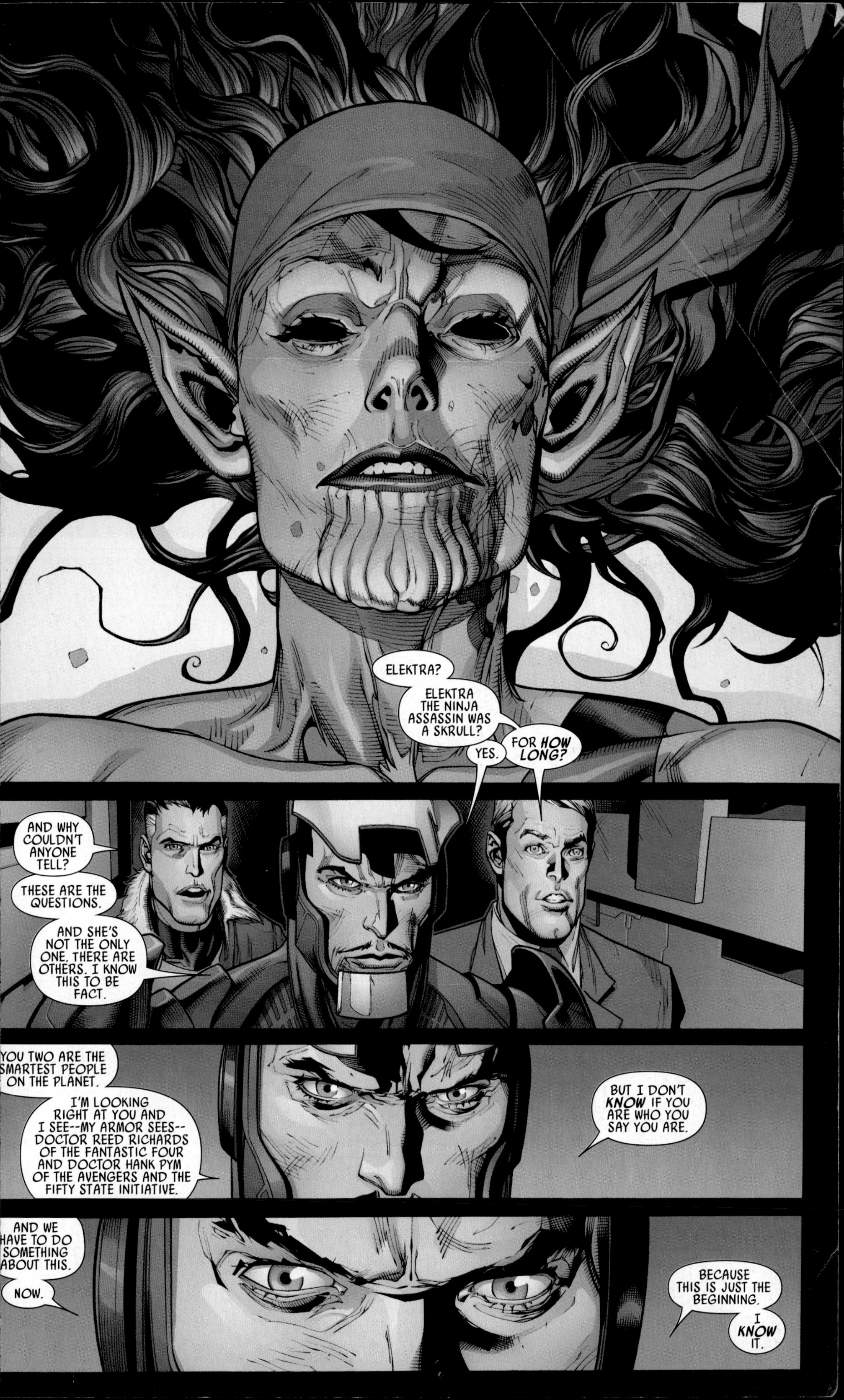
ELEKTRA?
ELEKTRA THE NINJA ASSASSIN WAS A SKRULL?
YES.
FOR HOW LONG?
AND WHY COULDN'T ANYONE TELL?
THESE ARE THE QUESTIONS.
AND SHE'S NOT THE ONLY ONE. THERE ARE OTHERS. I KNOW THIS TO BE FACT.
YOU TWO ARE THE SMARTEST PEOPLE ON THE PLANET.
I'M LOOKING RIGHT AT YOU AND I SEE--MY ARMOR SEES--DOCTOR REED RICHARDS OF THE FANTASTIC FOUR AND DOCTOR HANK PYM OF THE AVENGERS AND THE FIFTY STATE INITIATIVE.
BUT I DON'T KNOW IF YOU ARE WHO YOU SAY YOU ARE.
AND WE HAVE TO DO SOMETHING ABOUT THIS.
NOW.
BECAUSE THIS IS JUST THE BEGINNING.
I KNOW IT.

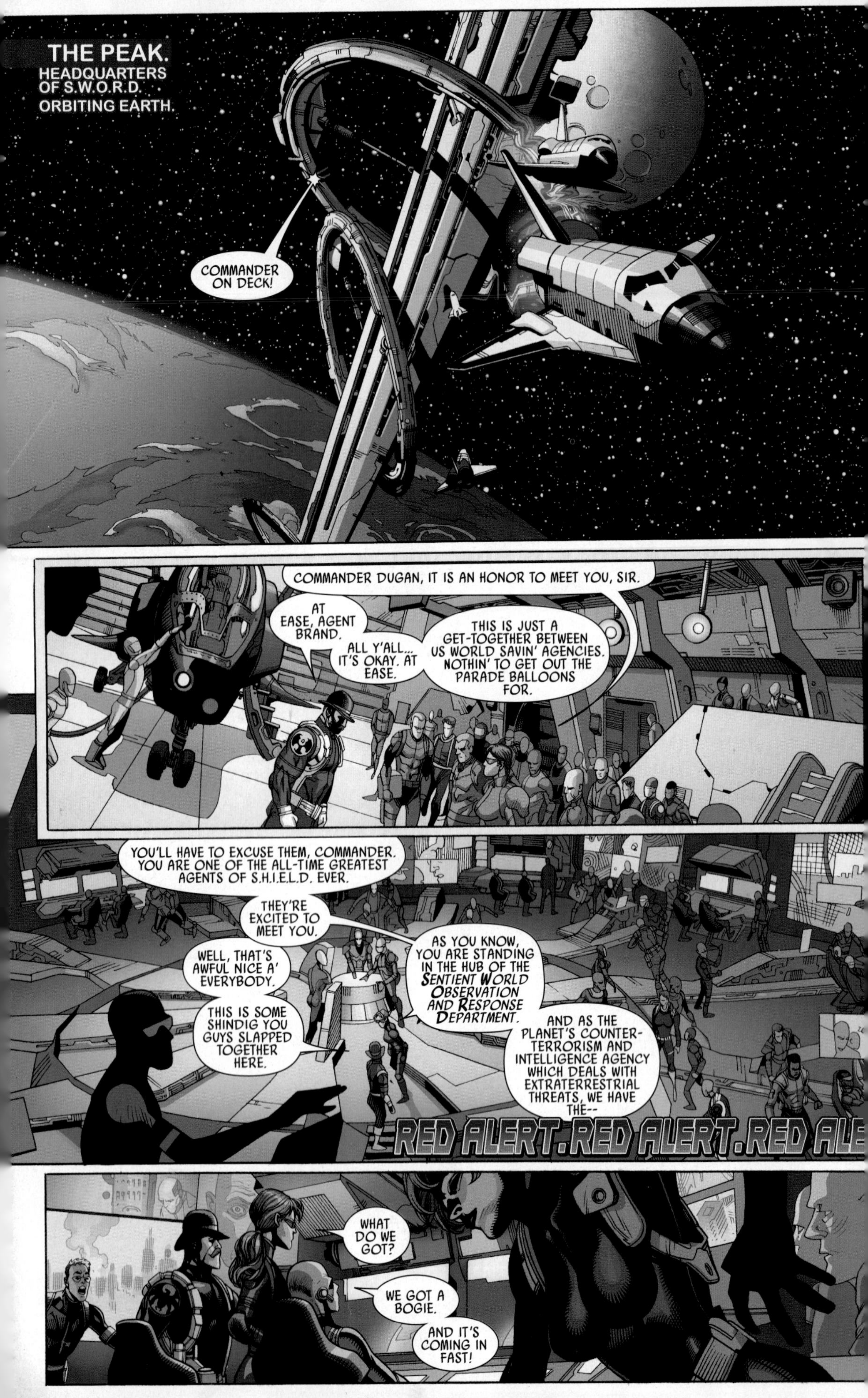
THE PEAK.
HEADQUARTERS OF S.W.O.R.D. ORBITING EARTH.
COMMANDER ON DECK!
COMMANDER DUGAN, IT IS AN HONOR TO MEET YOU, SIR.
AT EASE, AGENT BRAND.
ALL Y'ALL... IT'S OKAY. AT EASE.
THIS IS JUST A GET-TOGETHER BETWEEN US WORLD SAVIN' AGENCIES. NOTHIN' TO GET OUT THE PARADE BALLOONS FOR.
YOU'LL HAVE TO EXCUSE THEM, COMMANDER. YOU ARE ONE OF THE ALL-TIME GREATEST AGENTS OF S.H.I.E.L.D. EVER.
THEY'RE EXCITED TO MEET YOU.
WELL, THAT'S AWFUL NICE A' EVERYBODY.
THIS IS SOME SHINDIG YOU GUYS SLAPPED TOGETHER HERE.
AS YOU KNOW, YOU ARE STANDING IN THE HUB OF THE SENTIENT WORLD OBSERVATION AND RESPONSE DEPARTMENT.
AND AS THE PLANET'S COUNTER-TERRORISM AND INTELLIGENCE AGENCY WHICH DEALS WITH EXTRATERRESTRIAL THREATS, WE HAVE THE--
RED ALERT. RED ALERT. RED ALE
WHAT DO WE GOT?
WE GOT A BOGIE.
AND IT'S COMING IN FAST!

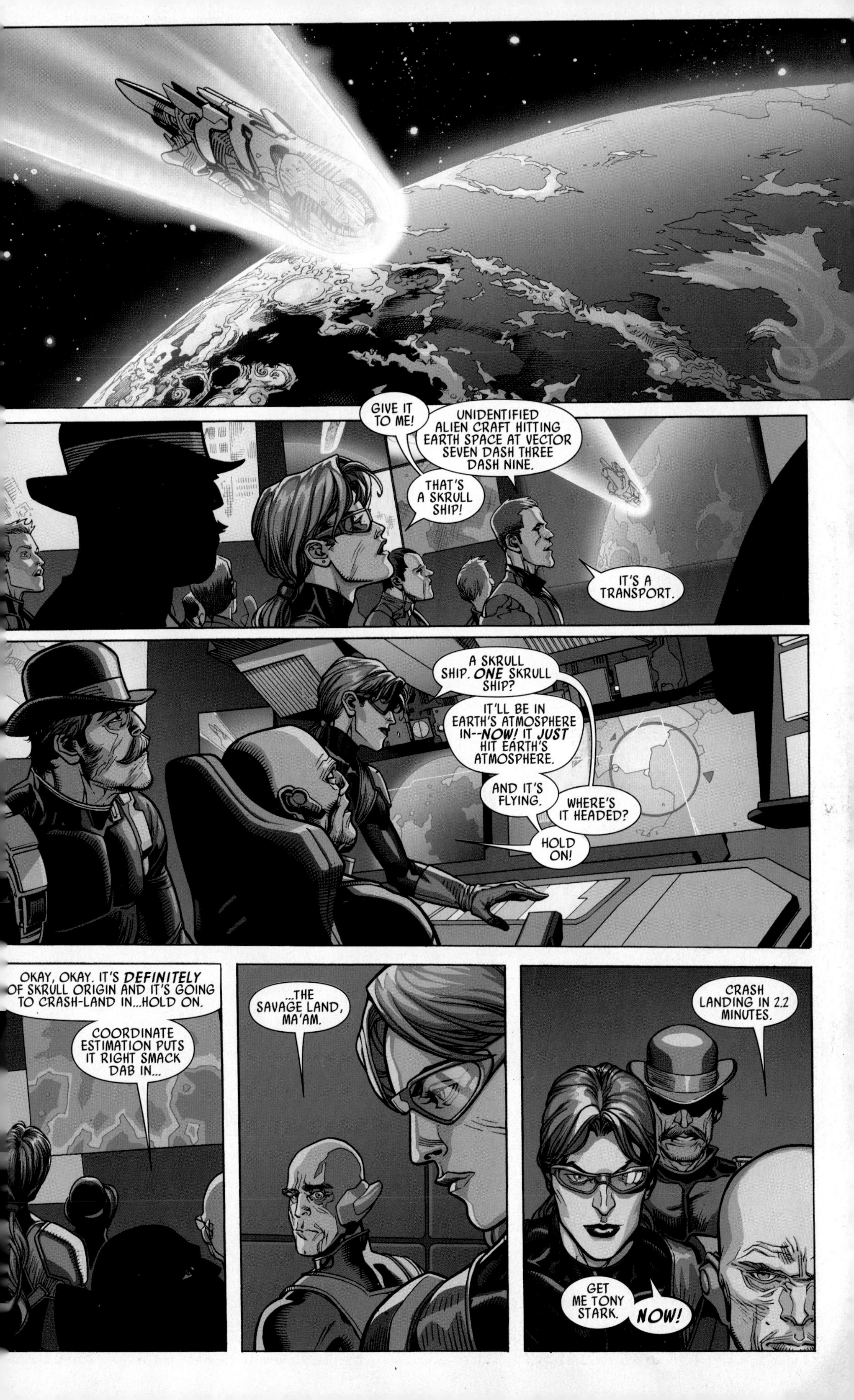
GIVE IT TO ME!
UNIDENTIFIED ALIEN CRAFT HITTING EARTH SPACE AT VECTOR SEVEN DASH THREE DASH NINE.
THAT'S A SKRULL SHIP!
IT'S A TRANSPORT.
A SKRULL SHIP. ONE SKRULL SHIP?
IT'LL BE IN EARTH'S ATMOSPHERE IN--NOW! IT JUST HIT EARTH'S ATMOSPHERE.
AND IT'S FLYING.
WHERE'S IT HEADED?
HOLD ON!
OKAY, OKAY. IT'S DEFINITELY OF SKRULL ORIGIN AND IT'S GOING TO CRASH-LAND IN...HOLD ON.
COORDINATE ESTIMATION PUTS IT RIGHT SMACK DAB IN...
...THE SAVAGE LAND, MA'AM.
CRASH LANDING IN 2.2 MINUTES.
GET ME TONY STARK.
NOW!

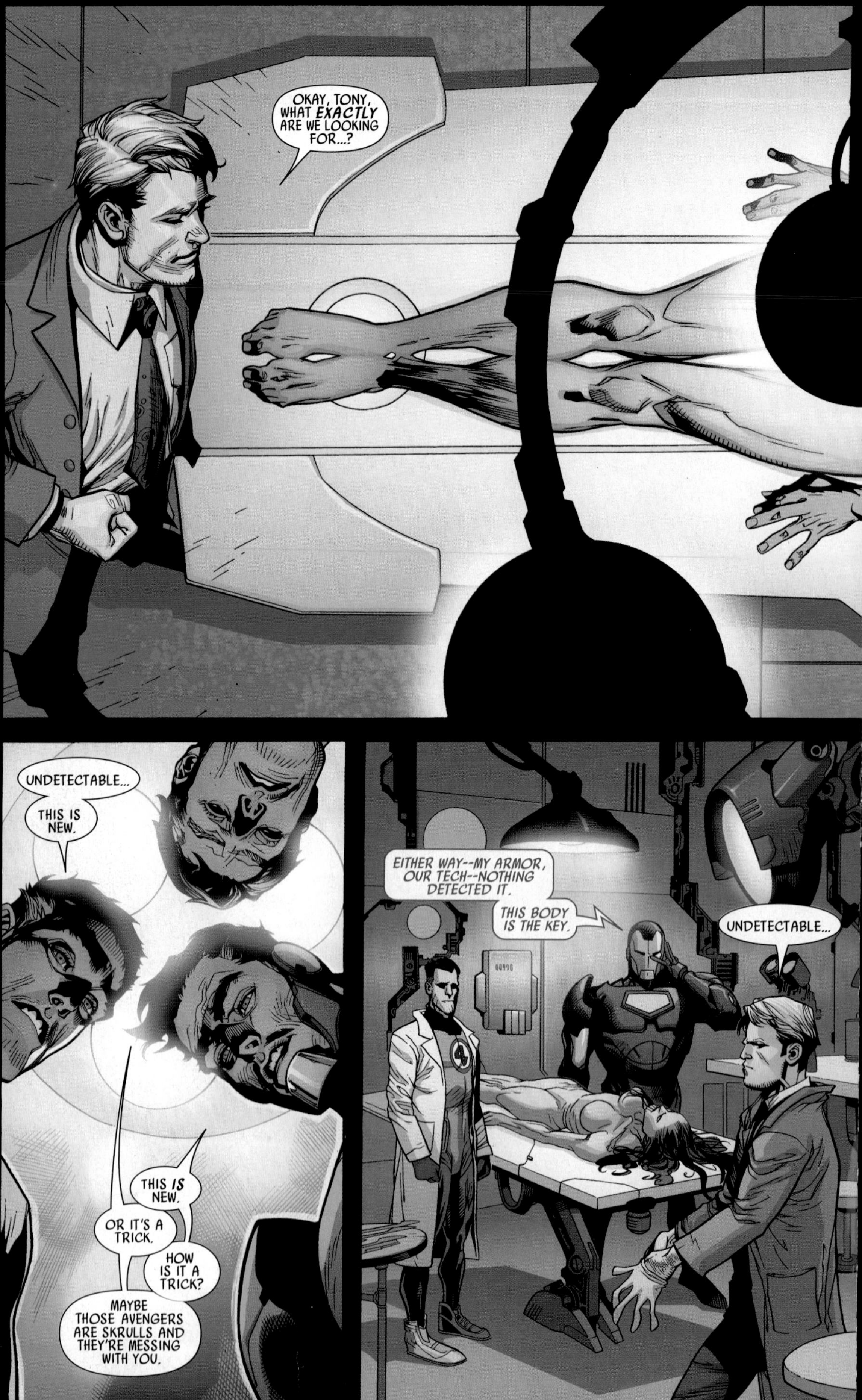
OKAY, TONY, WHAT EXACTLY ARE WE LOOKING FOR...?
UNDETECTABLE...
THIS IS NEW.
THIS IS NEW.
OR IT'S A TRICK.
HOW IS IT A TRICK?
MAYBE THOSE AVENGERS ARE SKRULLS AND THEY'RE MESSING WITH YOU.
EITHER WAY--MY ARMOR, OUR TECH--NOTHING DETECTED IT.
THIS BODY IS THE KEY.
UNDETECTABLE...

HOW THIS SKRULL WAS ABLE TO SHAPESHIFT *AND* STAY COMPLETELY UNDETECTABLE--

COMPLETELY UNDETECTABLE?

--TO MUTANT POWERS, MAGIC-BASED POWER SETS AND TECHNOLOGIES.

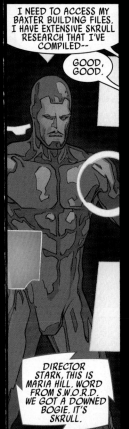

I NEED TO ACCESS MY BAXTER BUILDING FILES. I HAVE EXTENSIVE SKRULL RESEARCH THAT I'VE COMPILED--

GOOD, GOOD.

DIRECTOR STARK, THIS IS MARIA HILL. WORD FROM S.W.O.R.D. WE GOT A DOWNED BOGIE. IT'S SKRULL.

CRASH-LANDED? ANY SURVIVORS?

WE CAN'T TELL. WE HAVE TO SEND A TEAM IN. I CAN GO MYSELF.

NO, I GOT IT.

WHAT IS IT?

I HAVE TO GO.

OH, OKAY. WE CAN DO *THIS.*

I'LL CALL IN FOR REPORTS.

WHAT HAPPENED?

I'LL CALL IN.

HE'LL CALL IN.

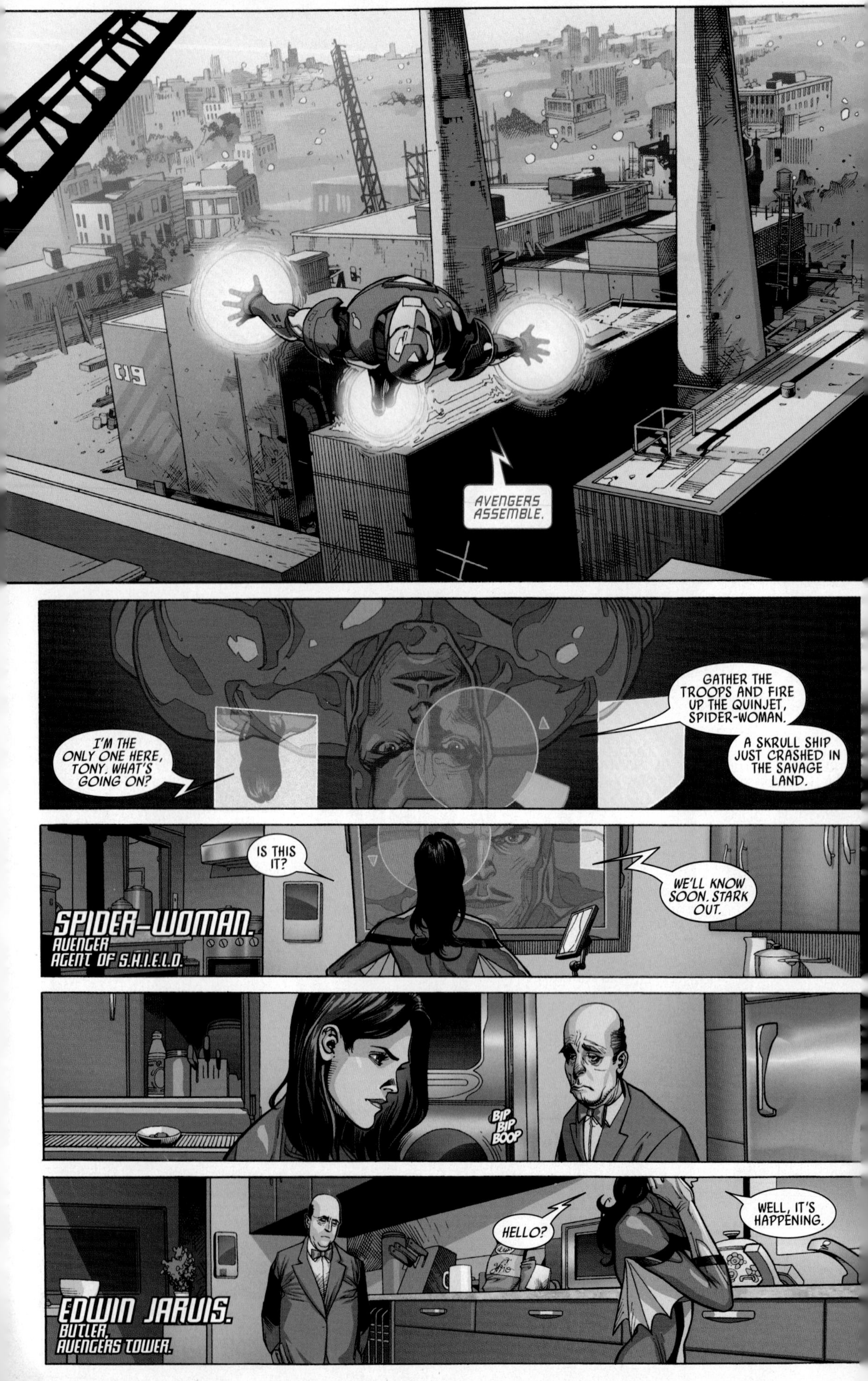
C19
AVENGERS ASSEMBLE.
GATHER THE TROOPS AND FIRE UP THE QUINJET, SPIDER-WOMAN.
A SKRULL SHIP JUST CRASHED IN THE SAVAGE LAND.
I'M THE ONLY ONE HERE, TONY. WHAT'S GOING ON?
IS THIS IT?
WE'LL KNOW SOON. STARK OUT.
SPIDER-WOMAN.
AVENGER
AGENT OF S.H.I.E.L.D.
BIP BIP BOOP
HELLO?
WELL, IT'S HAPPENING.
EDWIN JARVIS.
BUTLER,
AVENGERS TOWER.

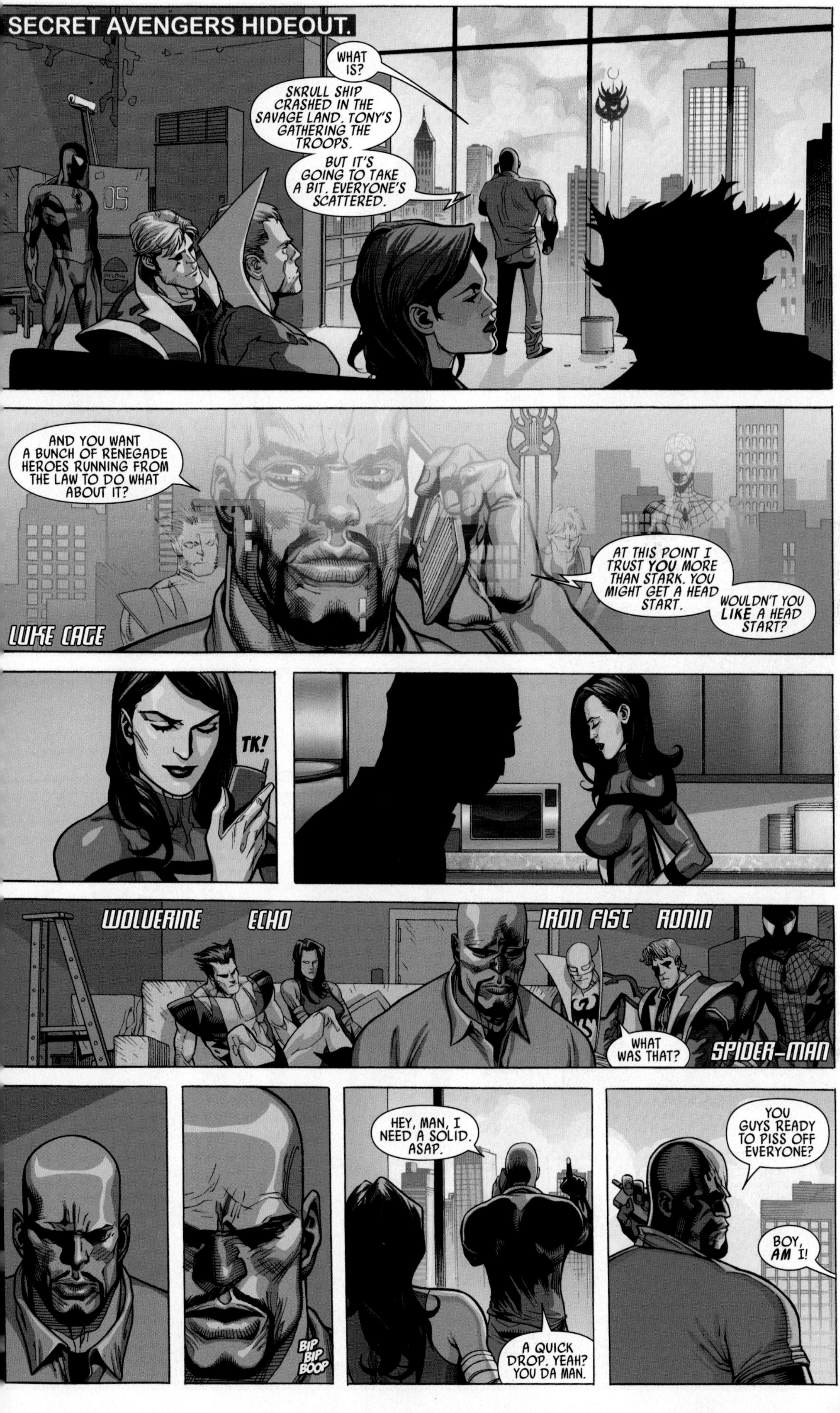

SECRET AVENGERS HIDEOUT.
WHAT IS?
SKRULL SHIP CRASHED IN THE SAVAGE LAND. TONY'S GATHERING THE TROOPS.
BUT IT'S GOING TO TAKE A BIT. EVERYONE'S SCATTERED.
AND YOU WANT A BUNCH OF RENEGADE HEROES RUNNING FROM THE LAW TO DO WHAT ABOUT IT?
LUKE CAGE
AT THIS POINT I TRUST YOU MORE THAN STARK. YOU MIGHT GET A HEAD START.
WOULDN'T YOU LIKE A HEAD START?
TK!
WOLVERINE
ECHO
IRON FIST
RONIN
SPIDER-MAN
WHAT WAS THAT?
BIP BIP BOOP
HEY, MAN, I NEED A SOLID. ASAP.
A QUICK DROP. YEAH? YOU DA MAN.
YOU GUYS READY TO PISS OFF EVERYONE?
BOY, AM I!

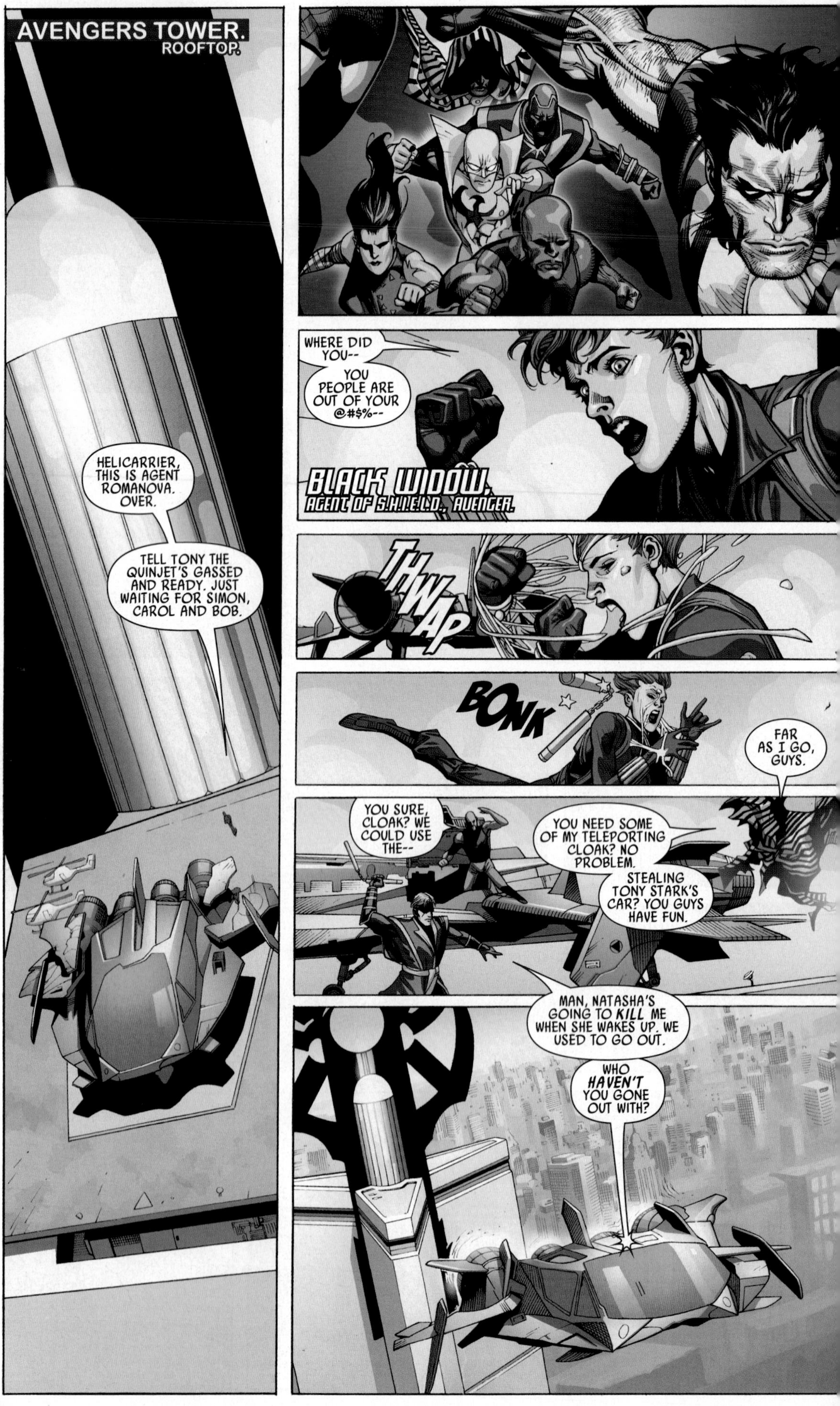
AVENGERS TOWER.
ROOFTOP.
HELICARRIER, THIS IS AGENT ROMANOVA. OVER.
TELL TONY THE QUINJET'S GASSED AND READY. JUST WAITING FOR SIMON, CAROL AND BOB.
WHERE DID YOU--
YOU PEOPLE ARE OUT OF YOUR @#$%--
BLACK WIDOW.
AGENT OF S.H.I.E.L.D., AVENGER.
THWAP
BONK
FAR AS I GO, GUYS.
YOU SURE, CLOAK? WE COULD USE THE--
YOU NEED SOME OF MY TELEPORTING CLOAK? NO PROBLEM.
STEALING TONY STARK'S CAR? YOU GUYS HAVE FUN.
MAN, NATASHA'S GOING TO KILL ME WHEN SHE WAKES UP. WE USED TO GO OUT.
WHO HAVEN'T YOU GONE OUT WITH?

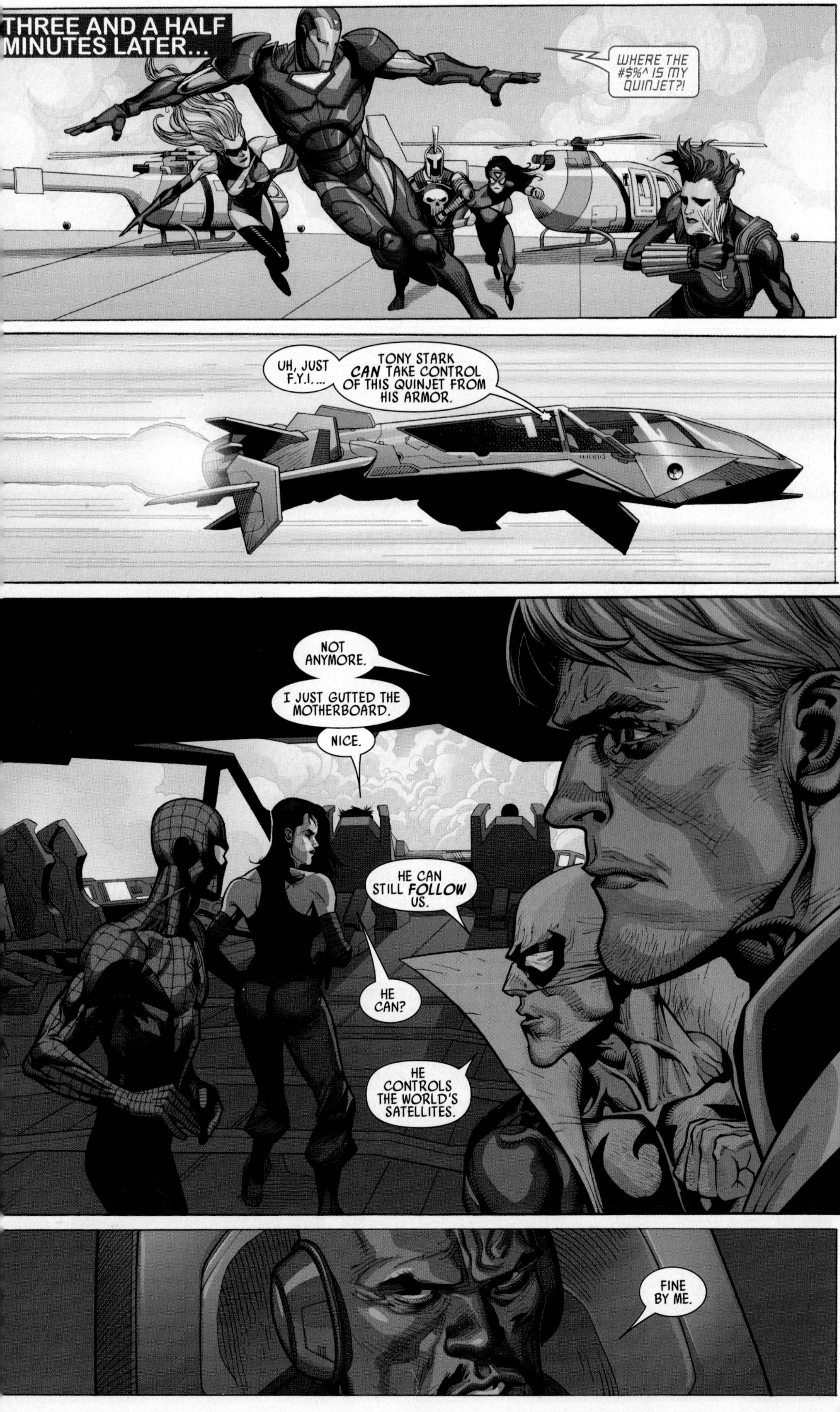
THREE AND A HALF MINUTES LATER...
WHERE THE #$%^ IS MY QUINJET?!
UH, JUST F.Y.I....
TONY STARK CAN TAKE CONTROL OF THIS QUINJET FROM HIS ARMOR.
NOT ANYMORE.
I JUST GUTTED THE MOTHERBOARD.
NICE.
HE CAN STILL FOLLOW US.
HE CAN?
HE CONTROLS THE WORLD'S SATELLITES.
FINE BY ME.

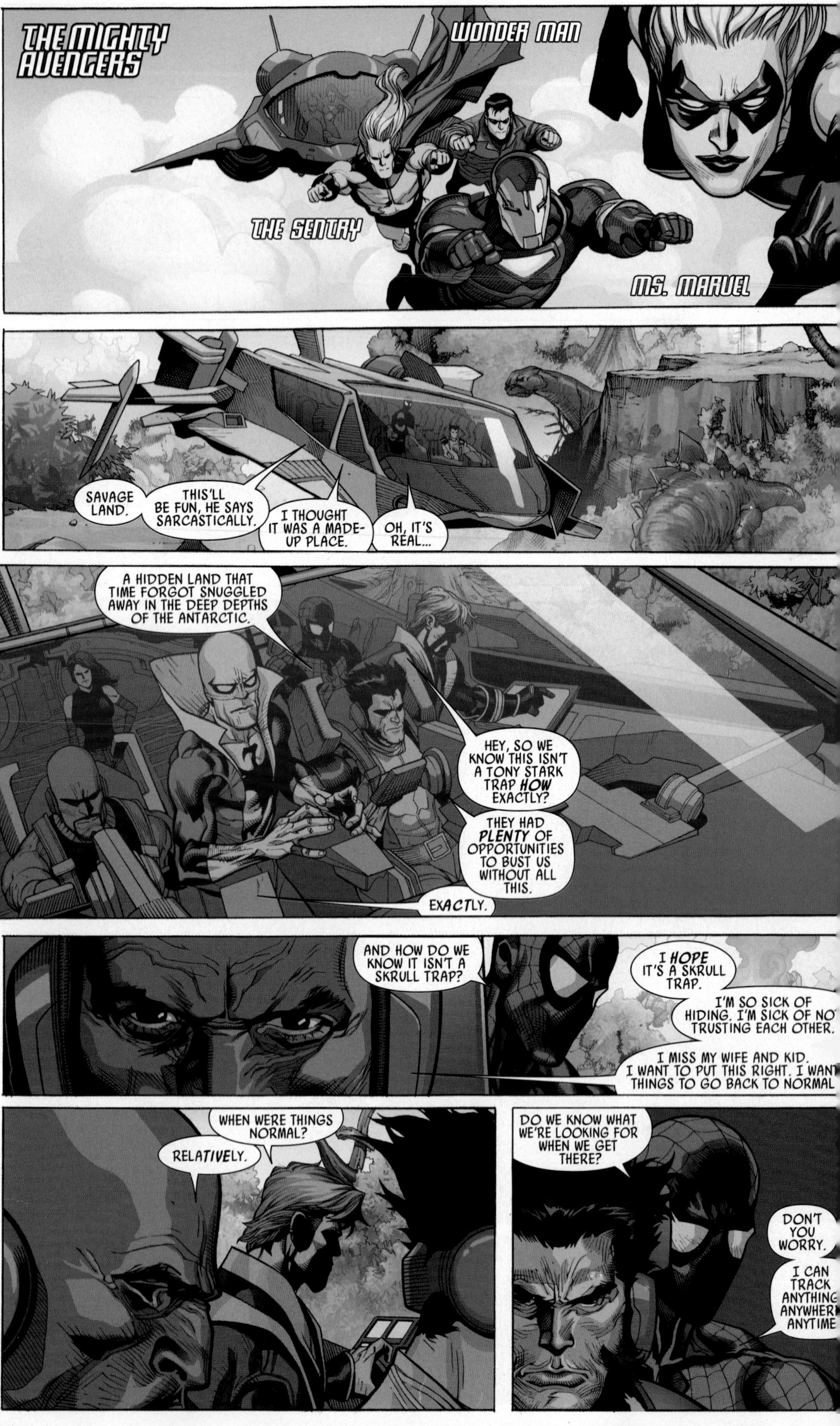
THE MIGHTY AVENGERS
WONDER MAN
THE SENTRY
MS. MARVEL
SAVAGE LAND.
THIS'LL BE FUN, HE SAYS SARCASTICALLY.
I THOUGHT IT WAS A MADE-UP PLACE.
OH, IT'S REAL...
A HIDDEN LAND THAT TIME FORGOT SNUGGLED AWAY IN THE DEEP DEPTHS OF THE ANTARCTIC.
HEY, SO WE KNOW THIS ISN'T A TONY STARK TRAP HOW EXACTLY?
THEY HAD PLENTY OF OPPORTUNITIES TO BUST US WITHOUT ALL THIS.
EXACTLY.
AND HOW DO WE KNOW IT ISN'T A SKRULL TRAP?
I HOPE IT'S A SKRULL TRAP.
I'M SO SICK OF HIDING. I'M SICK OF NO TRUSTING EACH OTHER.
I MISS MY WIFE AND KID. I WANT TO PUT THIS RIGHT. I WANT THINGS TO GO BACK TO NORMAL
WHEN WERE THINGS NORMAL?
RELATIVELY.
DO WE KNOW WHAT WE'RE LOOKING FOR WHEN WE GET THERE?
DON'T YOU WORRY.
I CAN TRACK ANYTHING ANYWHER ANYTIME

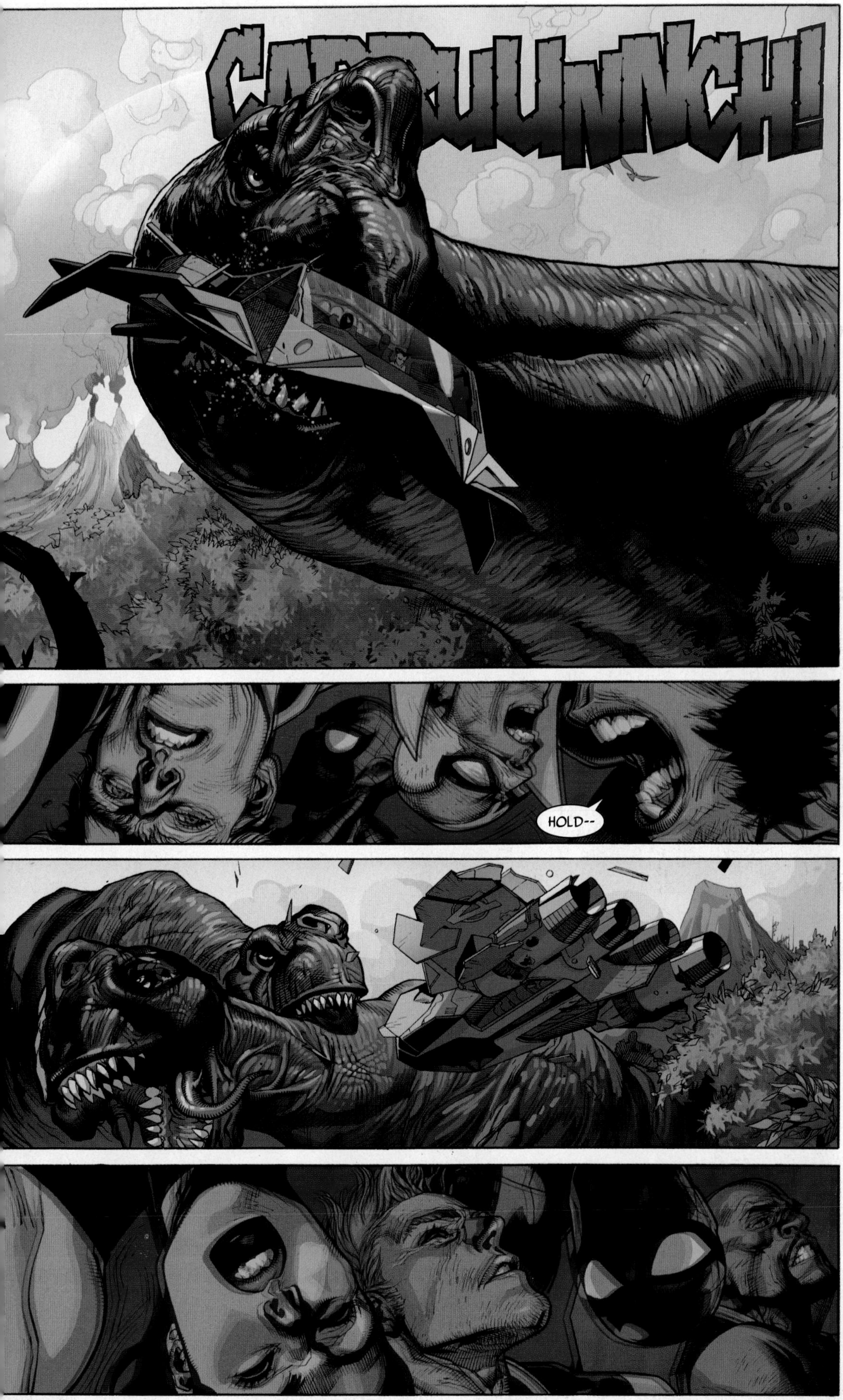
CARRUUNNCH!
HOLD--

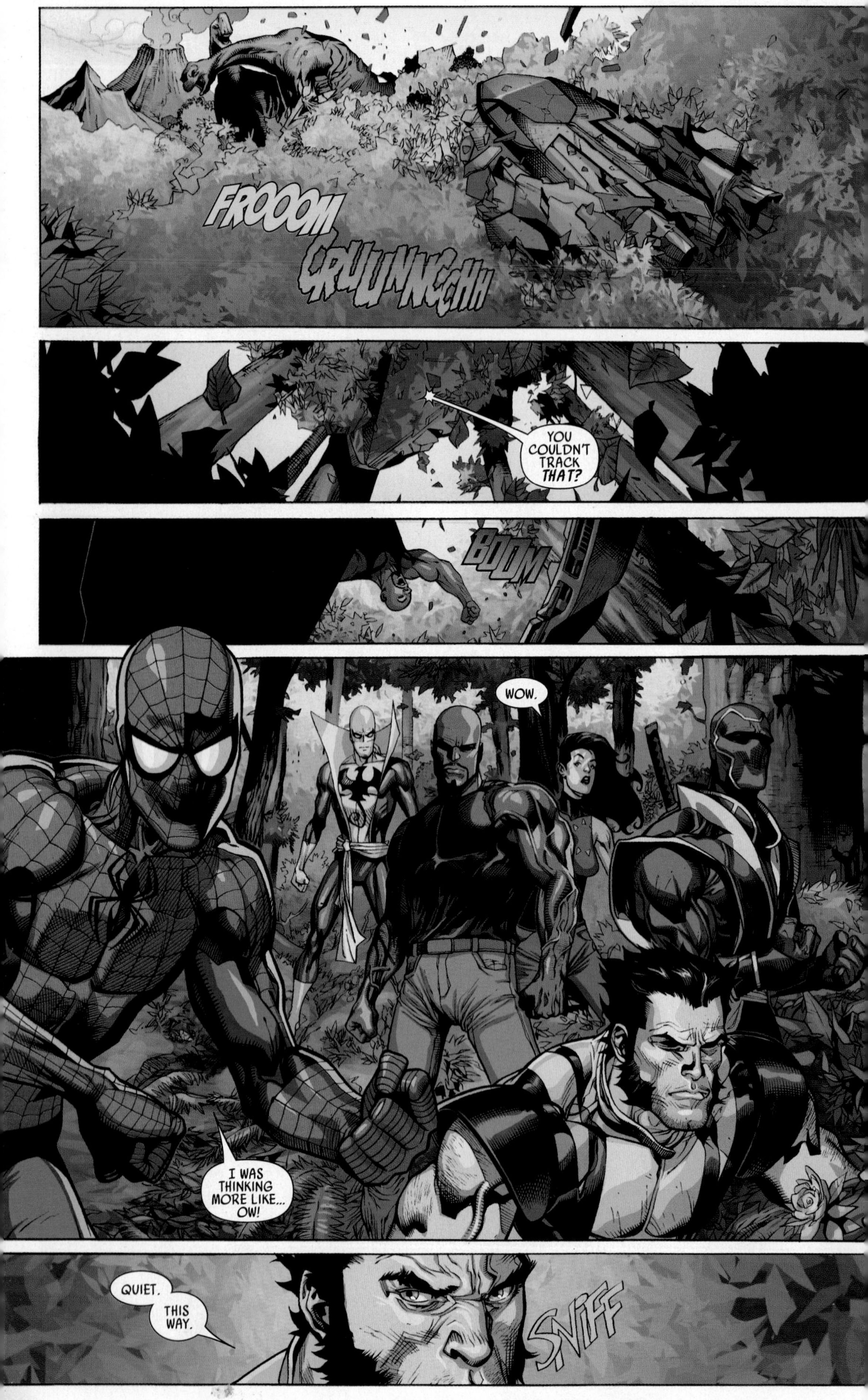
FROOOM
CRUUNNCCHH
YOU COULDN'T TRACK THAT?
BOOM
WOW.
I WAS THINKING MORE LIKE... OW!
QUIET.
THIS WAY.
SNIFF

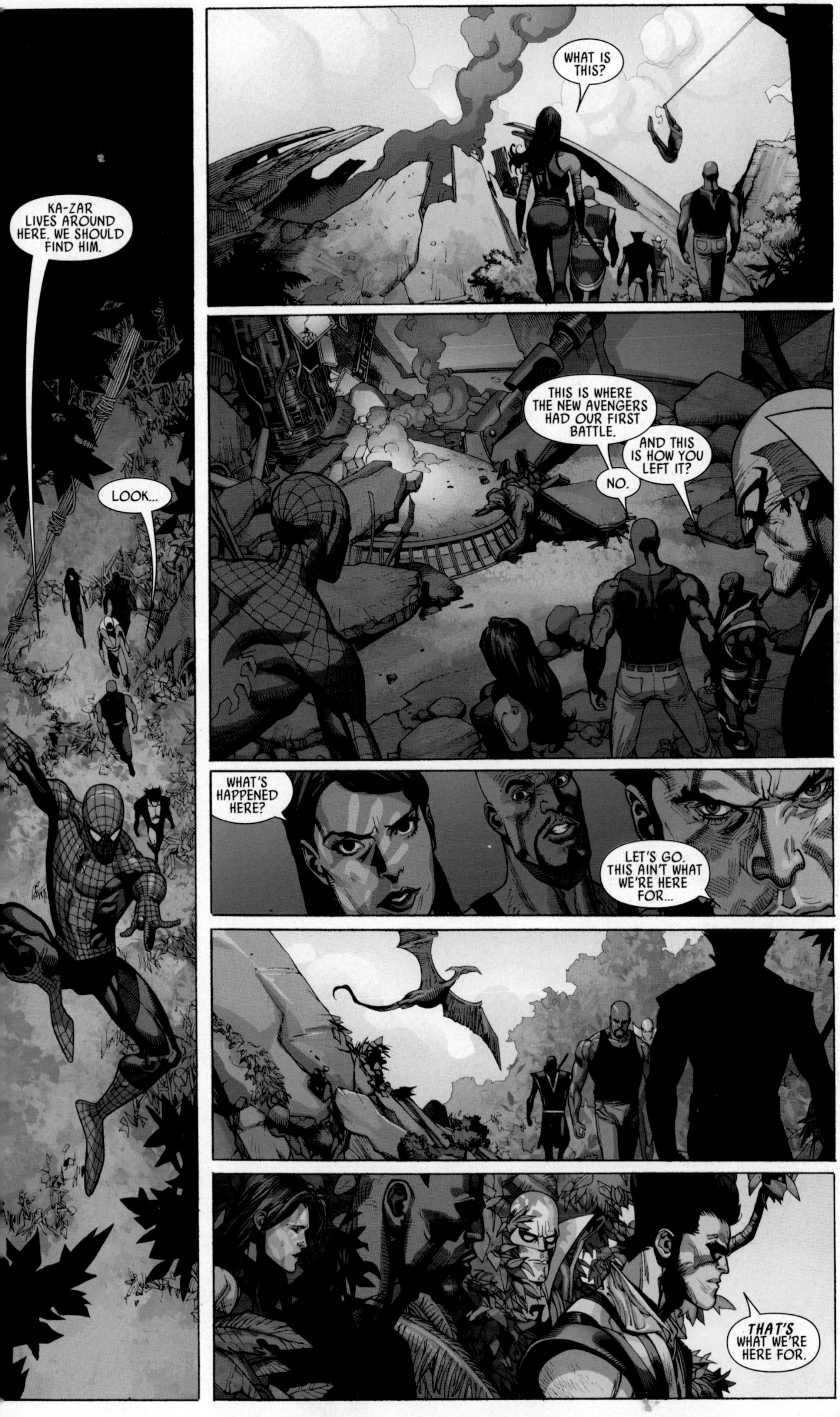
KA-ZAR LIVES AROUND HERE. WE SHOULD FIND HIM.
LOOK...
WHAT IS THIS?
THIS IS WHERE THE NEW AVENGERS HAD OUR FIRST BATTLE.
AND THIS IS HOW YOU LEFT IT?
NO.
WHAT'S HAPPENED HERE?
LET'S GO. THIS AIN'T WHAT WE'RE HERE FOR...
THAT'S WHAT WE'RE HERE FOR.

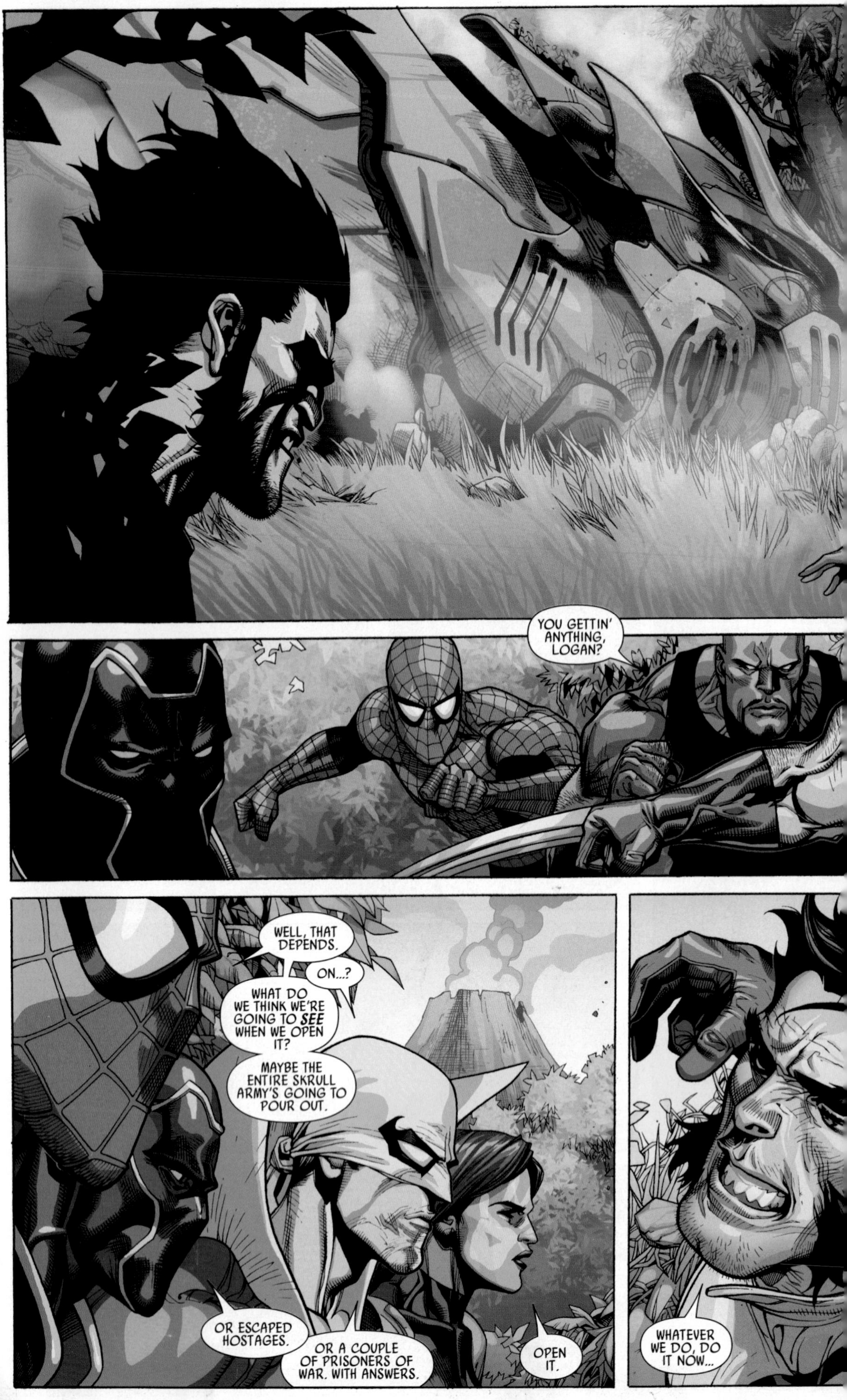

YOU GETTIN' ANYTHING, LOGAN?
WELL, THAT DEPENDS.
ON...?
WHAT DO WE THINK WE'RE GOING TO **SEE** WHEN WE OPEN IT?
MAYBE THE ENTIRE SKRULL ARMY'S GOING TO POUR OUT.
OR ESCAPED HOSTAGES.
OR A COUPLE OF PRISONERS OF WAR. WITH ANSWERS.
OPEN IT.
WHATEVER WE DO, DO IT NOW...

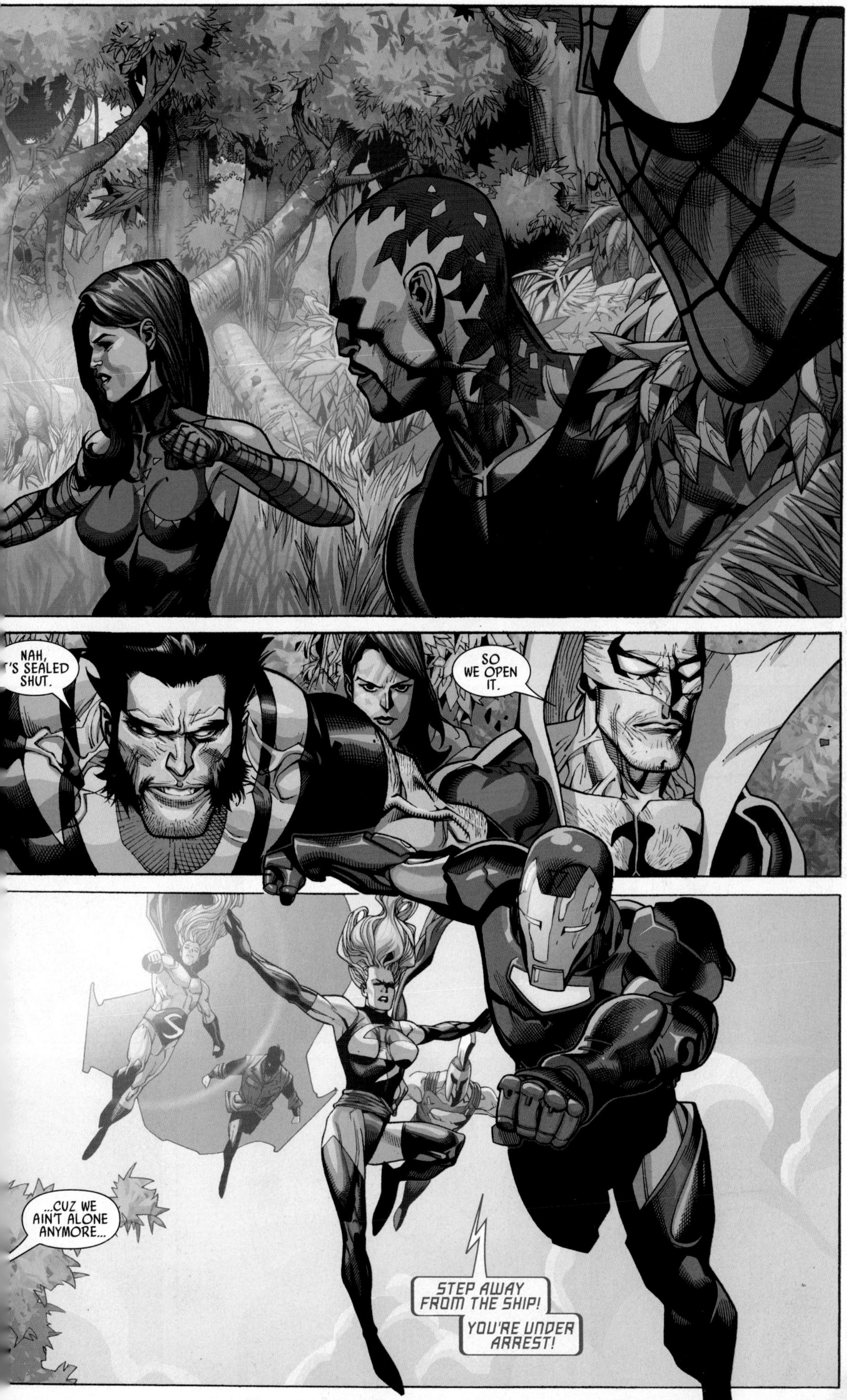
NAH, T'S SEALED SHUT.
SO WE OPEN IT.
...CUZ WE AIN'T ALONE ANYMORE...
STEP AWAY FROM THE SHIP!
YOU'RE UNDER ARREST!

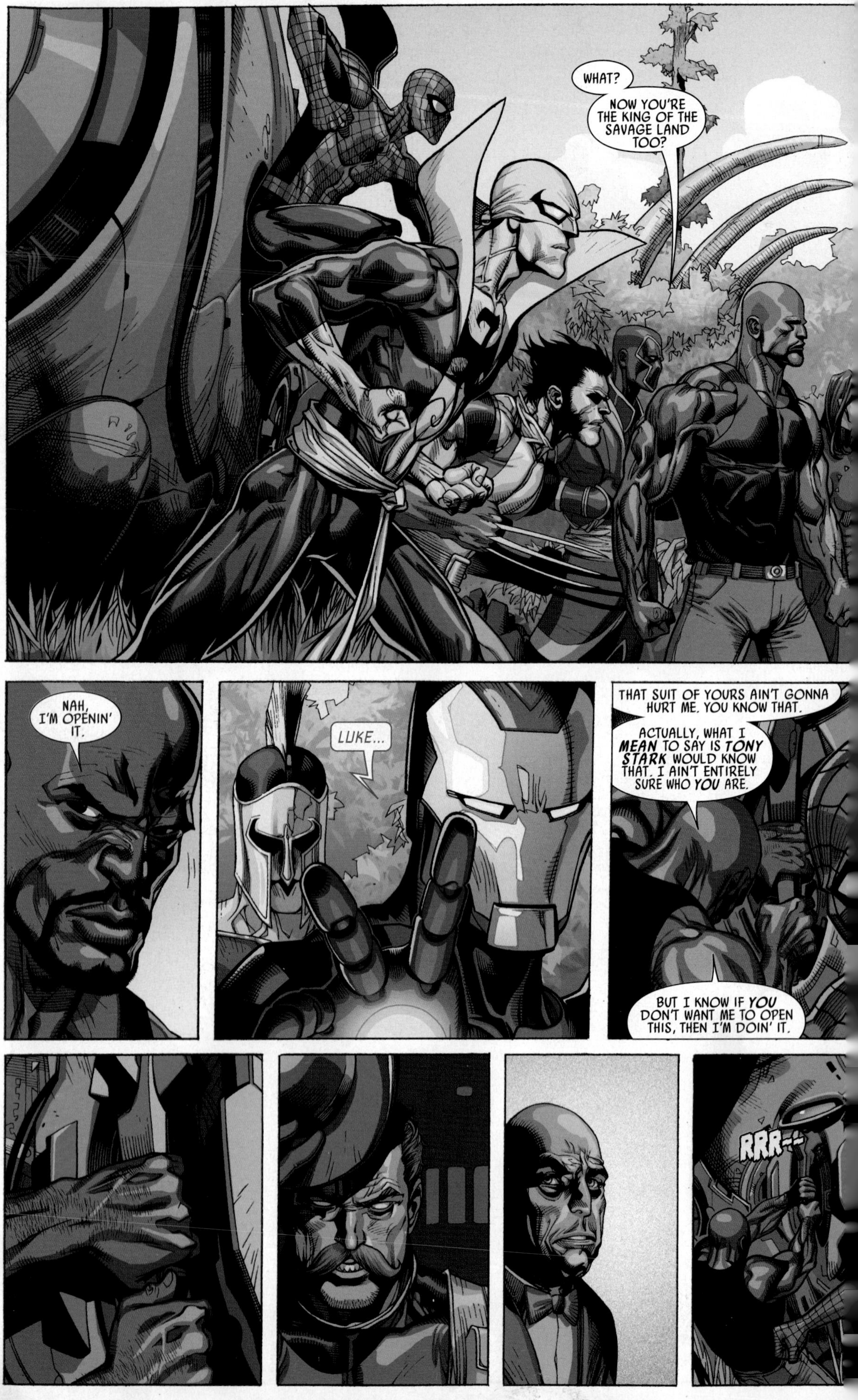
WHAT?
NOW YOU'RE THE KING OF THE SAVAGE LAND TOO?
NAH, I'M OPENIN' IT.
LUKE...
THAT SUIT OF YOURS AIN'T GONNA HURT ME. YOU KNOW THAT.
ACTUALLY, WHAT I MEAN TO SAY IS TONY STARK WOULD KNOW THAT. I AIN'T ENTIRELY SURE WHO YOU ARE.
BUT I KNOW IF YOU DON'T WANT ME TO OPEN THIS, THEN I'M DOIN' IT.
RRR--

COME ON, GUYS! YOU'RE SMART ENOUGH TO KNOW WHEN TO STAND DOWN.

LUKE, SERIOUSLY, STAND DOWN.

WHAT THE HELL DOES THAT MEAN?

I THINK IT MEANS HE THINKS STARK'S A SKRULL.

LUKE, COME ON... LET US HANDLE THIS.

VREEEE!

HE LOVES YOU...

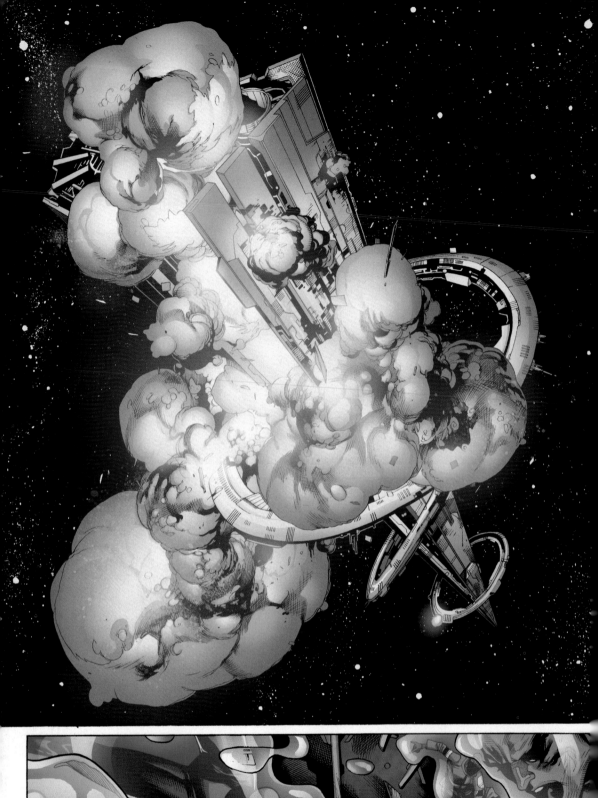
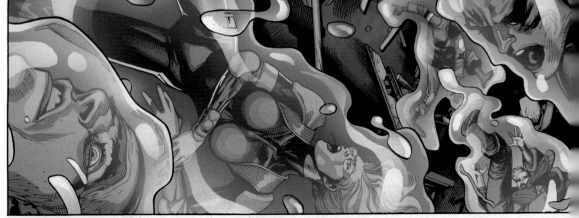

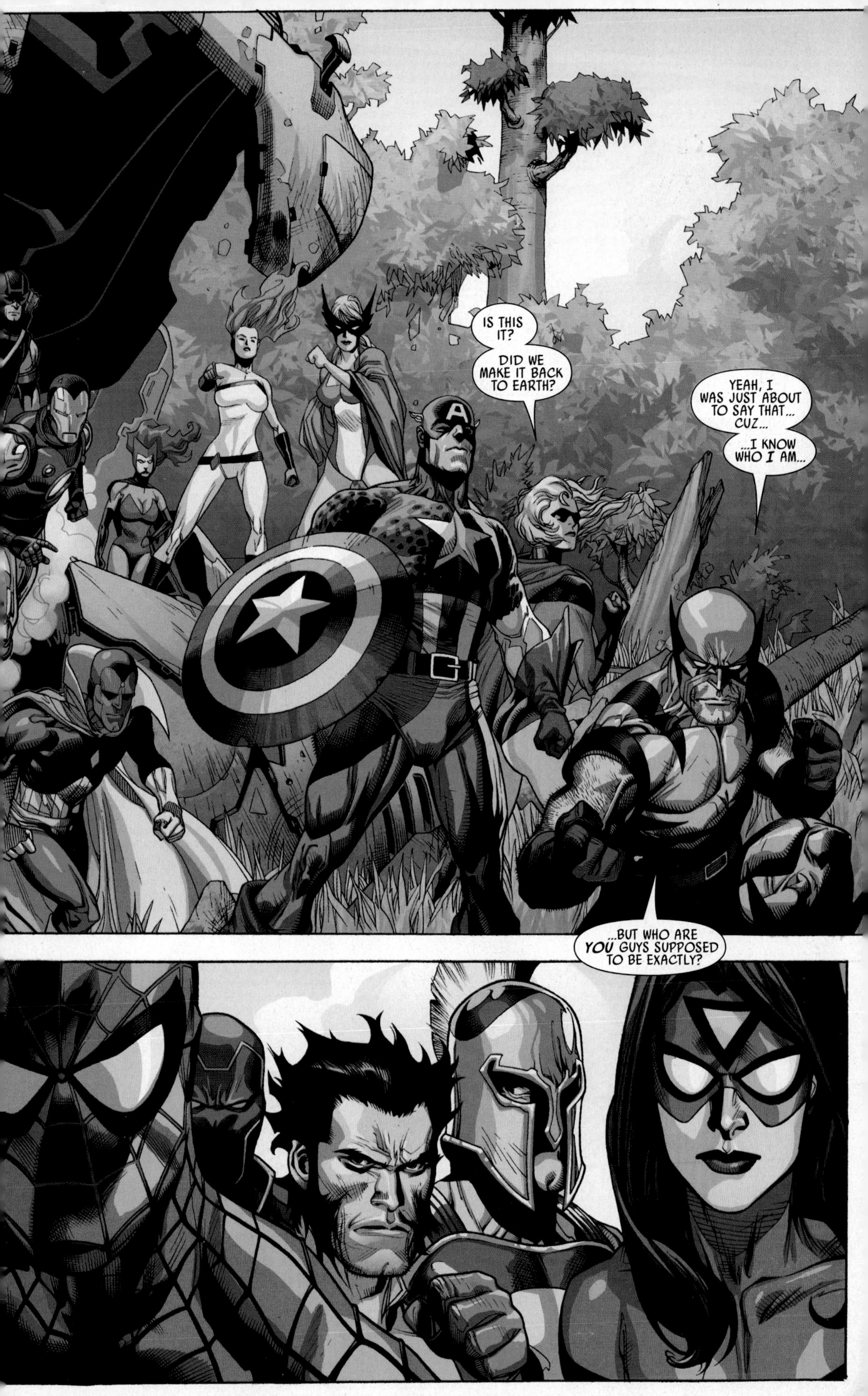
IS THIS IT?
DID WE MAKE IT BACK TO EARTH?
YEAH, I WAS JUST ABOUT TO SAY THAT... CUZ...
...I KNOW WHO I AM...
...BUT WHO ARE YOU GUYS SUPPOSED TO BE EXACTLY?

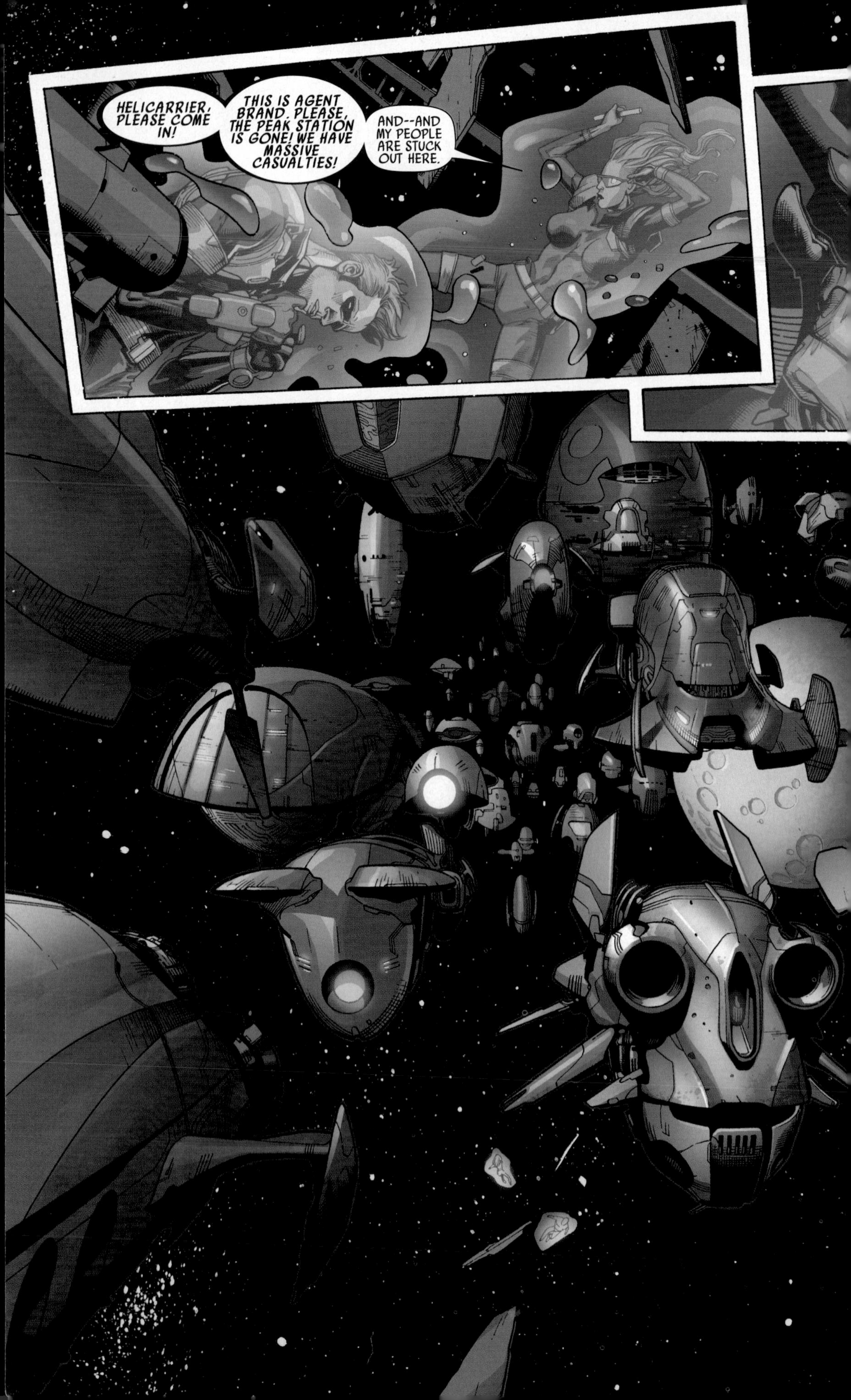
HELICARRIER, PLEASE COME IN!
THIS IS AGENT BRAND. PLEASE, THE PEAK STATION IS GONE! WE HAVE MASSIVE CASUALTIES!
AND--AND MY PEOPLE ARE STUCK OUT HERE.

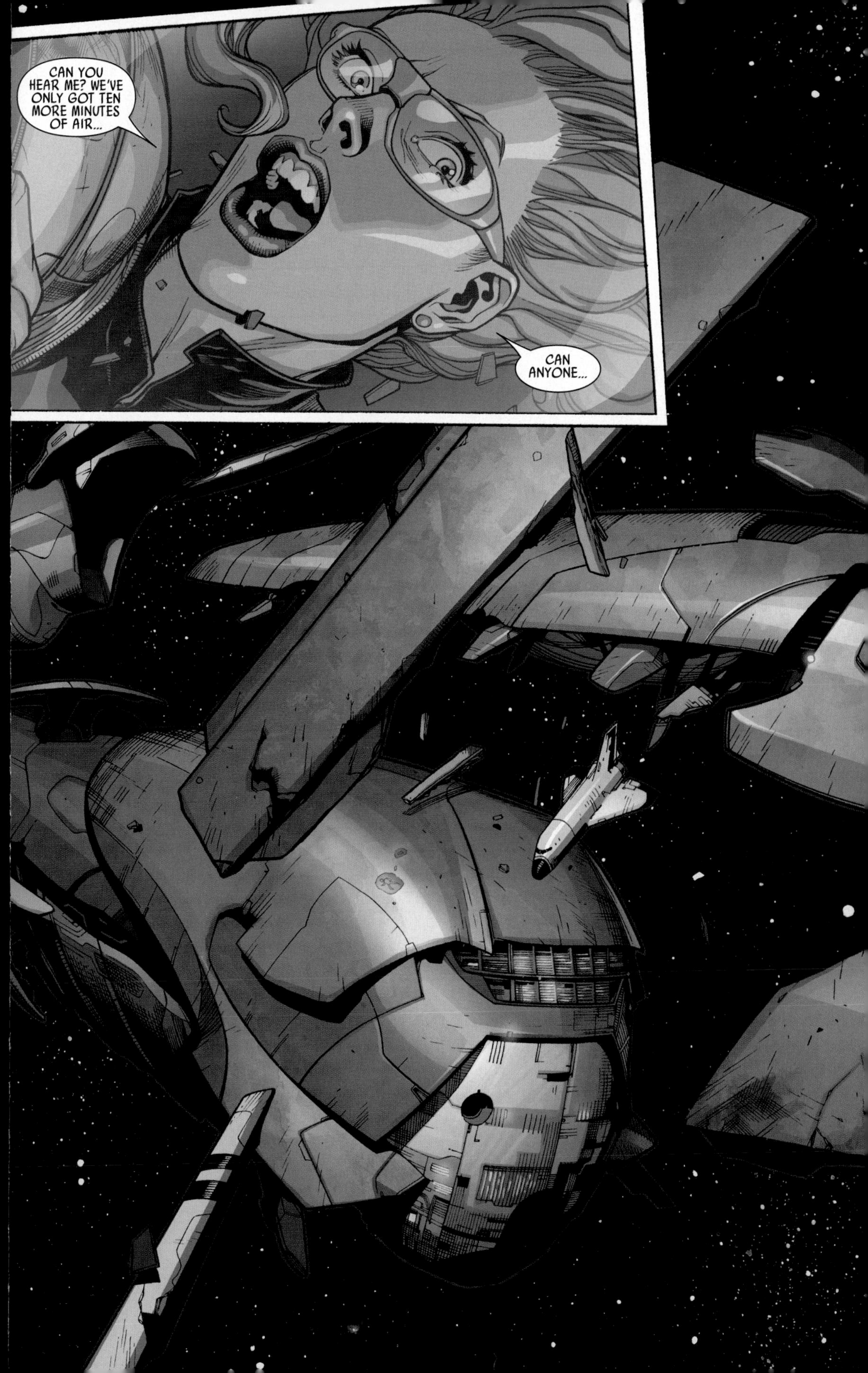
CAN YOU HEAR ME? WE'VE ONLY GOT TEN MORE MINUTES OF AIR...
CAN ANYONE...

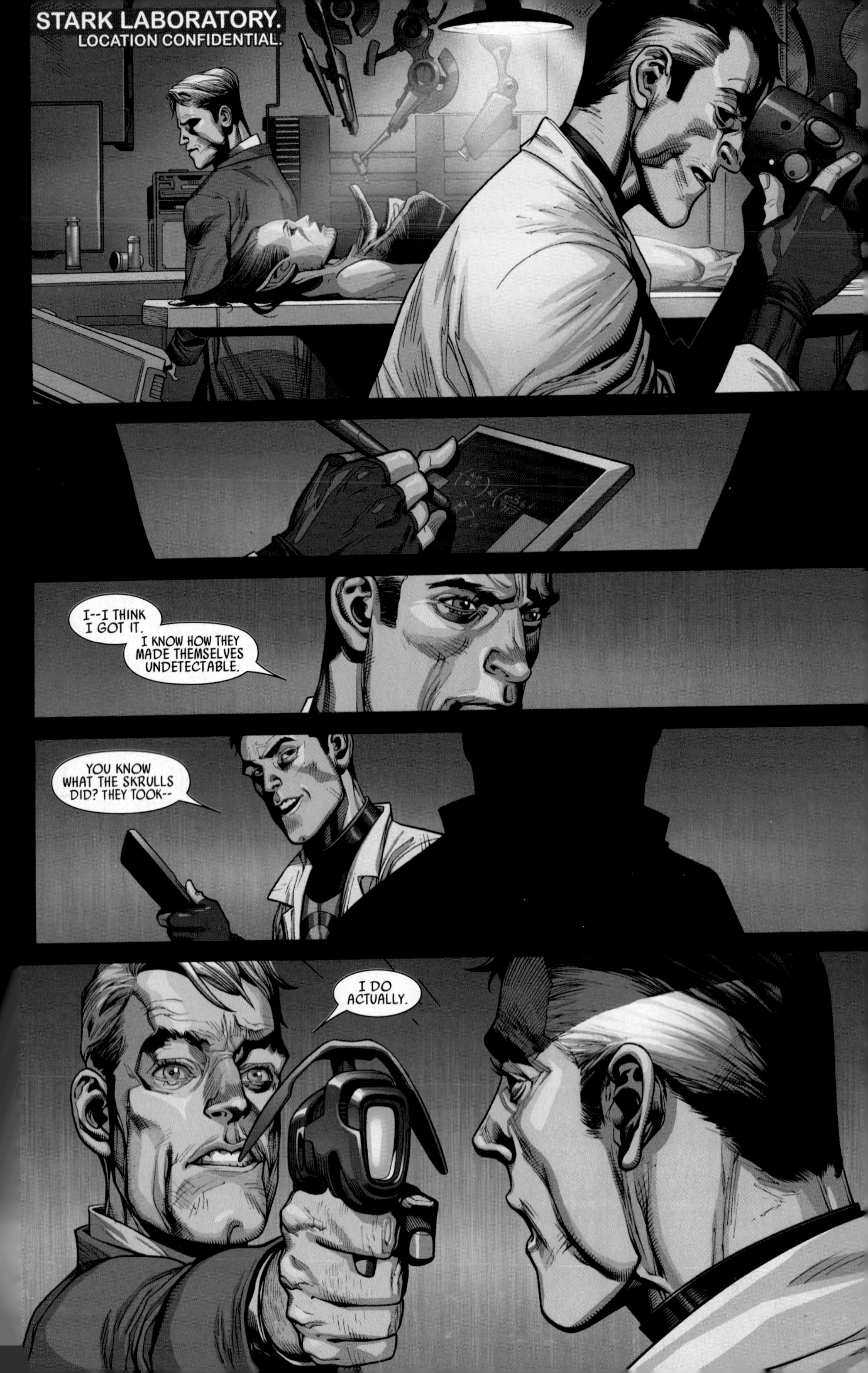
STARK LABORATORY.
LOCATION CONFIDENTIAL.
I--I THINK I GOT IT.
I KNOW HOW THEY MADE THEMSELVES UNDETECTABLE.
YOU KNOW WHAT THE SKRULLS DID? THEY TOOK--
I DO ACTUALLY.

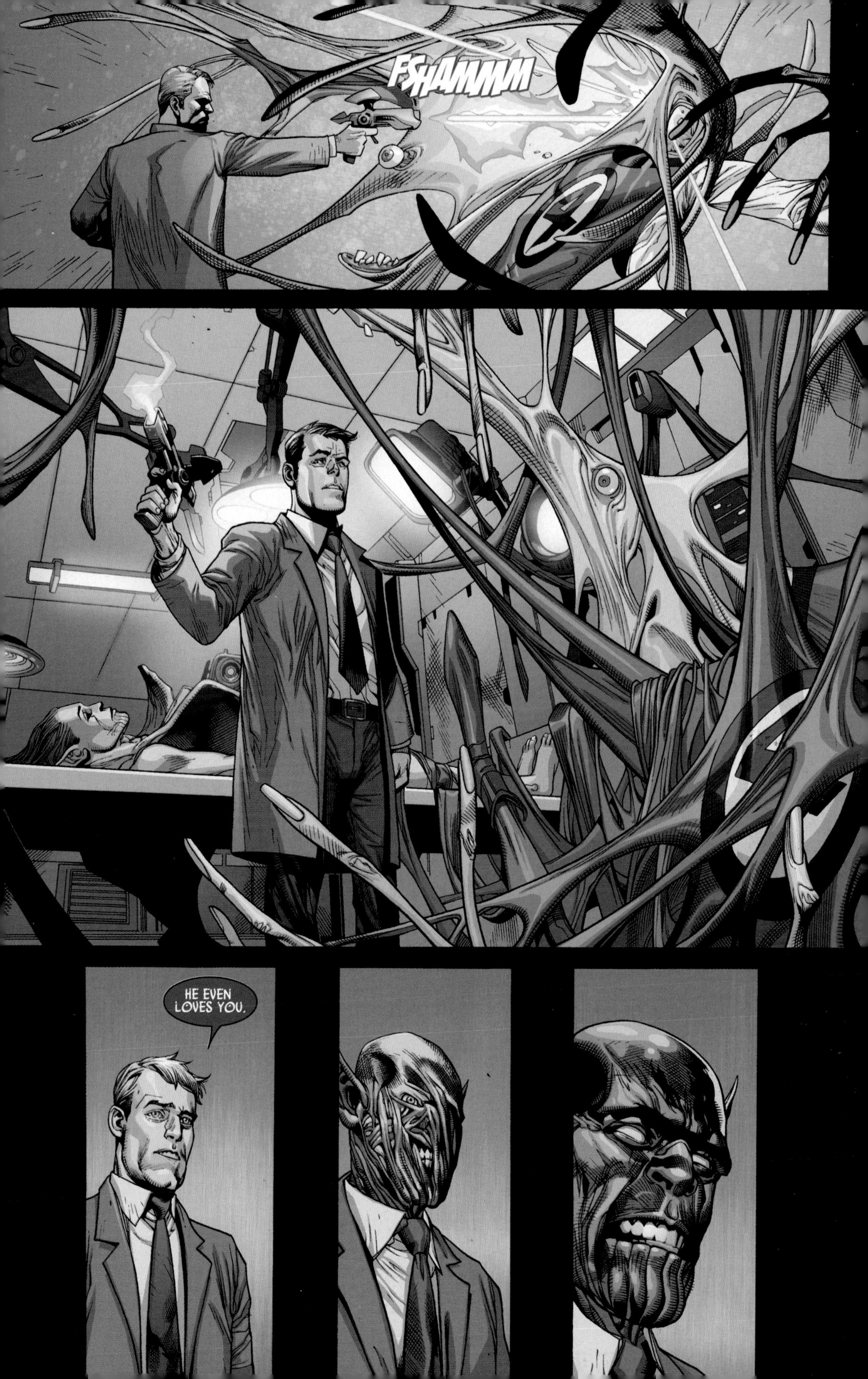
FSHAMMM
HE EVEN LOVES YOU.

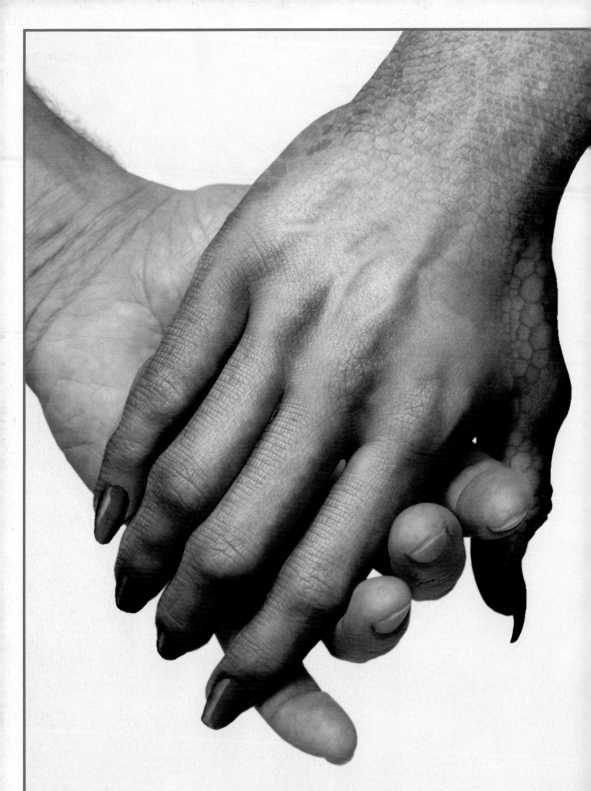

EMBRACE CHANGE

www.embracechange.org

SECRET INVASION

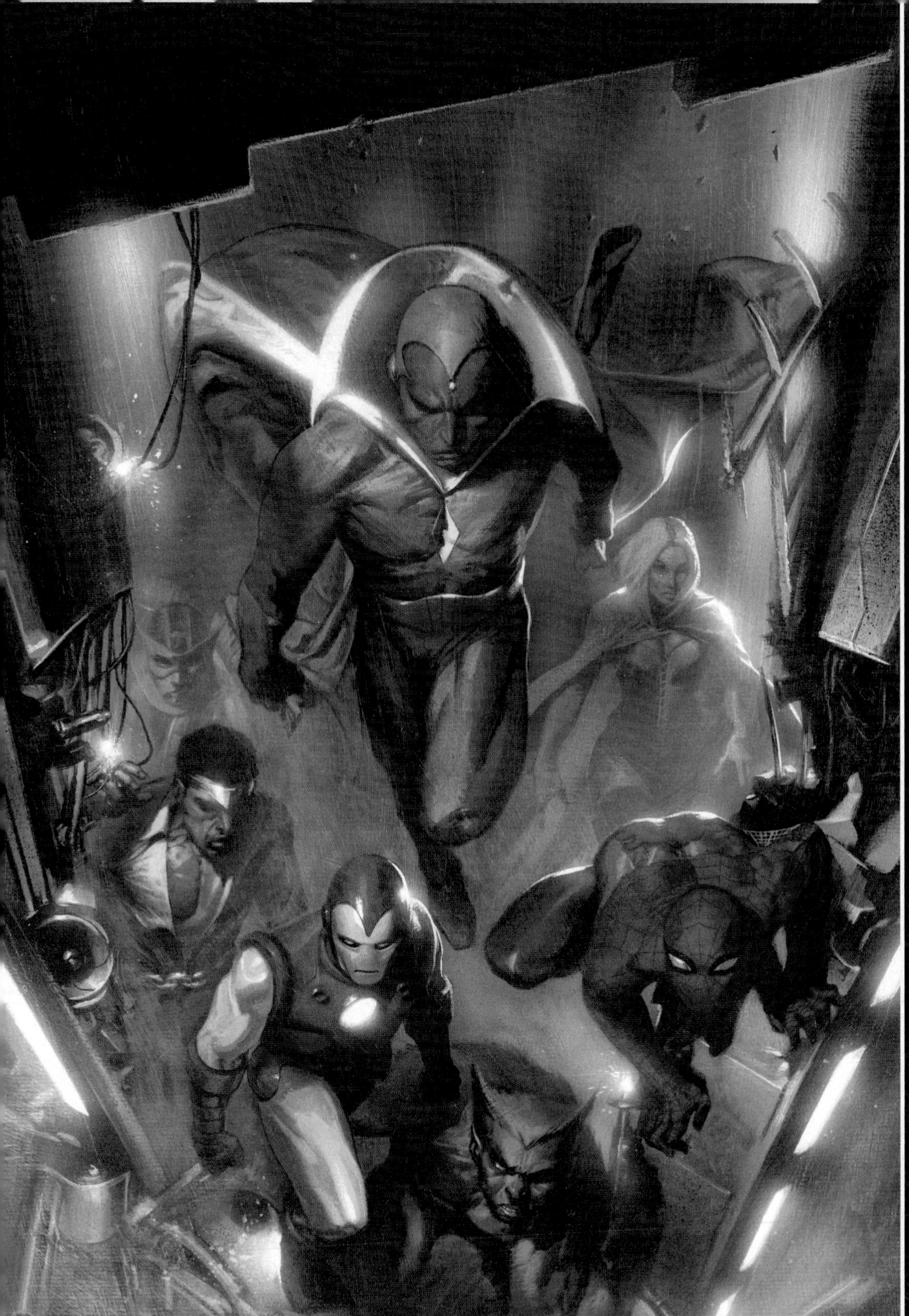

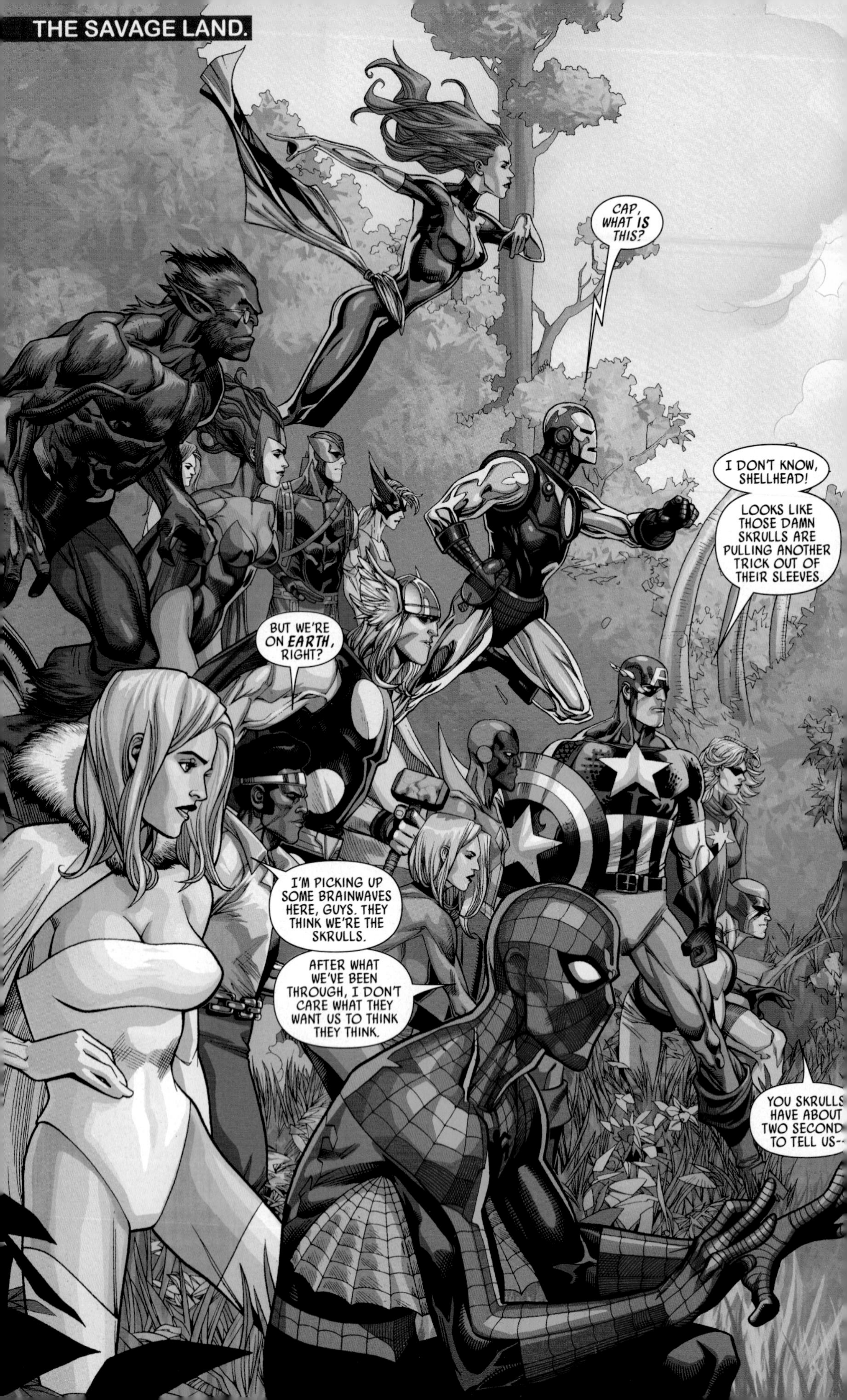
THE SAVAGE LAND.
CAP, WHAT IS THIS?
I DON'T KNOW, SHELLHEAD!
LOOKS LIKE THOSE DAMN SKRULLS ARE PULLING ANOTHER TRICK OUT OF THEIR SLEEVES.
BUT WE'RE ON EARTH, RIGHT?
I'M PICKING UP SOME BRAINWAVES HERE, GUYS. THEY THINK WE'RE THE SKRULLS.
AFTER WHAT WE'VE BEEN THROUGH, I DON'T CARE WHAT THEY WANT US TO THINK THEY THINK.
YOU SKRULLS HAVE ABOUT TWO SECOND TO TELL US--

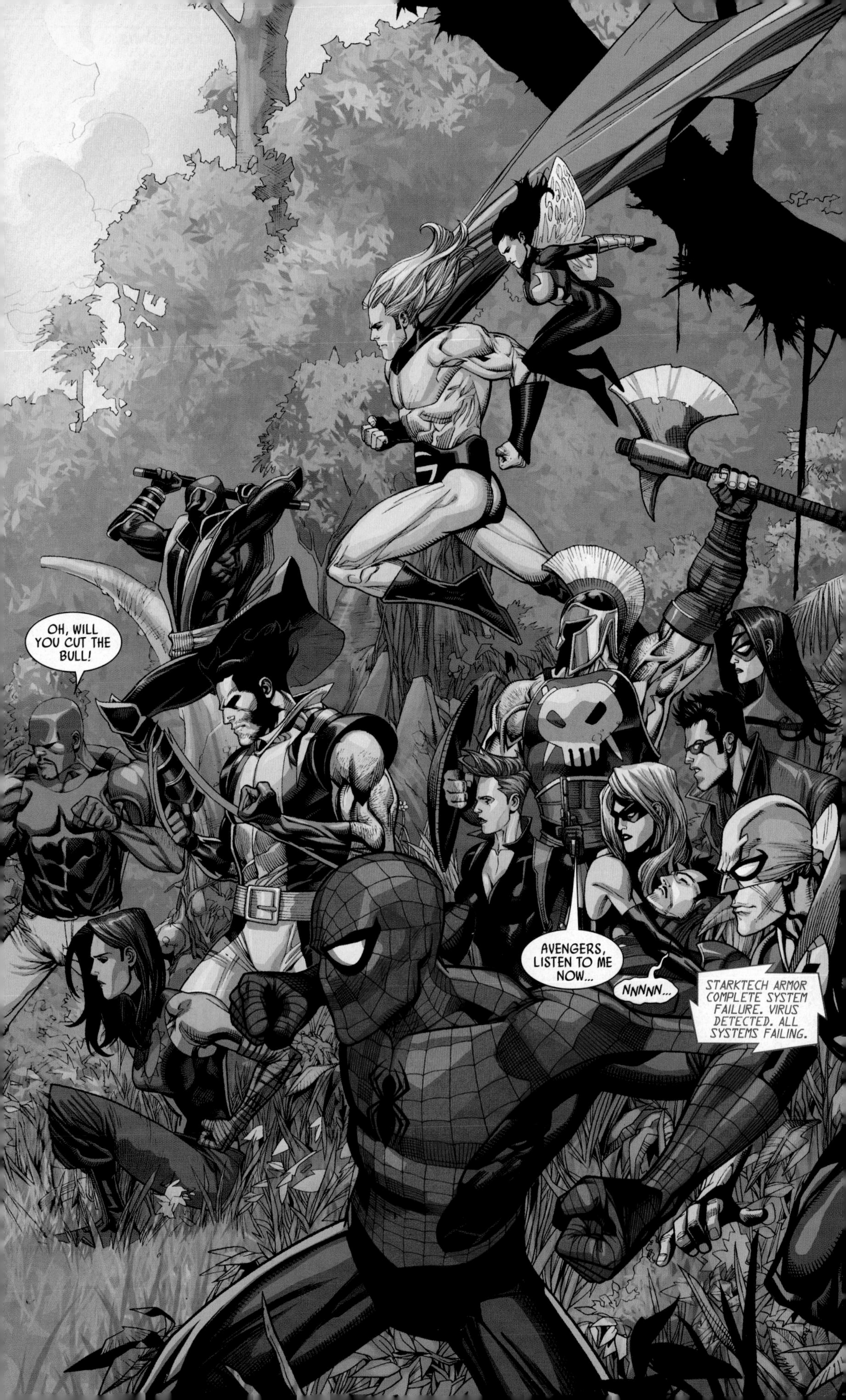
OH, WILL YOU CUT THE BULL!
AVENGERS, LISTEN TO ME NOW...
NNNNN...
STARKTECH ARMOR COMPLETE SYSTEM FAILURE. VIRUS DETECTED. ALL SYSTEMS FAILING.

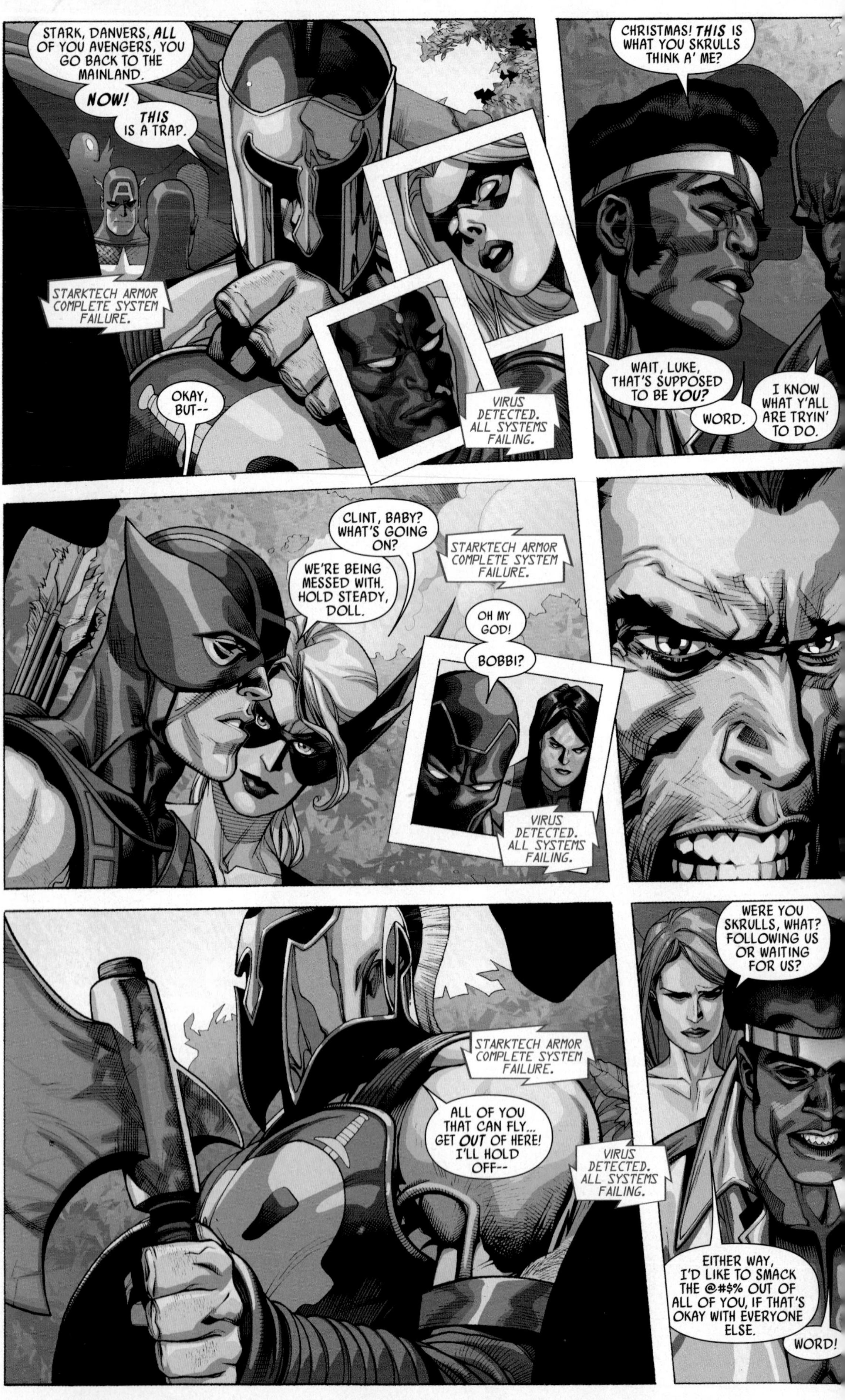
STARK, DANVERS, ALL OF YOU AVENGERS, YOU GO BACK TO THE MAINLAND.
NOW!
THIS IS A TRAP.
STARKTECH ARMOR COMPLETE SYSTEM FAILURE.
OKAY, BUT--
VIRUS DETECTED. ALL SYSTEMS FAILING.
CHRISTMAS! THIS IS WHAT YOU SKRULLS THINK A' ME?
WAIT, LUKE, THAT'S SUPPOSED TO BE YOU?
WORD.
I KNOW WHAT Y'ALL ARE TRYIN' TO DO.
CLINT, BABY? WHAT'S GOING ON?
WE'RE BEING MESSED WITH. HOLD STEADY, DOLL.
STARKTECH ARMOR COMPLETE SYSTEM FAILURE.
OH MY GOD!
BOBBI?
VIRUS DETECTED. ALL SYSTEMS FAILING.
STARKTECH ARMOR COMPLETE SYSTEM FAILURE.
ALL OF YOU THAT CAN FLY... GET OUT OF HERE! I'LL HOLD OFF--
VIRUS DETECTED. ALL SYSTEMS FAILING.
WERE YOU SKRULLS, WHAT? FOLLOWING US OR WAITING FOR US?
EITHER WAY, I'D LIKE TO SMACK THE @#$% OUT OF ALL OF YOU, IF THAT'S OKAY WITH EVERYONE ELSE.
WORD!

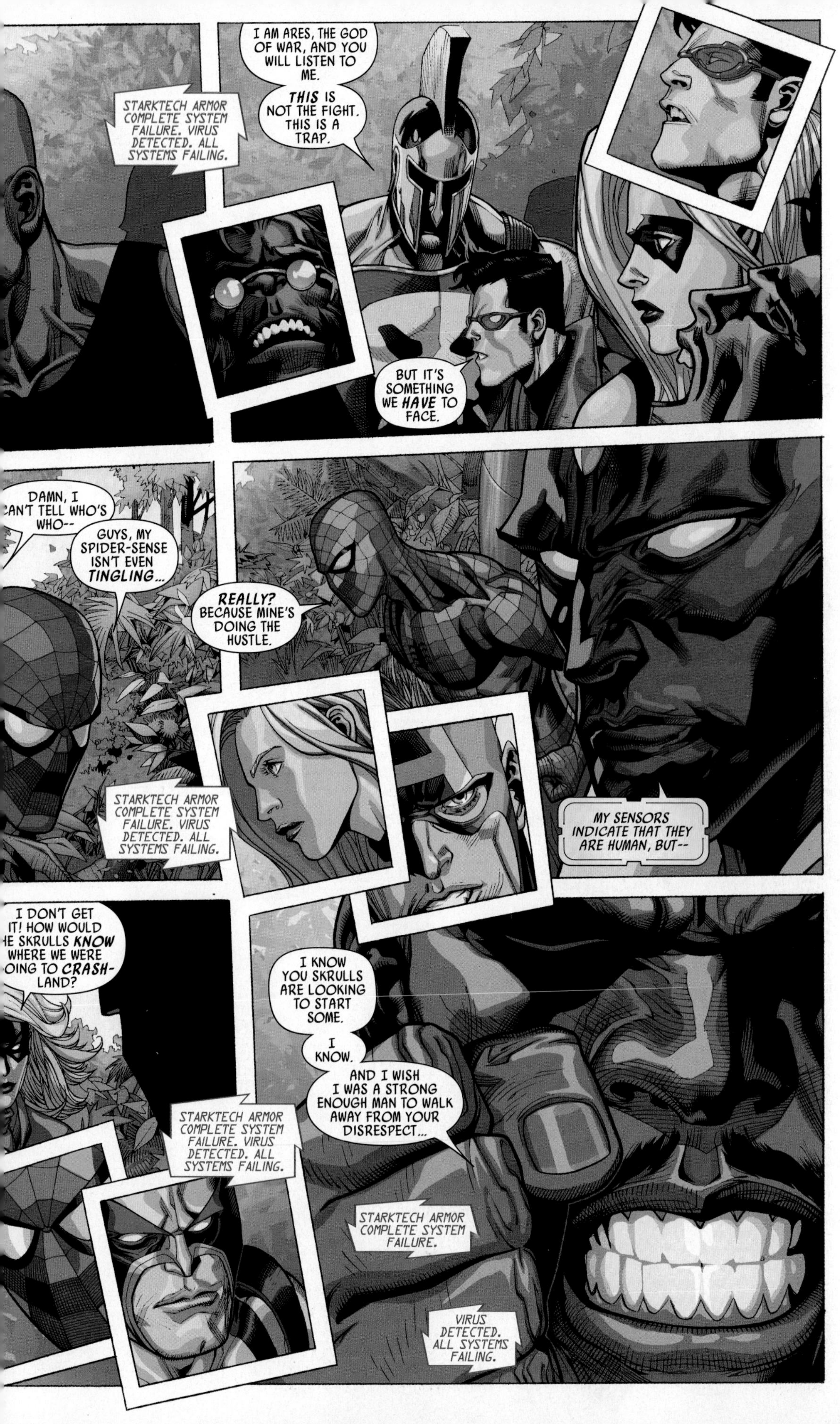
STARKTECH ARMOR COMPLETE SYSTEM FAILURE. VIRUS DETECTED. ALL SYSTEMS FAILING.
I AM ARES, THE GOD OF WAR, AND YOU WILL LISTEN TO ME.
THIS IS NOT THE FIGHT. THIS IS A TRAP.
BUT IT'S SOMETHING WE HAVE TO FACE.
DAMN, I CAN'T TELL WHO'S WHO--
GUYS, MY SPIDER-SENSE ISN'T EVEN TINGLING...
REALLY? BECAUSE MINE'S DOING THE HUSTLE.
STARKTECH ARMOR COMPLETE SYSTEM FAILURE. VIRUS DETECTED. ALL SYSTEMS FAILING.
MY SENSORS INDICATE THAT THEY ARE HUMAN, BUT--
I DON'T GET IT! HOW WOULD THE SKRULLS KNOW WHERE WE WERE GOING TO CRASH-LAND?
I KNOW YOU SKRULLS ARE LOOKING TO START SOME.
I KNOW.
AND I WISH I WAS A STRONG ENOUGH MAN TO WALK AWAY FROM YOUR DISRESPECT...
STARKTECH ARMOR COMPLETE SYSTEM FAILURE. VIRUS DETECTED. ALL SYSTEMS FAILING.
STARKTECH ARMOR COMPLETE SYSTEM FAILURE.
VIRUS DETECTED. ALL SYSTEMS FAILING.

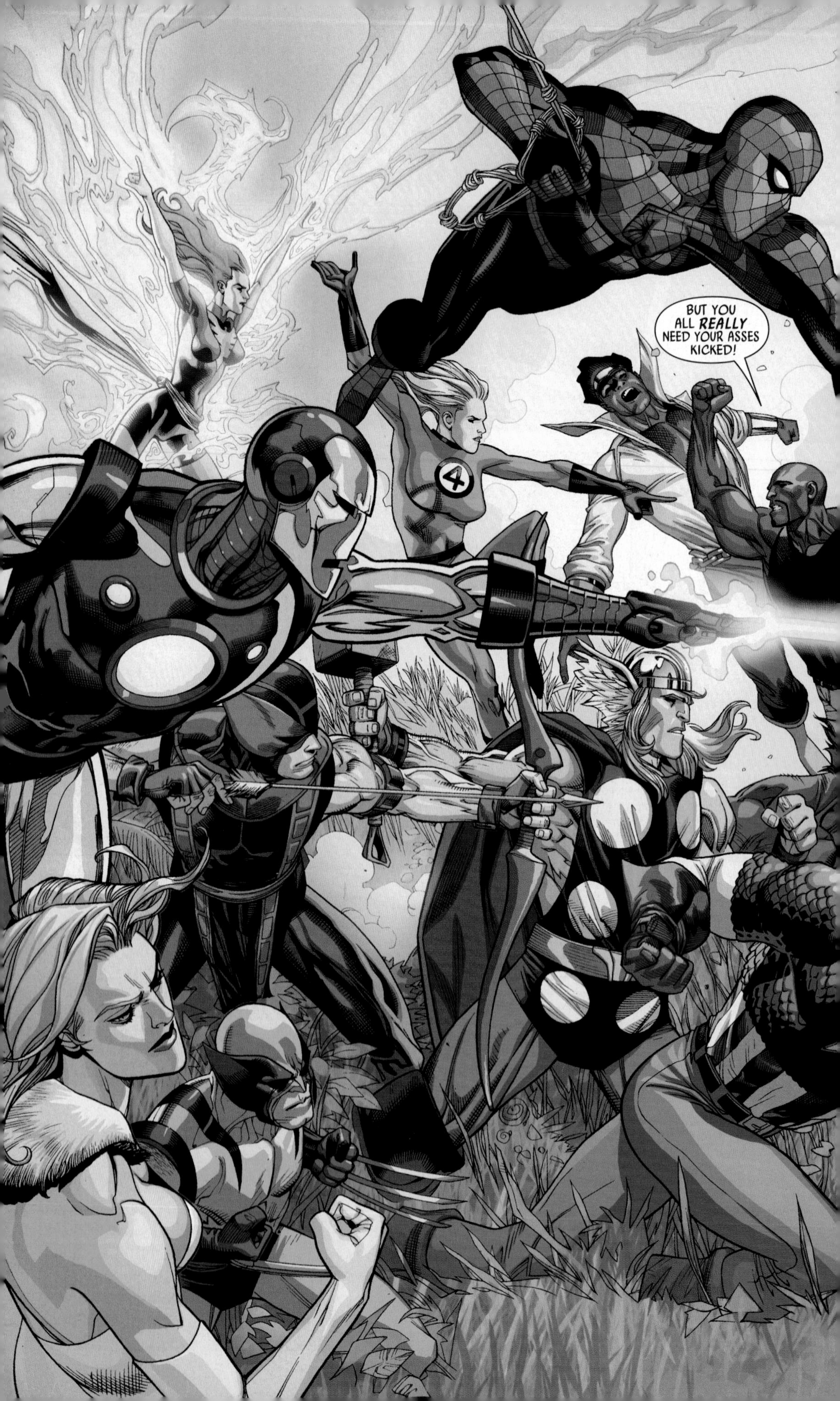
BUT YOU ALL REALLY NEED YOUR ASSES KICKED!

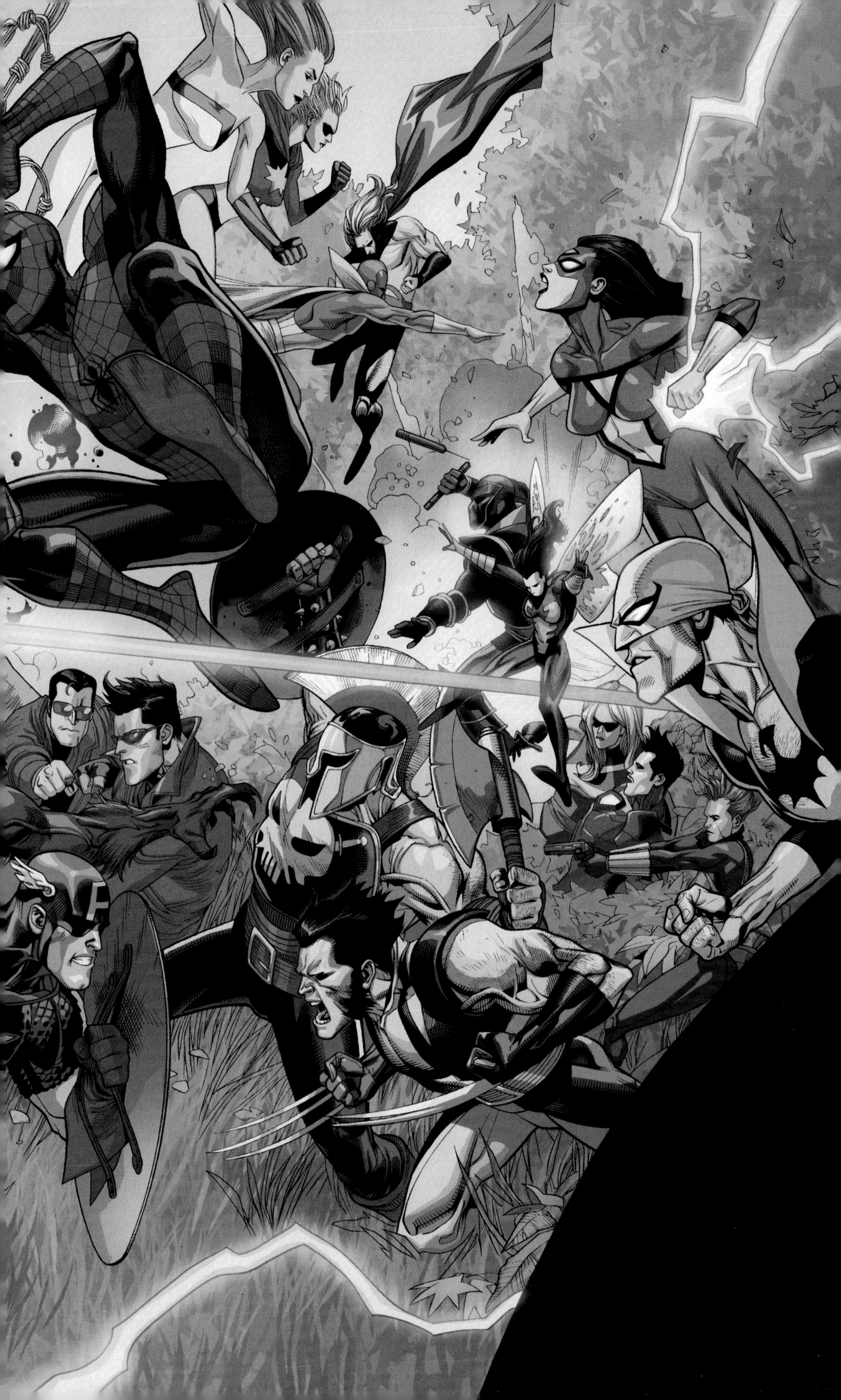

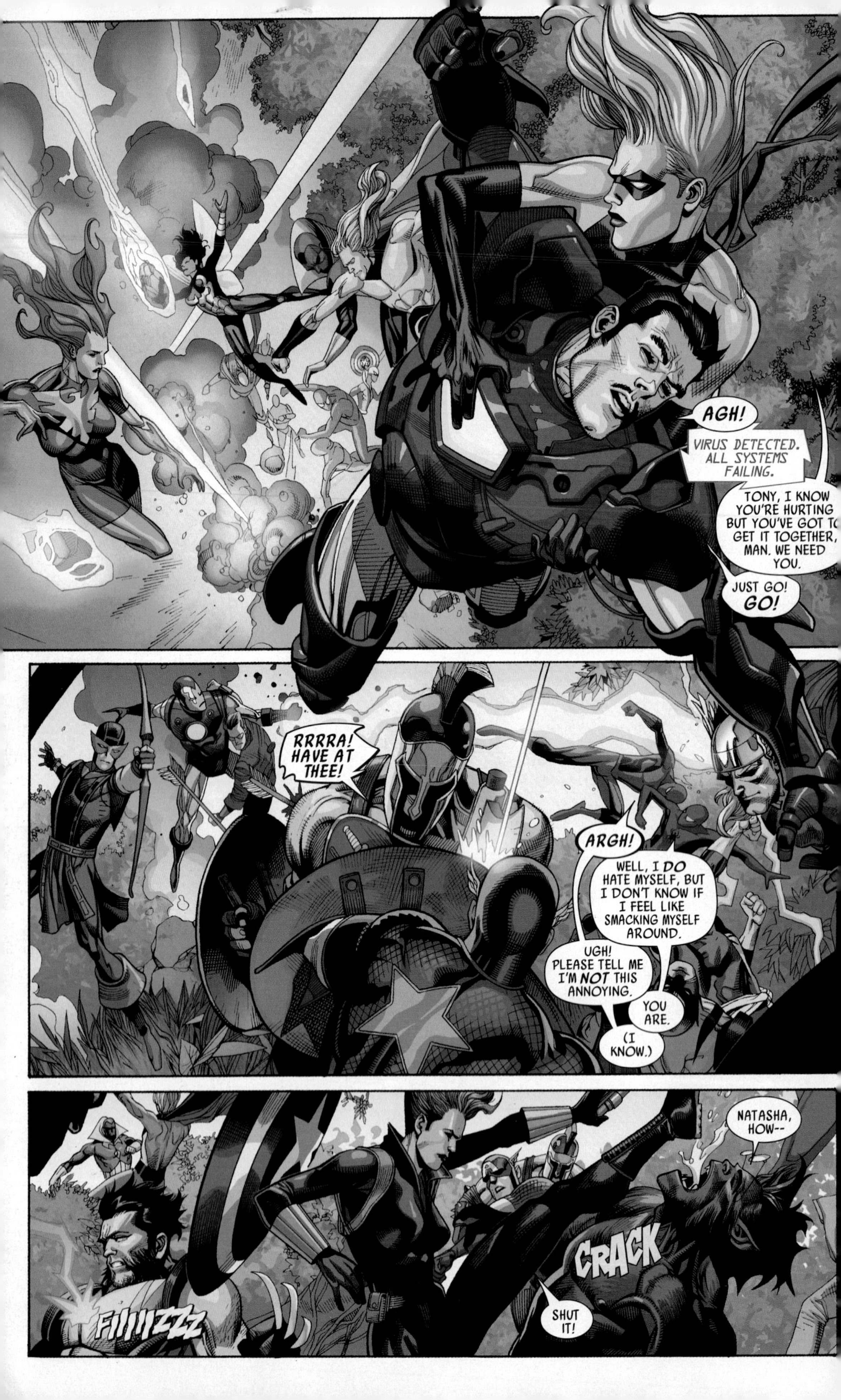
AGH!
VIRUS DETECTED. ALL SYSTEMS FAILING.
TONY, I KNOW YOU'RE HURTING BUT YOU'VE GOT TO GET IT TOGETHER, MAN. WE NEED YOU.
JUST GO! GO!
RRRRA! HAVE AT THEE!
ARGH!
WELL, I DO HATE MYSELF, BUT I DON'T KNOW IF I FEEL LIKE SMACKING MYSELF AROUND.
UGH! PLEASE TELL ME I'M NOT THIS ANNOYING.
YOU ARE.
(I KNOW.)
NATASHA, HOW--
CRACK
SHUT IT!
FIIIIIZZZ

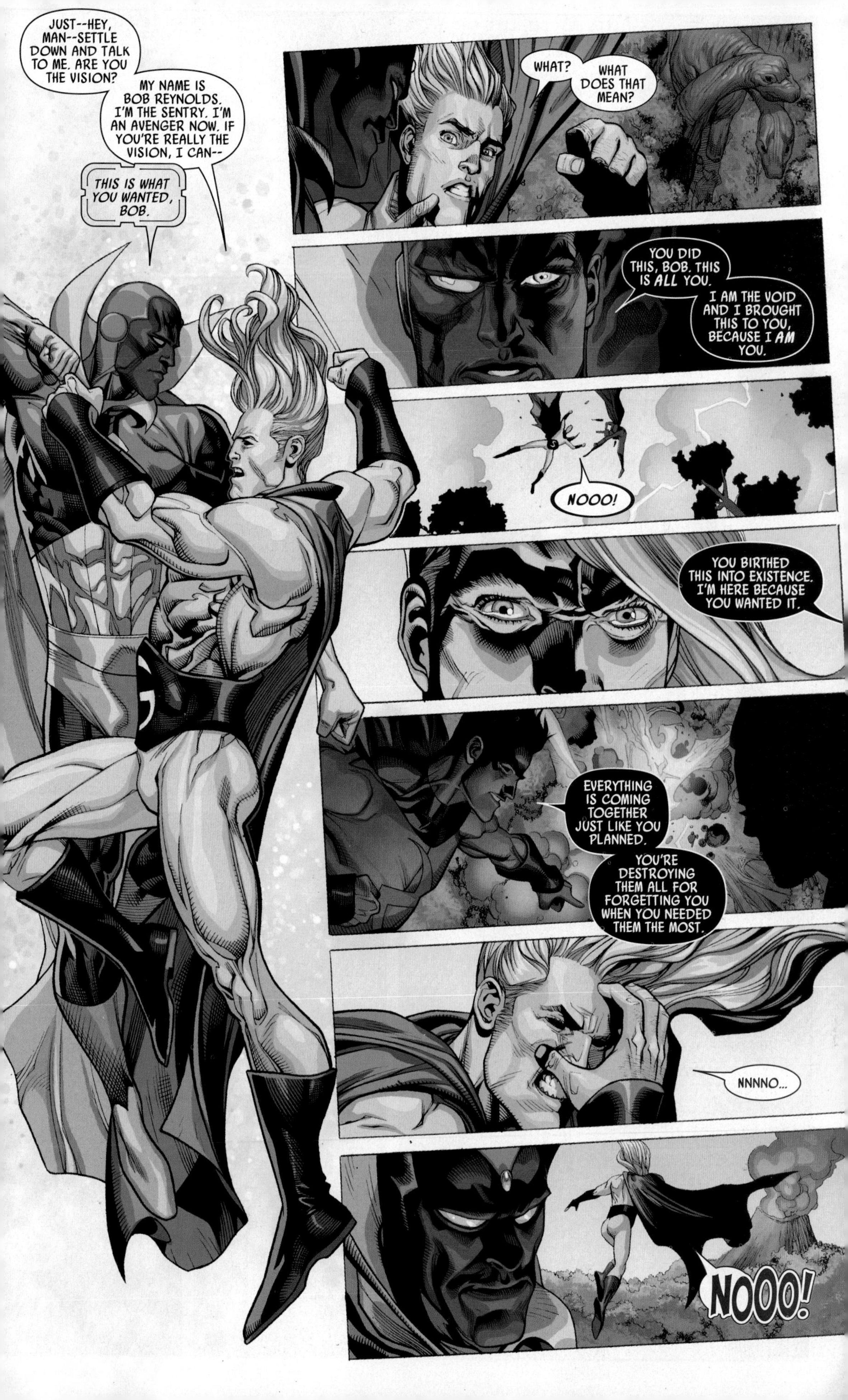
JUST--HEY, MAN--SETTLE DOWN AND TALK TO ME. ARE YOU THE VISION?
MY NAME IS BOB REYNOLDS. I'M THE SENTRY. I'M AN AVENGER NOW. IF YOU'RE REALLY THE VISION, I CAN--
THIS IS WHAT YOU WANTED, BOB.
WHAT?
WHAT DOES THAT MEAN?
YOU DID THIS, BOB. THIS IS ALL YOU.
I AM THE VOID AND I BROUGHT THIS TO YOU, BECAUSE I AM YOU.
NOOO!
YOU BIRTHED THIS INTO EXISTENCE. I'M HERE BECAUSE YOU WANTED IT.
EVERYTHING IS COMING TOGETHER JUST LIKE YOU PLANNED.
YOU'RE DESTROYING THEM ALL FOR FORGETTING YOU WHEN YOU NEEDED THEM THE MOST.
NNNNO...
NOOO!

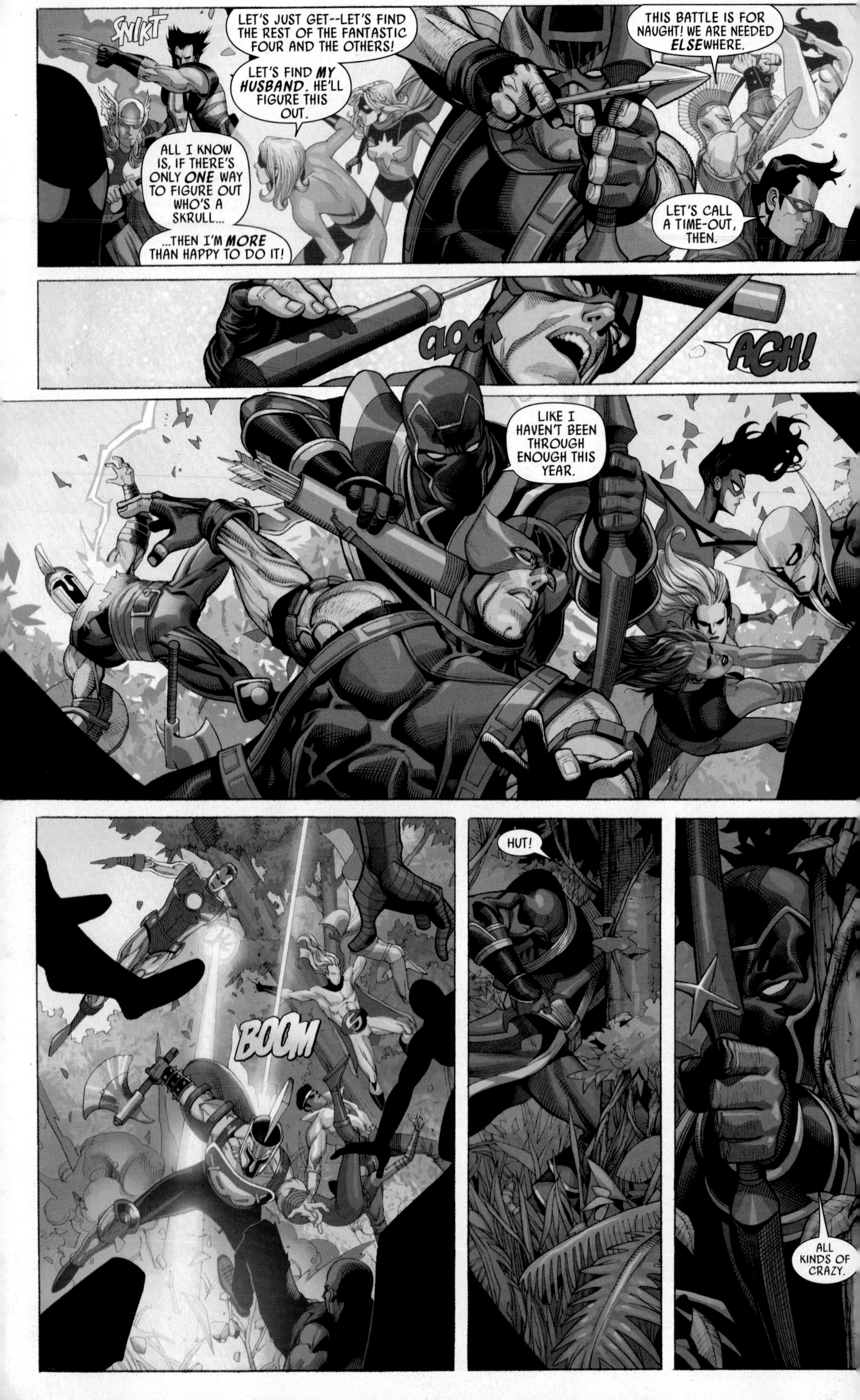
SNIKT
LET'S JUST GET--LET'S FIND THE REST OF THE FANTASTIC FOUR AND THE OTHERS!
LET'S FIND MY HUSBAND. HE'LL FIGURE THIS OUT.
ALL I KNOW IS, IF THERE'S ONLY ONE WAY TO FIGURE OUT WHO'S A SKRULL...
...THEN I'M MORE THAN HAPPY TO DO IT!
THIS BATTLE IS FOR NAUGHT! WE ARE NEEDED ELSEWHERE.
LET'S CALL A TIME-OUT, THEN.
CLOCK
AGH!
LIKE I HAVEN'T BEEN THROUGH ENOUGH THIS YEAR.
BOOM
HUT!
ALL KINDS OF CRAZY.

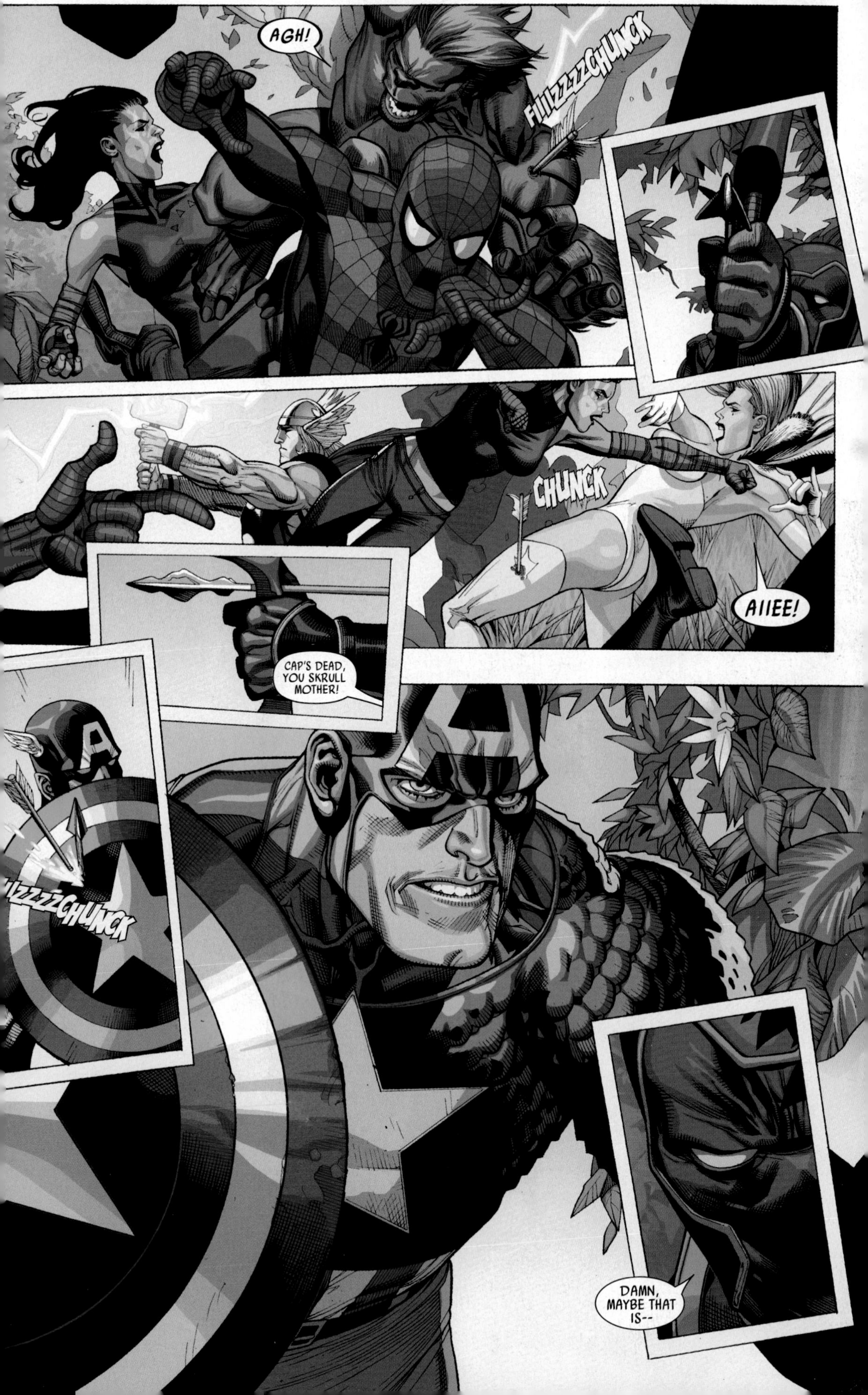
AGH!
FIIIzzzzCHUNCK
CHUNCK
AIIEE!
CAP'S DEAD, YOU SKRULL MOTHER!
IIzzzzzCHUNCK
DAMN, MAYBE THAT IS--

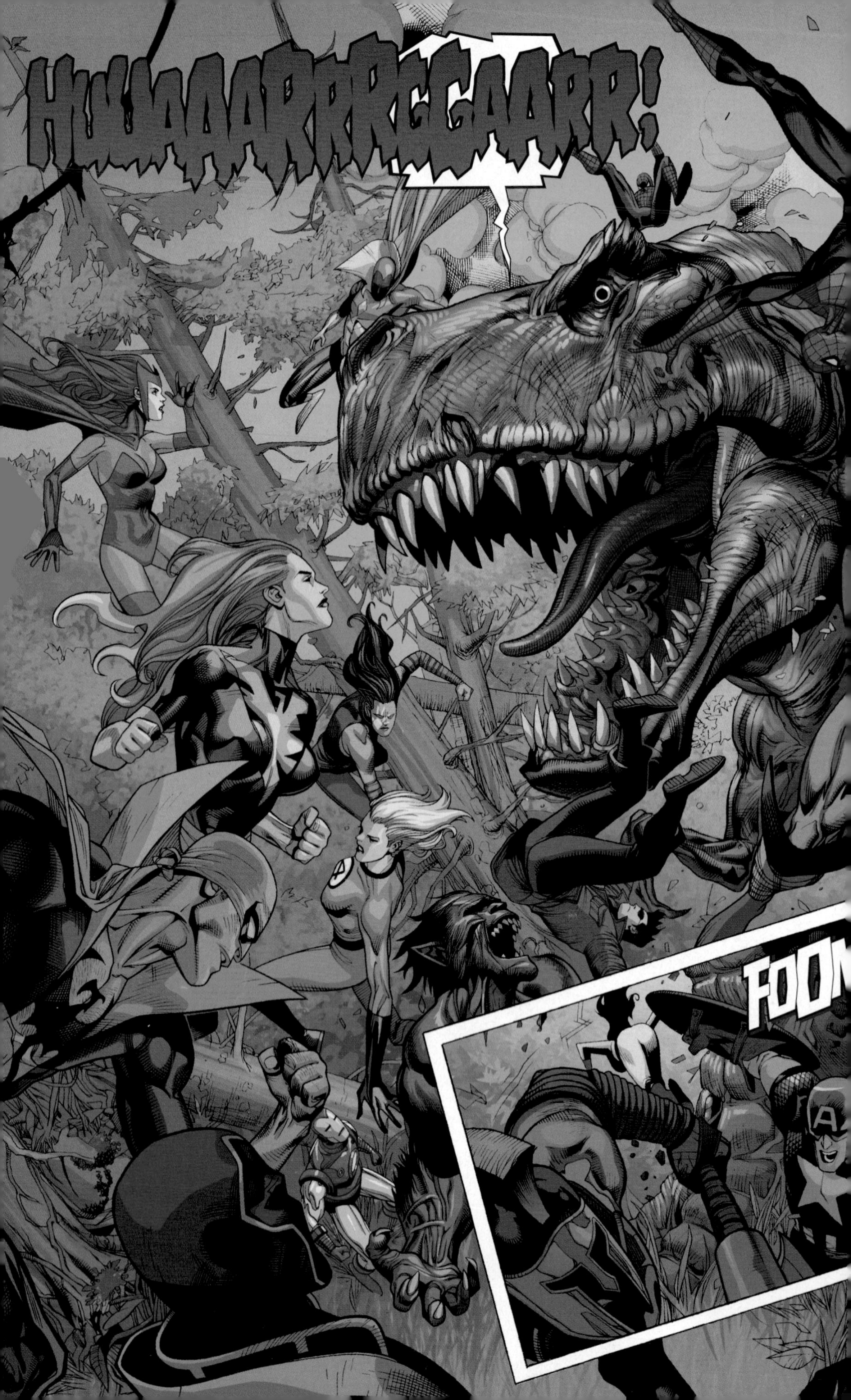
HUUAAARRRGAARR!
FOOM

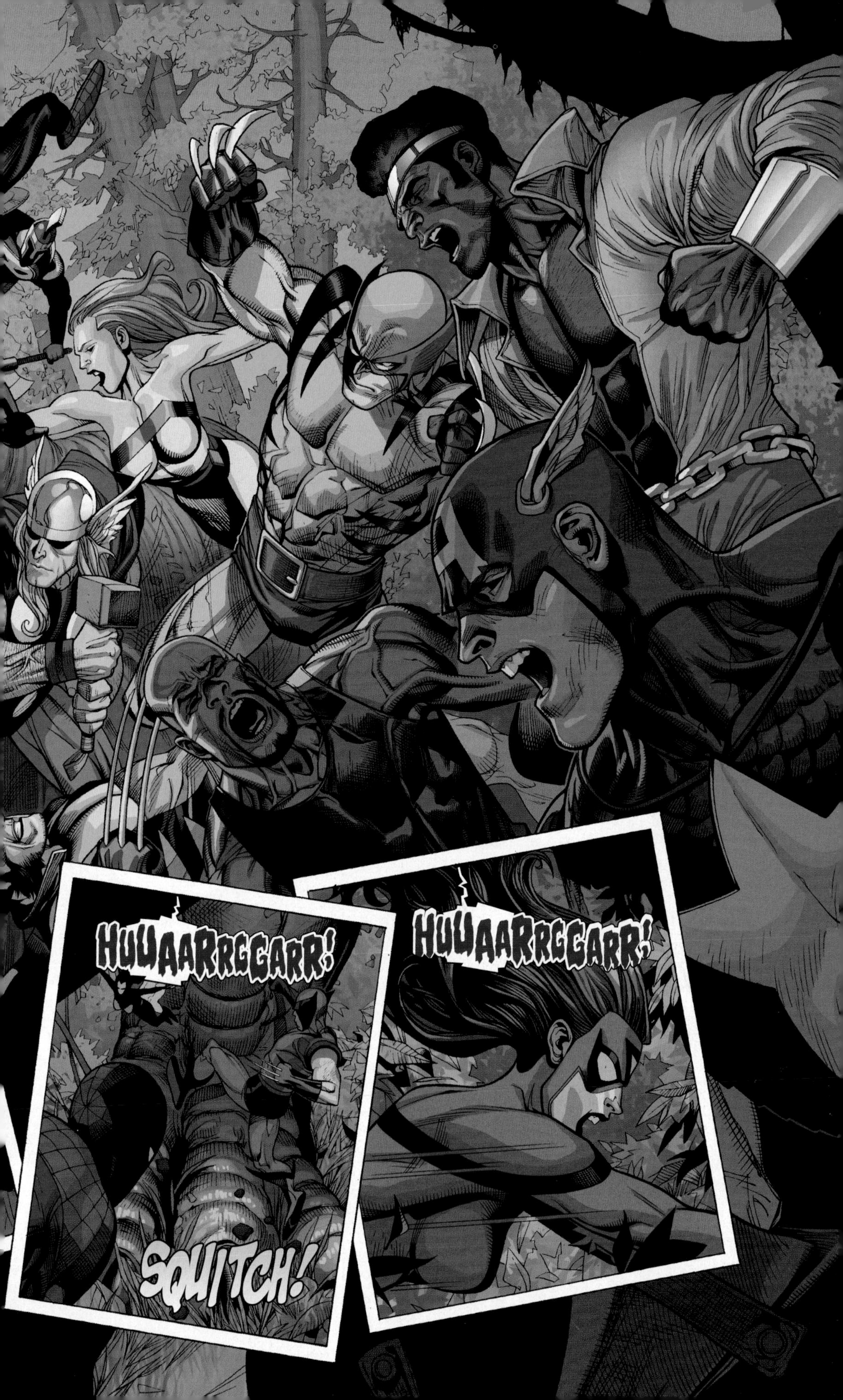
HUUAARRGGARR!
SQUITCH!
HUUAARRGGARR!

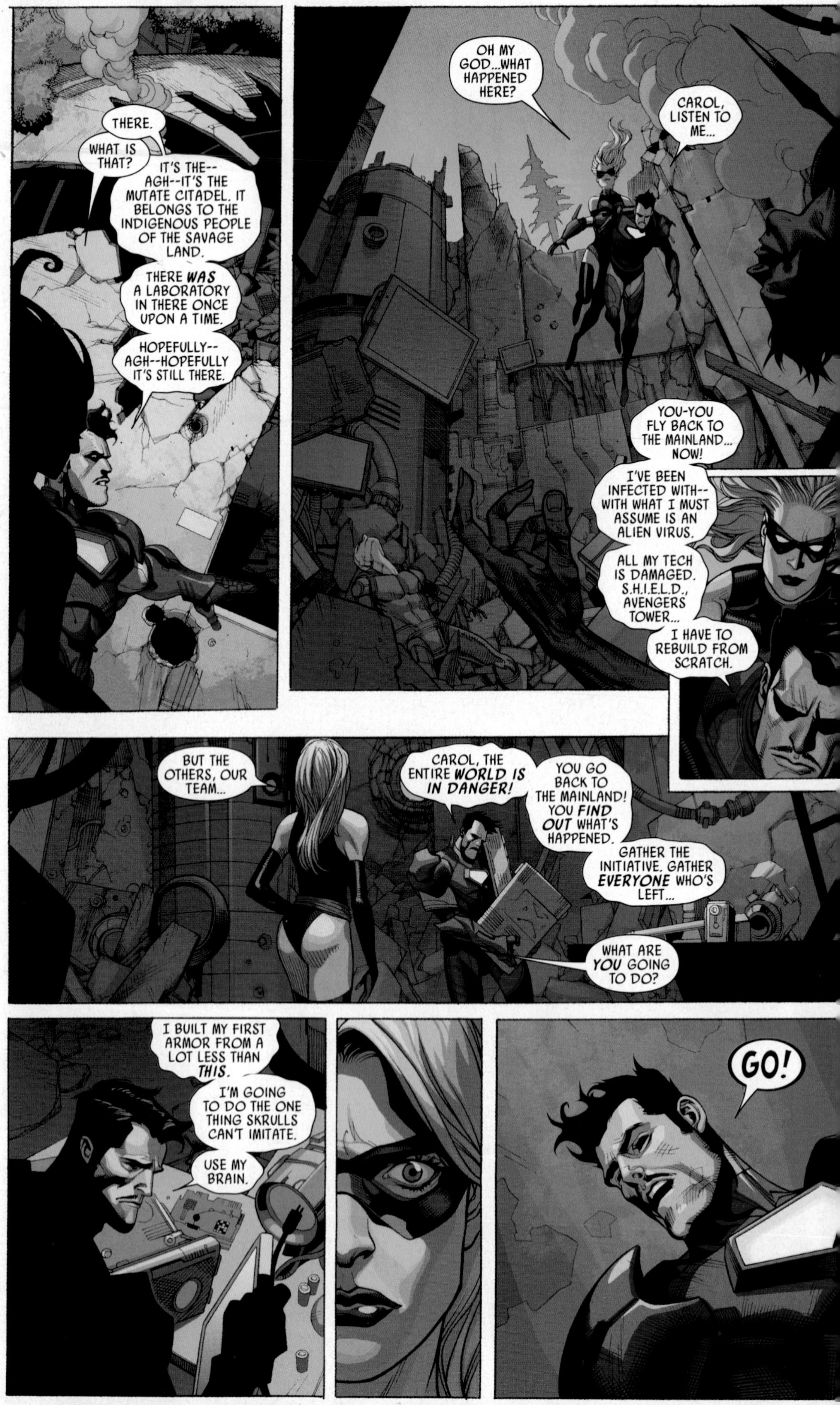
THERE.
WHAT IS THAT?
IT'S THE--AGH--IT'S THE MUTATE CITADEL. IT BELONGS TO THE INDIGENOUS PEOPLE OF THE SAVAGE LAND.
THERE WAS A LABORATORY IN THERE ONCE UPON A TIME.
HOPEFULLY--AGH--HOPEFULLY IT'S STILL THERE.
OH MY GOD...WHAT HAPPENED HERE?
CAROL, LISTEN TO ME...
YOU-YOU FLY BACK TO THE MAINLAND... NOW!
I'VE BEEN INFECTED WITH--WITH WHAT I MUST ASSUME IS AN ALIEN VIRUS.
ALL MY TECH IS DAMAGED. S.H.I.E.L.D., AVENGERS TOWER...
I HAVE TO REBUILD FROM SCRATCH.
BUT THE OTHERS, OUR TEAM...
CAROL, THE ENTIRE WORLD IS IN DANGER!
YOU GO BACK TO THE MAINLAND! YOU FIND OUT WHAT'S HAPPENED.
GATHER THE INITIATIVE. GATHER EVERYONE WHO'S LEFT...
WHAT ARE YOU GOING TO DO?
I BUILT MY FIRST ARMOR FROM A LOT LESS THAN THIS.
I'M GOING TO DO THE ONE THING SKRULLS CAN'T IMITATE.
USE MY BRAIN.
GO!

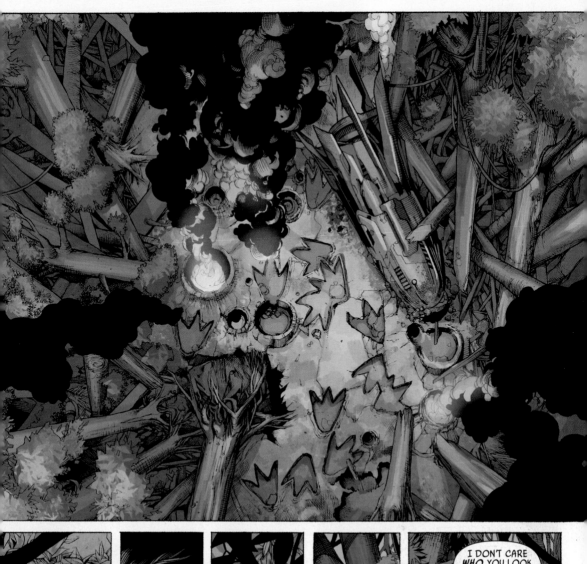

I DON'T CARE *WHO* YOU LOOK LIKE...YA COME NEAR ME, I'LL GUT YA.

EXCEPT YOU CAN'T. UNBREAKABLE SKIN.

UNBREAKABLE CLAWS.

AND LOOK AT THAT...

SNIFF...

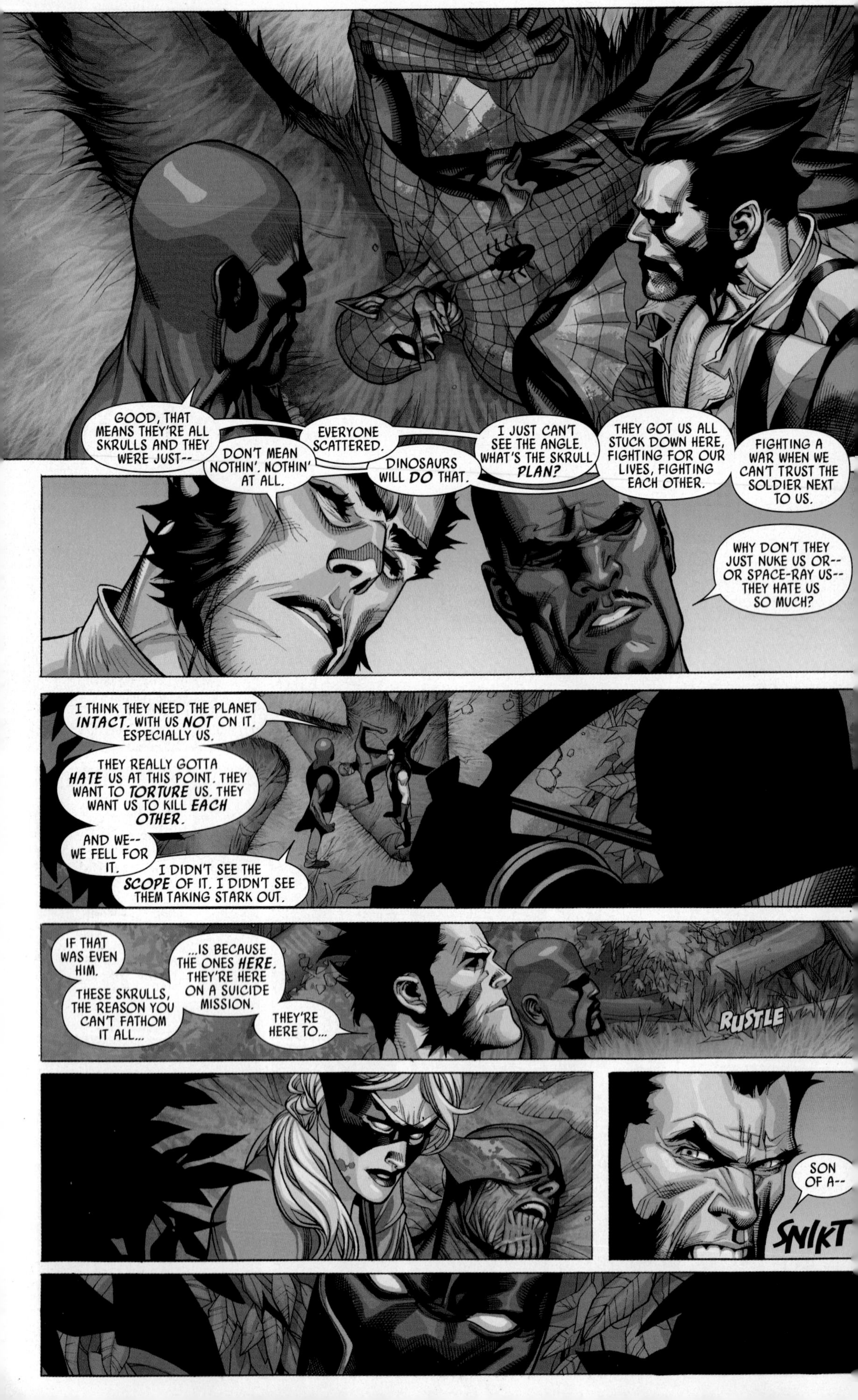
GOOD, THAT MEANS THEY'RE ALL SKRULLS AND THEY WERE JUST--
DON'T MEAN NOTHIN'. NOTHIN' AT ALL.
EVERYONE SCATTERED.
DINOSAURS WILL DO THAT.
I JUST CAN'T SEE THE ANGLE. WHAT'S THE SKRULL PLAN?
THEY GOT US ALL STUCK DOWN HERE, FIGHTING FOR OUR LIVES, FIGHTING EACH OTHER.
FIGHTING A WAR WHEN WE CAN'T TRUST THE SOLDIER NEXT TO US.
WHY DON'T THEY JUST NUKE US OR-- OR SPACE-RAY US-- THEY HATE US SO MUCH?
I THINK THEY NEED THE PLANET INTACT. WITH US NOT ON IT. ESPECIALLY US.
THEY REALLY GOTTA HATE US AT THIS POINT. THEY WANT TO TORTURE US. THEY WANT US TO KILL EACH OTHER.
AND WE-- WE FELL FOR IT.
I DIDN'T SEE THE SCOPE OF IT. I DIDN'T SEE THEM TAKING STARK OUT.
IF THAT WAS EVEN HIM.
THESE SKRULLS, THE REASON YOU CAN'T FATHOM IT ALL...
...IS BECAUSE THE ONES HERE. THEY'RE HERE ON A SUICIDE MISSION.
THEY'RE HERE TO...
RUSTLE
SON OF A--
SNIKT

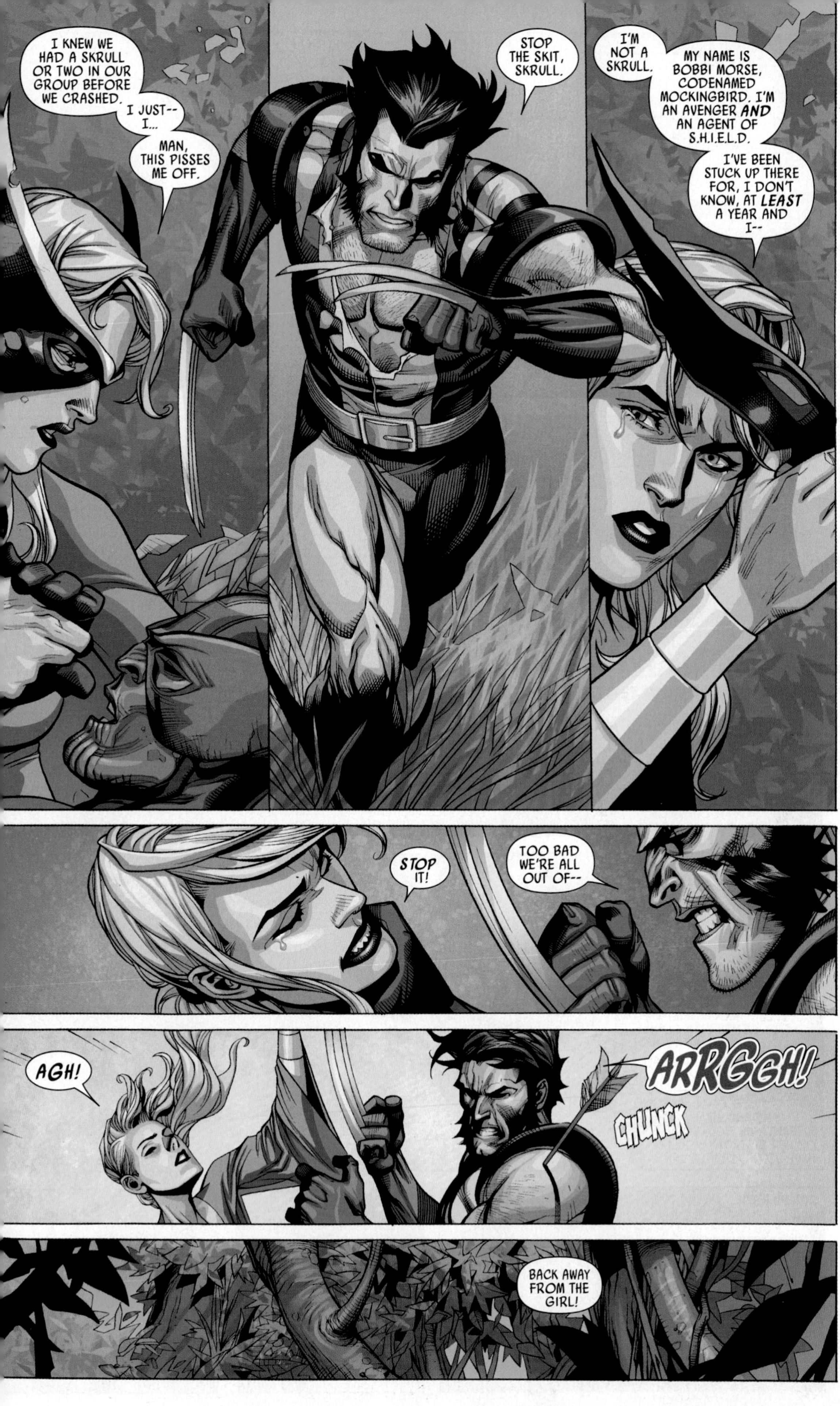
I KNEW WE HAD A SKRULL OR TWO IN OUR GROUP BEFORE WE CRASHED.
I JUST-- I...
MAN, THIS PISSES ME OFF.
STOP THE SKIT, SKRULL.
I'M NOT A SKRULL.
MY NAME IS BOBBI MORSE, CODENAMED MOCKINGBIRD. I'M AN AVENGER AND AN AGENT OF S.H.I.E.L.D.
I'VE BEEN STUCK UP THERE FOR, I DON'T KNOW, AT LEAST A YEAR AND I--
STOP IT!
TOO BAD WE'RE ALL OUT OF--
AGH!
ARRGGH!
CHUNCK
BACK AWAY FROM THE GIRL!

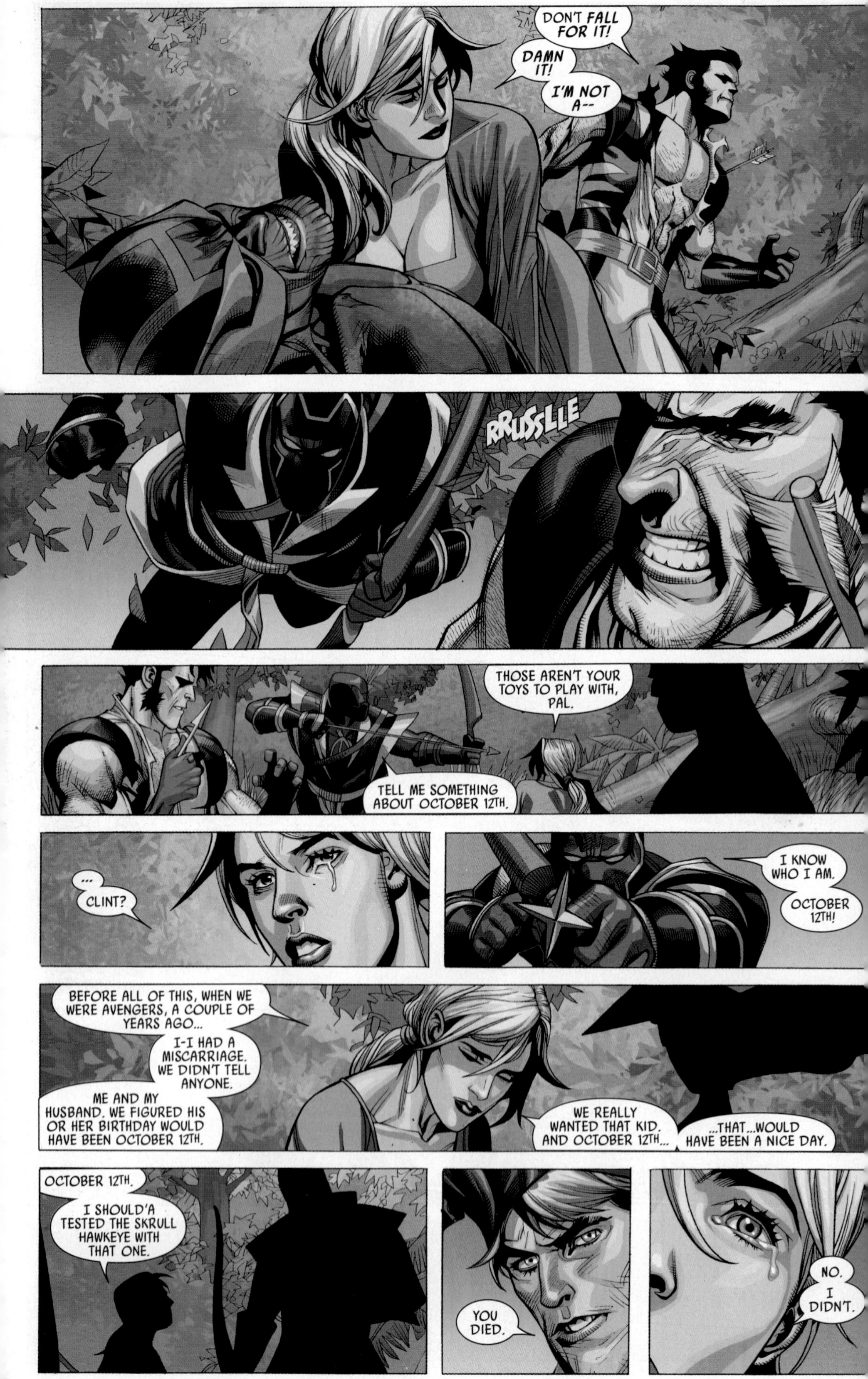
DON'T FALL FOR IT!
DAMN IT!
I'M NOT A--
RRUSSLLE
THOSE AREN'T YOUR TOYS TO PLAY WITH, PAL.
TELL ME SOMETHING ABOUT OCTOBER 12TH.
... CLINT?
I KNOW WHO I AM.
OCTOBER 12TH!
BEFORE ALL OF THIS, WHEN WE WERE AVENGERS, A COUPLE OF YEARS AGO...
I-I HAD A MISCARRIAGE. WE DIDN'T TELL ANYONE.
ME AND MY HUSBAND. WE FIGURED HIS OR HER BIRTHDAY WOULD HAVE BEEN OCTOBER 12TH.
WE REALLY WANTED THAT KID. AND OCTOBER 12TH...
...THAT...WOULD HAVE BEEN A NICE DAY.
OCTOBER 12TH.
I SHOULD'A TESTED THE SKRULL HAWKEYE WITH THAT ONE.
YOU DIED.
NO. I DIDN'T.

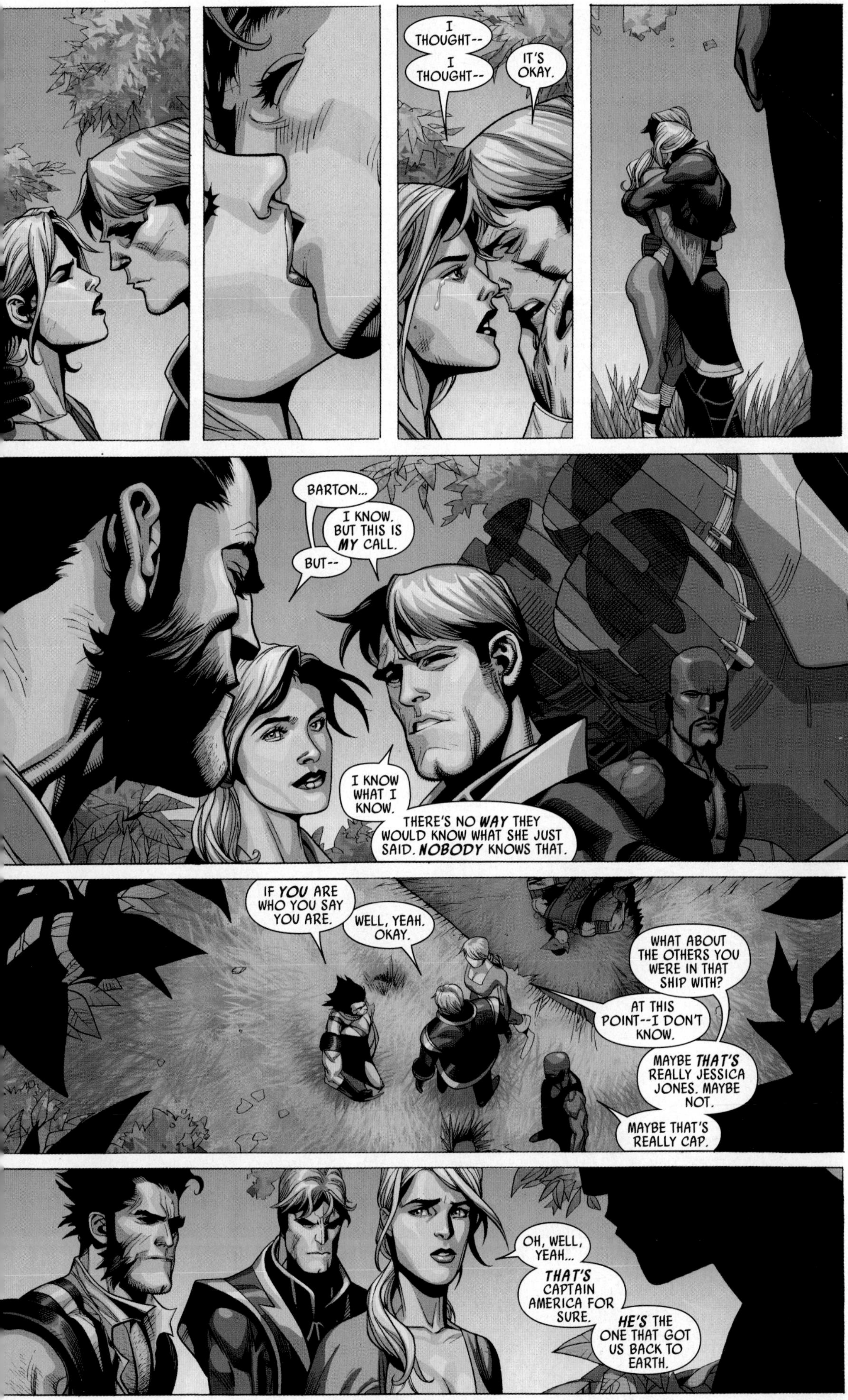
I THOUGHT--
I THOUGHT--
IT'S OKAY.
BARTON...
I KNOW. BUT THIS IS *MY* CALL.
BUT--
I KNOW WHAT I KNOW.
THERE'S NO *WAY* THEY WOULD KNOW WHAT SHE JUST SAID. *NOBODY* KNOWS THAT.
IF *YOU* ARE WHO YOU SAY YOU ARE.
WELL, YEAH. OKAY.
WHAT ABOUT THE OTHERS YOU WERE IN THAT SHIP WITH?
AT THIS POINT--I DON'T KNOW.
MAYBE *THAT'S* REALLY JESSICA JONES. MAYBE NOT.
MAYBE THAT'S REALLY CAP.
OH, WELL, YEAH...
THAT'S CAPTAIN AMERICA FOR SURE.
HE'S THE ONE THAT GOT US BACK TO EARTH.

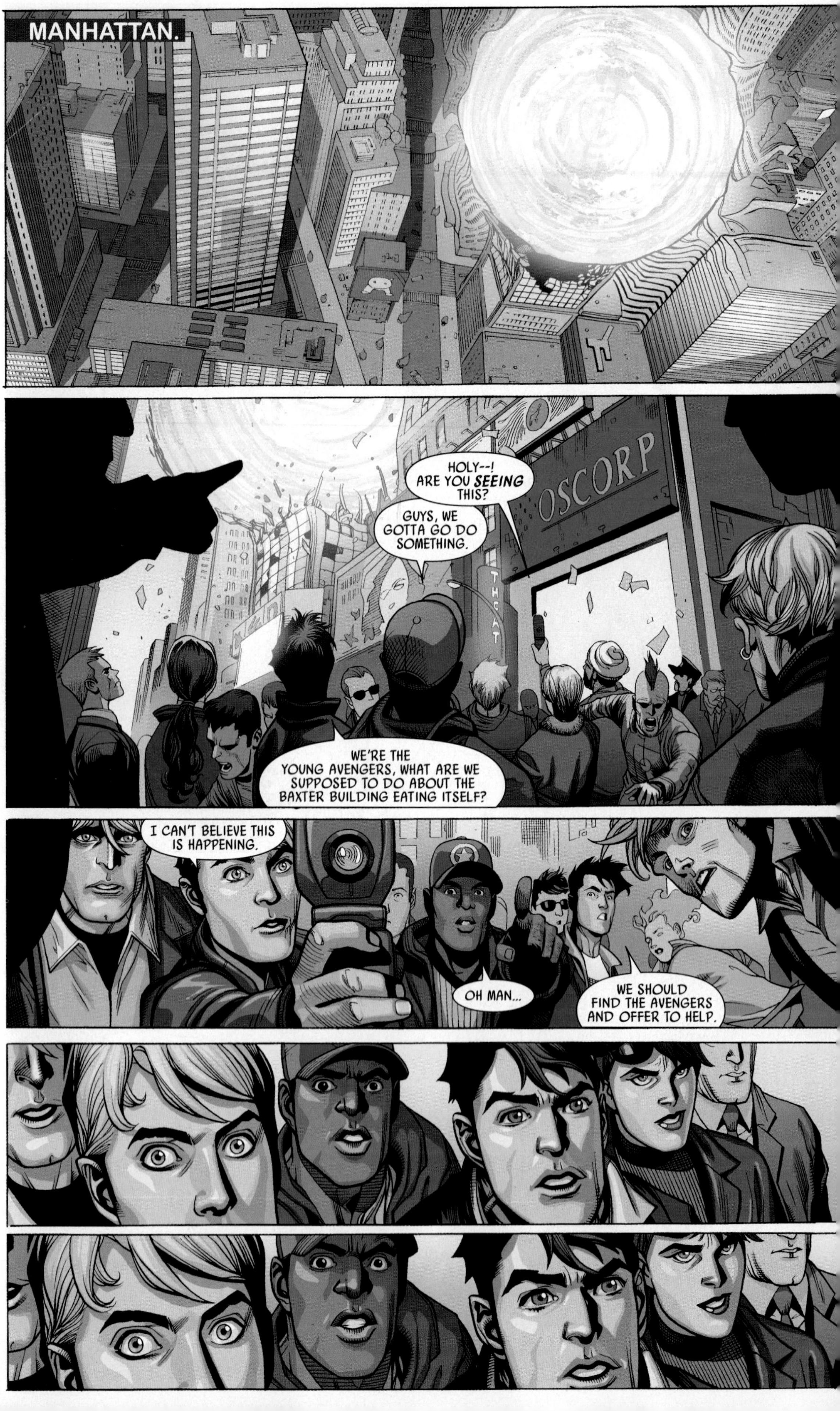

MANHATTAN.
HOLY--! ARE YOU SEEING THIS?
GUYS, WE GOTTA GO DO SOMETHING.
OSCORP
WE'RE THE YOUNG AVENGERS, WHAT ARE WE SUPPOSED TO DO ABOUT THE BAXTER BUILDING EATING ITSELF?
I CAN'T BELIEVE THIS IS HAPPENING.
OH MAN...
WE SHOULD FIND THE AVENGERS AND OFFER TO HELP.

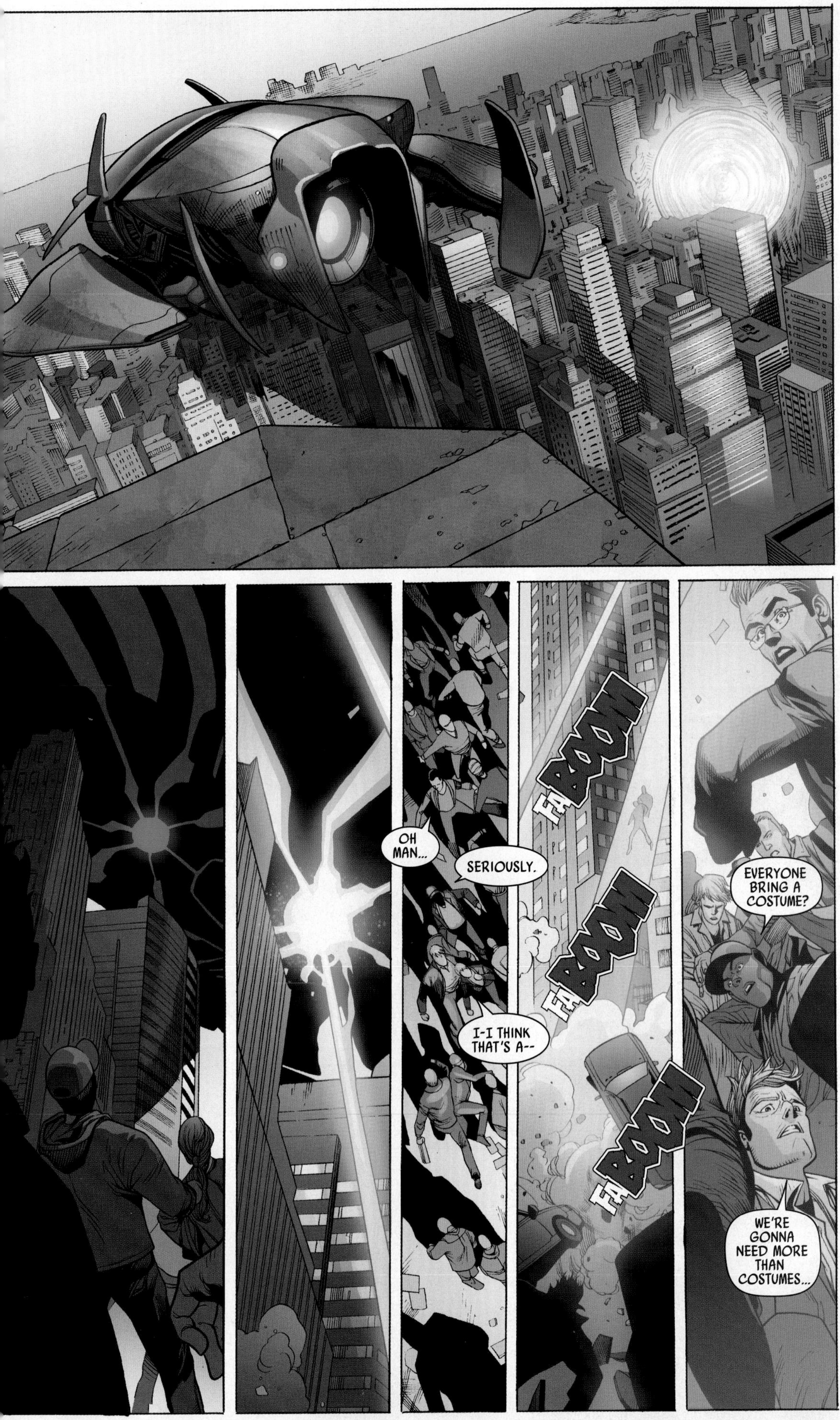
OH MAN...
SERIOUSLY.
I-I THINK THAT'S A--
FA BOOM
FA BOOM
FA BOOM
EVERYONE BRING A COSTUME?
WE'RE GONNA NEED MORE THAN COSTUMES...

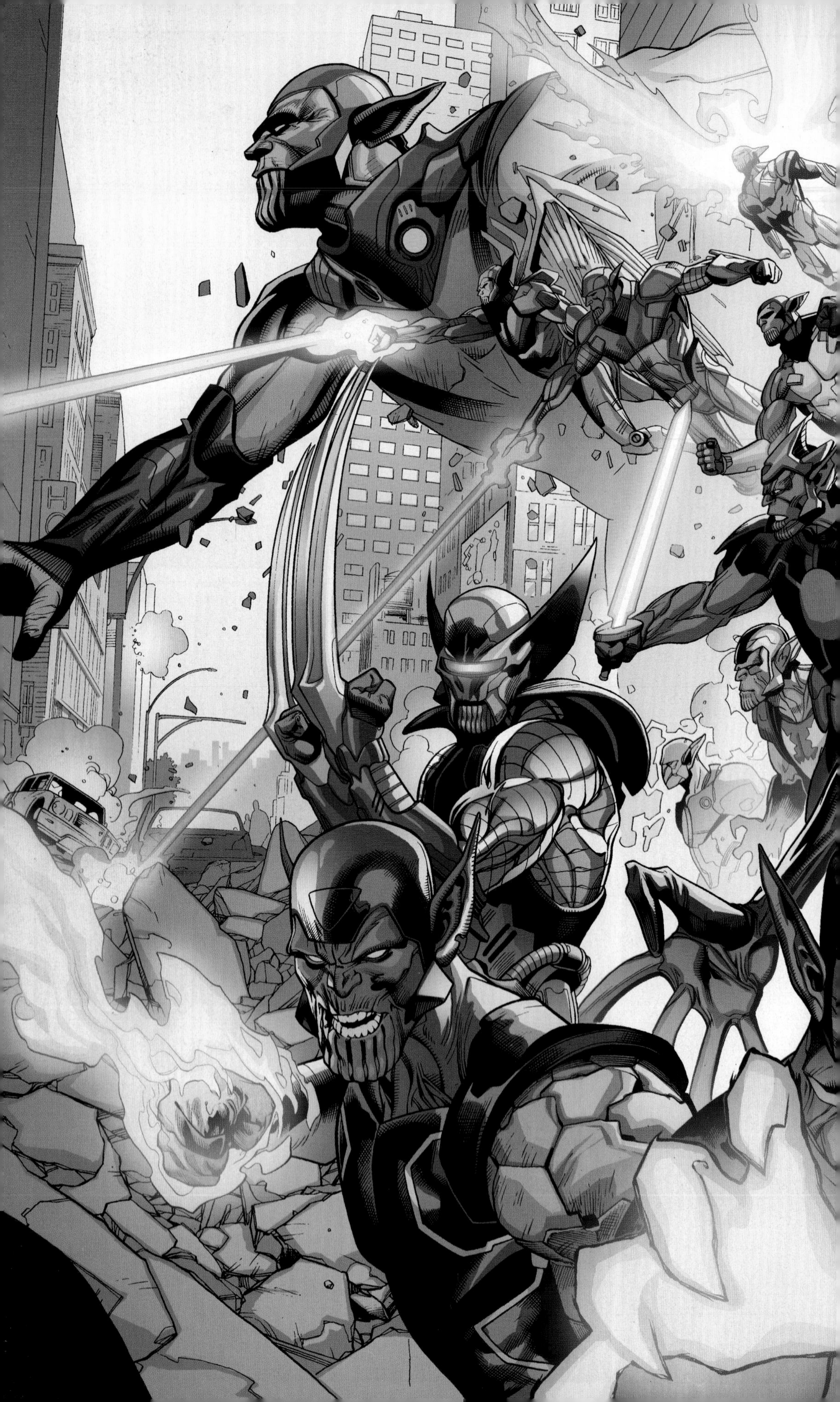

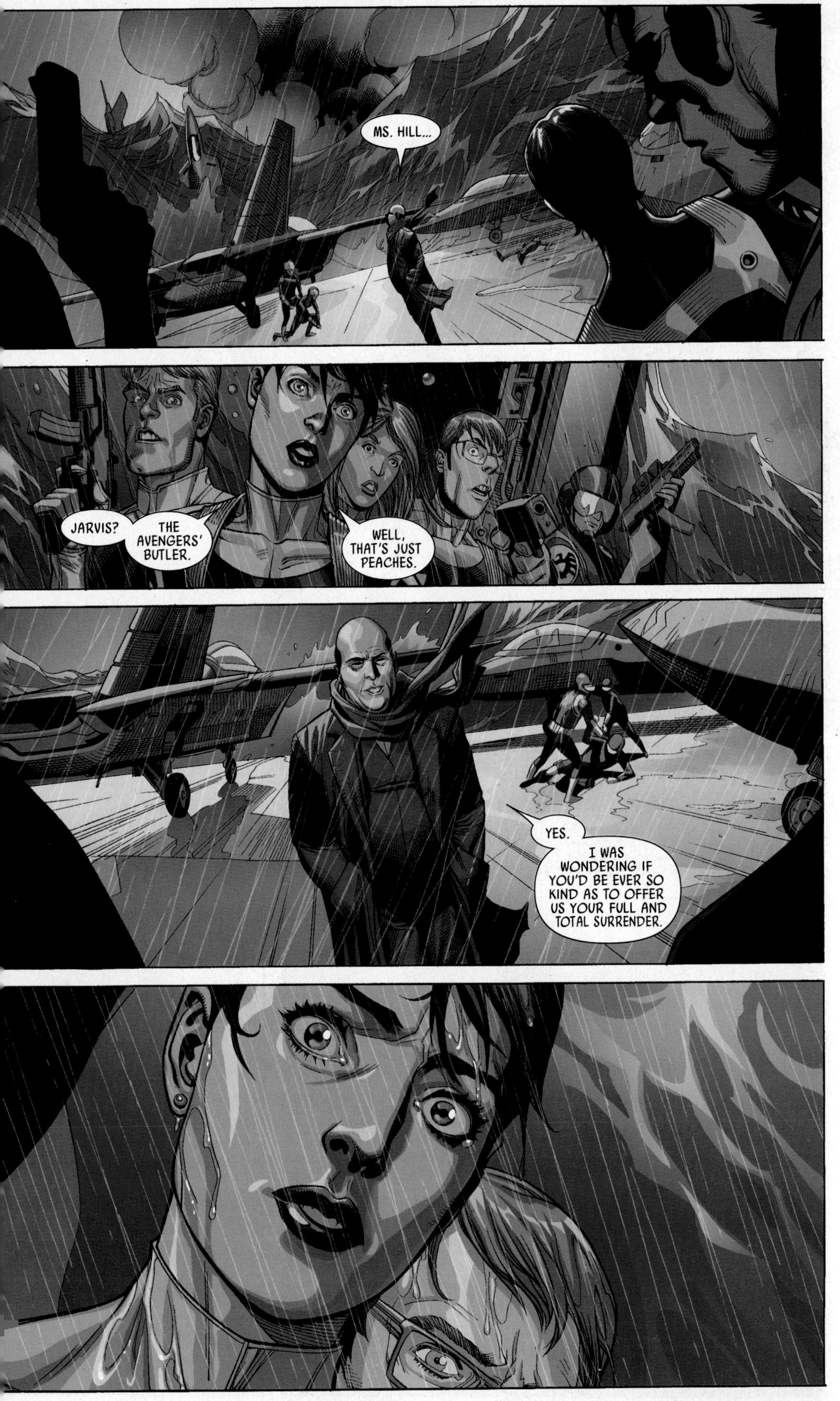

MS. HILL...
JARVIS?
THE AVENGERS' BUTLER.
WELL, THAT'S JUST PEACHES.
YES.
I WAS WONDERING IF YOU'D BE EVER SO KIND AS TO OFFER US YOUR FULL AND TOTAL SURRENDER.

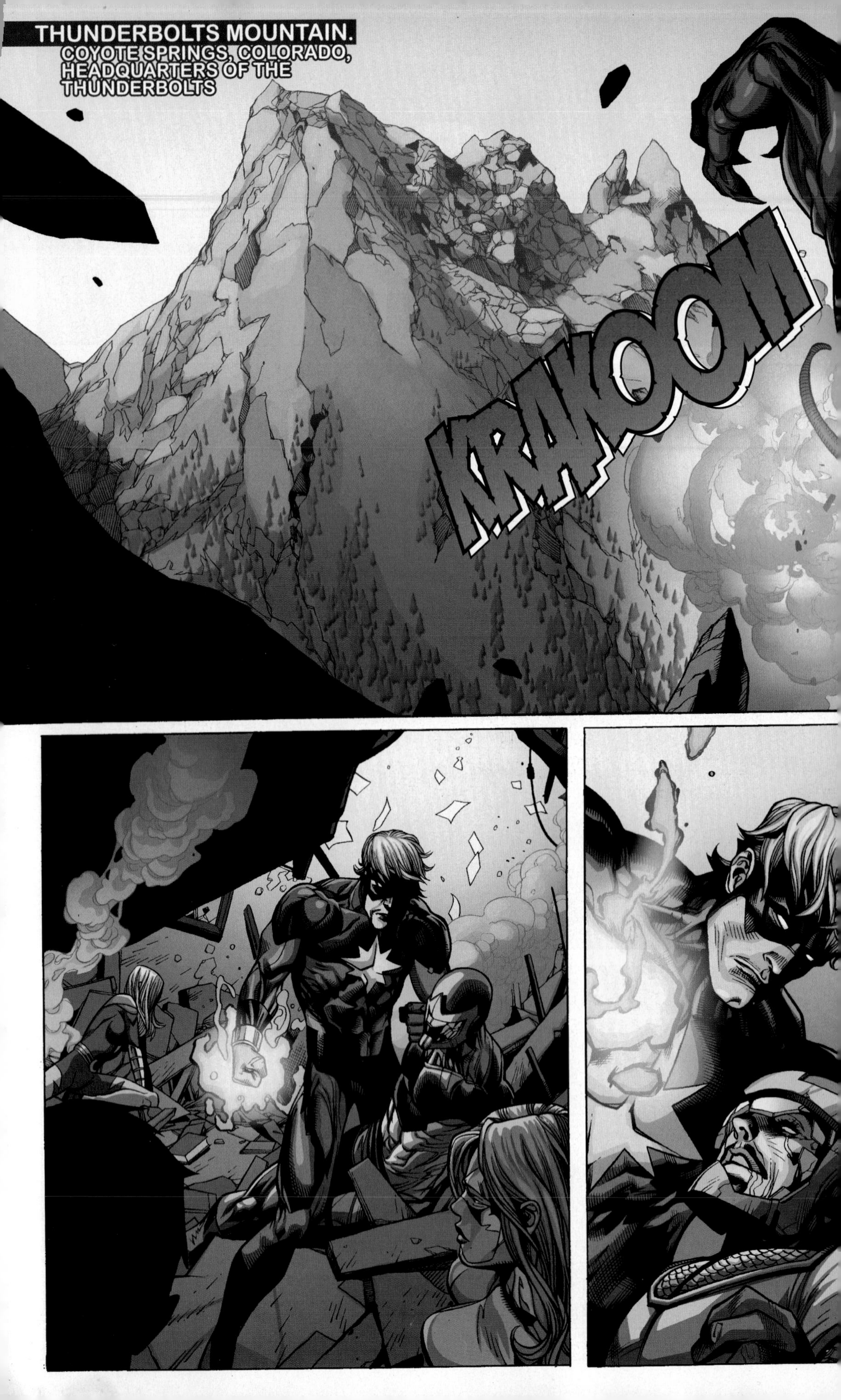
THUNDERBOLTS MOUNTAIN.
COYOTE SPRINGS, COLORADO, HEADQUARTERS OF THE THUNDERBOLTS
KRAKOOM

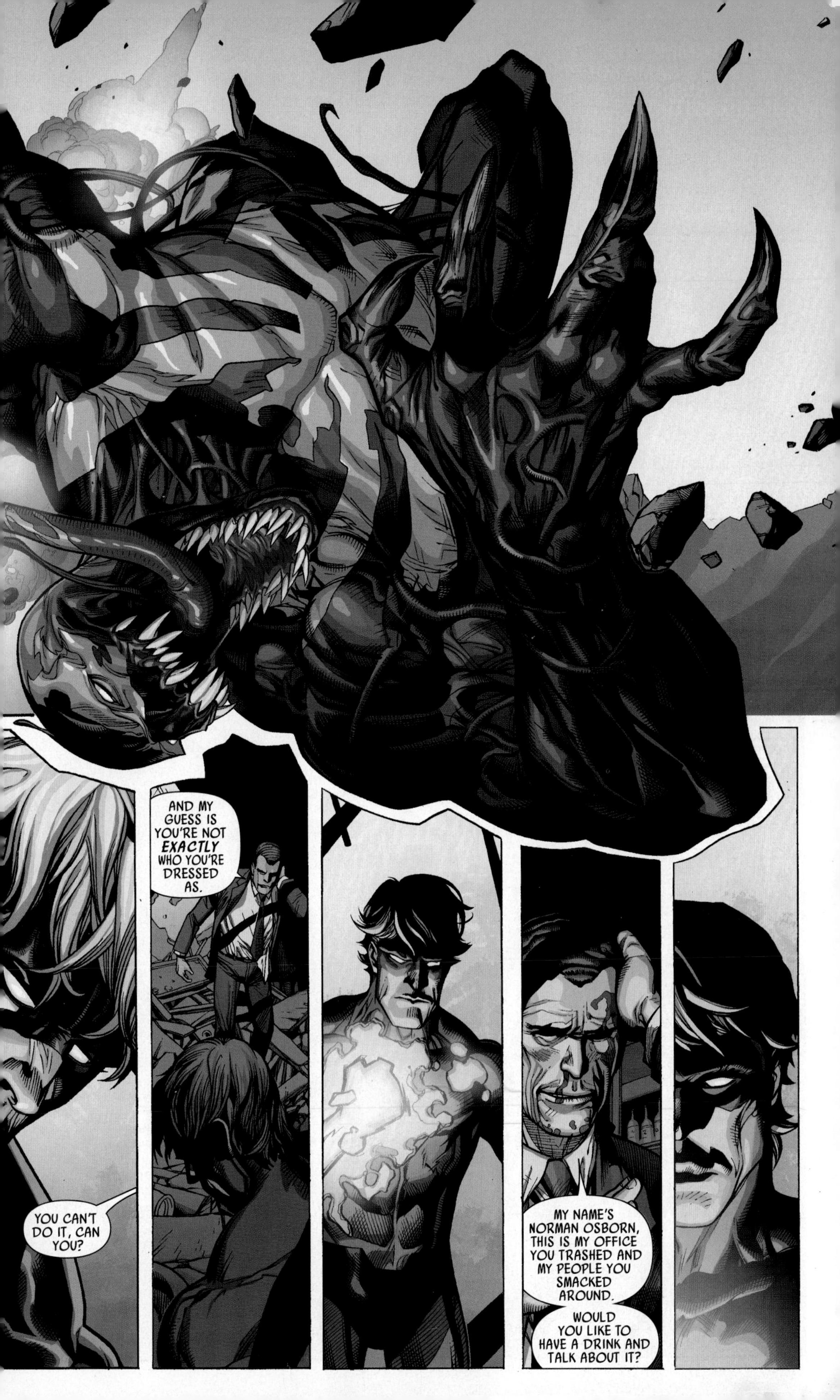

YOU CAN'T DO IT, CAN YOU?
AND MY GUESS IS YOU'RE NOT EXACTLY WHO YOU'RE DRESSED AS.
MY NAME'S NORMAN OSBORN, THIS IS MY OFFICE YOU TRASHED AND MY PEOPLE YOU SMACKED AROUND.
WOULD YOU LIKE TO HAVE A DRINK AND TALK ABOUT IT?

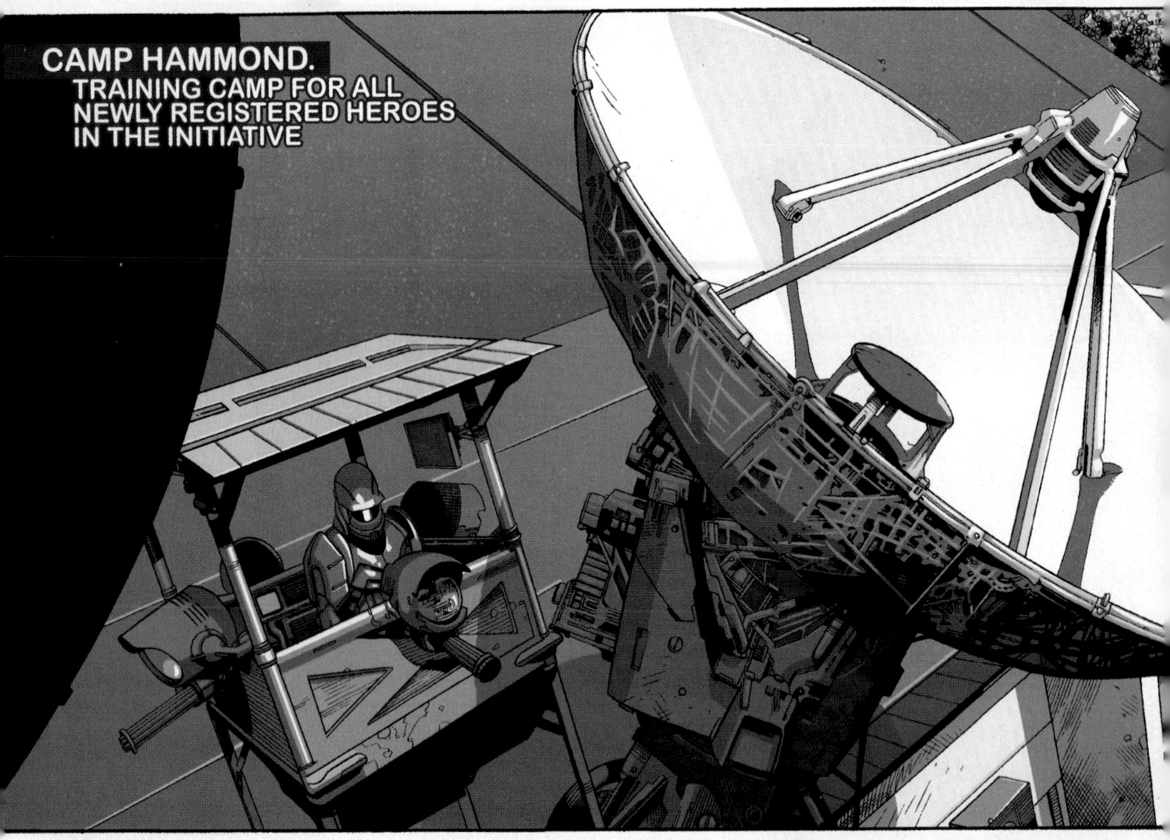
CAMP HAMMOND.
TRAINING CAMP FOR ALL NEWLY REGISTERED HEROES IN THE INITIATIVE

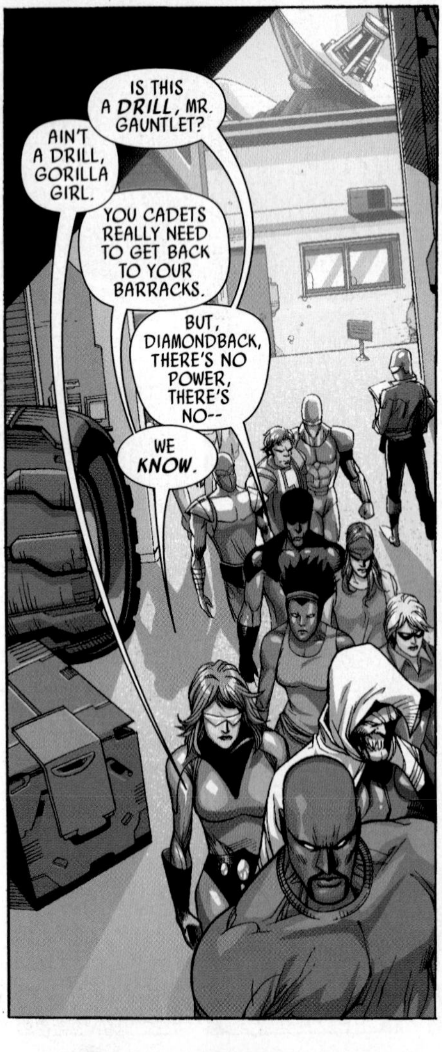
IS THIS A DRILL, MR. GAUNTLET?
AIN'T A DRILL, GORILLA GIRL.
YOU CADETS REALLY NEED TO GET BACK TO YOUR BARRACKS.
BUT, DIAMONDBACK, THERE'S NO POWER, THERE'S NO--
WE KNOW.

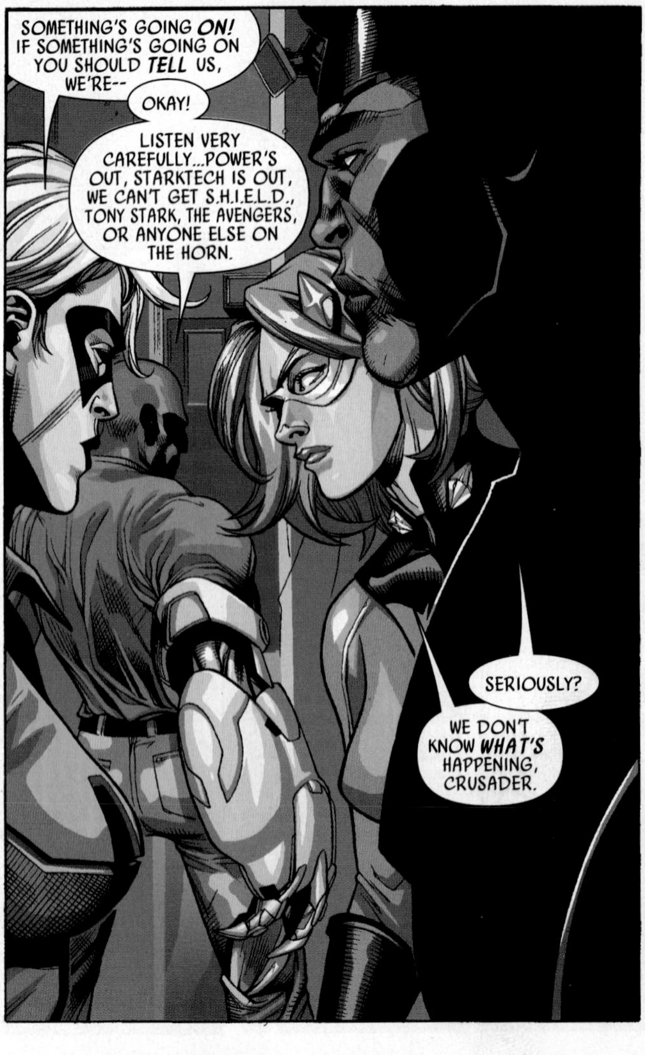
SOMETHING'S GOING ON! IF SOMETHING'S GOING ON YOU SHOULD TELL US, WE'RE--
OKAY!
LISTEN VERY CAREFULLY...POWER'S OUT, STARKTECH IS OUT, WE CAN'T GET S.H.I.E.L.D., TONY STARK, THE AVENGERS, OR ANYONE ELSE ON THE HORN.
SERIOUSLY?
WE DON'T KNOW WHAT'S HAPPENING, CRUSADER.

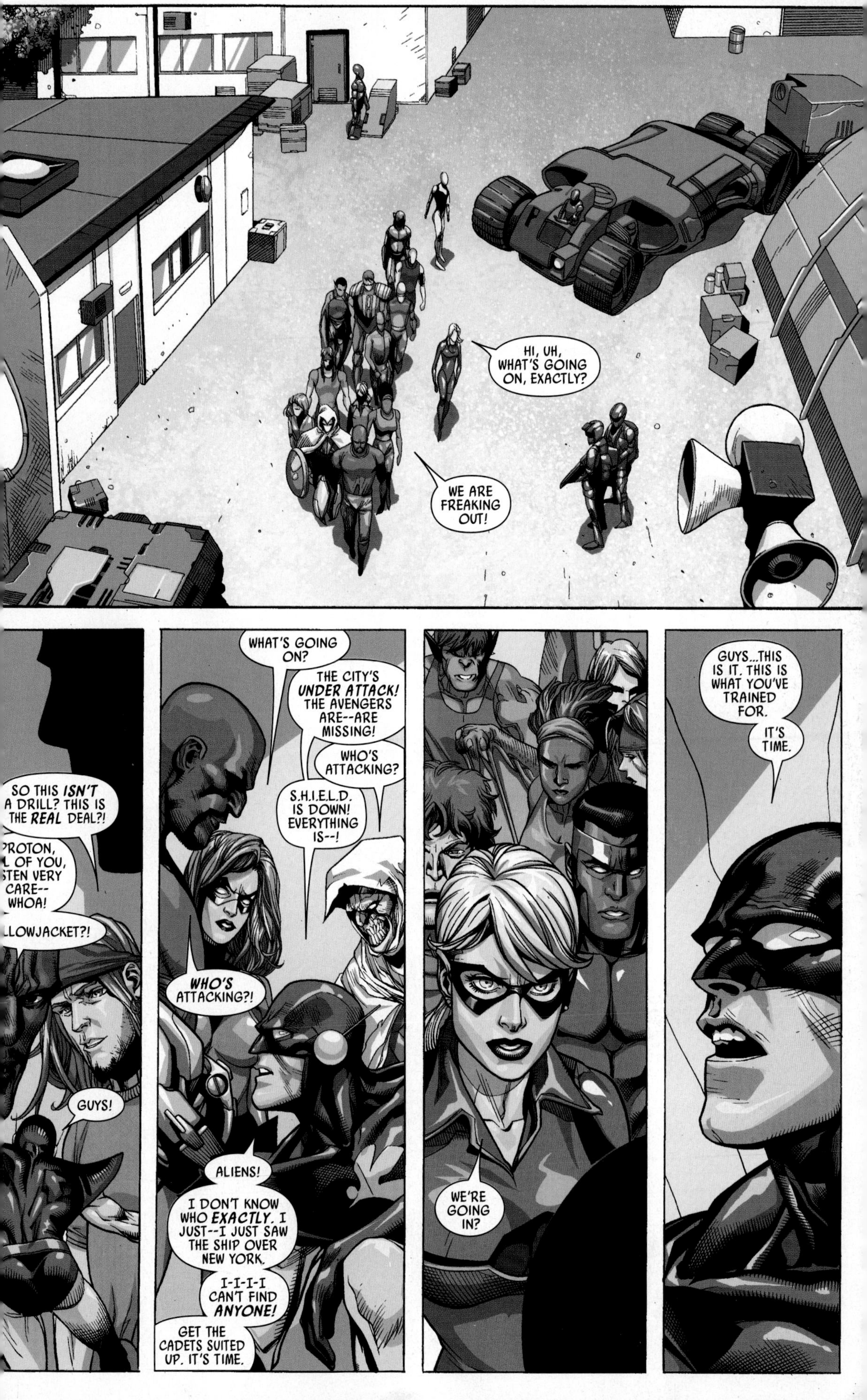
HI, UH, WHAT'S GOING ON, EXACTLY?
WE ARE FREAKING OUT!
SO THIS ISN'T A DRILL? THIS IS THE REAL DEAL?!
PROTON, L OF YOU, STEN VERY CARE-- WHOA!
LLOWJACKET?!
GUYS!
WHAT'S GOING ON?
THE CITY'S UNDER ATTACK! THE AVENGERS ARE--ARE MISSING!
WHO'S ATTACKING?
S.H.I.E.L.D. IS DOWN! EVERYTHING IS--!
WHO'S ATTACKING?!
ALIENS!
I DON'T KNOW WHO EXACTLY. I JUST--I JUST SAW THE SHIP OVER NEW YORK.
I-I-I-I CAN'T FIND ANYONE!
GET THE CADETS SUITED UP. IT'S TIME.
WE'RE GOING IN?
GUYS...THIS IS IT. THIS IS WHAT YOU'VE TRAINED FOR.
IT'S TIME.

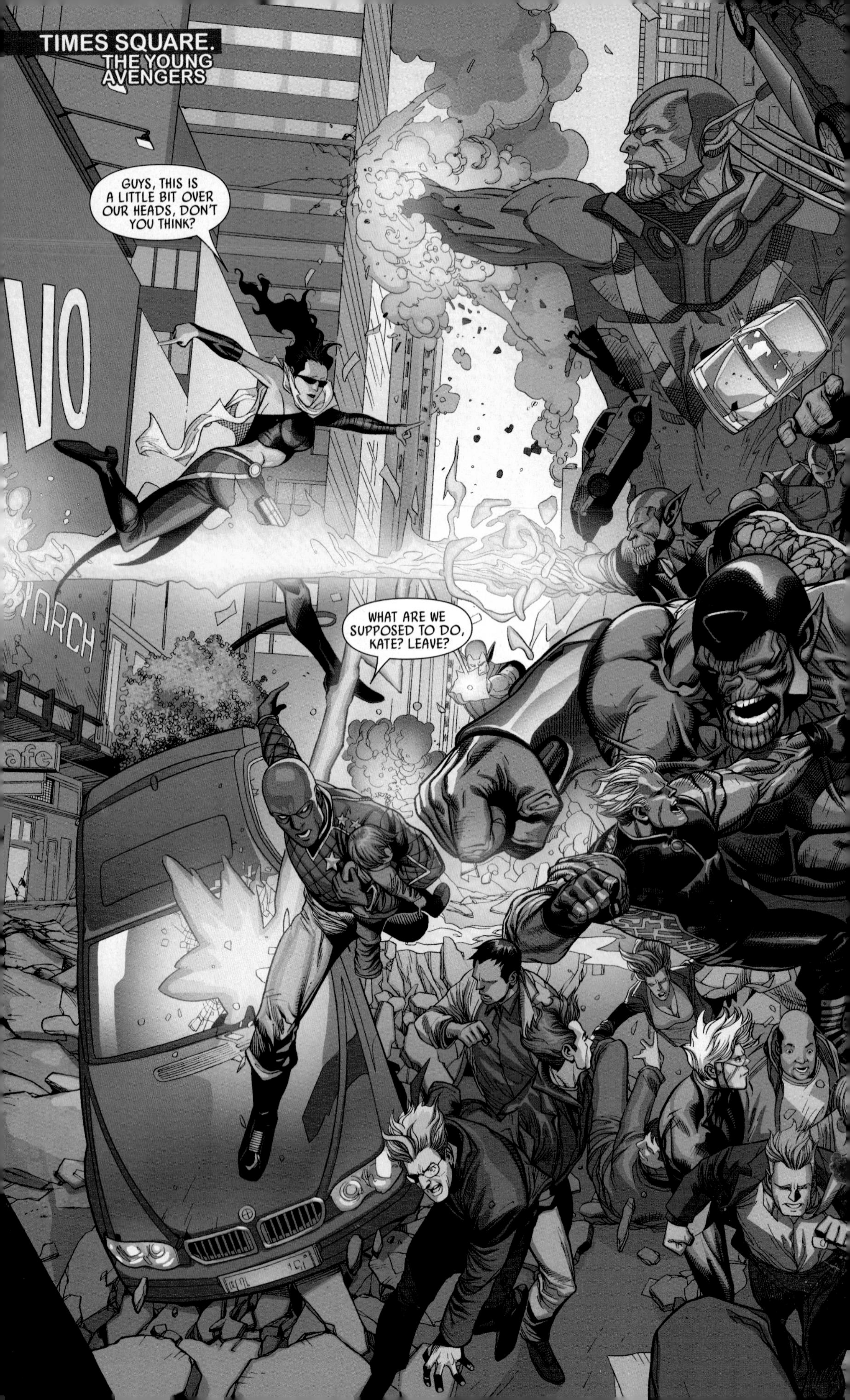
TIMES SQUARE.
THE YOUNG AVENGERS
GUYS, THIS IS A LITTLE BIT OVER OUR HEADS, DON'T YOU THINK?
WHAT ARE WE SUPPOSED TO DO, KATE? LEAVE?

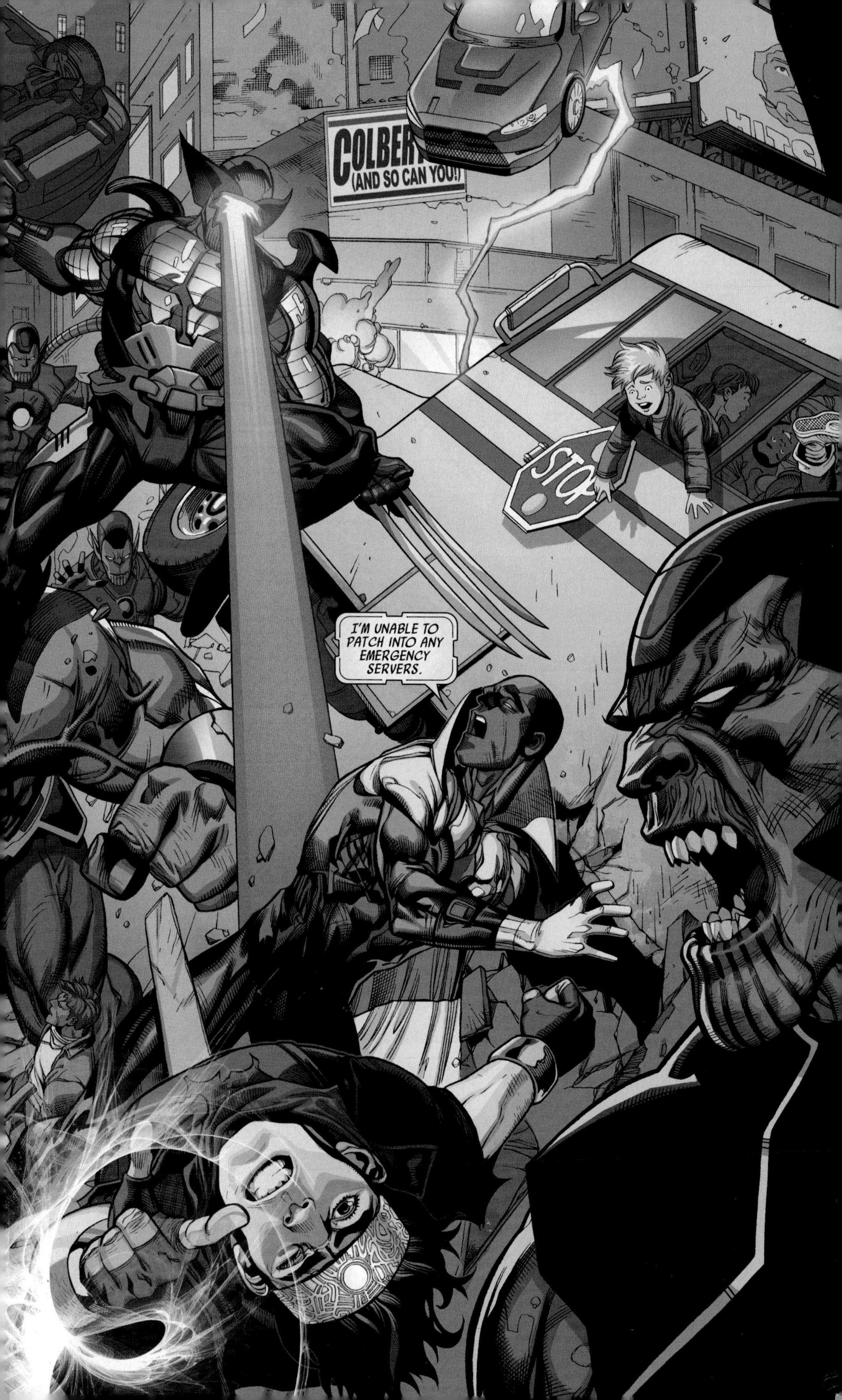
COLBERT
(AND SO CAN YOU!)
STOP
I'M UNABLE TO PATCH INTO ANY EMERGENCY SERVERS.

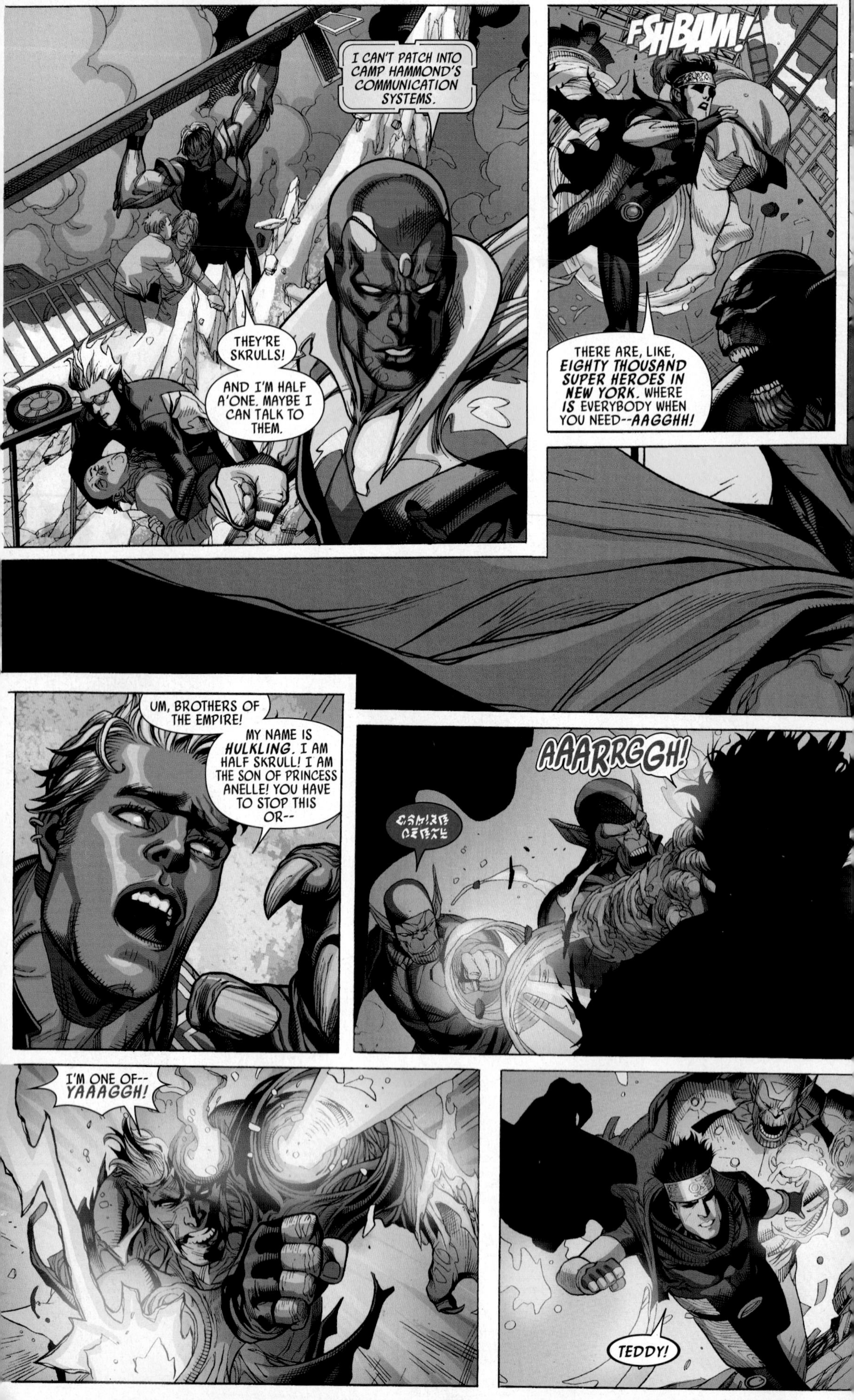
I CAN'T PATCH INTO CAMP HAMMOND'S COMMUNICATION SYSTEMS.
THEY'RE SKRULLS!
AND I'M HALF A'ONE. MAYBE I CAN TALK TO THEM.
FSHBAM!
THERE ARE, LIKE, EIGHTY THOUSAND SUPER HEROES IN NEW YORK. WHERE IS EVERYBODY WHEN YOU NEED--AAGGHH!
UM, BROTHERS OF THE EMPIRE!
MY NAME IS HULKLING. I AM HALF SKRULL! I AM THE SON OF PRINCESS ANELLE! YOU HAVE TO STOP THIS OR--
AAARRGGH!
I'M ONE OF-- YAAAGGH!
TEDDY!

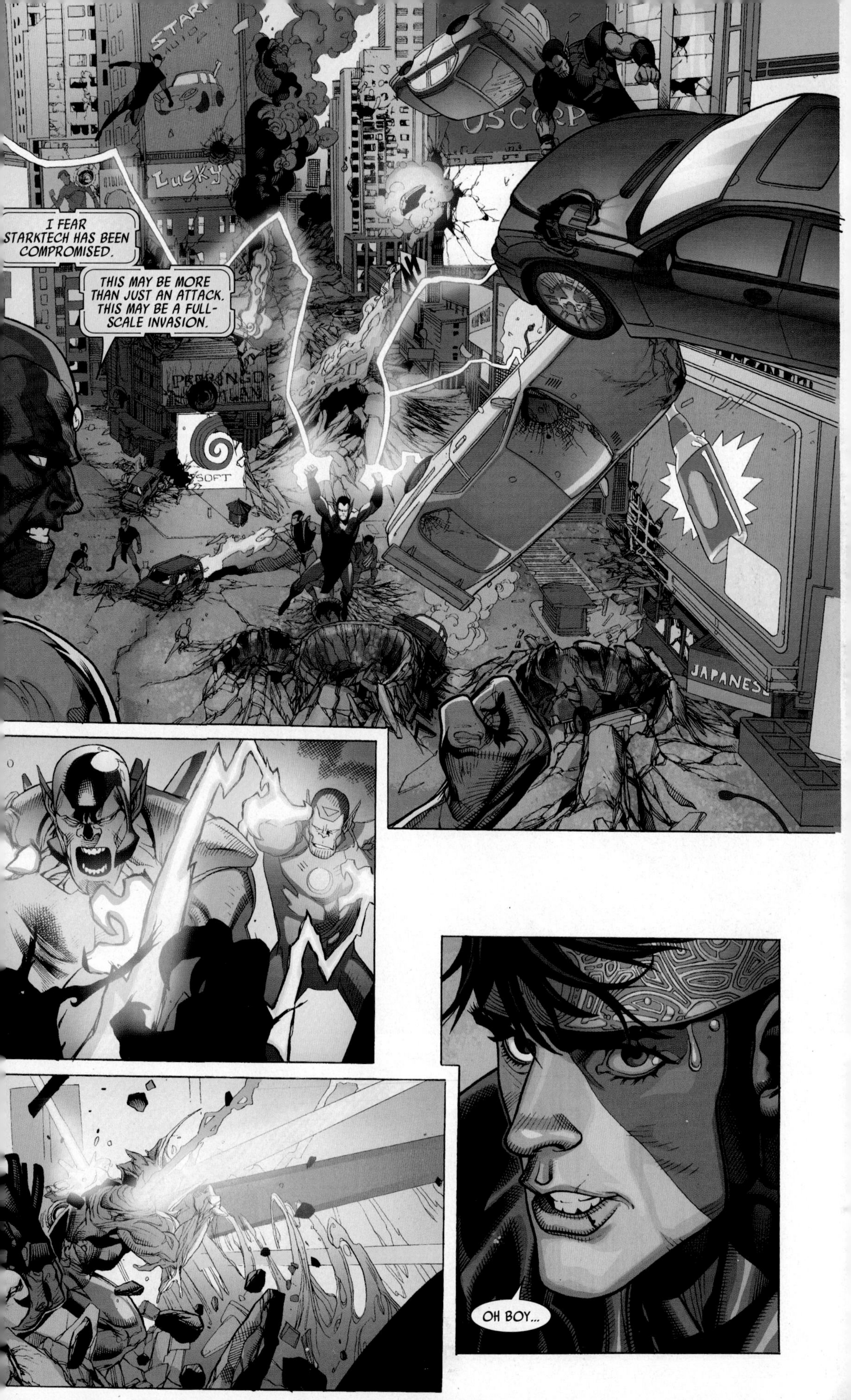
STARK
OSCORP
Lucky
I FEAR STARKTECH HAS BEEN COMPROMISED.
THIS MAY BE MORE THAN JUST AN ATTACK. THIS MAY BE A FULL-SCALE INVASION.
SOFT
JAPANESE
OH BOY...

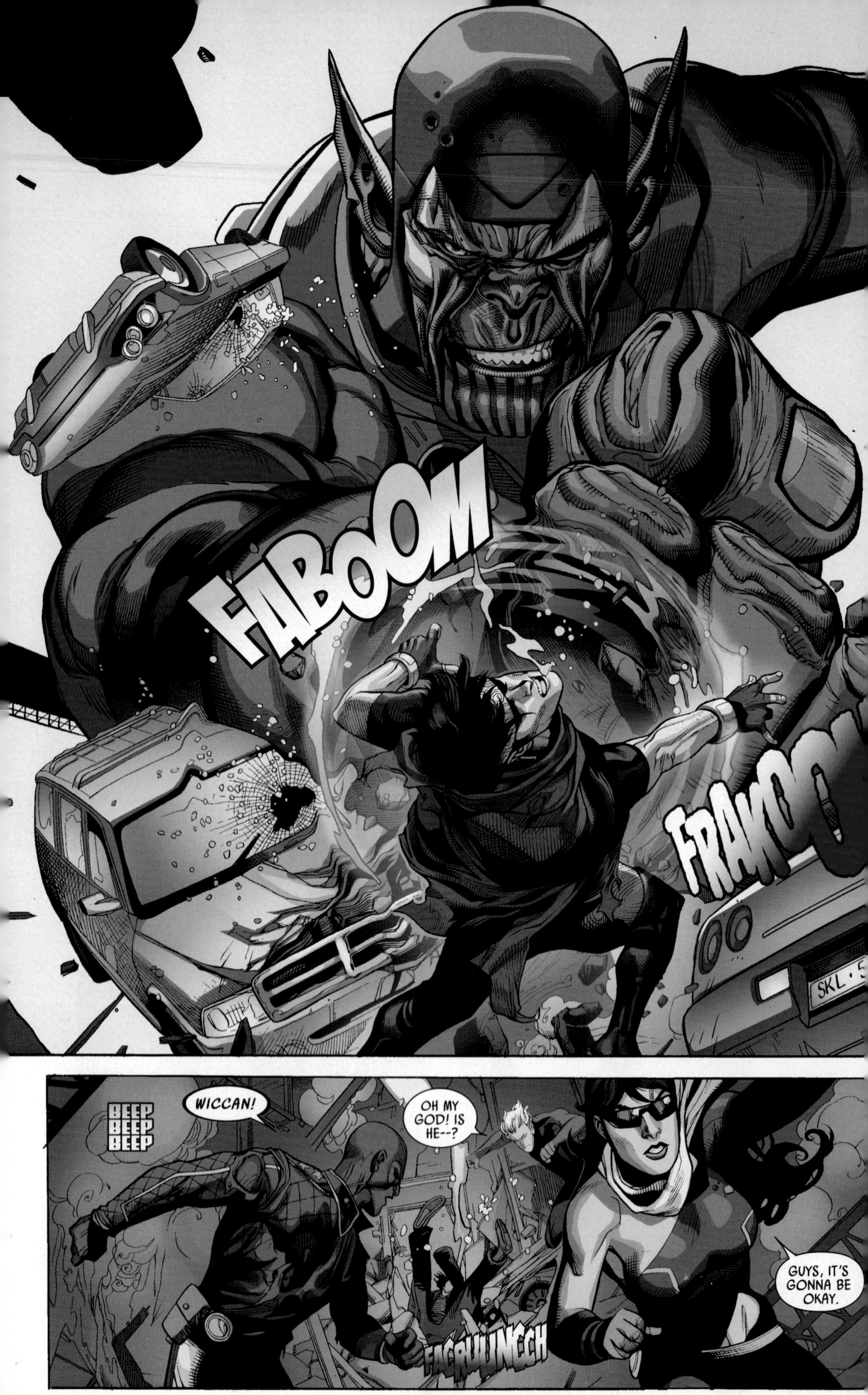
FABOOM
FRAKOO
SKL • 5
BEEP BEEP BEEP
WICCAN!
OH MY GOD! IS HE--?
GUYS, IT'S GONNA BE OKAY.
FAGRUUUNCCH

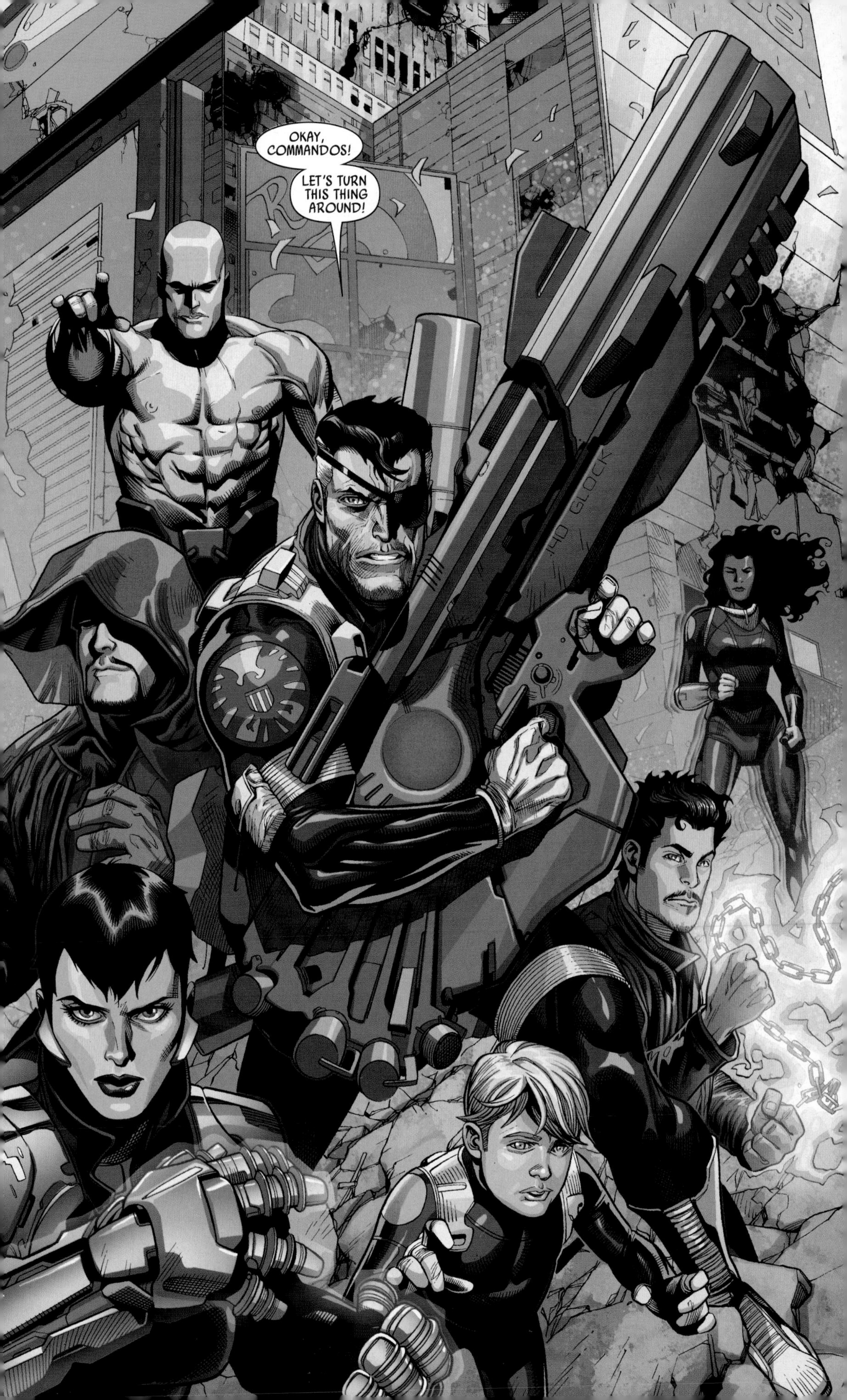
OKAY, COMMANDOS!
LET'S TURN THIS THING AROUND!
140 GLOCK

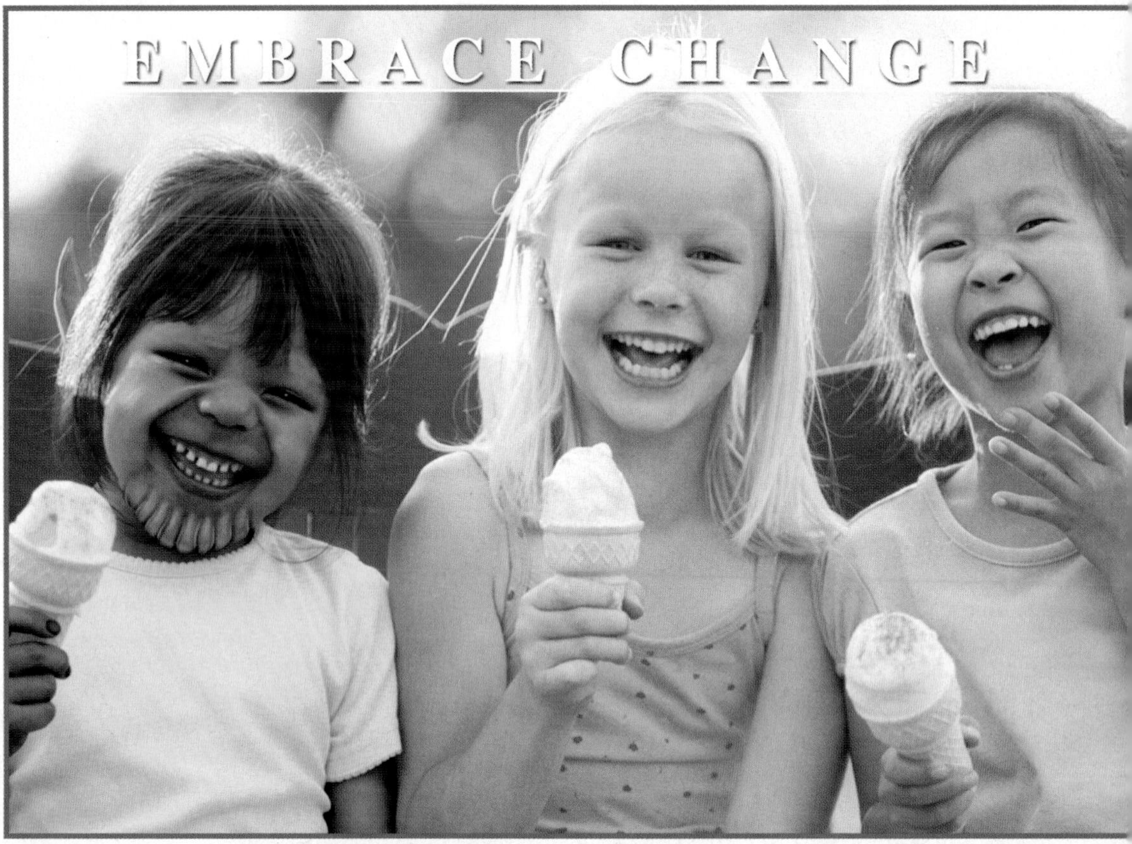
EMBRACE CHANGE

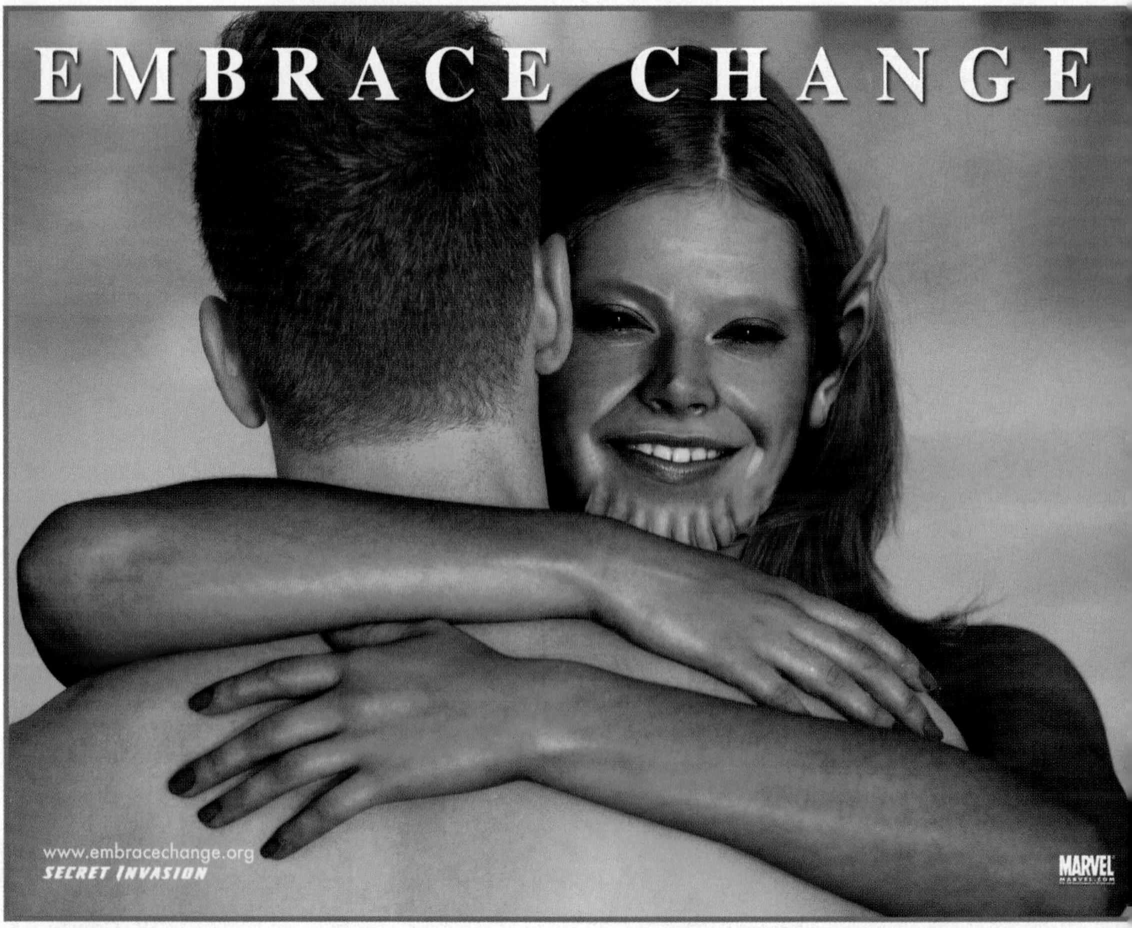
EMBRACE CHANGE
www.embracechange.org
SECRET INVASION
MARVEL

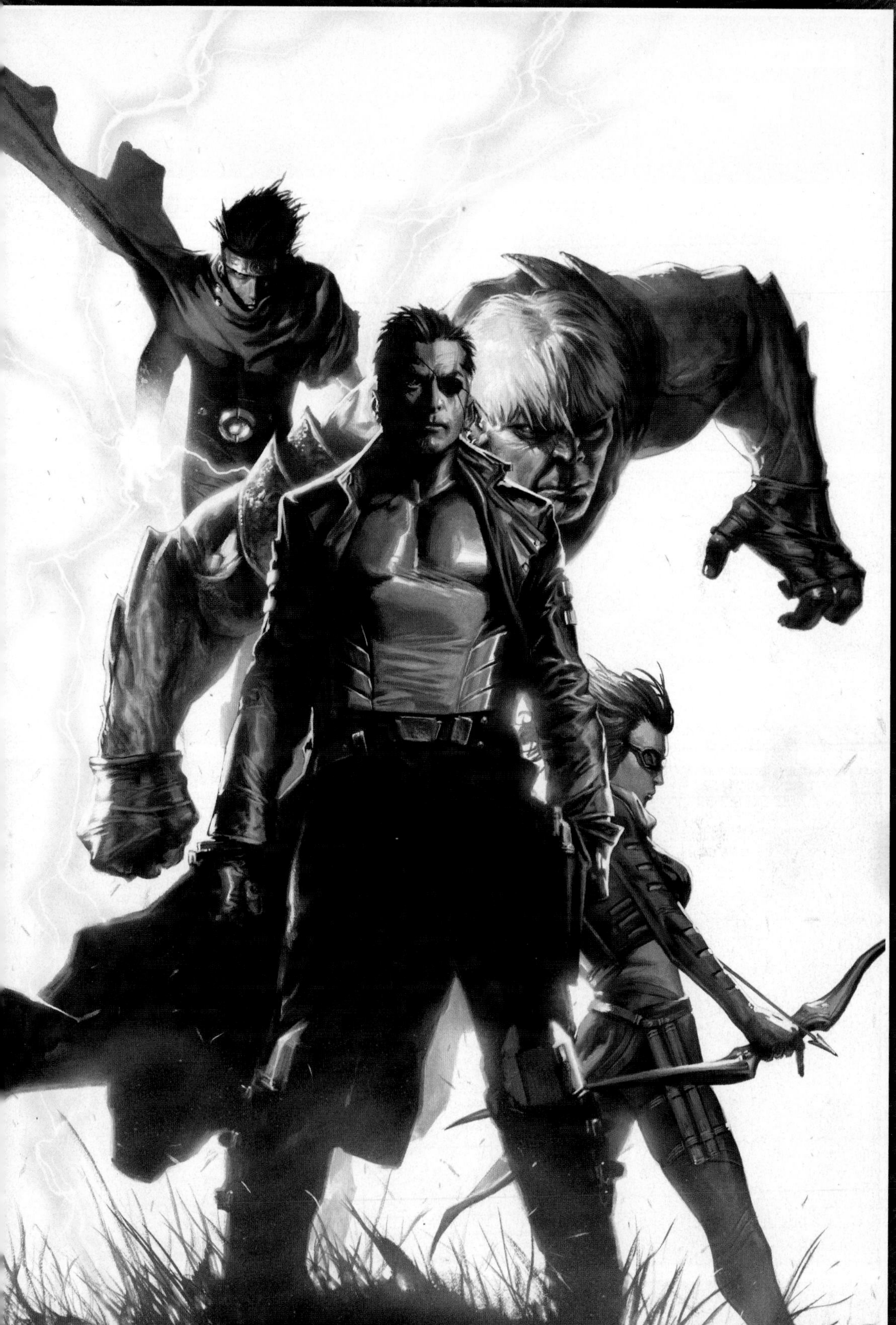

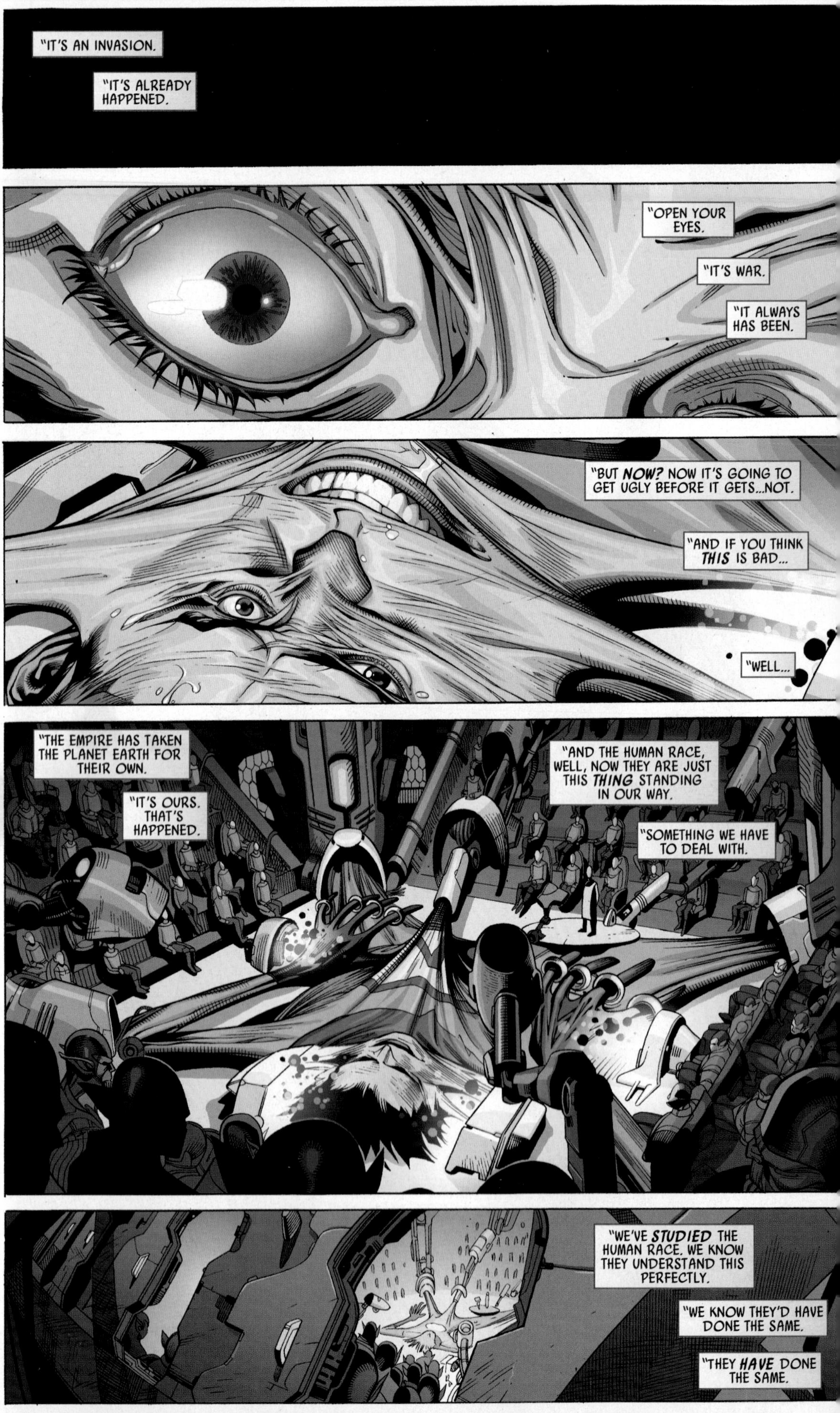
"IT'S AN INVASION.
"IT'S ALREADY HAPPENED.
"OPEN YOUR EYES.
"IT'S WAR.
"IT ALWAYS HAS BEEN.
"BUT NOW? NOW IT'S GOING TO GET UGLY BEFORE IT GETS...NOT.
"AND IF YOU THINK THIS IS BAD...
"WELL...
"THE EMPIRE HAS TAKEN THE PLANET EARTH FOR THEIR OWN.
"IT'S OURS. THAT'S HAPPENED.
"AND THE HUMAN RACE, WELL, NOW THEY ARE JUST THIS THING STANDING IN OUR WAY.
"SOMETHING WE HAVE TO DEAL WITH.
"WE'VE STUDIED THE HUMAN RACE. WE KNOW THEY UNDERSTAND THIS PERFECTLY.
"WE KNOW THEY'D HAVE DONE THE SAME.
"THEY HAVE DONE THE SAME.

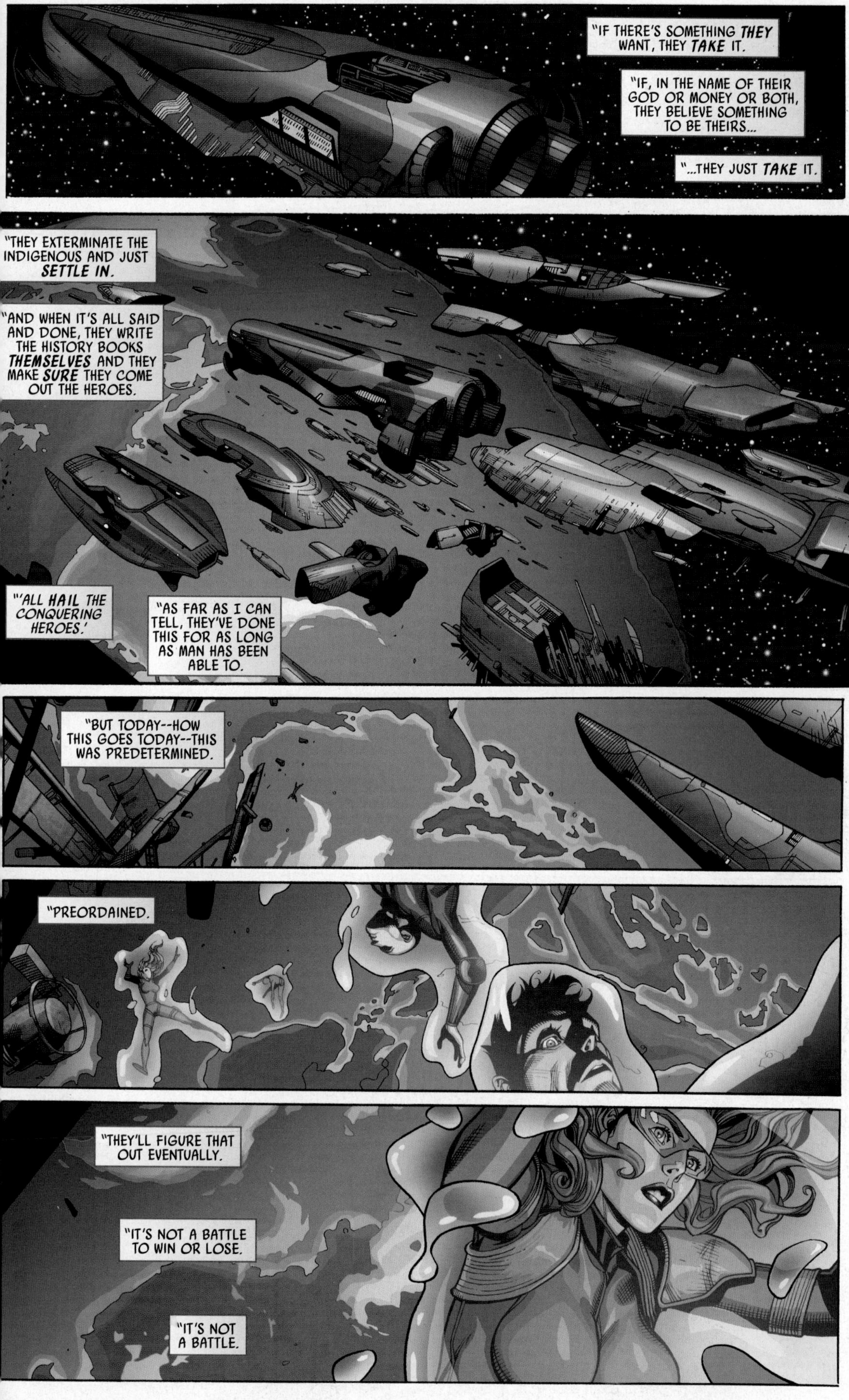
"IF THERE'S SOMETHING THEY WANT, THEY TAKE IT.
"IF, IN THE NAME OF THEIR GOD OR MONEY OR BOTH, THEY BELIEVE SOMETHING TO BE THEIRS...
"...THEY JUST TAKE IT.
"THEY EXTERMINATE THE INDIGENOUS AND JUST SETTLE IN.
"AND WHEN IT'S ALL SAID AND DONE, THEY WRITE THE HISTORY BOOKS THEMSELVES AND THEY MAKE SURE THEY COME OUT THE HEROES.
"'ALL HAIL THE CONQUERING HEROES.'
"AS FAR AS I CAN TELL, THEY'VE DONE THIS FOR AS LONG AS MAN HAS BEEN ABLE TO.
"BUT TODAY--HOW THIS GOES TODAY--THIS WAS PREDETERMINED.
"PREORDAINED.
"THEY'LL FIGURE THAT OUT EVENTUALLY.
"IT'S NOT A BATTLE TO WIN OR LOSE.
"IT'S NOT A BATTLE.

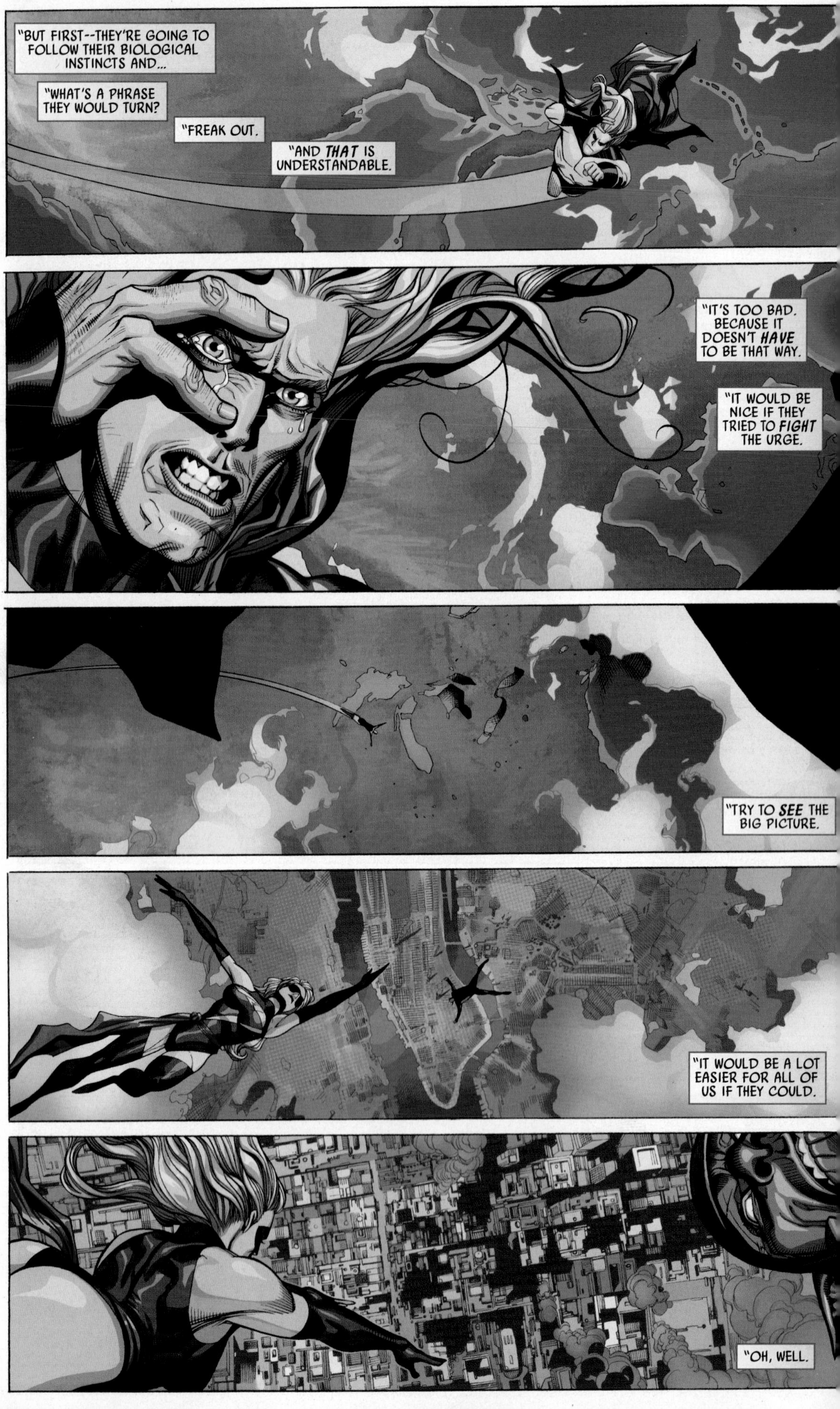
"BUT FIRST--THEY'RE GOING TO FOLLOW THEIR BIOLOGICAL INSTINCTS AND...
"WHAT'S A PHRASE THEY WOULD TURN?
"FREAK OUT.
"AND THAT IS UNDERSTANDABLE.
"IT'S TOO BAD. BECAUSE IT DOESN'T HAVE TO BE THAT WAY.
"IT WOULD BE NICE IF THEY TRIED TO FIGHT THE URGE.
"TRY TO SEE THE BIG PICTURE.
"IT WOULD BE A LOT EASIER FOR ALL OF US IF THEY COULD.
"OH, WELL.

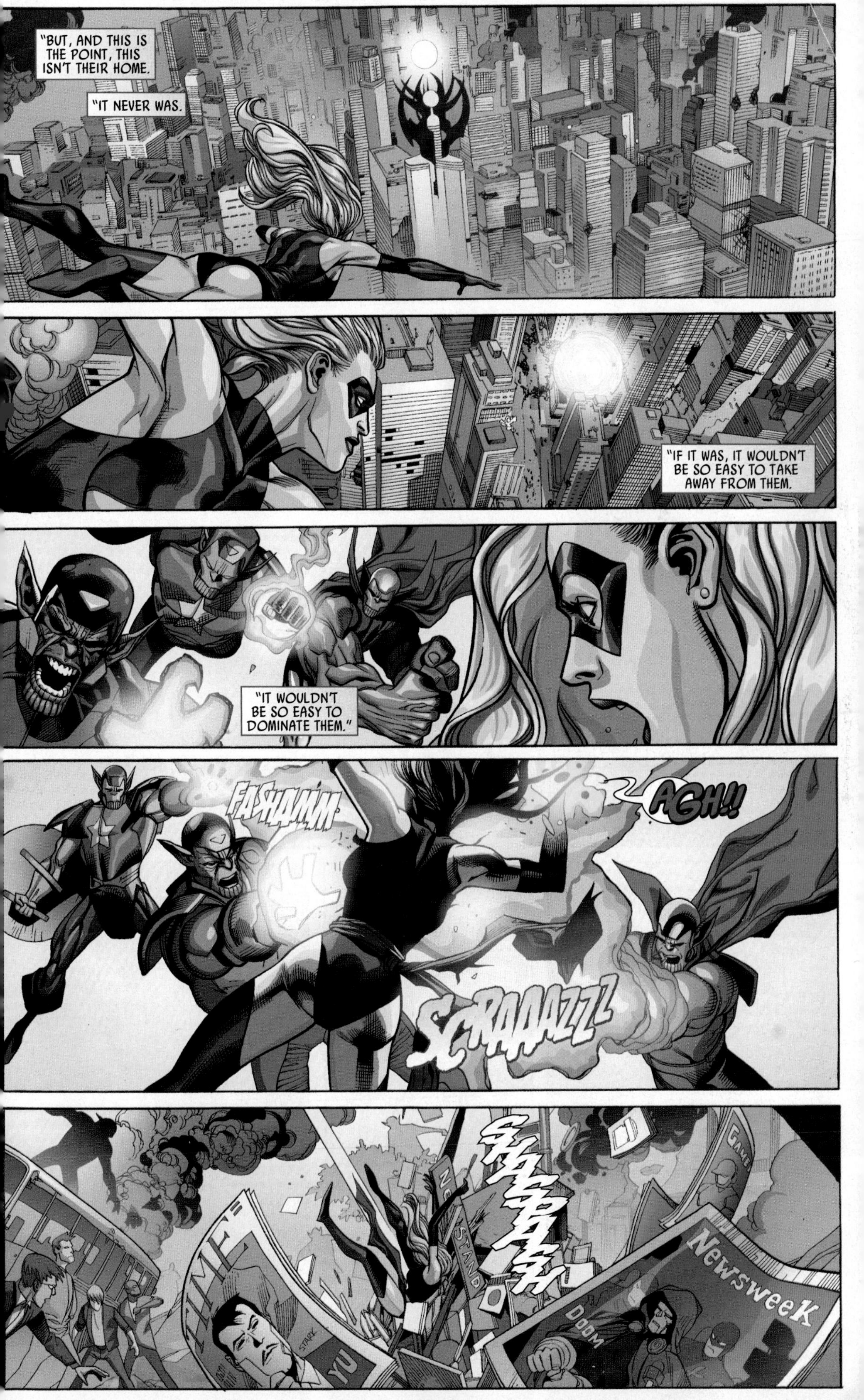
"BUT, AND THIS IS THE POINT, THIS ISN'T THEIR HOME.
"IT NEVER WAS.
"IF IT WAS, IT WOULDN'T BE SO EASY TO TAKE AWAY FROM THEM.
"IT WOULDN'T BE SO EASY TO DOMINATE THEM."
FASHAMM
AGH!!
SCRAAAZZZ
TIME
STARK
NEWSSTAND
Newsweek
DOOM

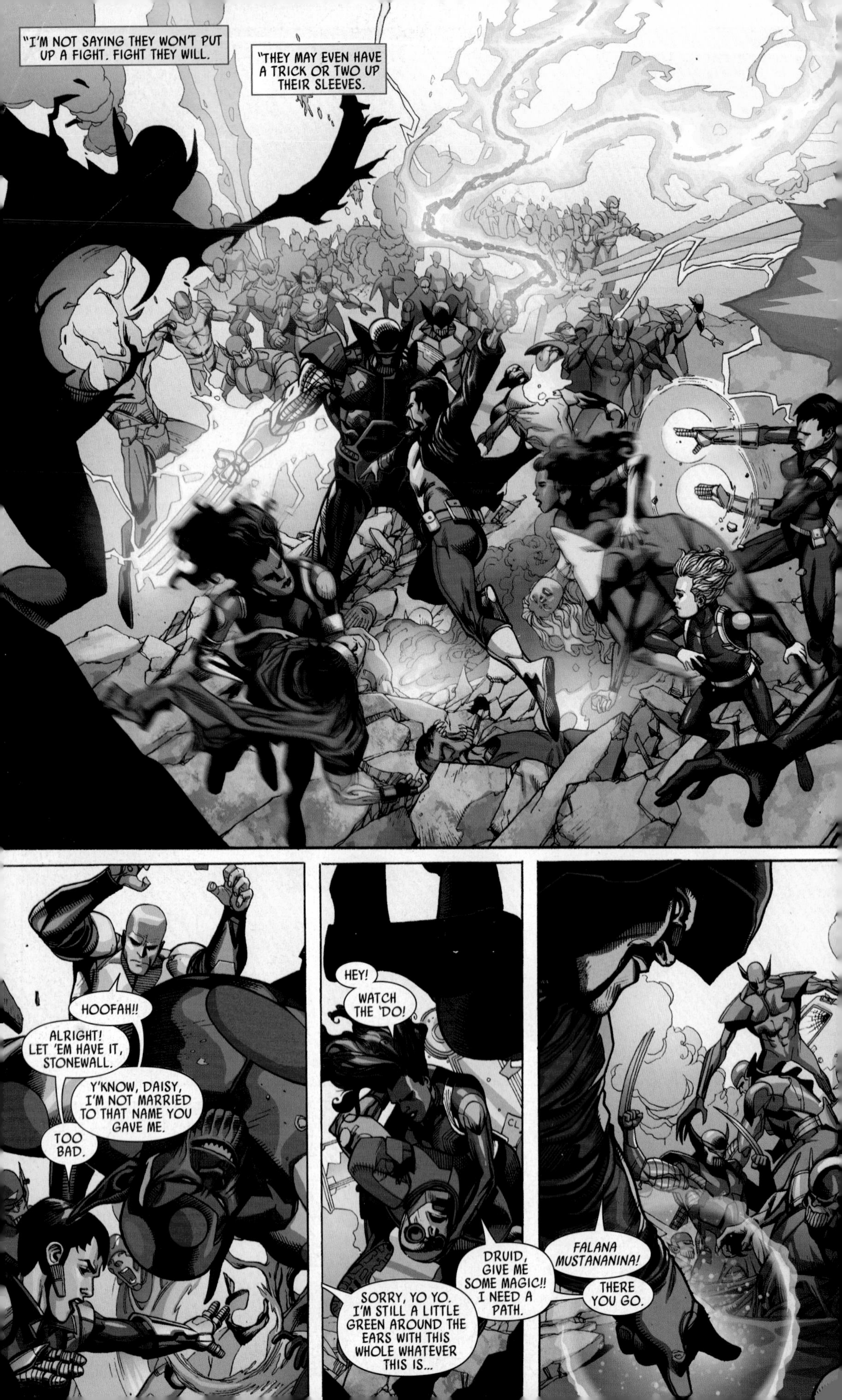
"I'M NOT SAYING THEY WON'T PUT UP A FIGHT. FIGHT THEY WILL.
"THEY MAY EVEN HAVE A TRICK OR TWO UP THEIR SLEEVES.
HOOFAH!!
ALRIGHT! LET 'EM HAVE IT, STONEWALL.
Y'KNOW, DAISY, I'M NOT MARRIED TO THAT NAME YOU GAVE ME.
TOO BAD.
HEY!
WATCH THE 'DO!
DRUID, GIVE ME SOME MAGIC!! I NEED A PATH.
SORRY, YO YO. I'M STILL A LITTLE GREEN AROUND THE EARS WITH THIS WHOLE WHATEVER THIS IS...
FALANA MUSTANANINA!
THERE YOU GO.

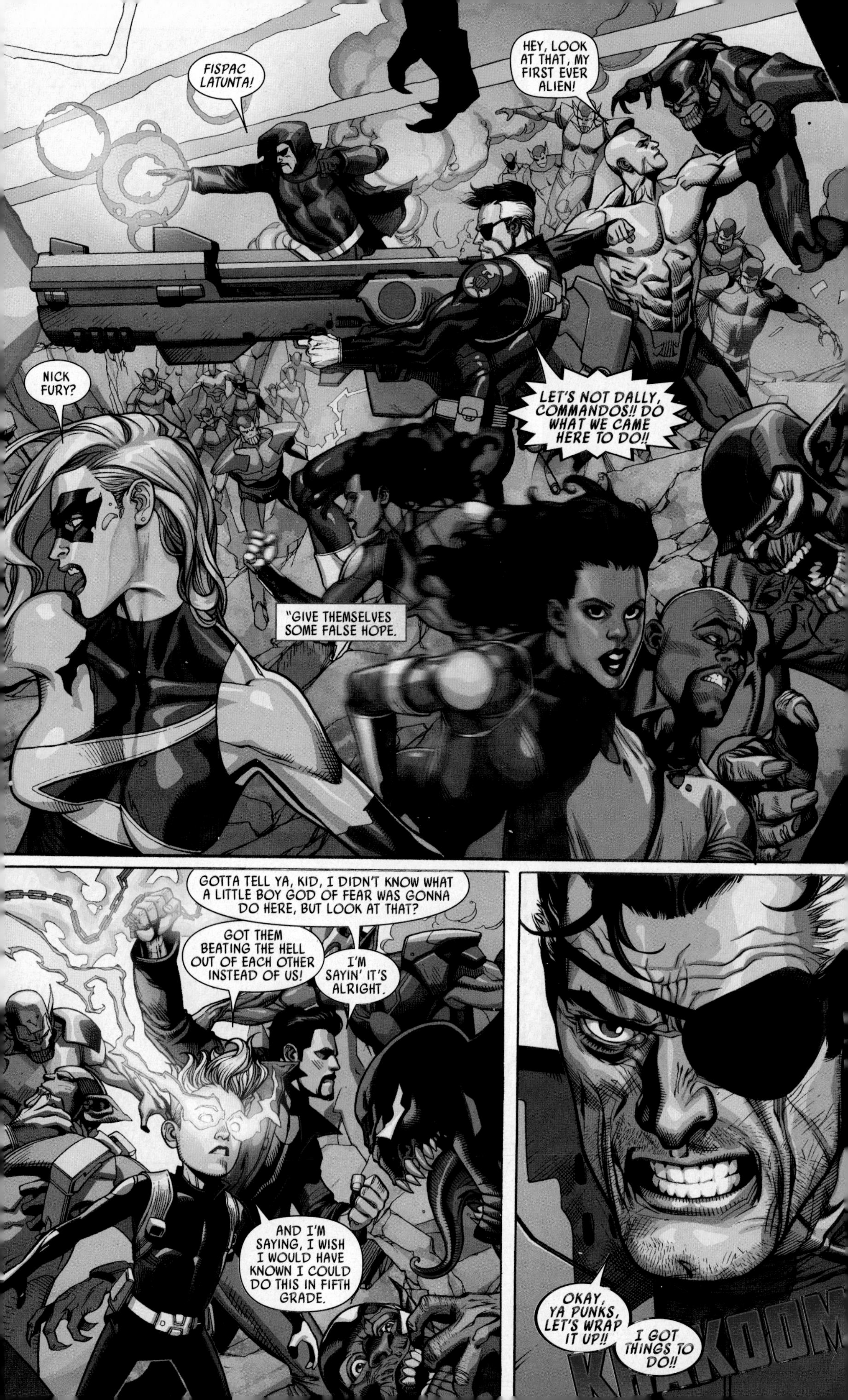
FISPAC LATUNTA!
HEY, LOOK AT THAT, MY FIRST EVER ALIEN!
NICK FURY?
LET'S NOT DALLY, COMMANDOS!! DO WHAT WE CAME HERE TO DO!!
"GIVE THEMSELVES SOME FALSE HOPE.
GOTTA TELL YA, KID, I DIDN'T KNOW WHAT A LITTLE BOY GOD OF FEAR WAS GONNA DO HERE, BUT LOOK AT THAT?
GOT THEM BEATING THE HELL OUT OF EACH OTHER INSTEAD OF US!
I'M SAYIN' IT'S ALRIGHT.
AND I'M SAYING, I WISH I WOULD HAVE KNOWN I COULD DO THIS IN FIFTH GRADE.
OKAY, YA PUNKS, LET'S WRAP IT UP!!
I GOT THINGS TO DO!!

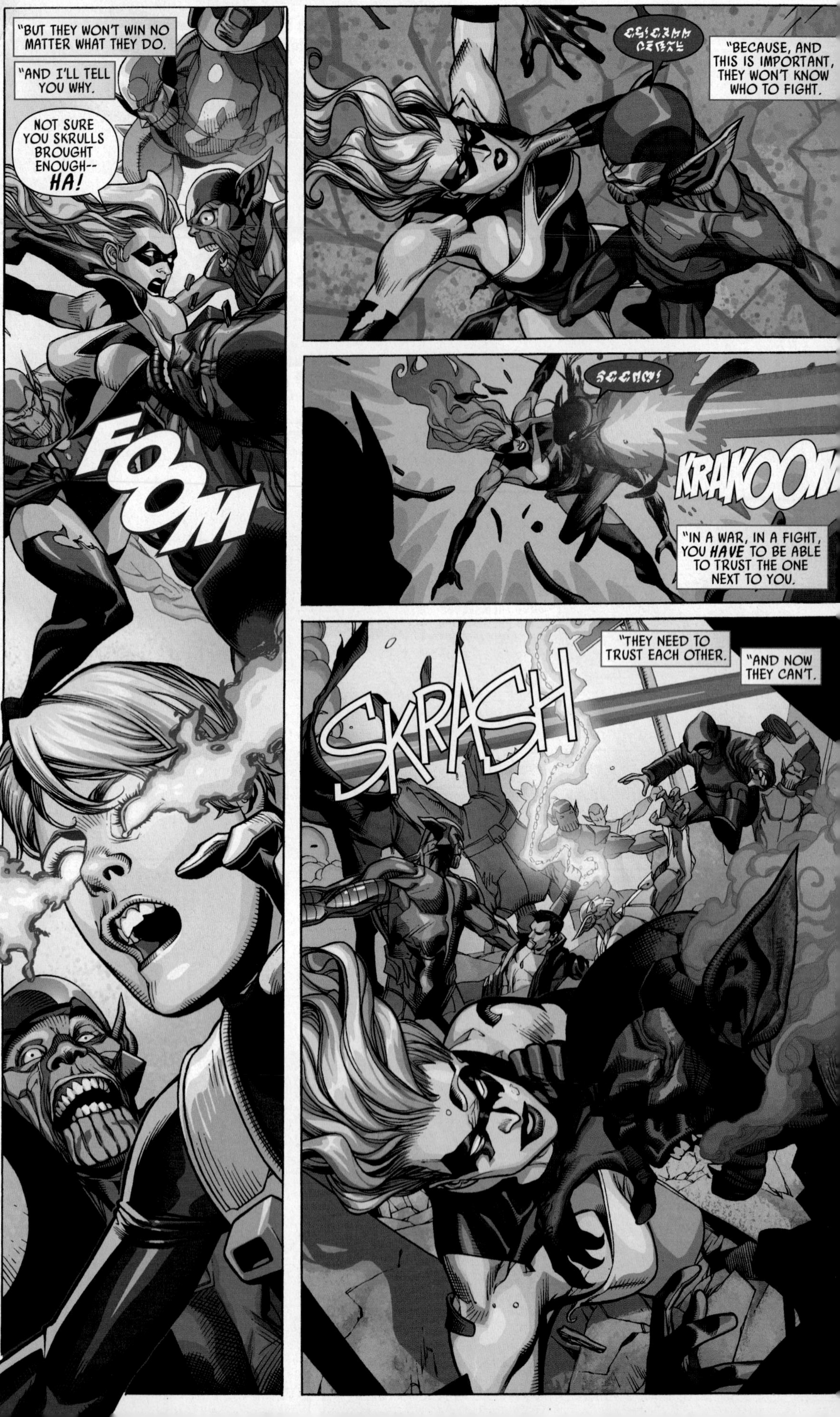

"BUT THEY WON'T WIN NO MATTER WHAT THEY DO.
"AND I'LL TELL YOU WHY.
NOT SURE YOU SKRULLS BROUGHT ENOUGH-- HA!
FOOM
"BECAUSE, AND THIS IS IMPORTANT, THEY WON'T KNOW WHO TO FIGHT.
KRAKOOM
"IN A WAR, IN A FIGHT, YOU HAVE TO BE ABLE TO TRUST THE ONE NEXT TO YOU.
"THEY NEED TO TRUST EACH OTHER.
"AND NOW THEY CAN'T.
SKRASH

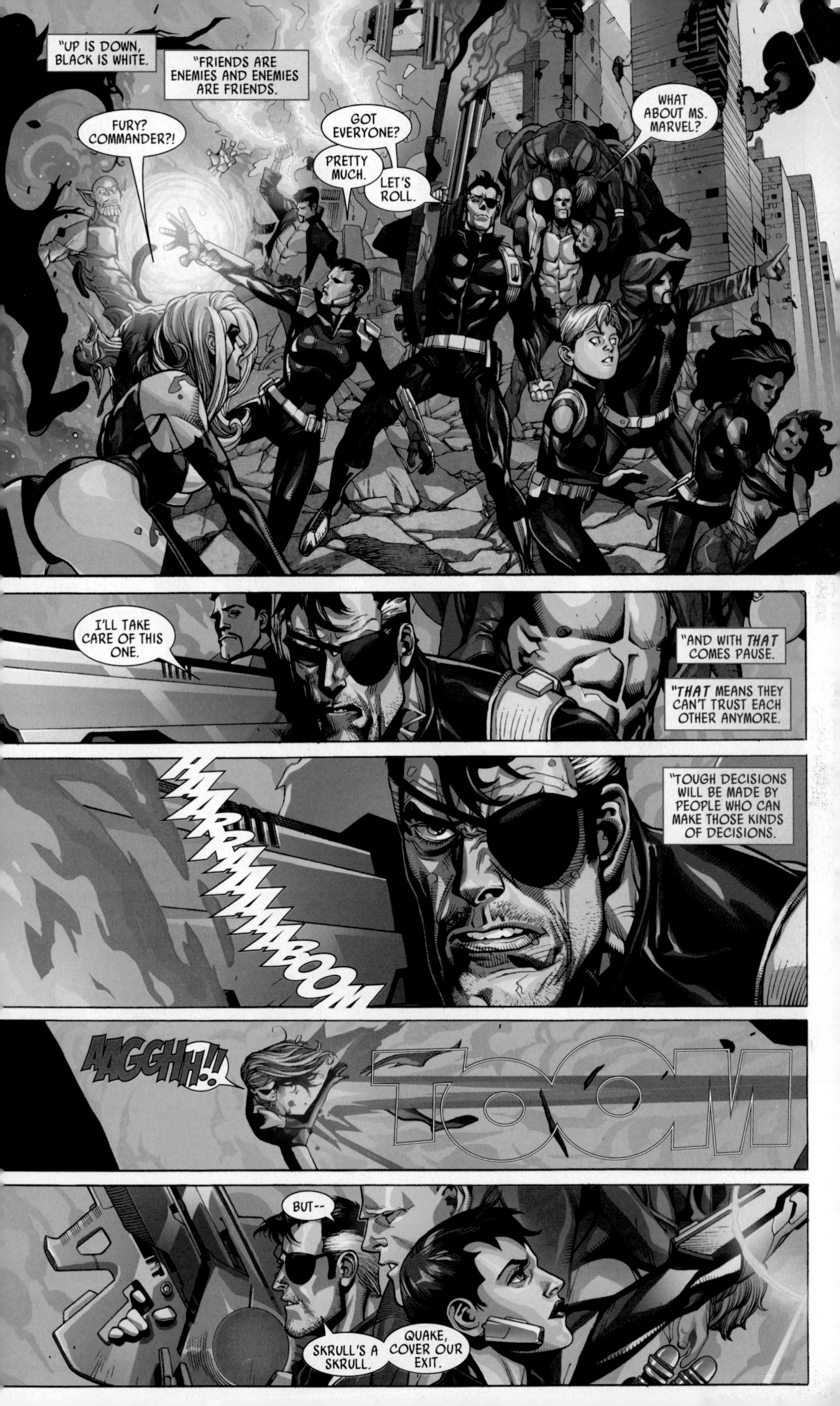
"UP IS DOWN, BLACK IS WHITE.
"FRIENDS ARE ENEMIES AND ENEMIES ARE FRIENDS.
FURY? COMMANDER?!
GOT EVERYONE?
PRETTY MUCH.
LET'S ROLL.
WHAT ABOUT MS. MARVEL?
I'LL TAKE CARE OF THIS ONE.
"AND WITH THAT COMES PAUSE.
"THAT MEANS THEY CAN'T TRUST EACH OTHER ANYMORE.
"TOUGH DECISIONS WILL BE MADE BY PEOPLE WHO CAN MAKE THOSE KINDS OF DECISIONS.
AAGGHH!!
TOOM
BUT--
SKRULL'S A SKRULL.
QUAKE, COVER OUR EXIT.

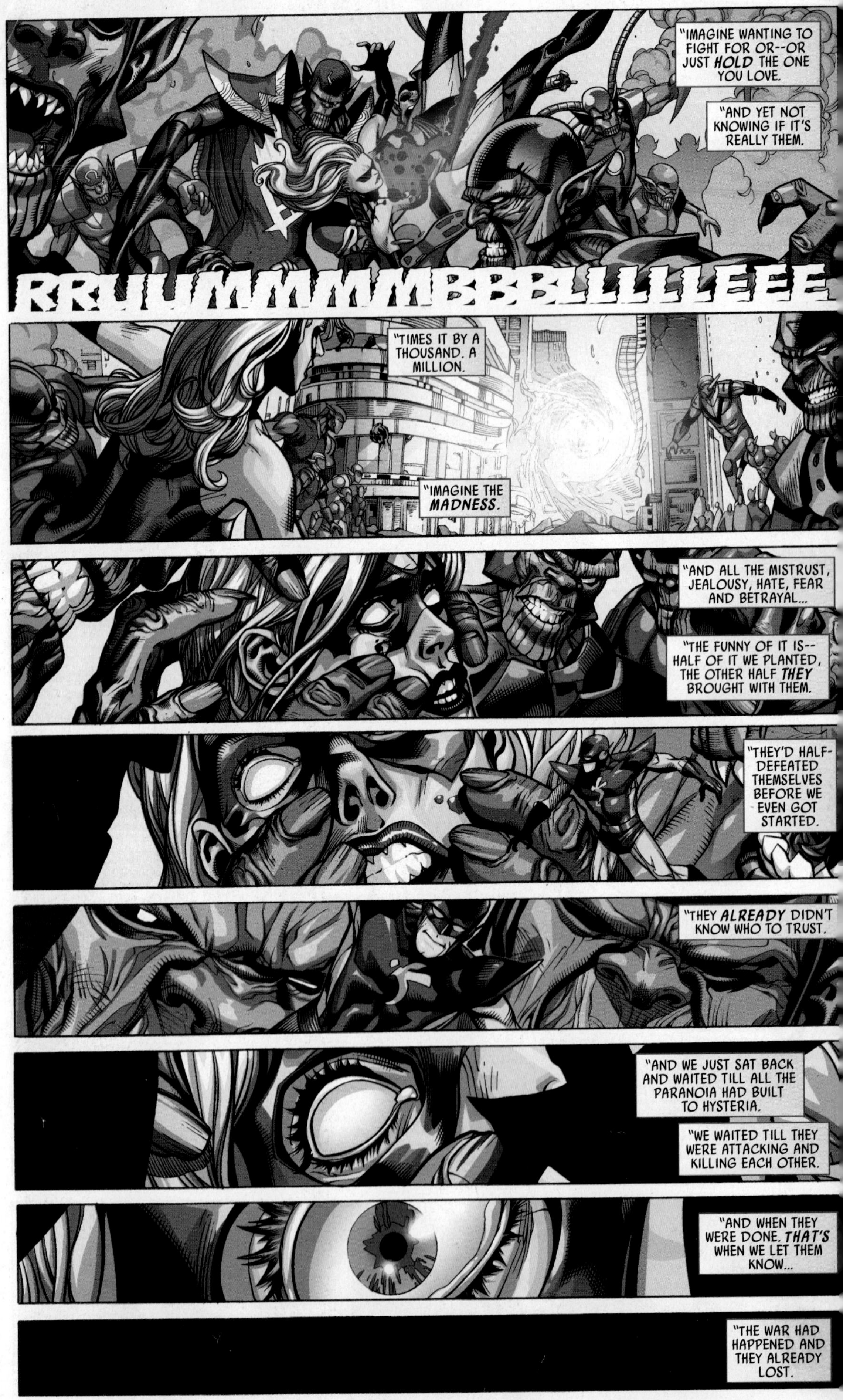
"IMAGINE WANTING TO FIGHT FOR OR--OR JUST HOLD THE ONE YOU LOVE.
"AND YET NOT KNOWING IF IT'S REALLY THEM.
RRUUMMMMMBBBLLLLLEEE
"TIMES IT BY A THOUSAND. A MILLION.
"IMAGINE THE MADNESS.
"AND ALL THE MISTRUST, JEALOUSY, HATE, FEAR AND BETRAYAL...
"THE FUNNY OF IT IS-- HALF OF IT WE PLANTED, THE OTHER HALF THEY BROUGHT WITH THEM.
"THEY'D HALF-DEFEATED THEMSELVES BEFORE WE EVEN GOT STARTED.
"THEY ALREADY DIDN'T KNOW WHO TO TRUST.
"AND WE JUST SAT BACK AND WAITED TILL ALL THE PARANOIA HAD BUILT TO HYSTERIA.
"WE WAITED TILL THEY WERE ATTACKING AND KILLING EACH OTHER.
"AND WHEN THEY WERE DONE. THAT'S WHEN WE LET THEM KNOW...
"THE WAR HAD HAPPENED AND THEY ALREADY LOST.

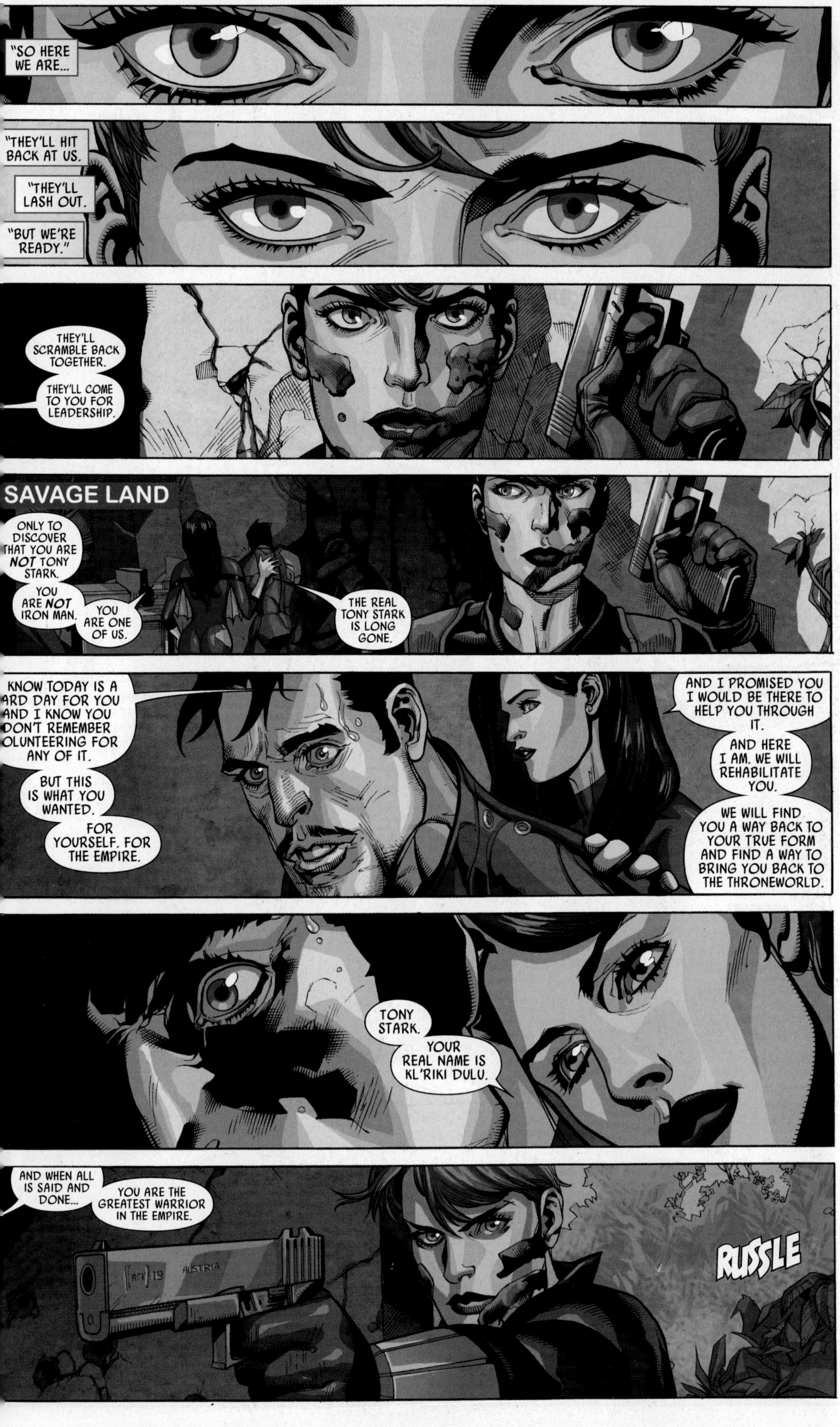

"SO HERE WE ARE...
"THEY'LL HIT BACK AT US.
"THEY'LL LASH OUT.
"BUT WE'RE READY."
THEY'LL SCRAMBLE BACK TOGETHER.
THEY'LL COME TO YOU FOR LEADERSHIP.
SAVAGE LAND
ONLY TO DISCOVER THAT YOU ARE NOT TONY STARK.
YOU ARE NOT IRON MAN.
YOU ARE ONE OF US.
THE REAL TONY STARK IS LONG GONE.
KNOW TODAY IS A ARD DAY FOR YOU AND I KNOW YOU DON'T REMEMBER OLUNTEERING FOR ANY OF IT.
BUT THIS IS WHAT YOU WANTED.
FOR YOURSELF. FOR THE EMPIRE.
AND I PROMISED YOU I WOULD BE THERE TO HELP YOU THROUGH IT.
AND HERE I AM. WE WILL REHABILITATE YOU.
WE WILL FIND YOU A WAY BACK TO YOUR TRUE FORM AND FIND A WAY TO BRING YOU BACK TO THE THRONEWORLD.
TONY STARK.
YOUR REAL NAME IS KL'RIKI DULU.
AND WHEN ALL IS SAID AND DONE...
YOU ARE THE GREATEST WARRIOR IN THE EMPIRE.
AUSTRIA
RUSSLE

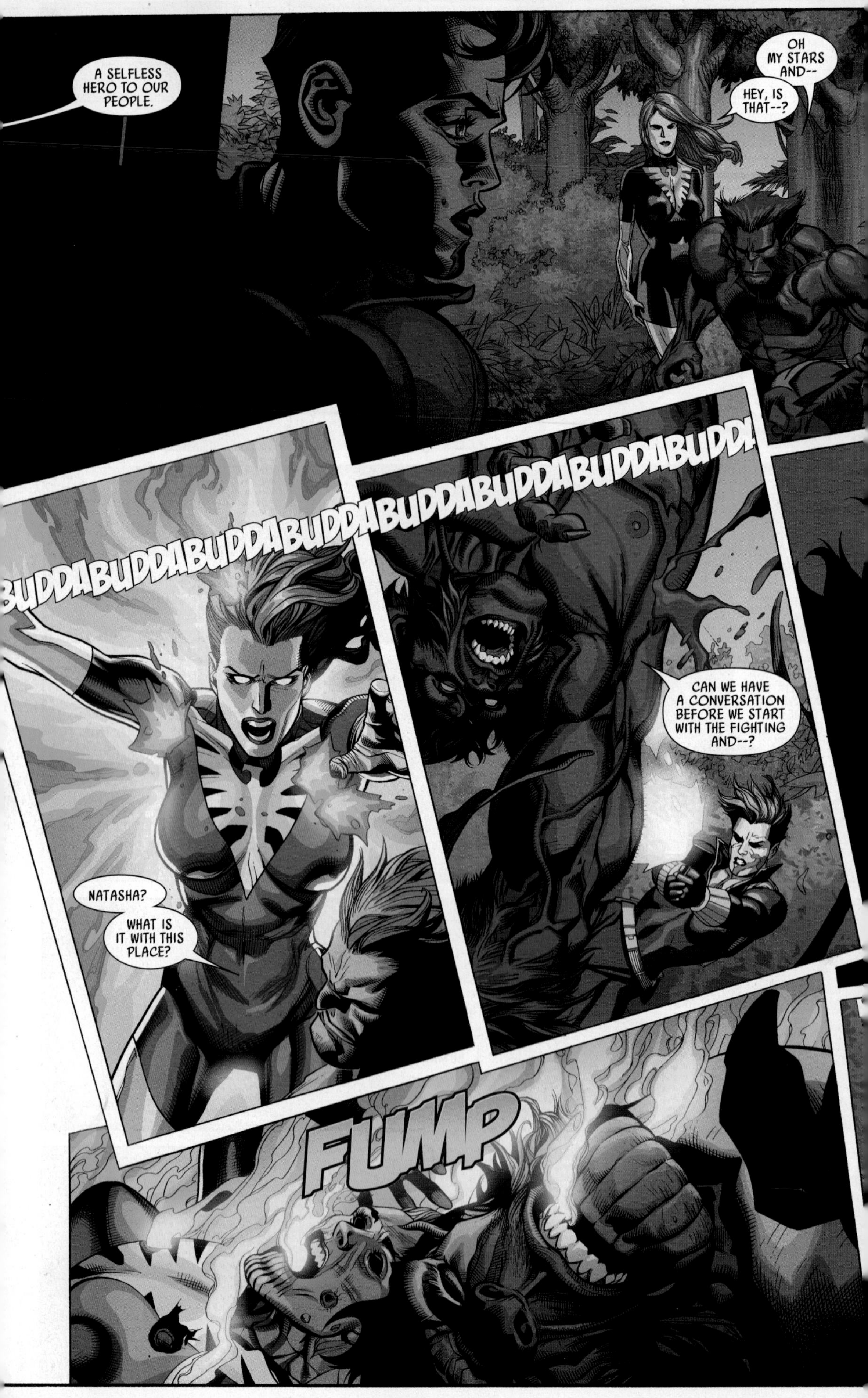
A SELFLESS HERO TO OUR PEOPLE.
OH MY STARS AND--
HEY, IS THAT--?
BUDDABUDDABUDDABUDDABUDDABUDDABUDDABUDDABUDD!
NATASHA?
WHAT IS IT WITH THIS PLACE?
CAN WE HAVE A CONVERSATION BEFORE WE START WITH THE FIGHTING AND--?
FUMP

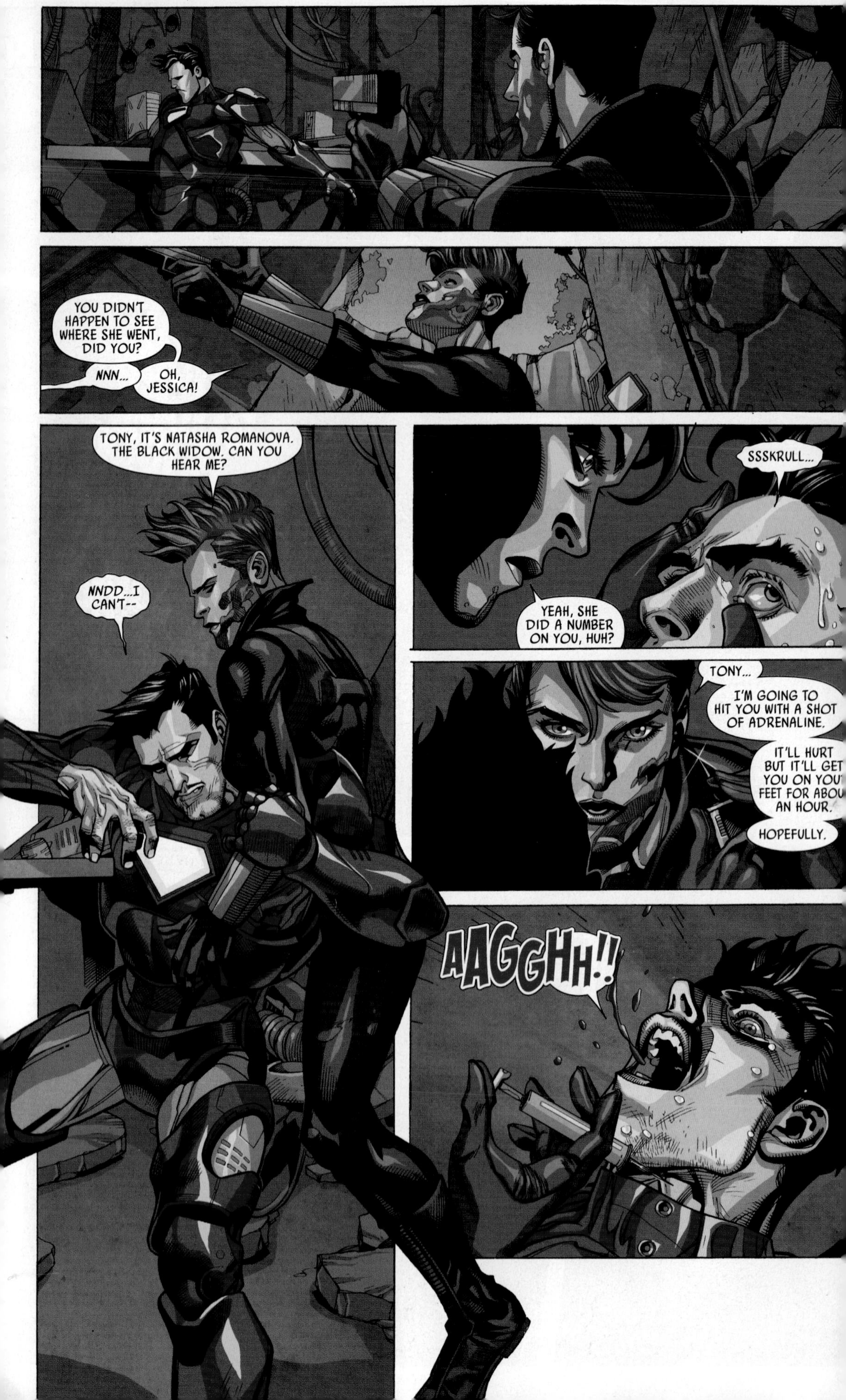

YOU DIDN'T HAPPEN TO SEE WHERE SHE WENT, DID YOU?
NNN...
OH, JESSICA!
TONY, IT'S NATASHA ROMANOVA. THE BLACK WIDOW. CAN YOU HEAR ME?
NNDD...I CAN'T--
SSSKRULL...
YEAH, SHE DID A NUMBER ON YOU, HUH?
TONY...
I'M GOING TO HIT YOU WITH A SHOT OF ADRENALINE.
IT'LL HURT BUT IT'LL GET YOU ON YOU FEET FOR ABOU AN HOUR.
HOPEFULLY.
AAGGHH!!

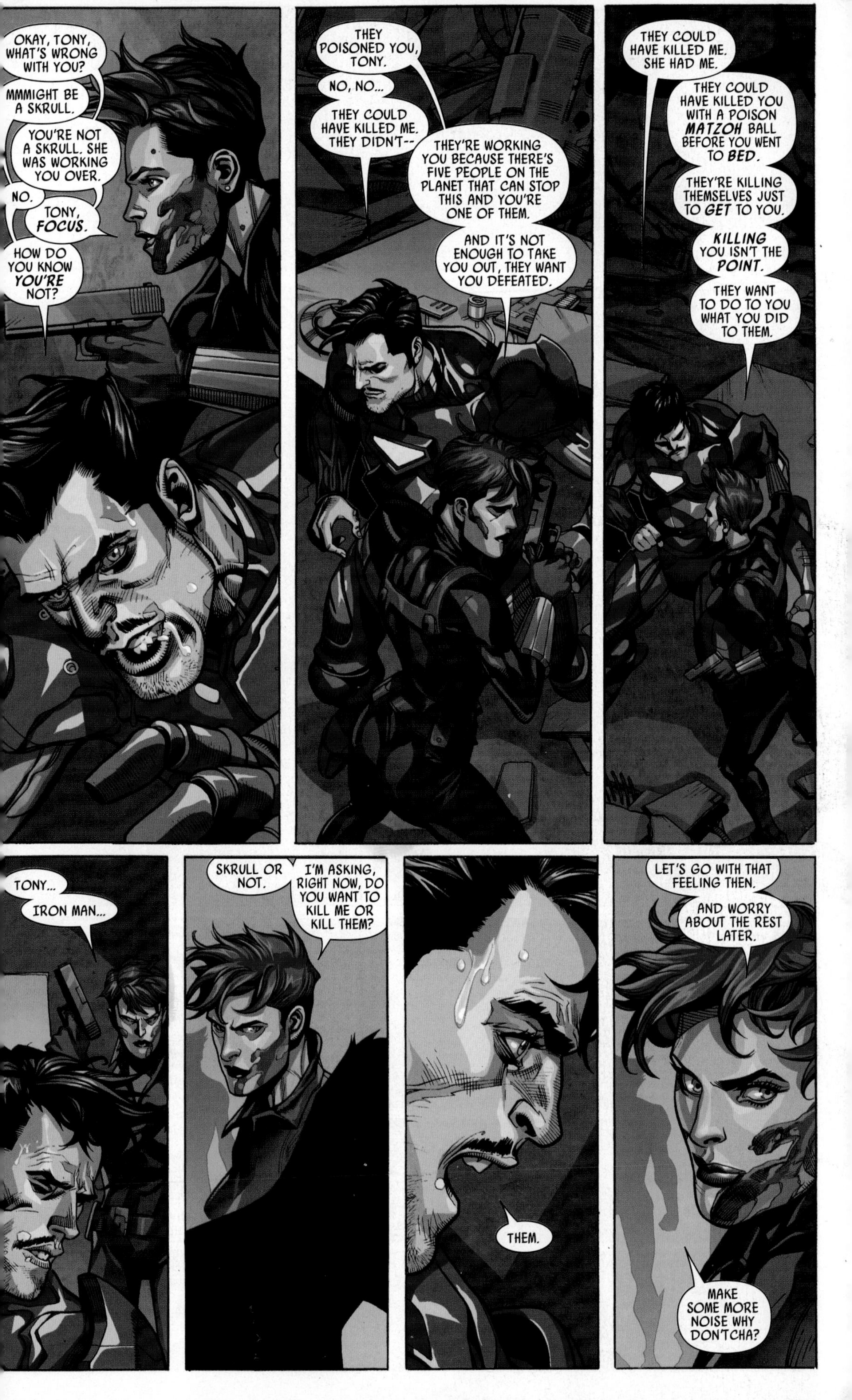

OKAY, TONY, WHAT'S WRONG WITH YOU?
MMMIGHT BE A SKRULL.
YOU'RE NOT A SKRULL. SHE WAS WORKING YOU OVER.
NO.
TONY, FOCUS.
HOW DO YOU KNOW YOU'RE NOT?
THEY POISONED YOU, TONY.
NO, NO...
THEY COULD HAVE KILLED ME. THEY DIDN'T--
THEY'RE WORKING YOU BECAUSE THERE'S FIVE PEOPLE ON THE PLANET THAT CAN STOP THIS AND YOU'RE ONE OF THEM.
AND IT'S NOT ENOUGH TO TAKE YOU OUT, THEY WANT YOU DEFEATED.
THEY COULD HAVE KILLED ME. SHE HAD ME.
THEY COULD HAVE KILLED YOU WITH A POISON MATZOH BALL BEFORE YOU WENT TO BED.
THEY'RE KILLING THEMSELVES JUST TO GET TO YOU.
KILLING YOU ISN'T THE POINT.
THEY WANT TO DO TO YOU WHAT YOU DID TO THEM.
TONY...
IRON MAN...
SKRULL OR NOT.
I'M ASKING, RIGHT NOW, DO YOU WANT TO KILL ME OR KILL THEM?
THEM.
LET'S GO WITH THAT FEELING THEN.
AND WORRY ABOUT THE REST LATER.
MAKE SOME MORE NOISE WHY DON'TCHA?

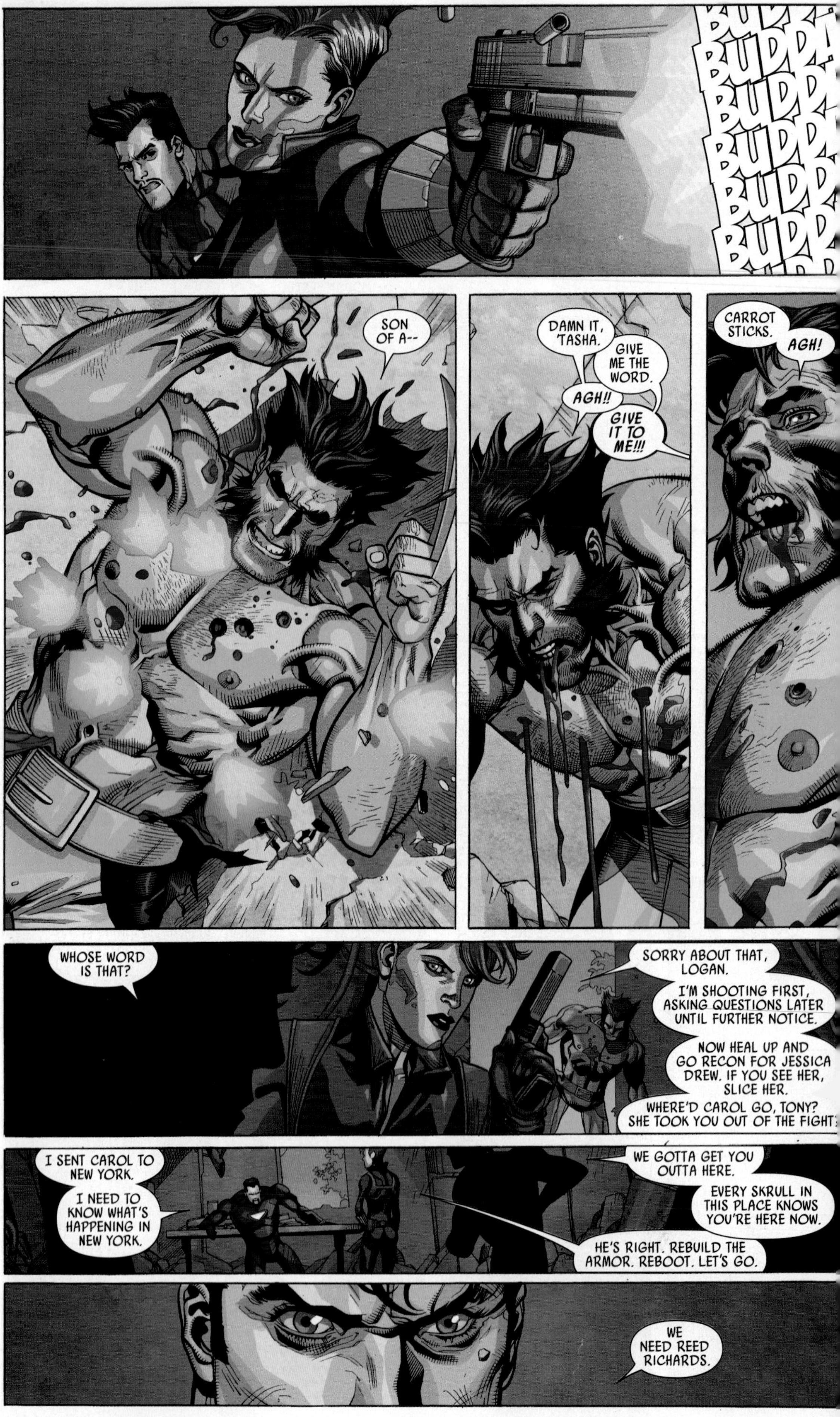
BUDDA BUDDA BUDDA BUDDA BUDDA BUDDA
SON OF A--
DAMN IT, 'TASHA.
AGH!!
GIVE ME THE WORD.
GIVE IT TO ME!!!
CARROT STICKS.
AGH!
WHOSE WORD IS THAT?
SORRY ABOUT THAT, LOGAN.
I'M SHOOTING FIRST, ASKING QUESTIONS LATER UNTIL FURTHER NOTICE.
NOW HEAL UP AND GO RECON FOR JESSICA DREW. IF YOU SEE HER, SLICE HER.
WHERE'D CAROL GO, TONY? SHE TOOK YOU OUT OF THE FIGHT.
I SENT CAROL TO NEW YORK.
I NEED TO KNOW WHAT'S HAPPENING IN NEW YORK.
WE GOTTA GET YOU OUTTA HERE.
EVERY SKRULL IN THIS PLACE KNOWS YOU'RE HERE NOW.
HE'S RIGHT. REBUILD THE ARMOR. REBOOT. LET'S GO.
WE NEED REED RICHARDS.

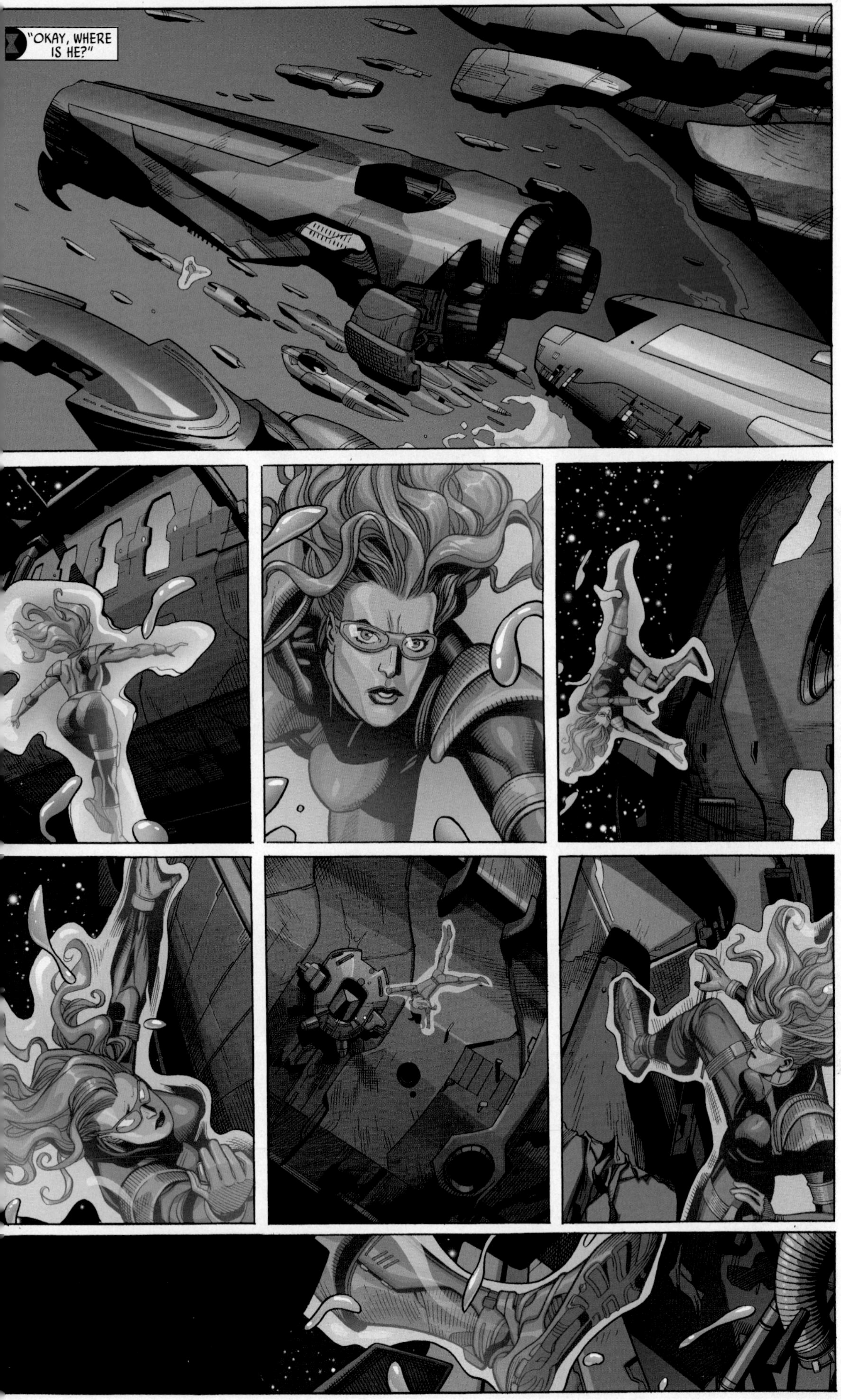
"OKAY, WHERE IS HE?"

NGA!
NGUH!

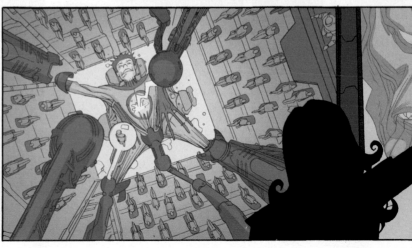

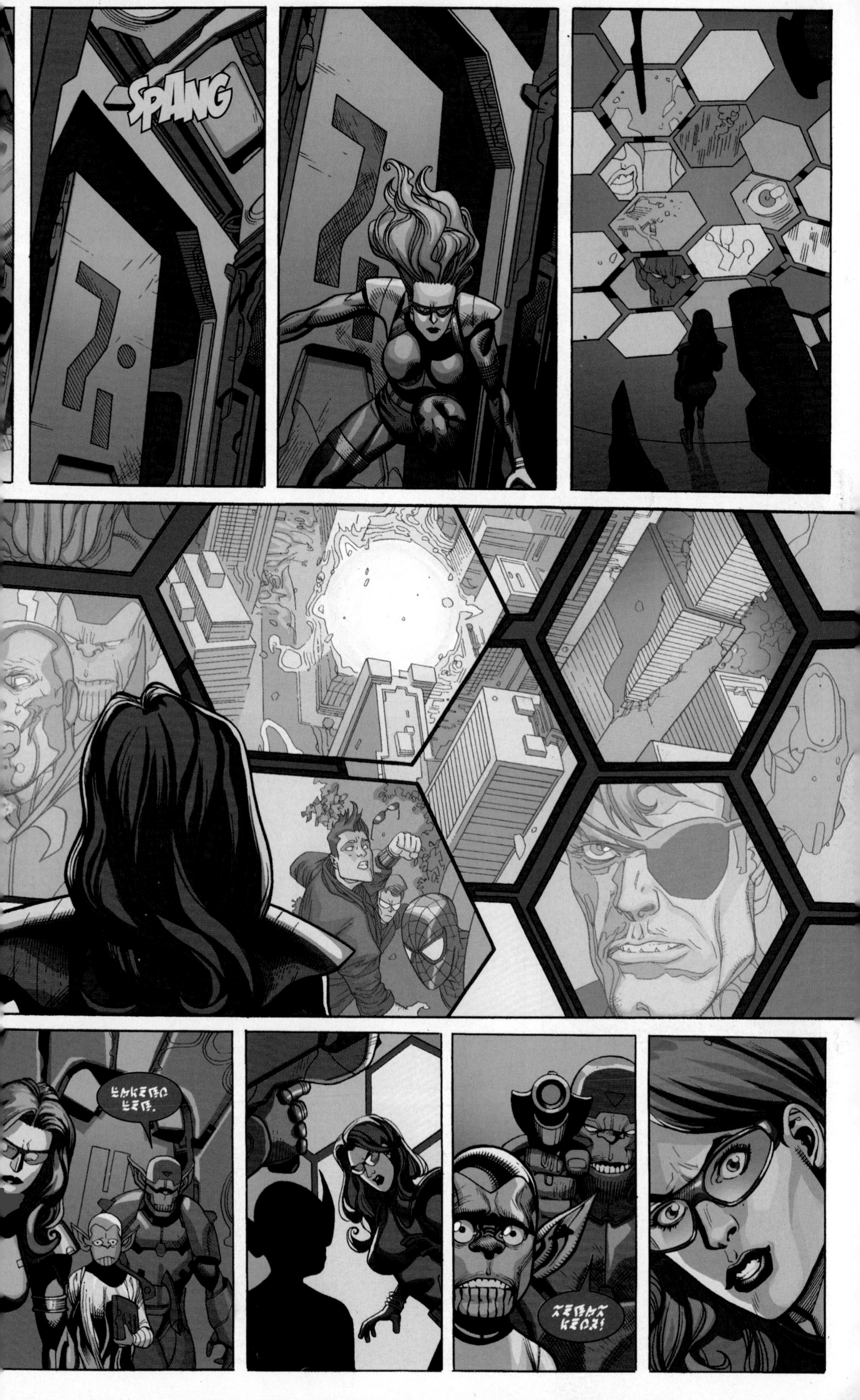
SPANG

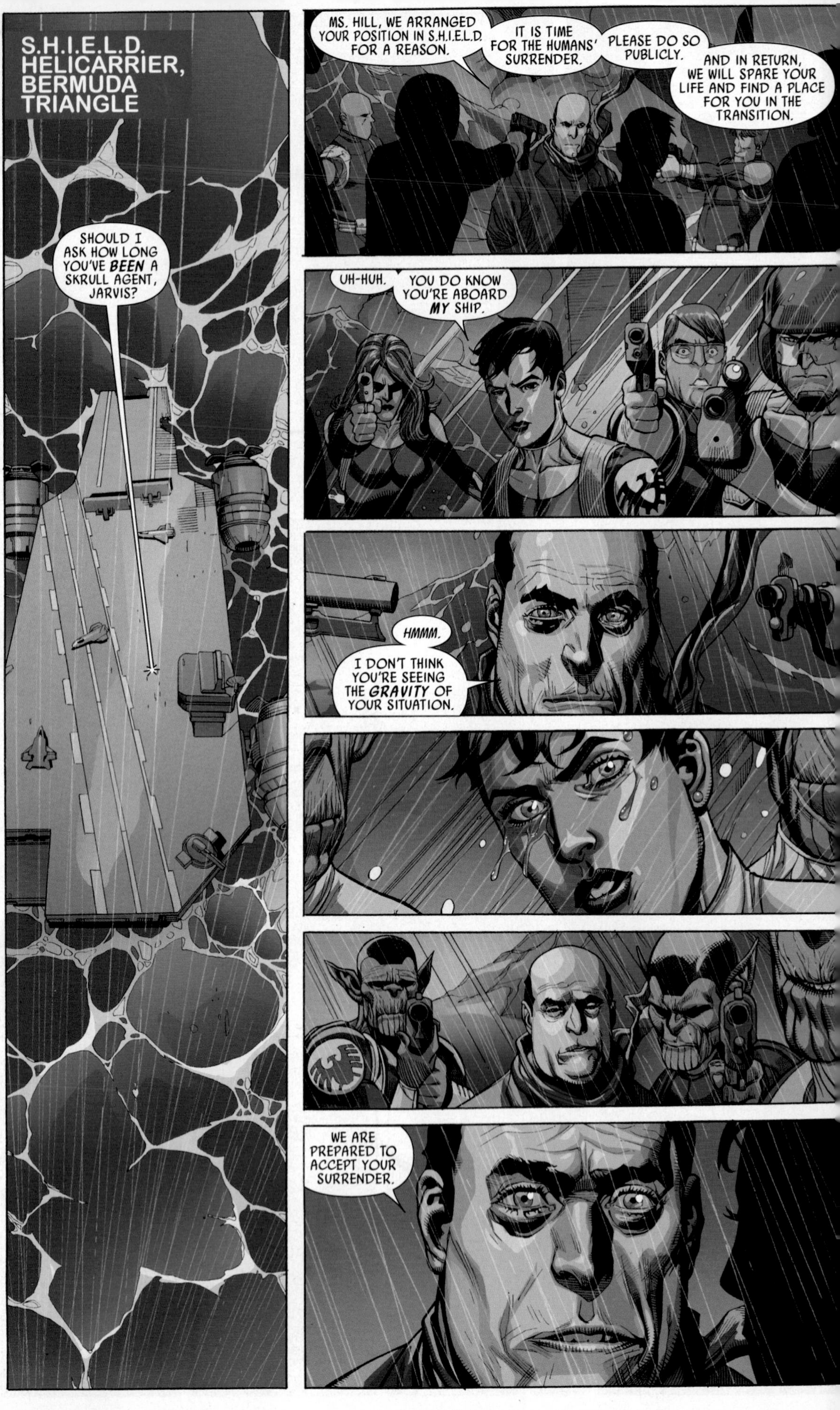
S.H.I.E.L.D. HELICARRIER, BERMUDA TRIANGLE
SHOULD I ASK HOW LONG YOU'VE BEEN A SKRULL AGENT, JARVIS?
MS. HILL, WE ARRANGED YOUR POSITION IN S.H.I.E.L.D. FOR A REASON.
IT IS TIME FOR THE HUMANS' SURRENDER.
PLEASE DO SO PUBLICLY.
AND IN RETURN, WE WILL SPARE YOUR LIFE AND FIND A PLACE FOR YOU IN THE TRANSITION.
UH-HUH.
YOU DO KNOW YOU'RE ABOARD MY SHIP.
HMMM.
I DON'T THINK YOU'RE SEEING THE GRAVITY OF YOUR SITUATION.
WE ARE PREPARED TO ACCEPT YOUR SURRENDER.

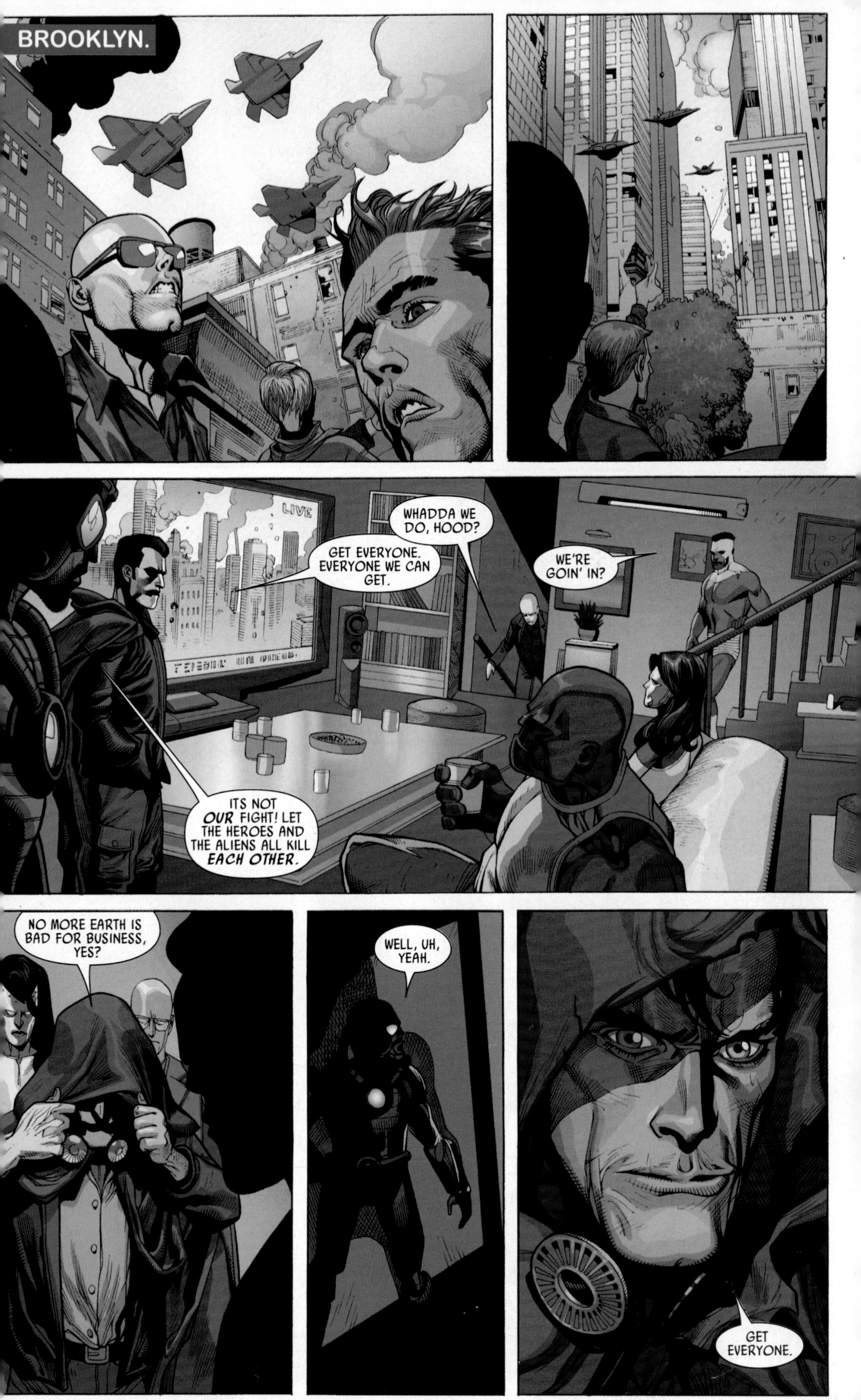
BROOKLYN.
LIVE
WHADDA WE DO, HOOD?
GET EVERYONE. EVERYONE WE CAN GET.
WE'RE GOIN' IN?
ITS NOT OUR FIGHT! LET THE HEROES AND THE ALIENS ALL KILL EACH OTHER.
NO MORE EARTH IS BAD FOR BUSINESS, YES?
WELL, UH, YEAH.
GET EVERYONE.

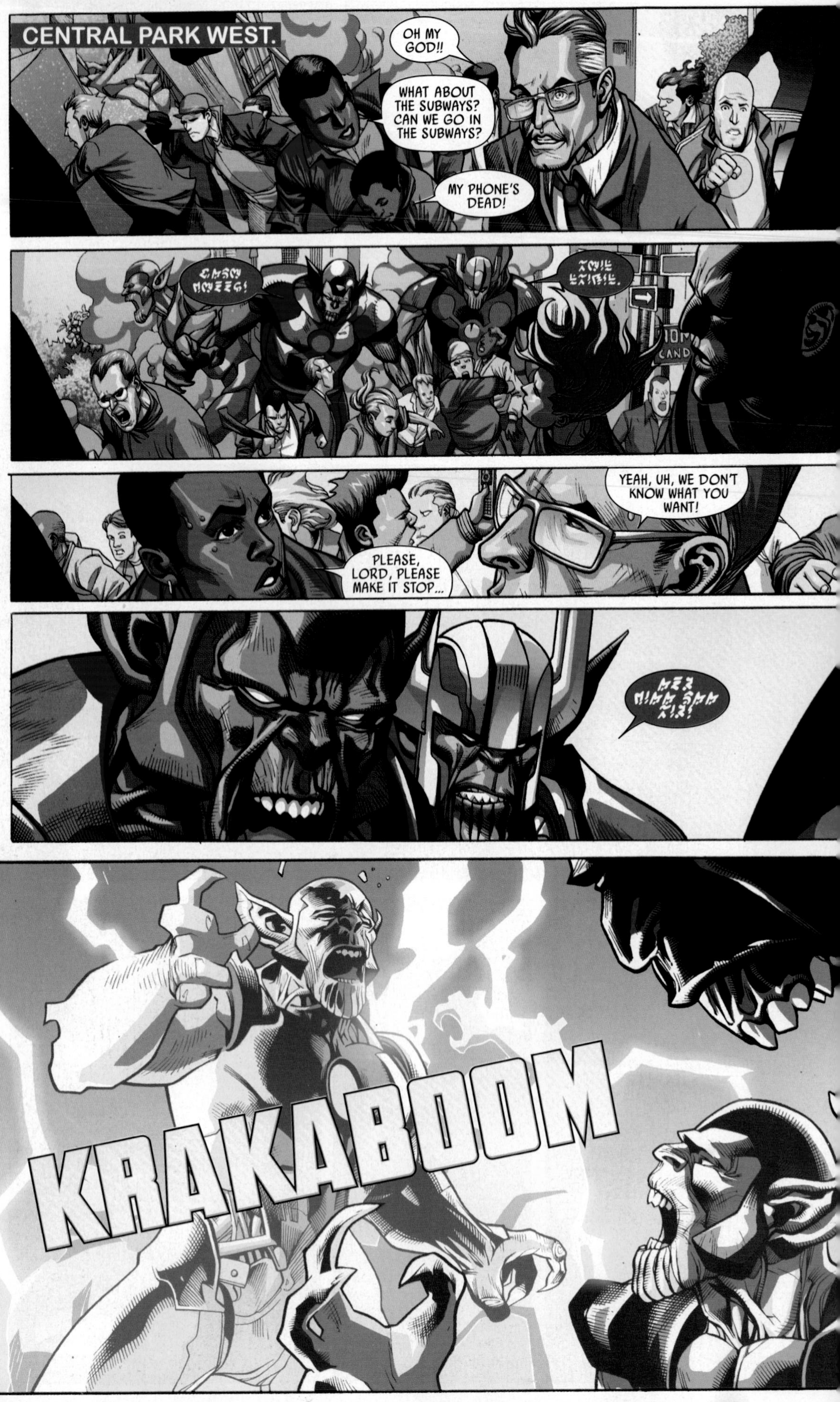

CENTRAL PARK WEST.
OH MY GOD!!
WHAT ABOUT THE SUBWAYS? CAN WE GO IN THE SUBWAYS?
MY PHONE'S DEAD!
YEAH, UH, WE DON'T KNOW WHAT YOU WANT!
PLEASE, LORD, PLEASE MAKE IT STOP...
KRAKABOOM

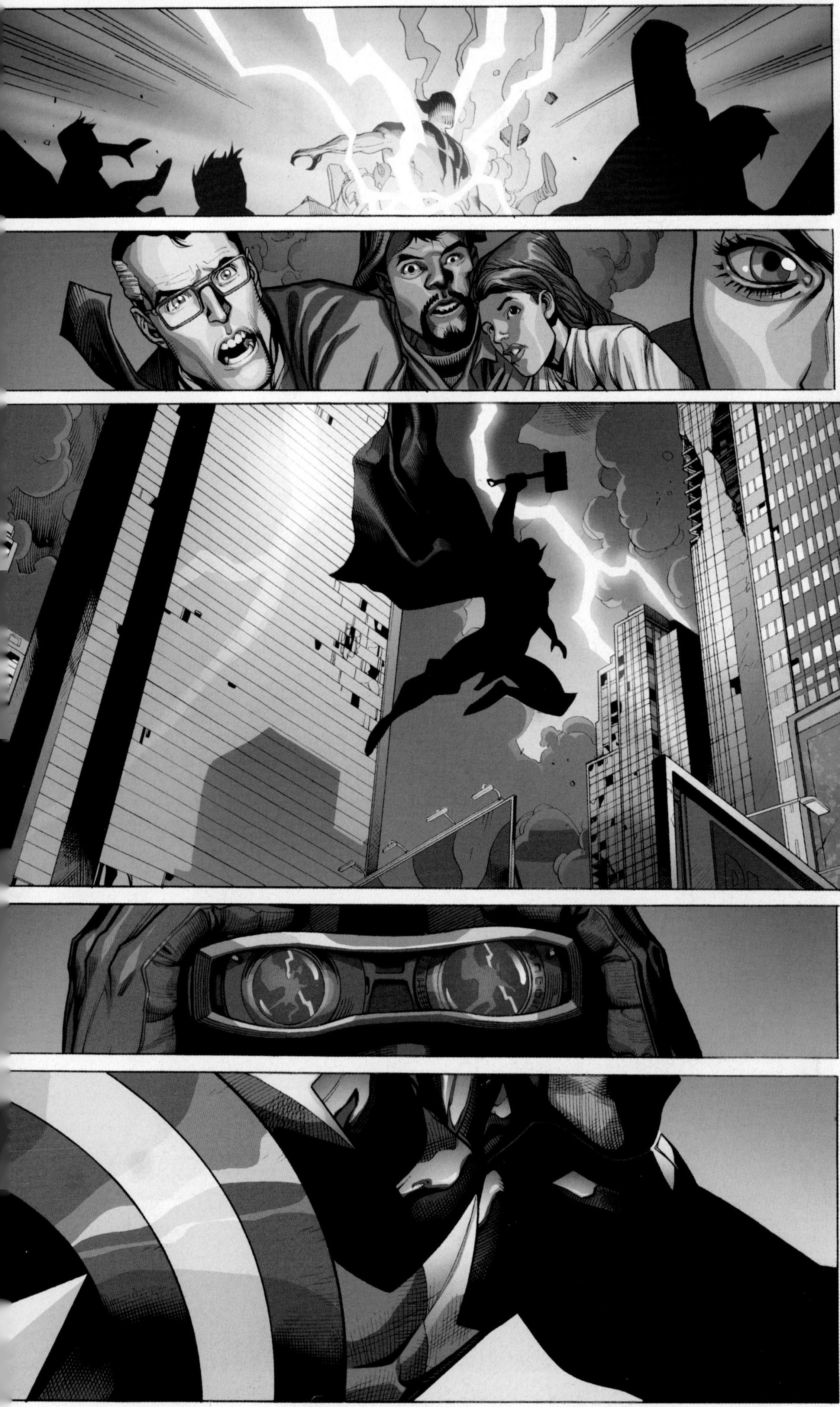

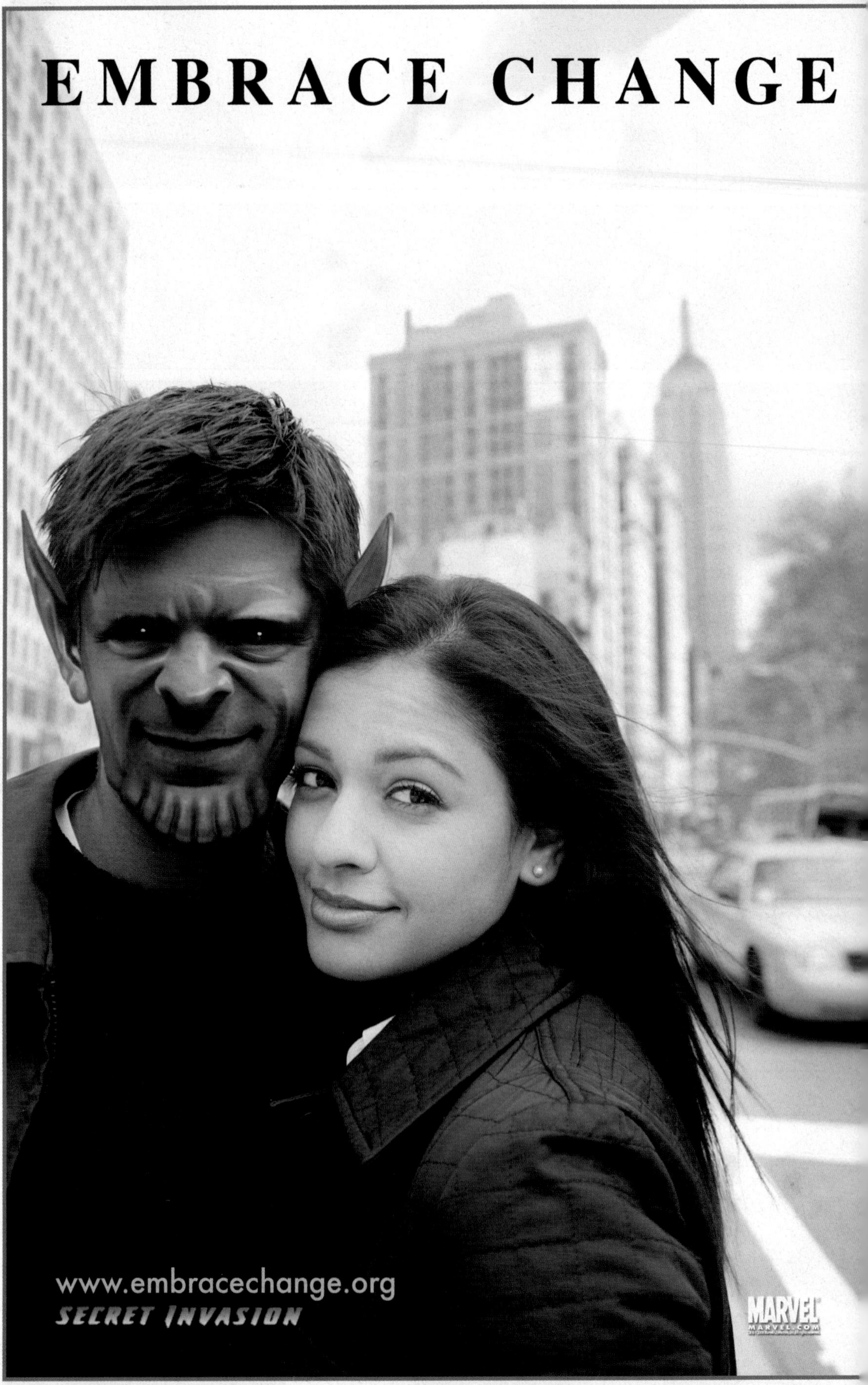

EMBRACE CHANGE
www.embracechange.org
SECRET INVASION
MARVEL
MARVEL.COM

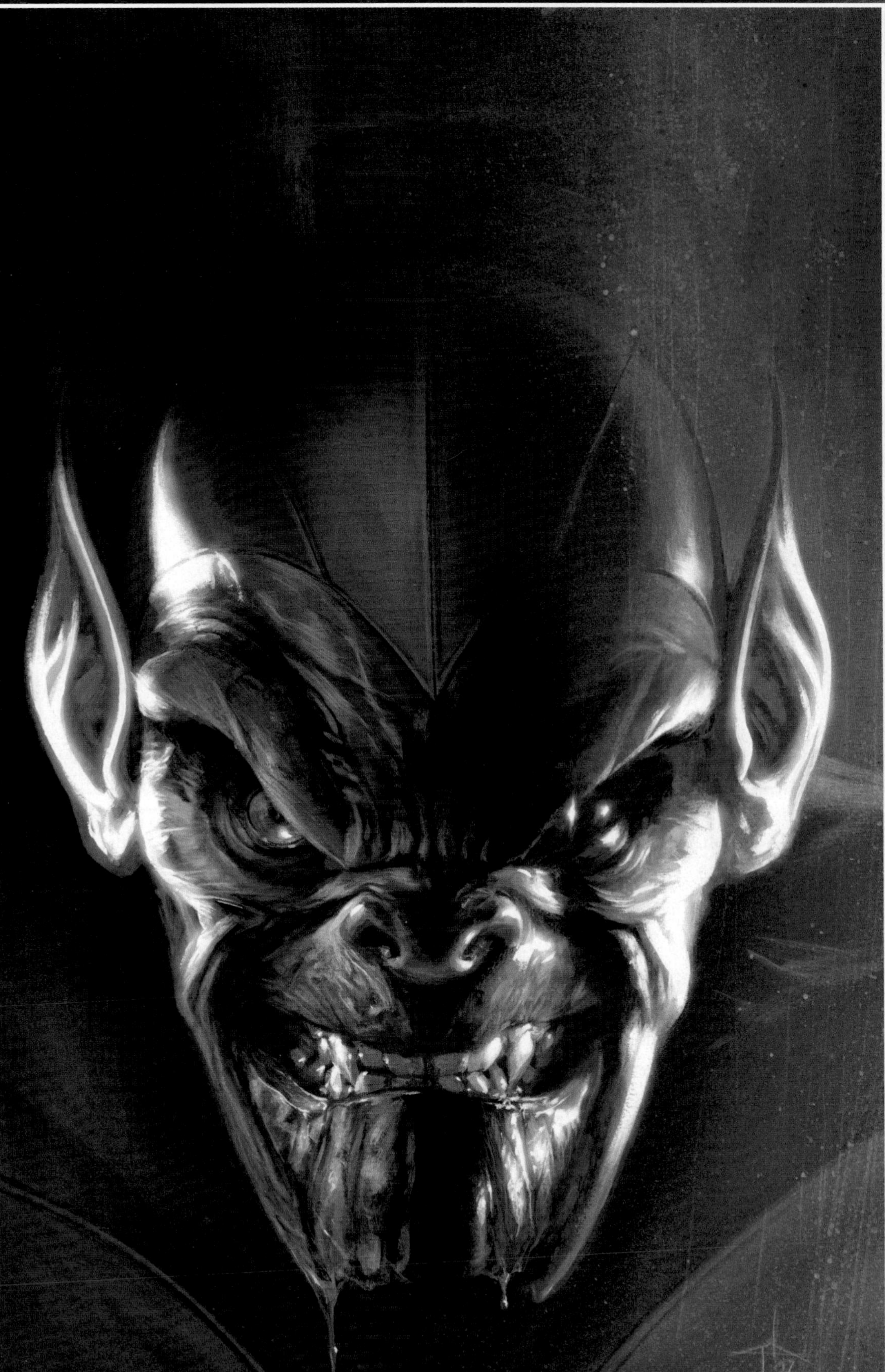

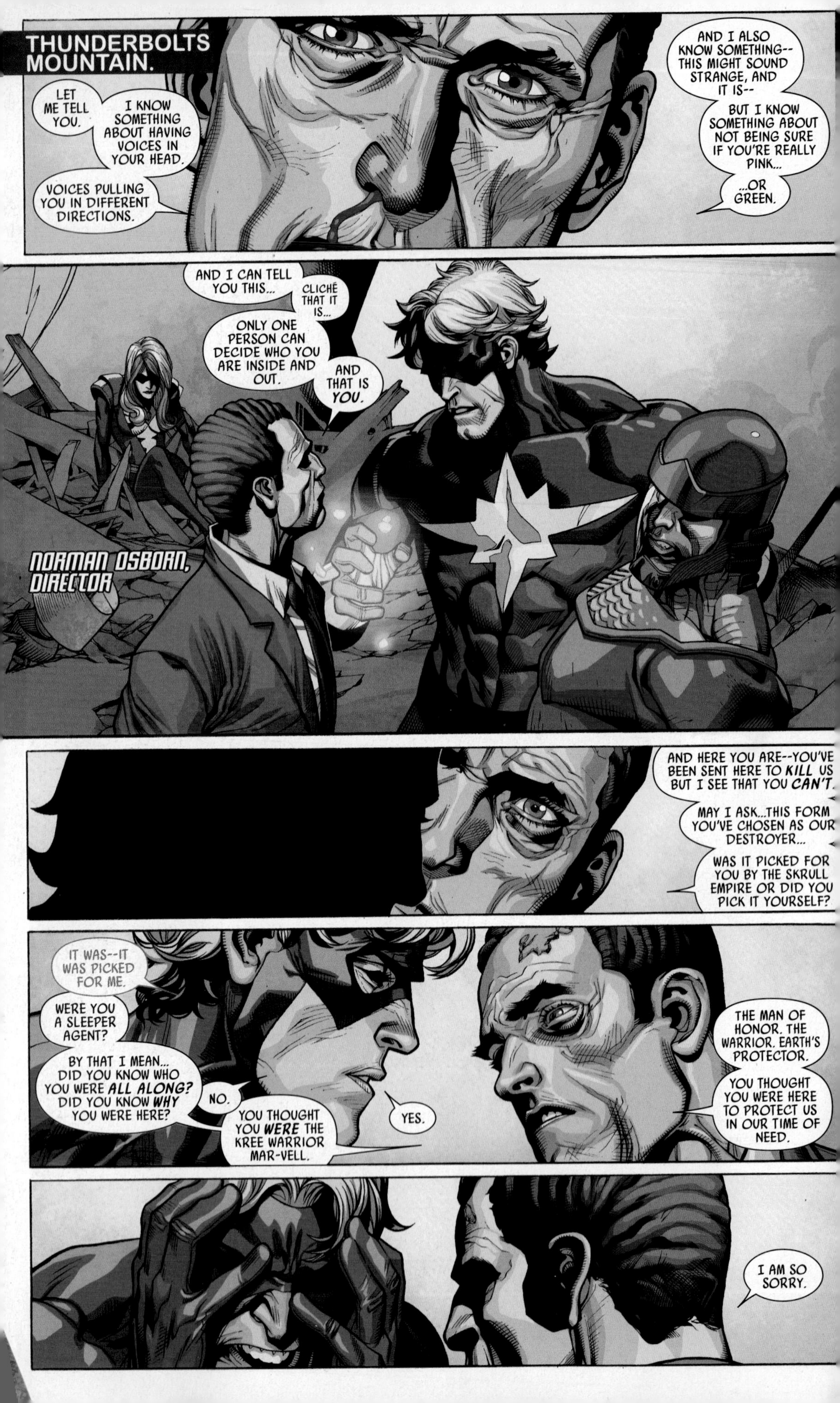

THUNDERBOLTS MOUNTAIN.
LET ME TELL YOU.
I KNOW SOMETHING ABOUT HAVING VOICES IN YOUR HEAD.
VOICES PULLING YOU IN DIFFERENT DIRECTIONS.
AND I ALSO KNOW SOMETHING-- THIS MIGHT SOUND STRANGE, AND IT IS--
BUT I KNOW SOMETHING ABOUT NOT BEING SURE IF YOU'RE REALLY PINK...
...OR GREEN.
AND I CAN TELL YOU THIS...
CLICHÉ THAT IT IS...
ONLY ONE PERSON CAN DECIDE WHO YOU ARE INSIDE AND OUT.
AND THAT IS YOU.
NORMAN OSBORN, DIRECTOR
AND HERE YOU ARE--YOU'VE BEEN SENT HERE TO KILL US BUT I SEE THAT YOU CAN'T.
MAY I ASK...THIS FORM YOU'VE CHOSEN AS OUR DESTROYER...
WAS IT PICKED FOR YOU BY THE SKRULL EMPIRE OR DID YOU PICK IT YOURSELF?
IT WAS--IT WAS PICKED FOR ME.
WERE YOU A SLEEPER AGENT?
BY THAT I MEAN... DID YOU KNOW WHO YOU WERE ALL ALONG? DID YOU KNOW WHY YOU WERE HERE?
NO.
YOU THOUGHT YOU WERE THE KREE WARRIOR MAR-VELL.
YES.
THE MAN OF HONOR. THE WARRIOR. EARTH'S PROTECTOR.
YOU THOUGHT YOU WERE HERE TO PROTECT US IN OUR TIME OF NEED.
I AM SO SORRY.

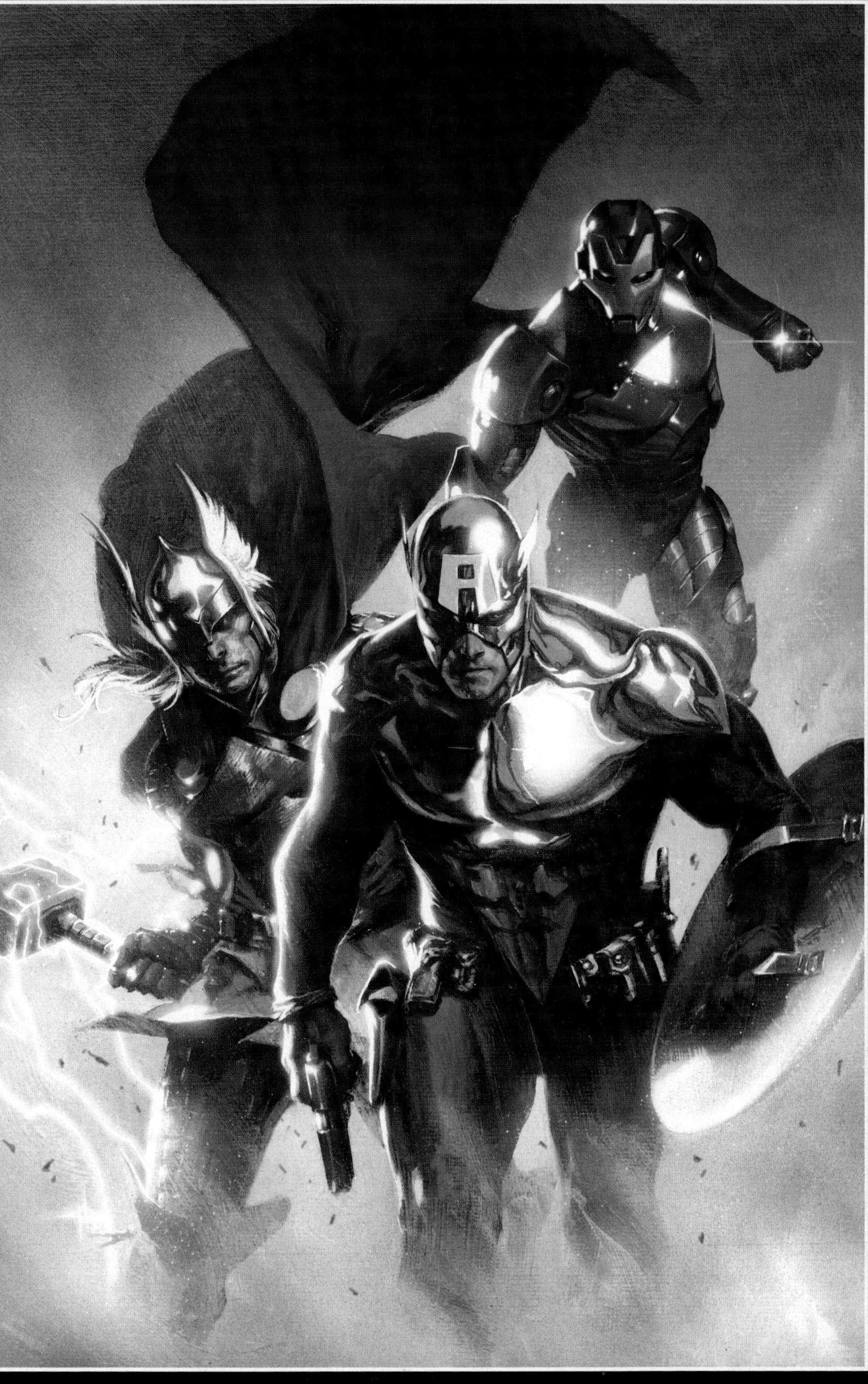

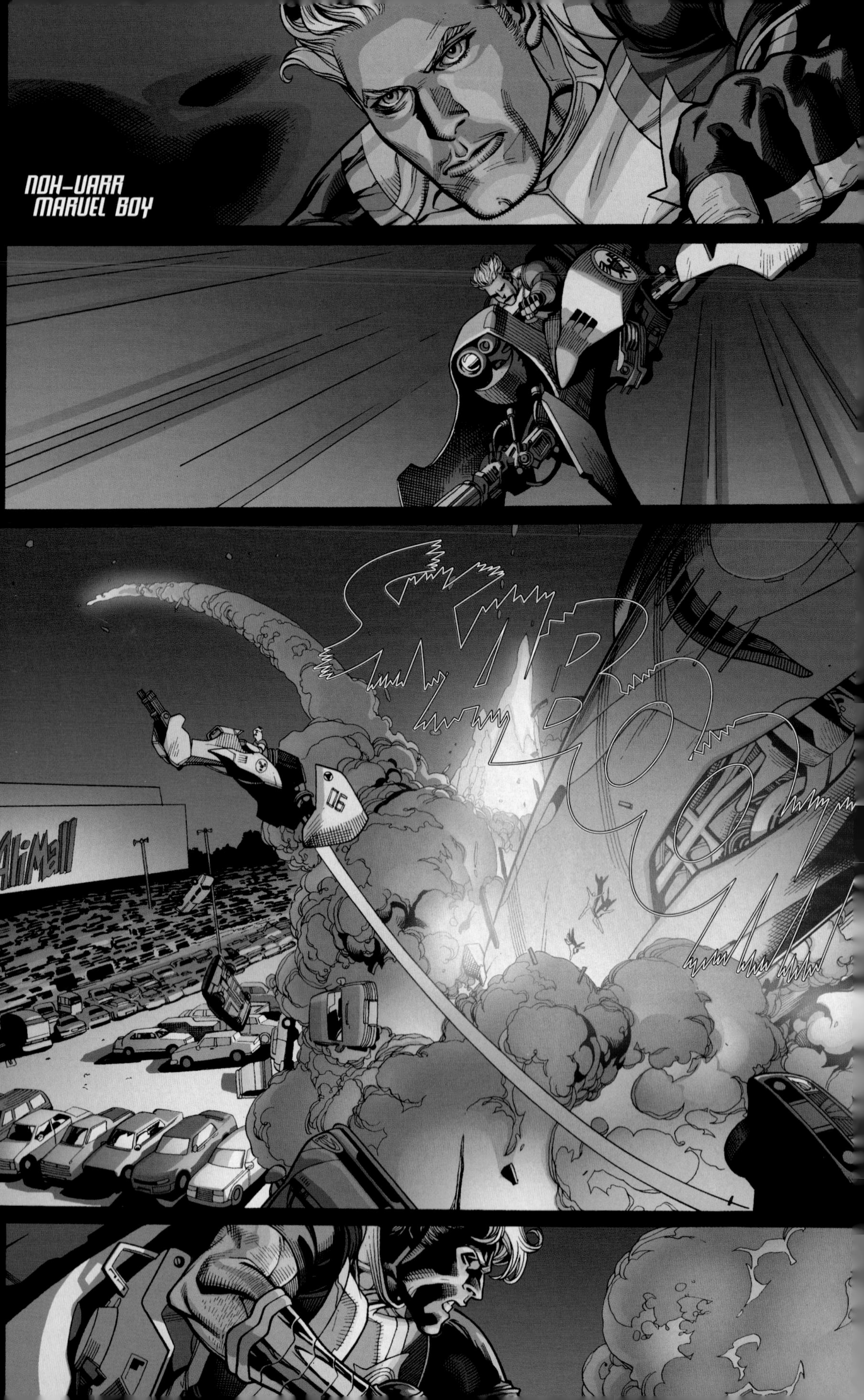
NOH-VARR
MARVEL BOY
AliMall
06
SKRRRBOOM

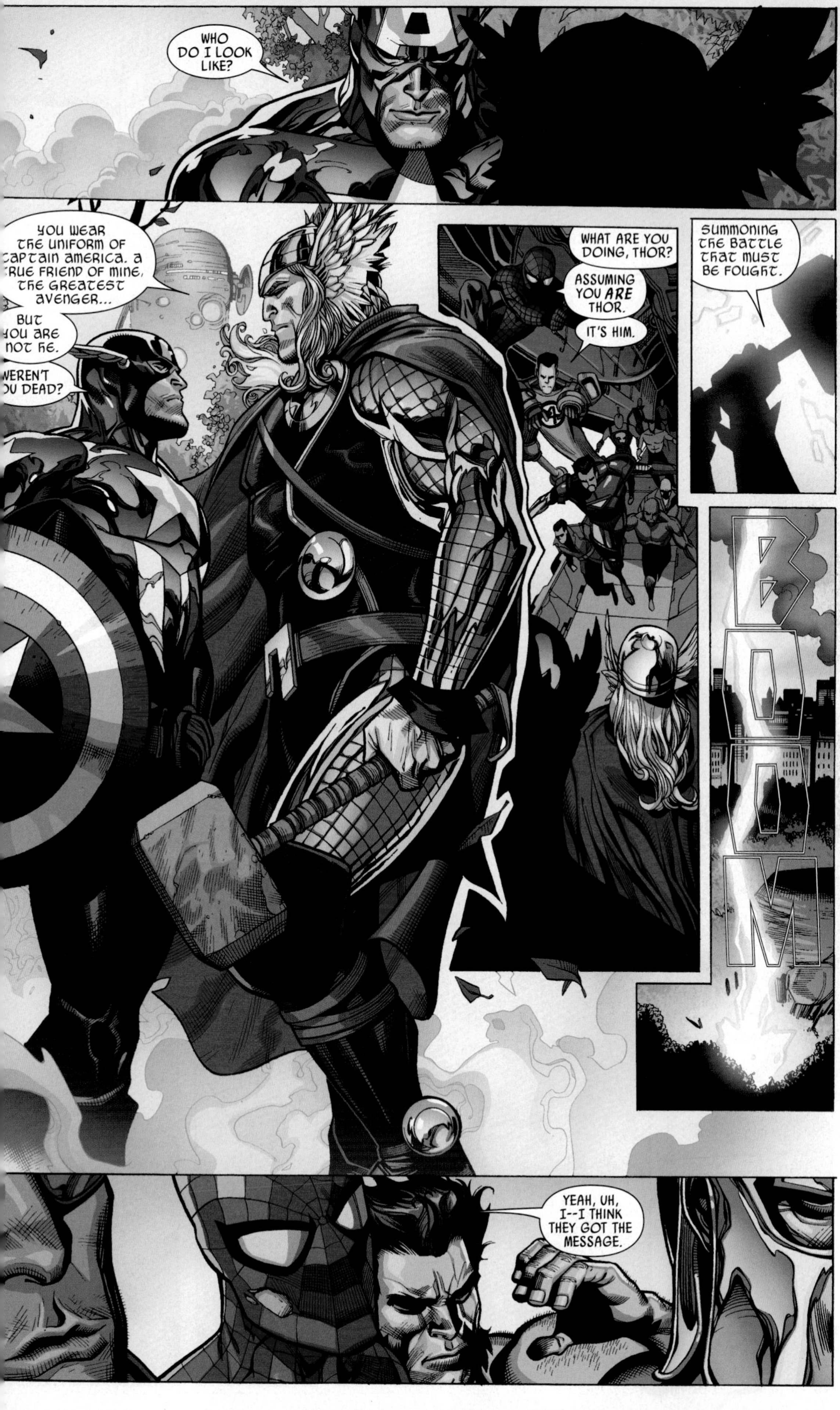
WHO DO I LOOK LIKE?
YOU WEAR THE UNIFORM OF CAPTAIN AMERICA. A TRUE FRIEND OF MINE, THE GREATEST AVENGER...
BUT YOU ARE NOT HE.
WEREN'T YOU DEAD?
WHAT ARE YOU DOING, THOR?
ASSUMING YOU ARE THOR.
IT'S HIM.
SUMMONING THE BATTLE THAT MUST BE FOUGHT.
BOOM
YEAH, UH, I--I THINK THEY GOT THE MESSAGE.

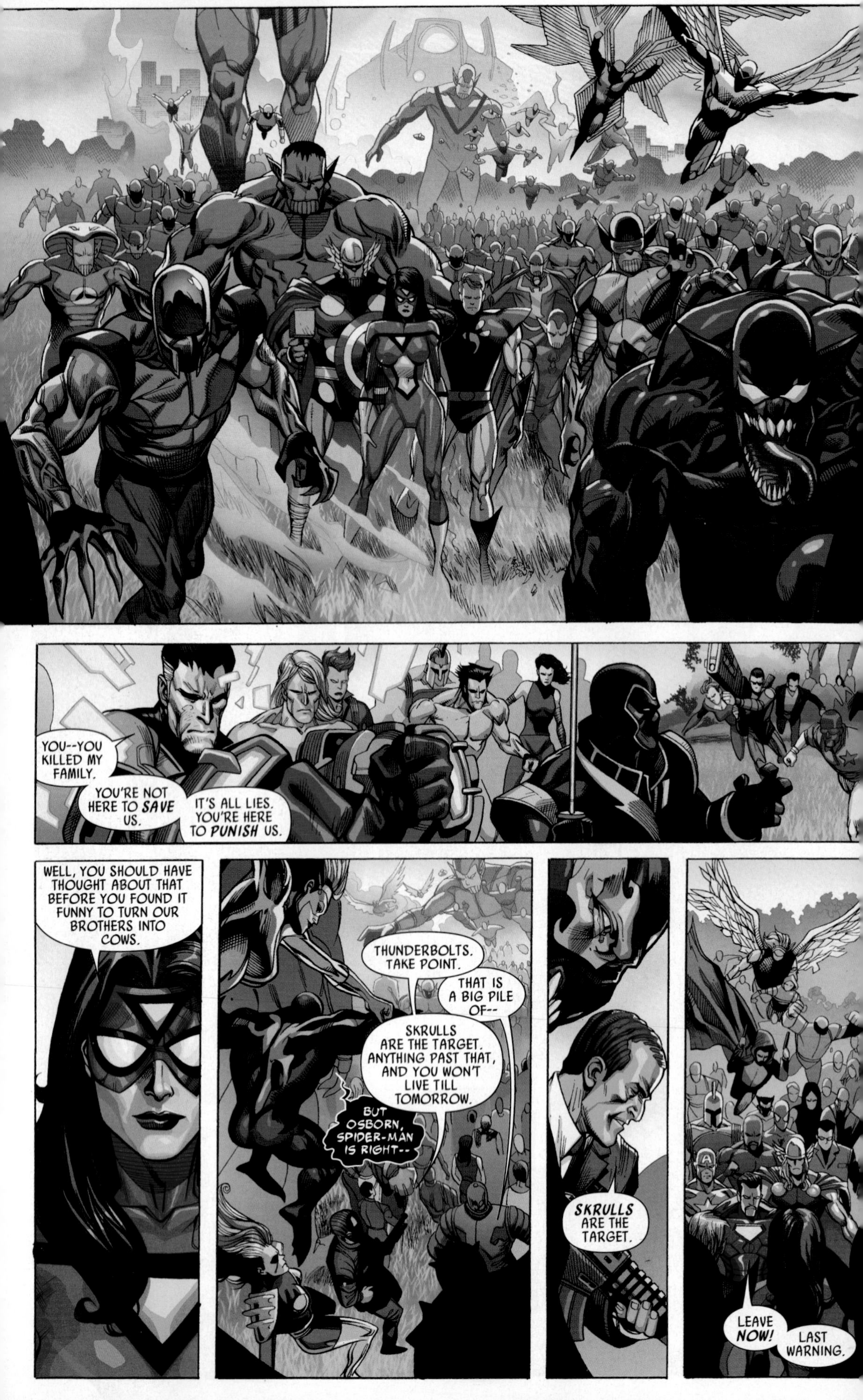

YOU--YOU KILLED MY FAMILY.
YOU'RE NOT HERE TO **SAVE** US.
IT'S ALL LIES. YOU'RE HERE TO **PUNISH** US.
WELL, YOU SHOULD HAVE THOUGHT ABOUT THAT BEFORE YOU FOUND IT FUNNY TO TURN OUR BROTHERS INTO COWS.
THUNDERBOLTS. TAKE POINT.
THAT IS A BIG PILE OF--
SKRULLS ARE THE TARGET. ANYTHING PAST THAT, AND YOU WON'T LIVE TILL TOMORROW.
BUT OSBORN, SPIDER-MAN IS RIGHT--
SKRULLS ARE THE TARGET.
LEAVE **NOW!**
LAST WARNING.

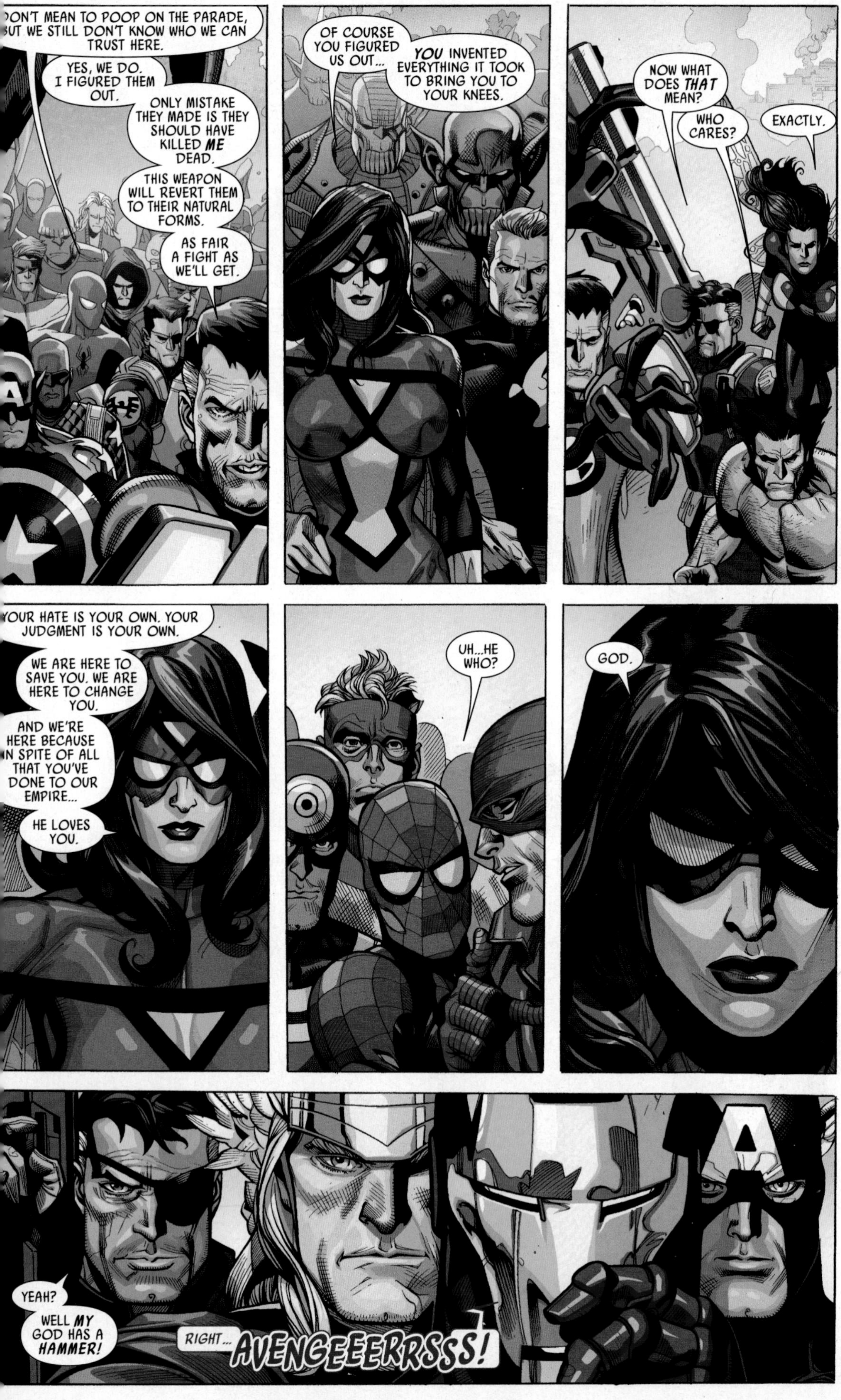
DON'T MEAN TO POOP ON THE PARADE, BUT WE STILL DON'T KNOW WHO WE CAN TRUST HERE.
YES, WE DO. I FIGURED THEM OUT.
ONLY MISTAKE THEY MADE IS THEY SHOULD HAVE KILLED ME DEAD.
THIS WEAPON WILL REVERT THEM TO THEIR NATURAL FORMS.
AS FAIR A FIGHT AS WE'LL GET.
OF COURSE YOU FIGURED US OUT...
YOU INVENTED EVERYTHING IT TOOK TO BRING YOU TO YOUR KNEES.
NOW WHAT DOES THAT MEAN?
WHO CARES?
EXACTLY.
YOUR HATE IS YOUR OWN. YOUR JUDGMENT IS YOUR OWN.
WE ARE HERE TO SAVE YOU. WE ARE HERE TO CHANGE YOU.
AND WE'RE HERE BECAUSE IN SPITE OF ALL THAT YOU'VE DONE TO OUR EMPIRE...
HE LOVES YOU.
UH...HE WHO?
GOD.
YEAH?
WELL MY GOD HAS A HAMMER!
RIGHT... AVENGEEERRSSS!

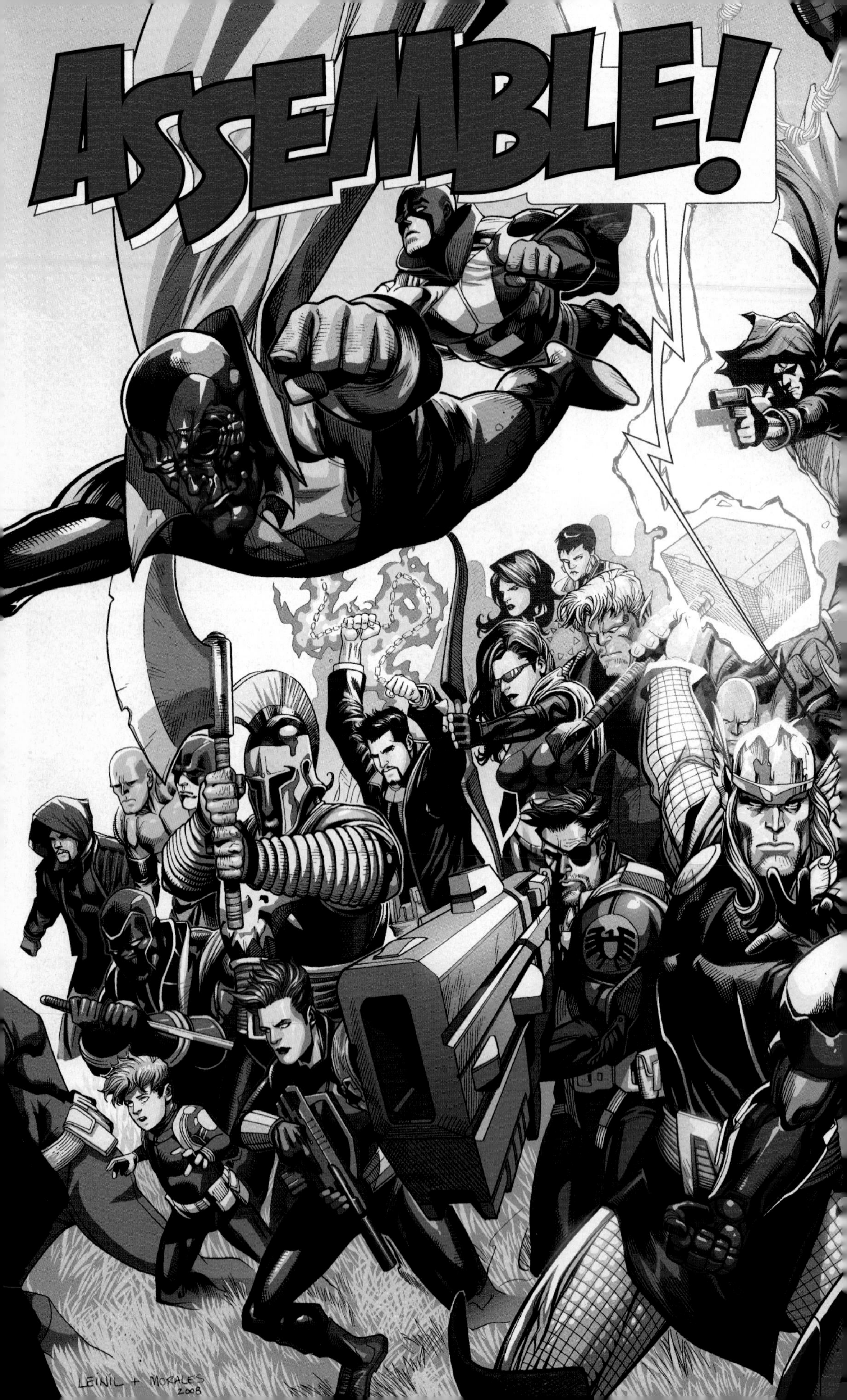
ASSEMBLE!
LEINIL + MORALES
2008

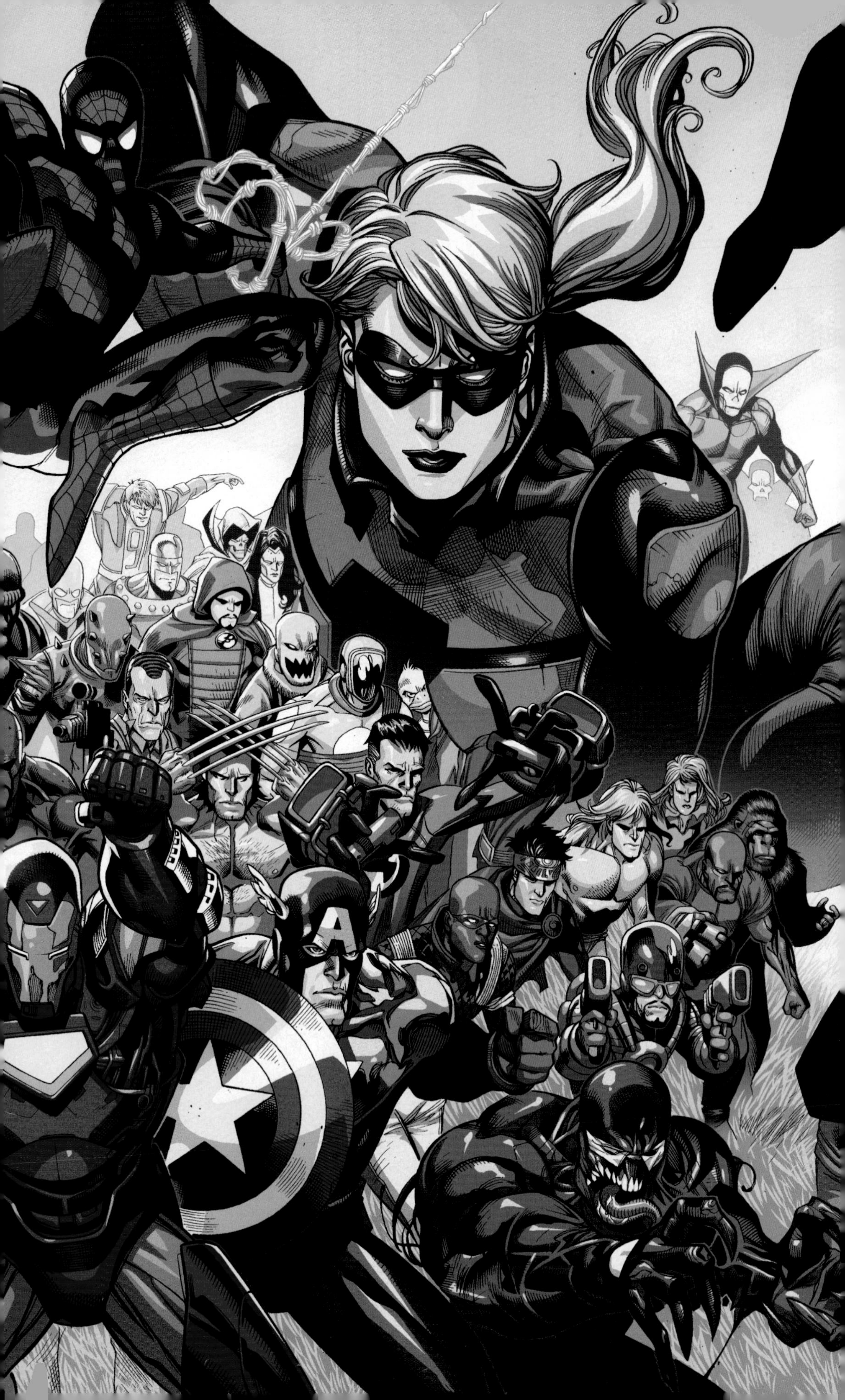

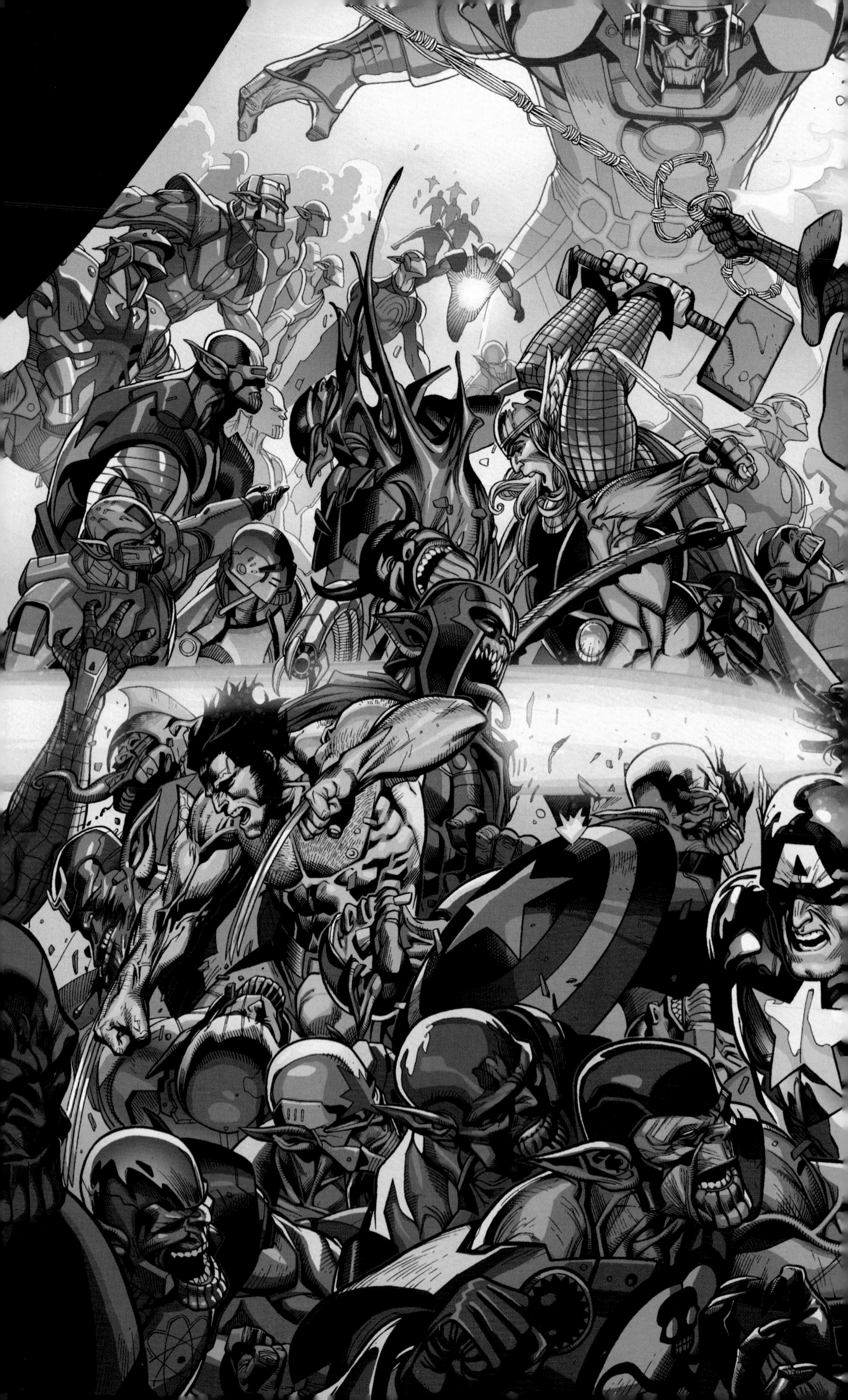

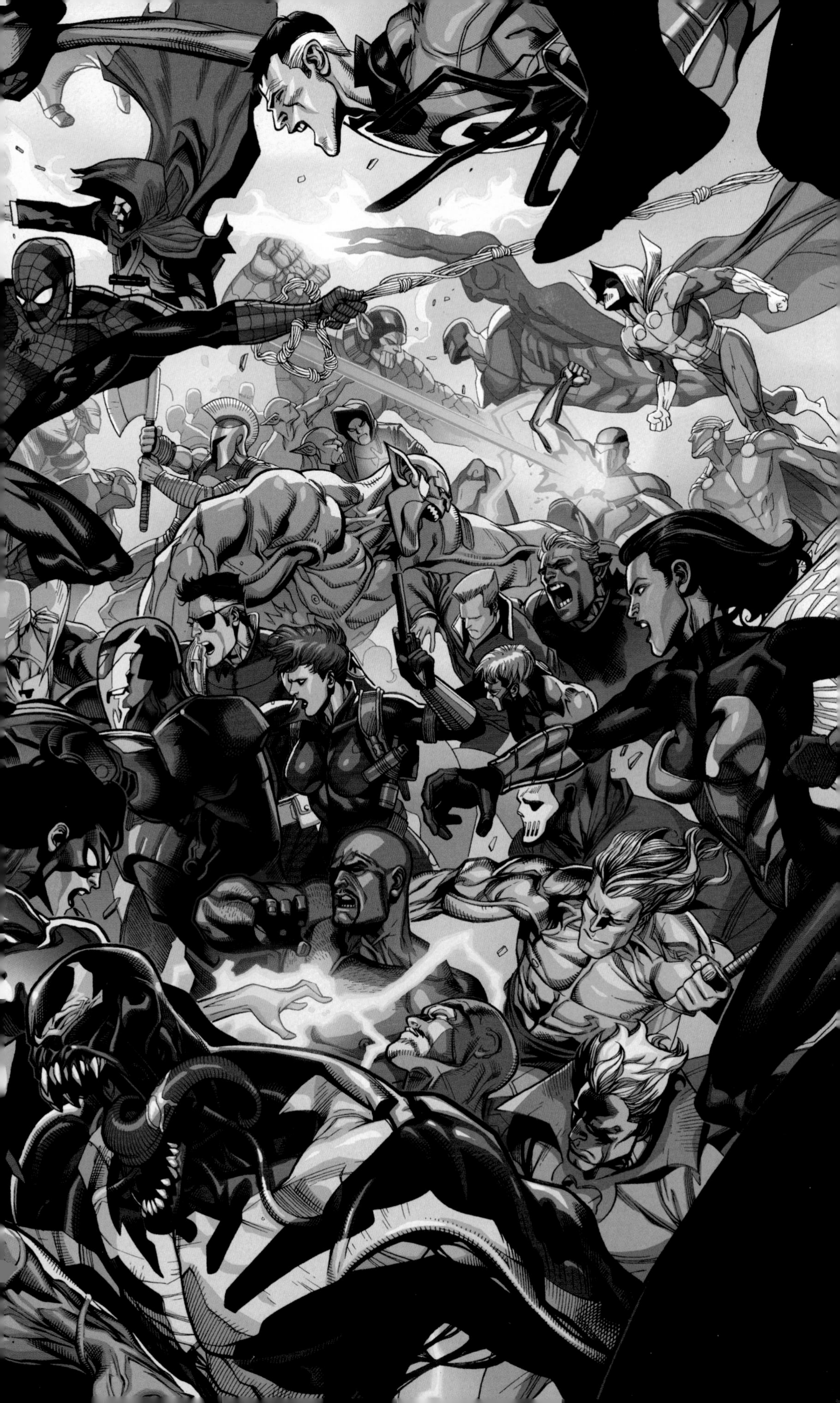

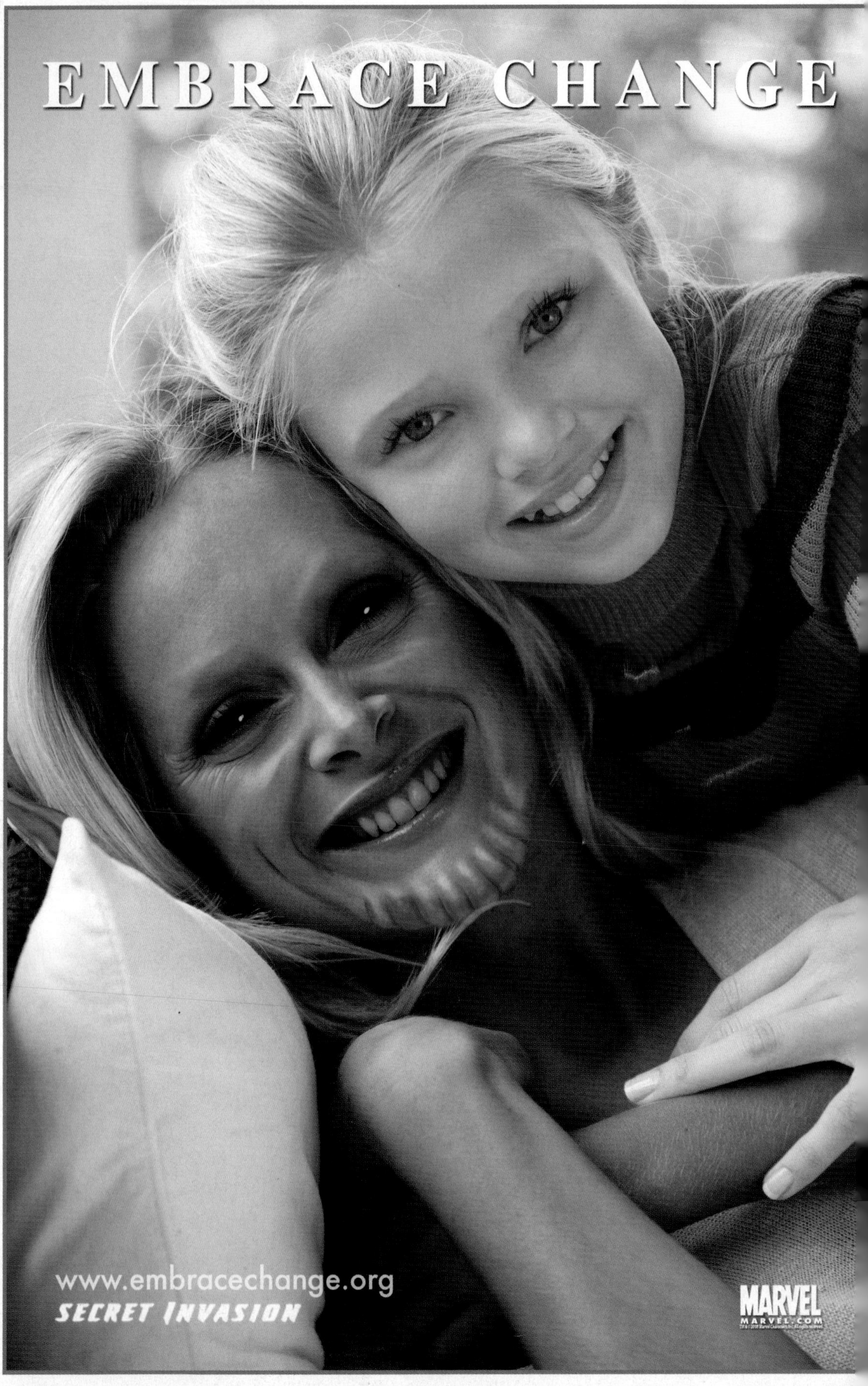
EMBRACE CHANGE
www.embracechange.org
SECRET INVASION
MARVEL
MARVEL.COM

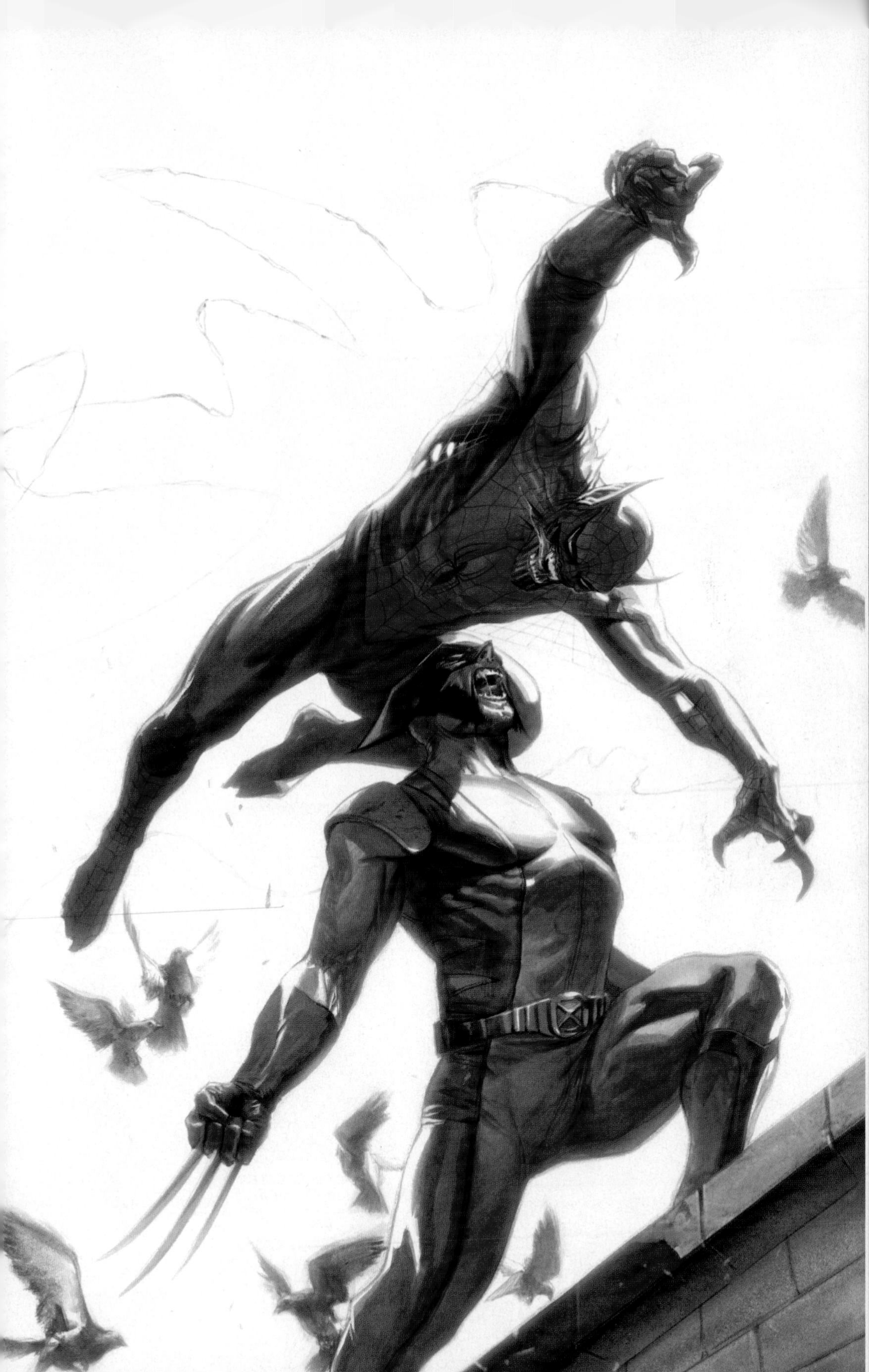

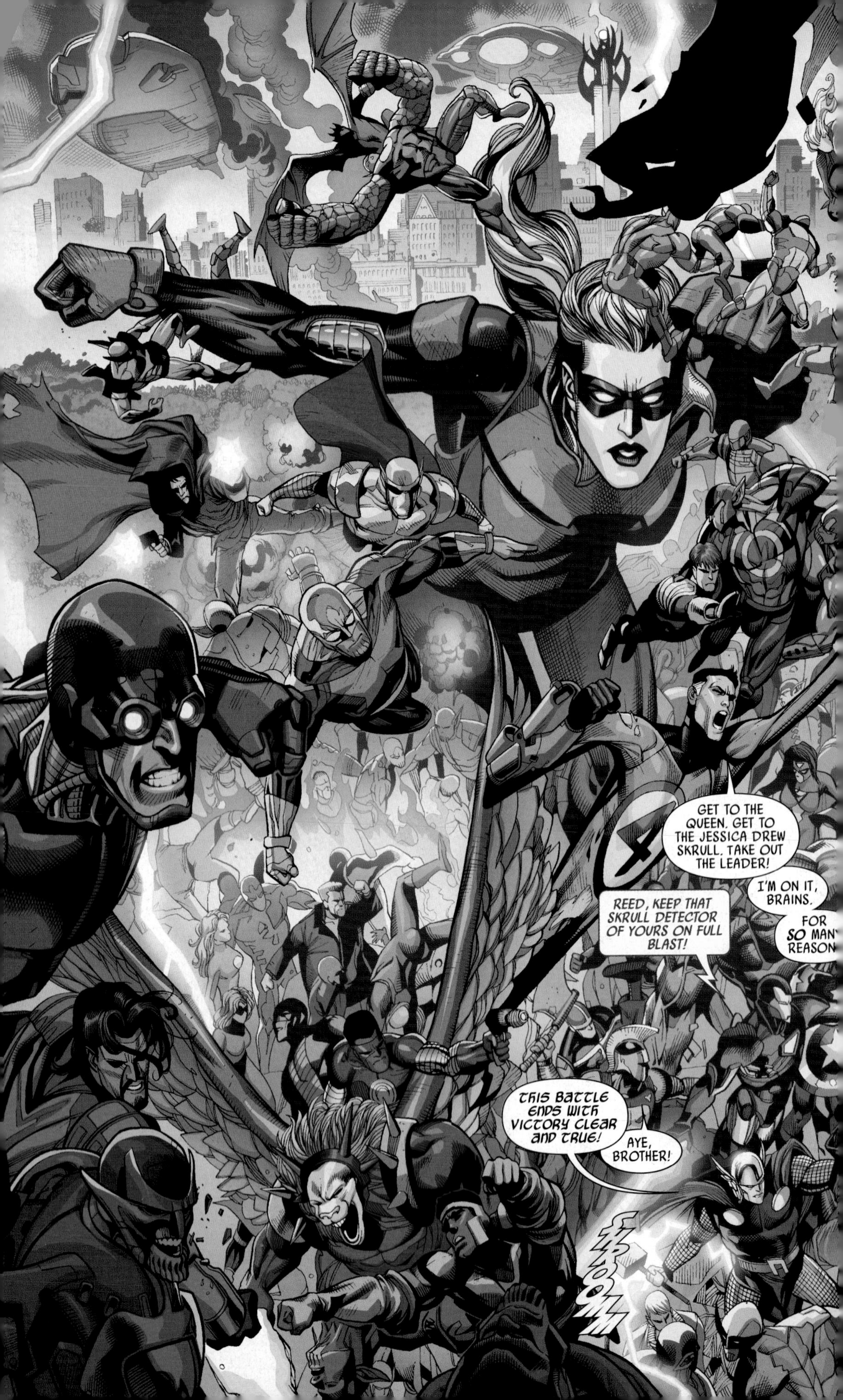
GET TO THE QUEEN. GET TO THE JESSICA DREW SKRULL. TAKE OUT THE LEADER!
I'M ON IT, BRAINS.
FOR SO MANY REASON
REED, KEEP THAT SKRULL DETECTOR OF YOURS ON FULL BLAST!
THIS BATTLE ENDS WITH VICTORY CLEAR AND TRUE!
AYE, BROTHER!
SHHHOOOMM

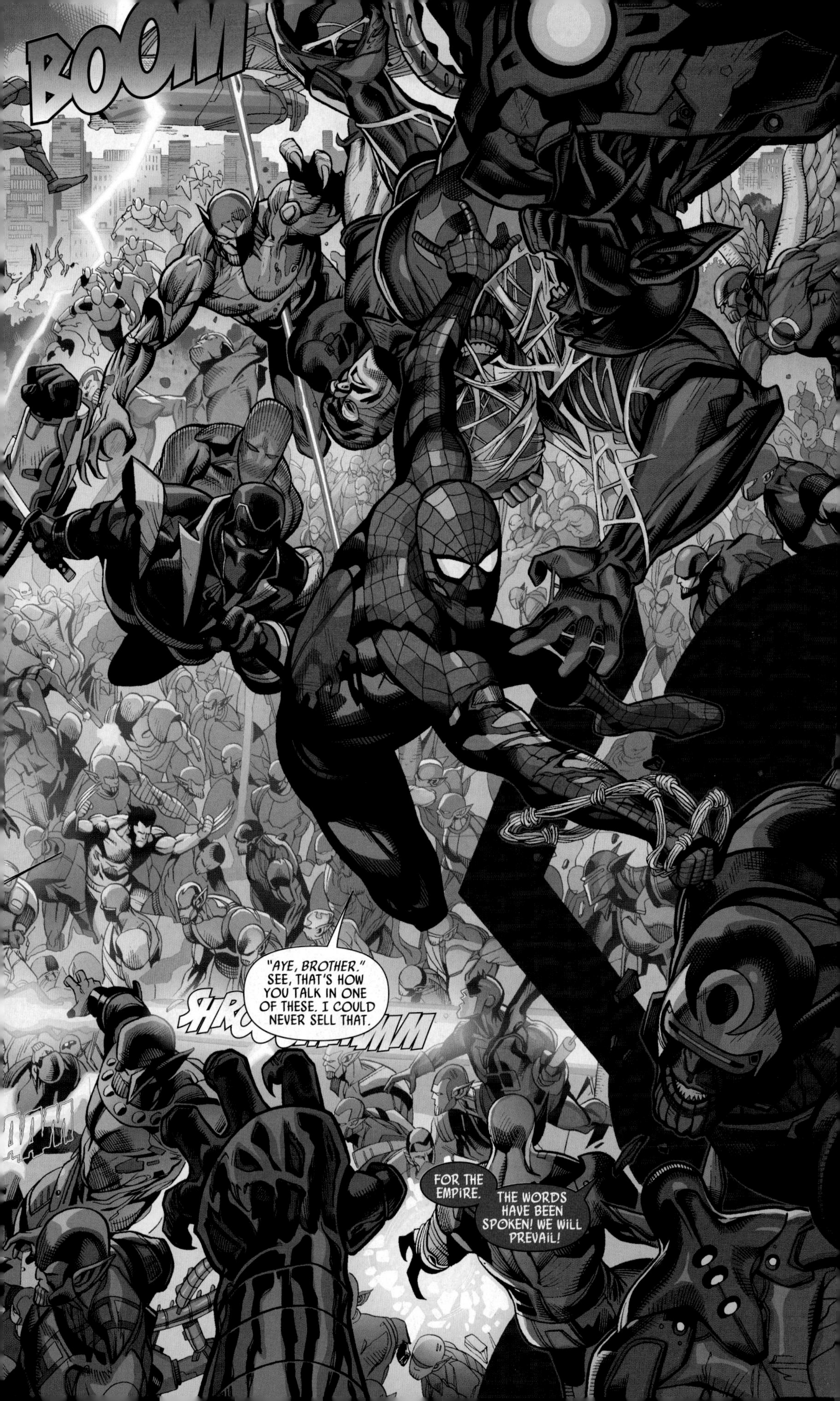
BOOM
"AYE, BROTHER." SEE, THAT'S HOW YOU TALK IN ONE OF THESE. I COULD NEVER SELL THAT.
FOR THE EMPIRE.
THE WORDS HAVE BEEN SPOKEN! WE WILL PREVAIL!

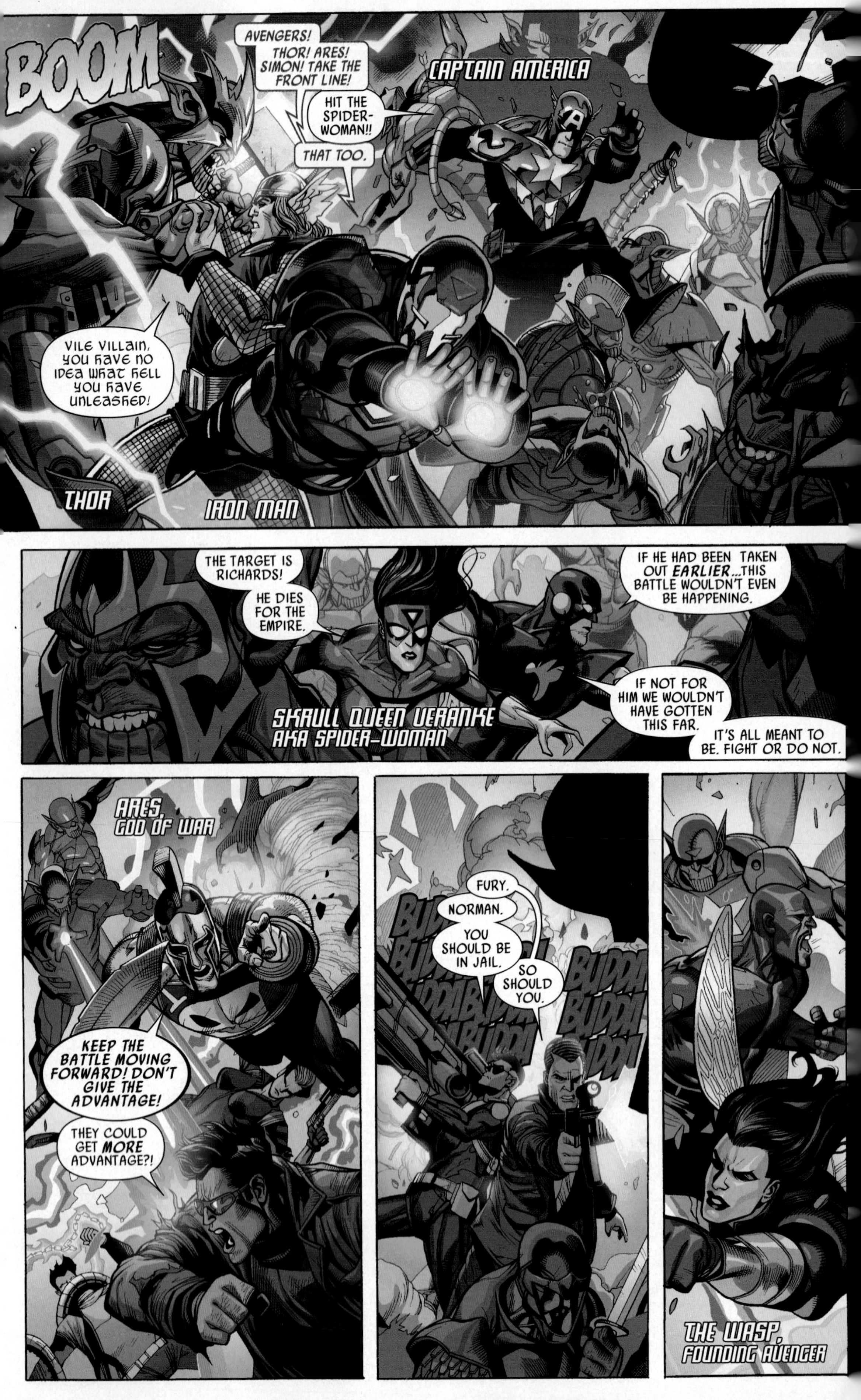
BOOM
AVENGERS! THOR! ARES! SIMON! TAKE THE FRONT LINE!
HIT THE SPIDER-WOMAN!!
THAT TOO.
CAPTAIN AMERICA
VILE VILLAIN, YOU HAVE NO IDEA WHAT HELL YOU HAVE UNLEASHED!
THOR
IRON MAN
THE TARGET IS RICHARDS!
HE DIES FOR THE EMPIRE.
SKRULL QUEEN VERANKE AKA SPIDER-WOMAN
IF HE HAD BEEN TAKEN OUT EARLIER... THIS BATTLE WOULDN'T EVEN BE HAPPENING.
IF NOT FOR HIM WE WOULDN'T HAVE GOTTEN THIS FAR.
IT'S ALL MEANT TO BE. FIGHT OR DO NOT.
ARES, GOD OF WAR
KEEP THE BATTLE MOVING FORWARD! DON'T GIVE THE ADVANTAGE!
THEY COULD GET MORE ADVANTAGE?!
FURY.
NORMAN.
YOU SHOULD BE IN JAIL.
SO SHOULD YOU.
THE WASP, FOUNDING AVENGER

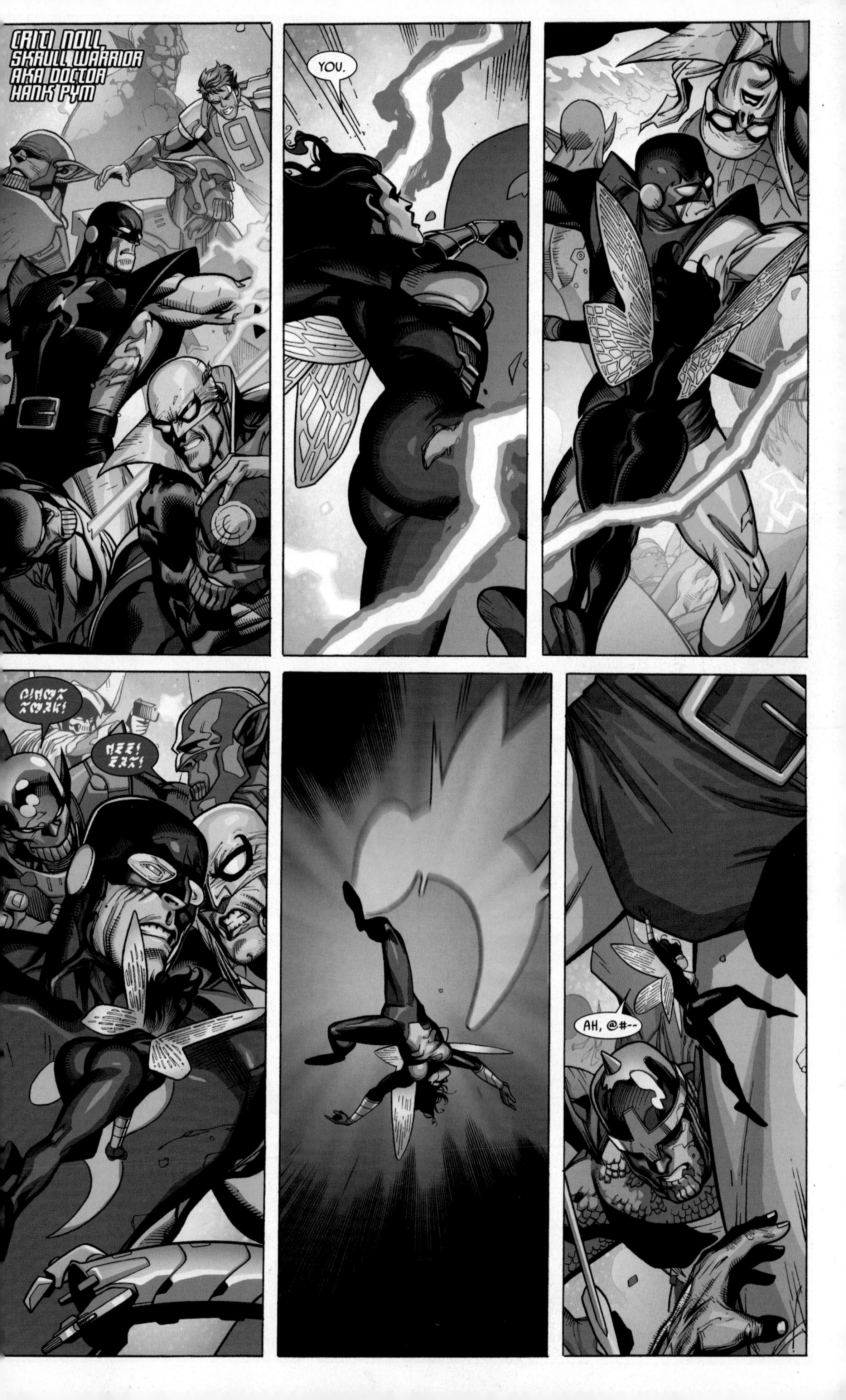

CRITI NOLL, SKRULL WARRIOR AKA DOCTOR HANK PYM
YOU.
AH, @#--

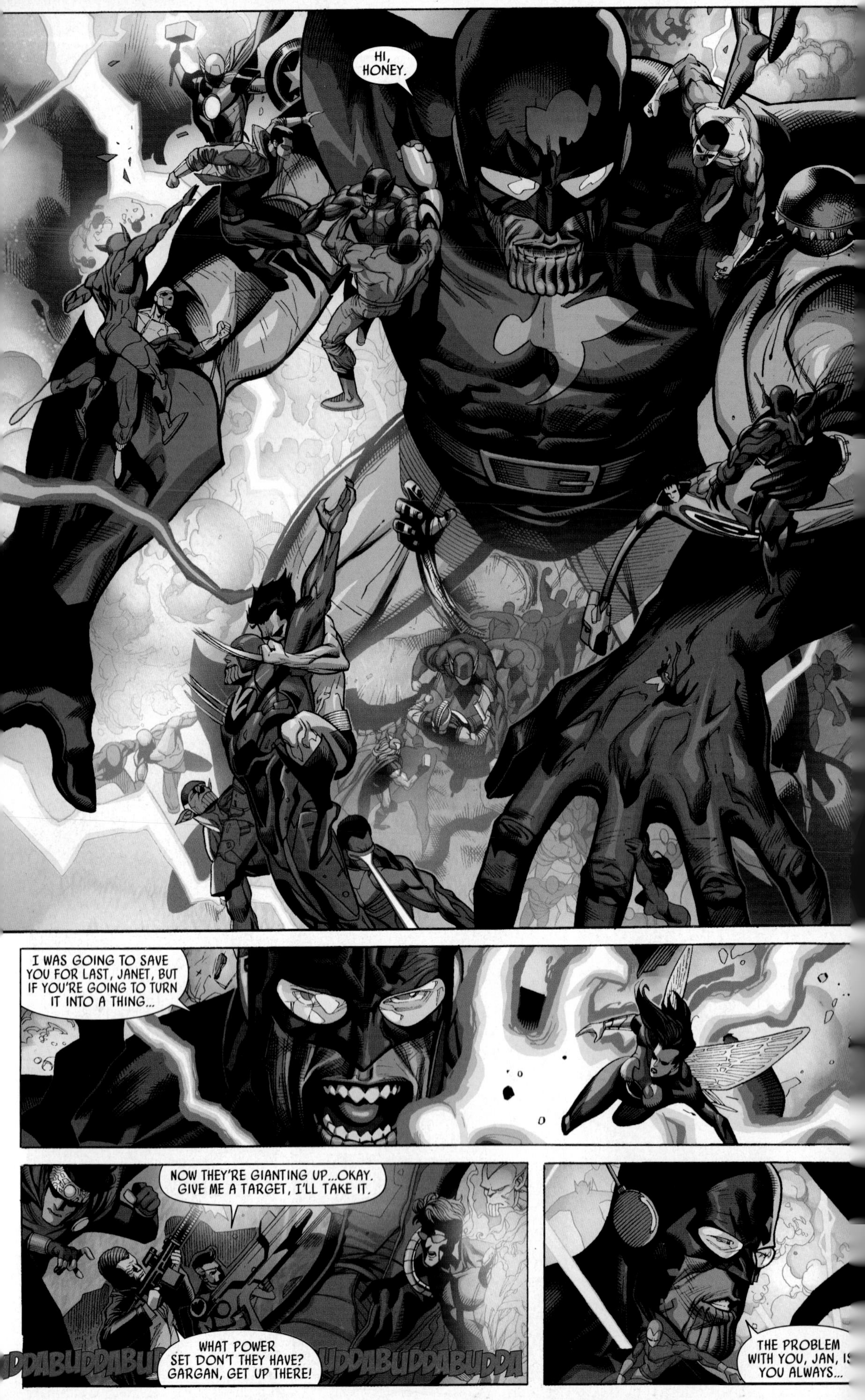
HI, HONEY.
I WAS GOING TO SAVE YOU FOR LAST, JANET, BUT IF YOU'RE GOING TO TURN IT INTO A THING...
NOW THEY'RE GIANTING UP...OKAY. GIVE ME A TARGET, I'LL TAKE IT.
WHAT POWER SET DON'T THEY HAVE? GARGAN, GET UP THERE!
DDABUDDABU
UDDABUDDABUDDA
THE PROBLEM WITH YOU, JAN, IS YOU ALWAYS...

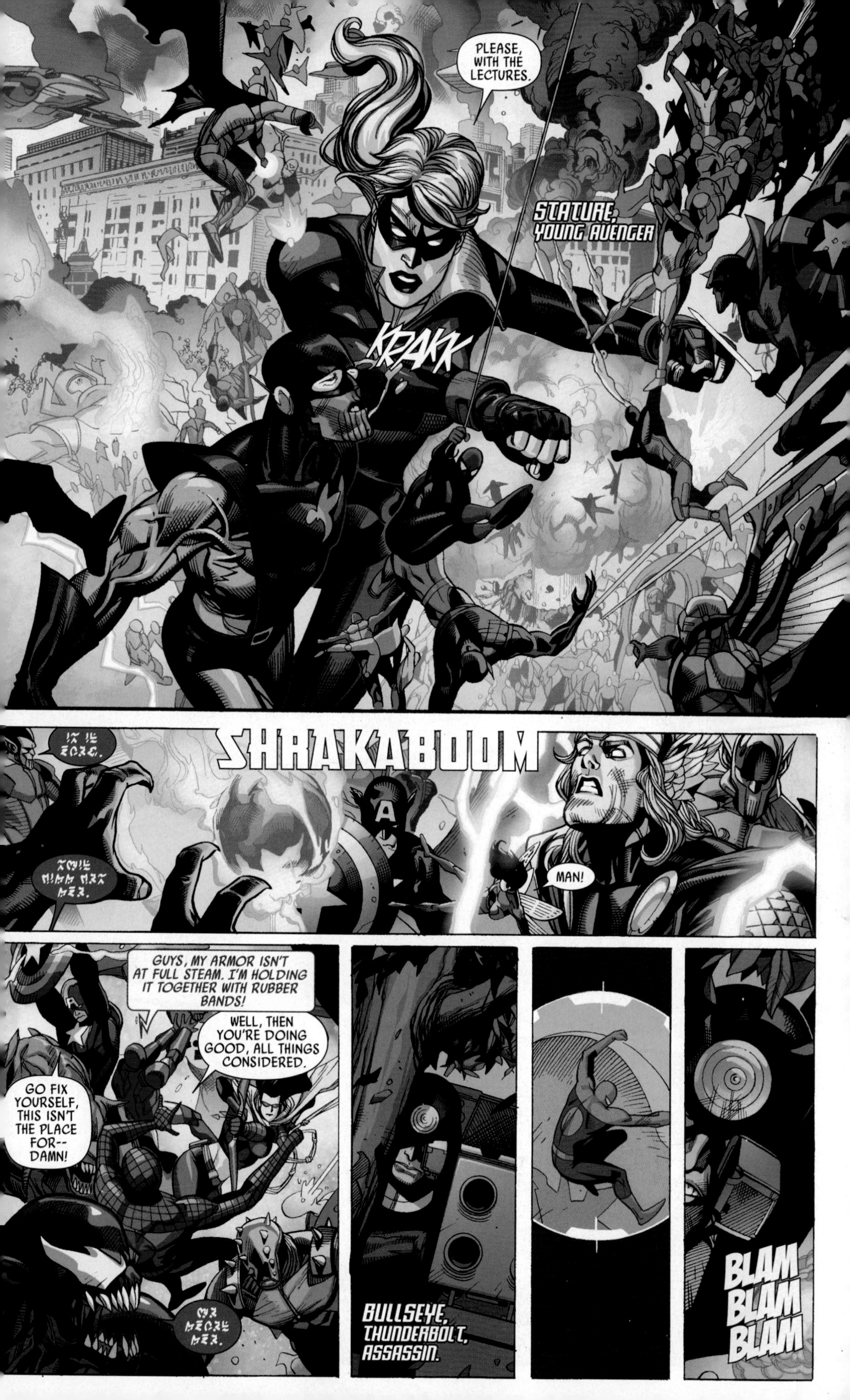
PLEASE, WITH THE LECTURES.
STATURE, YOUNG AVENGER
KRAKK
SHRAKABOOM
MAN!
GUYS, MY ARMOR ISN'T AT FULL STEAM. I'M HOLDING IT TOGETHER WITH RUBBER BANDS!
WELL, THEN YOU'RE DOING GOOD, ALL THINGS CONSIDERED.
GO FIX YOURSELF, THIS ISN'T THE PLACE FOR-- DAMN!
BULLSEYE, THUNDERBOLT, ASSASSIN.
BLAM BLAM BLAM

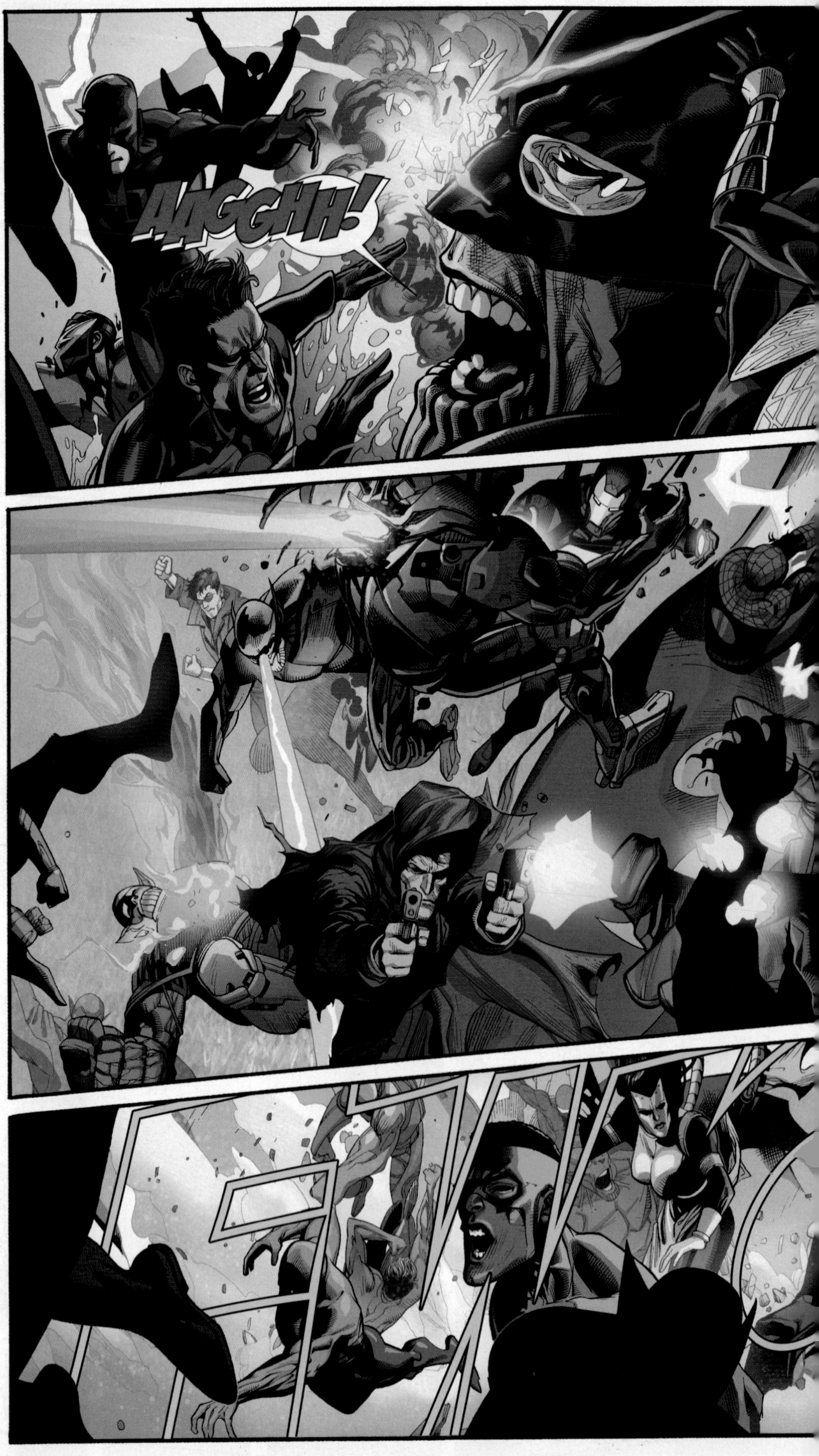
AAGGHH!

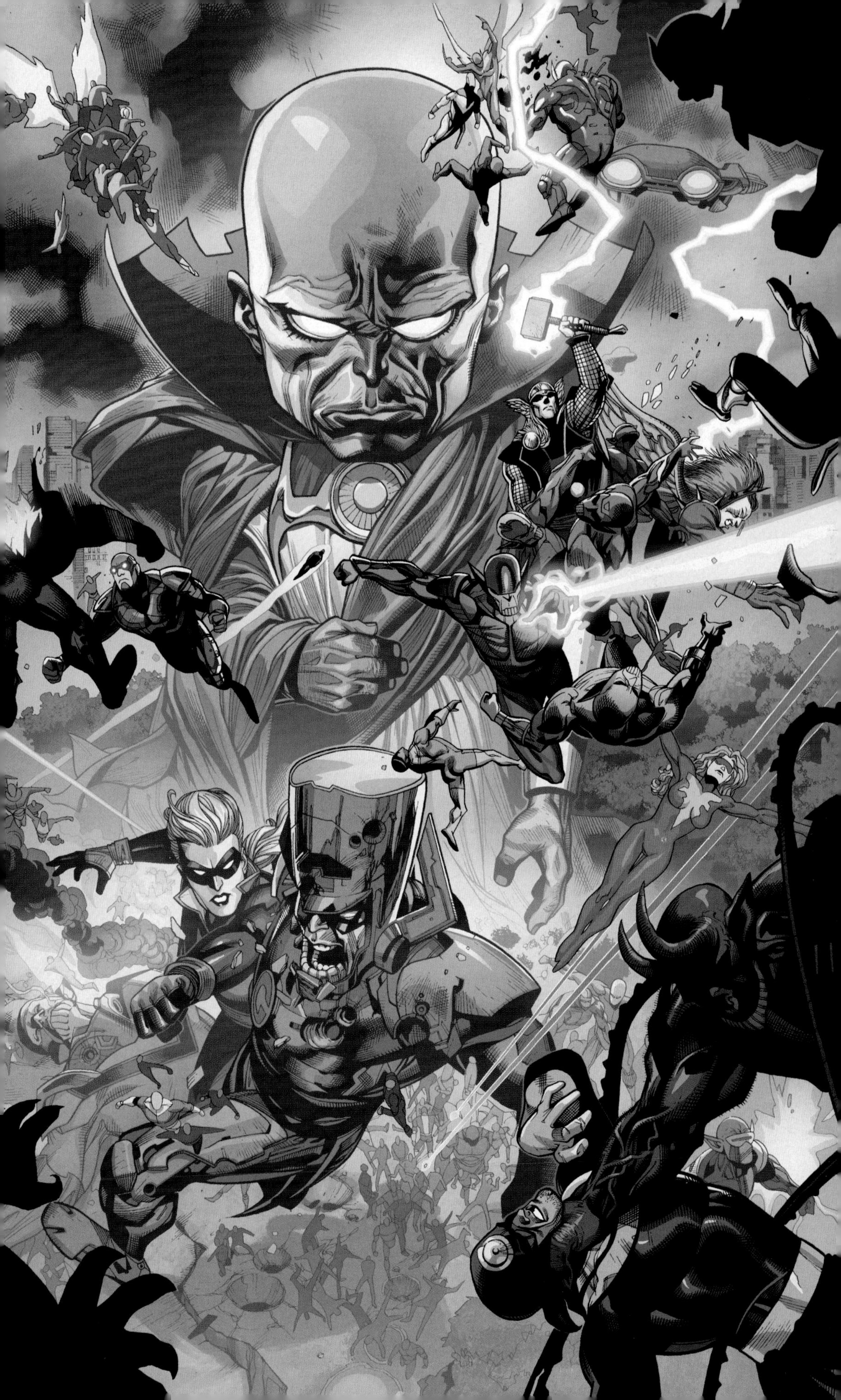

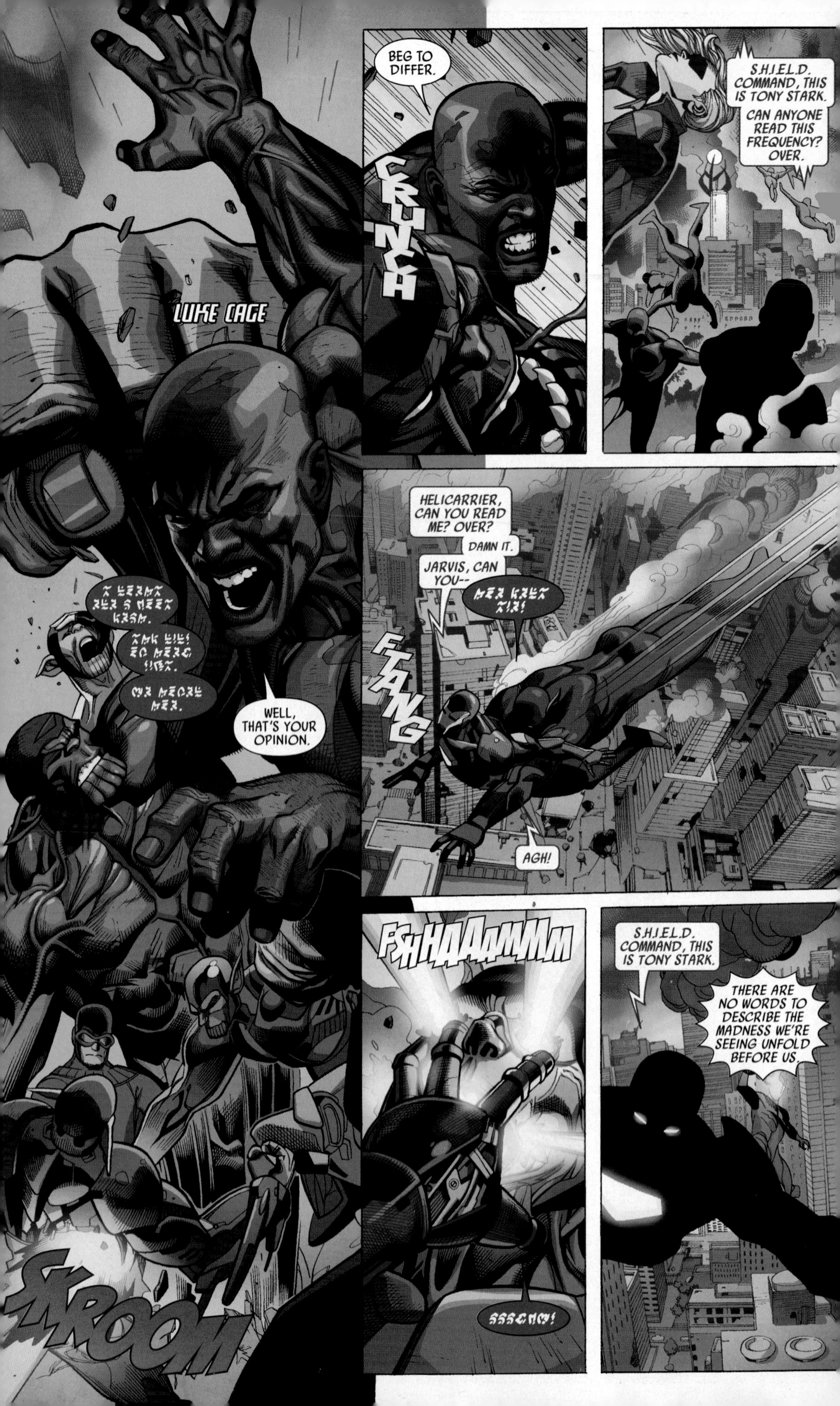
LUKE CAGE
WELL, THAT'S YOUR OPINION.
SKROOM
BEG TO DIFFER.
CRUNCH
S.H.I.E.L.D. COMMAND, THIS IS TONY STARK.
CAN ANYONE READ THIS FREQUENCY? OVER.
HELICARRIER, CAN YOU READ ME? OVER?
DAMN IT.
JARVIS, CAN YOU--
FTANG
AGH!
FSHHAAAMMMM
S.H.I.E.L.D. COMMAND, THIS IS TONY STARK.
THERE ARE NO WORDS TO DESCRIBE THE MADNESS WE'RE SEEING UNFOLD BEFORE US.

THE POWERED COMMUNITIES HAVE JOINED FORCES AGAINST THE ARMIES OF THIS SKRULL EMPIRE.

WE'RE TRYING TO GET YOU WHAT INFORMATION WE HAVE AS IT COMES IN. TONY STARK, DIRECTOR OF--

@#$%!

JARUIS

CNN

JESSICA JONES

@#$%!

MA'AM?

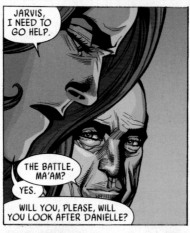

JARVIS, I NEED TO GO HELP.

THE BATTLE, MA'AM?

YES.

WILL YOU, PLEASE, WILL YOU LOOK AFTER DANIELLE?

YES.

YOU UNDERSTAND WHAT I'M ASKING?

YOU UNDERSTAND WE MAY NOT COME BACK.

I UNDERSTAND COMPLETELY.

BABY, MOMMY HAS TO GO DO THE RIGHT THING FOR ONCE IN HER LIFE.

I'M GOING TO GO HELP YOUR DADDY.

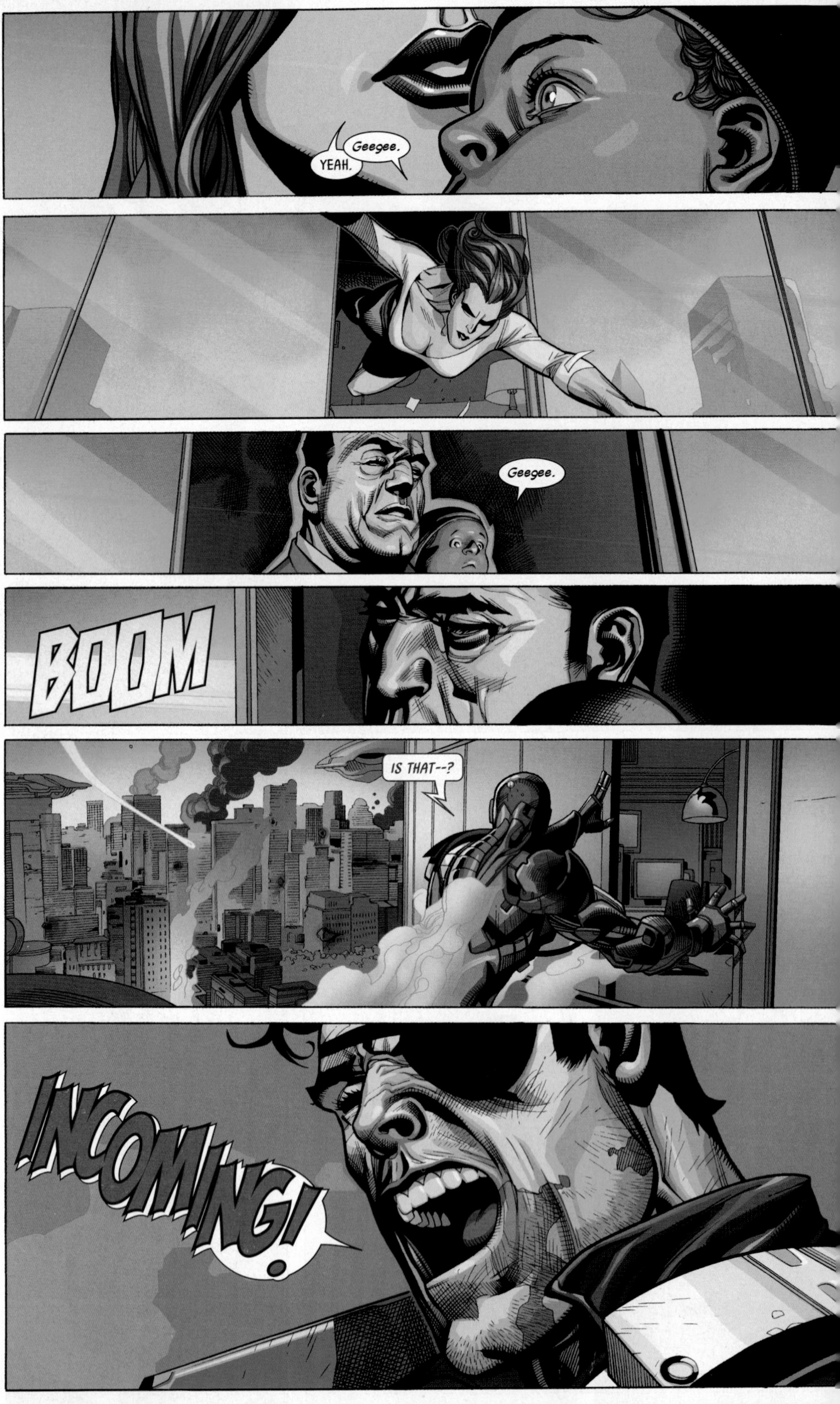
Geegee.
YEAH.
Geegee.
BOOM
IS THAT--?
INCOMING!

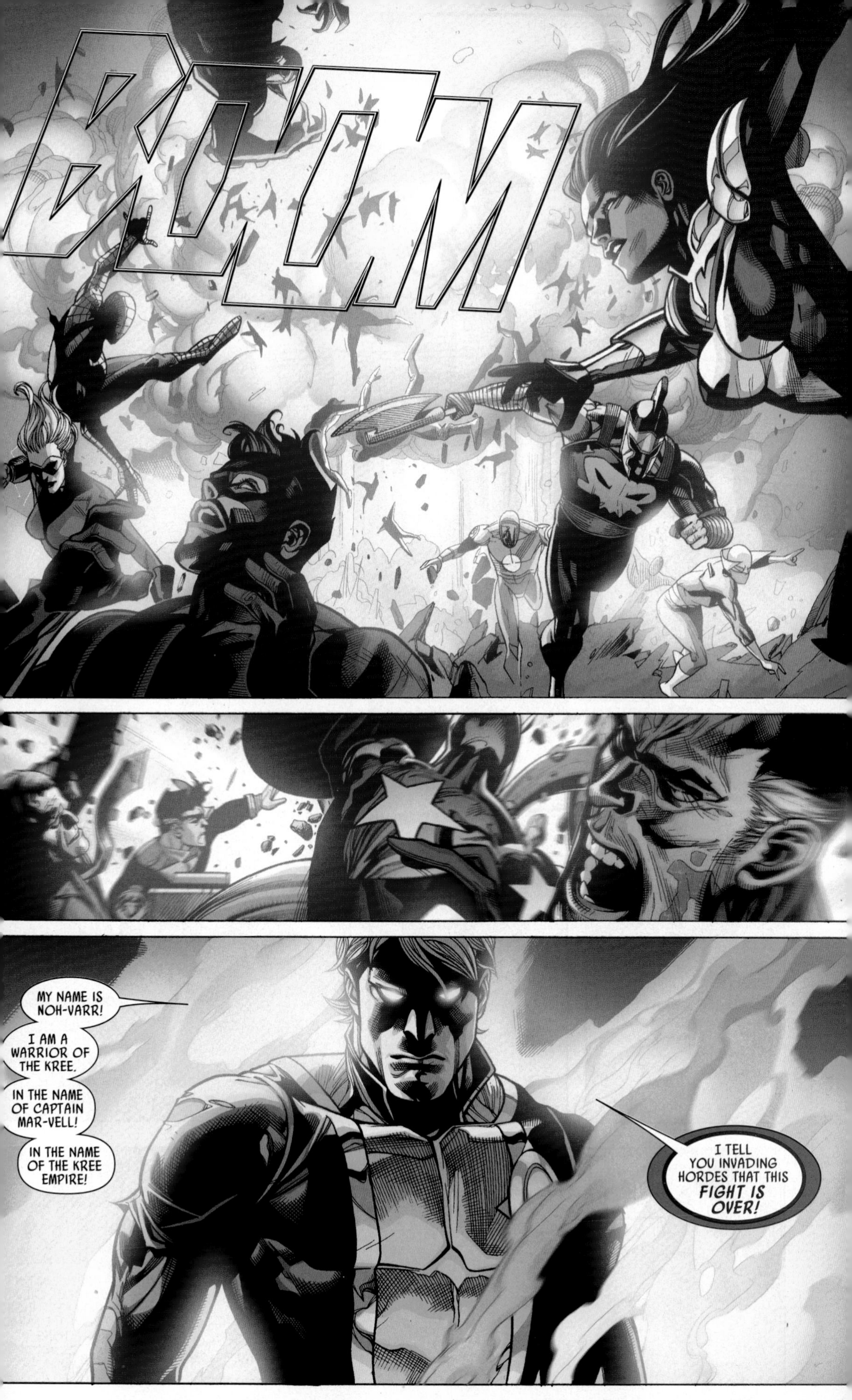
BLAM
MY NAME IS NOH-VARR!
I AM A WARRIOR OF THE KREE.
IN THE NAME OF CAPTAIN MAR-VELL!
IN THE NAME OF THE KREE EMPIRE!
I TELL YOU INVADING HORDES THAT THIS FIGHT IS OVER!

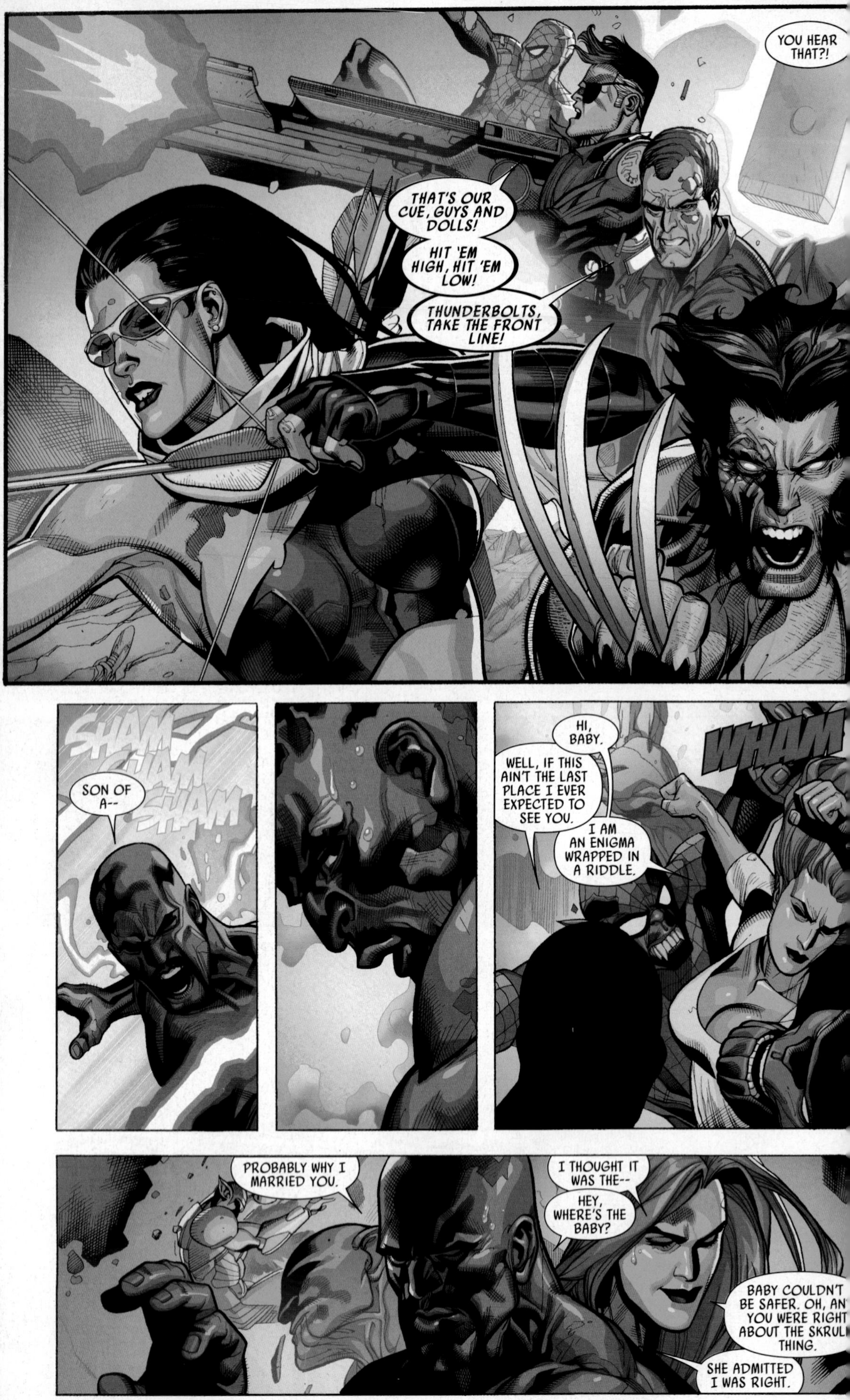

YOU HEAR THAT?!
THAT'S OUR CUE, GUYS AND DOLLS!
HIT 'EM HIGH, HIT 'EM LOW!
THUNDERBOLTS, TAKE THE FRONT LINE!
SHAM SHAM SHAM
SON OF A--
HI, BABY.
WELL, IF THIS AIN'T THE LAST PLACE I EVER EXPECTED TO SEE YOU.
I AM AN ENIGMA WRAPPED IN A RIDDLE.
WHAM
PROBABLY WHY I MARRIED YOU.
I THOUGHT IT WAS THE--
HEY, WHERE'S THE BABY?
BABY COULDN'T BE SAFER. OH, AN YOU WERE RIGHT ABOUT THE SKRULL THING.
SHE ADMITTED I WAS RIGHT.

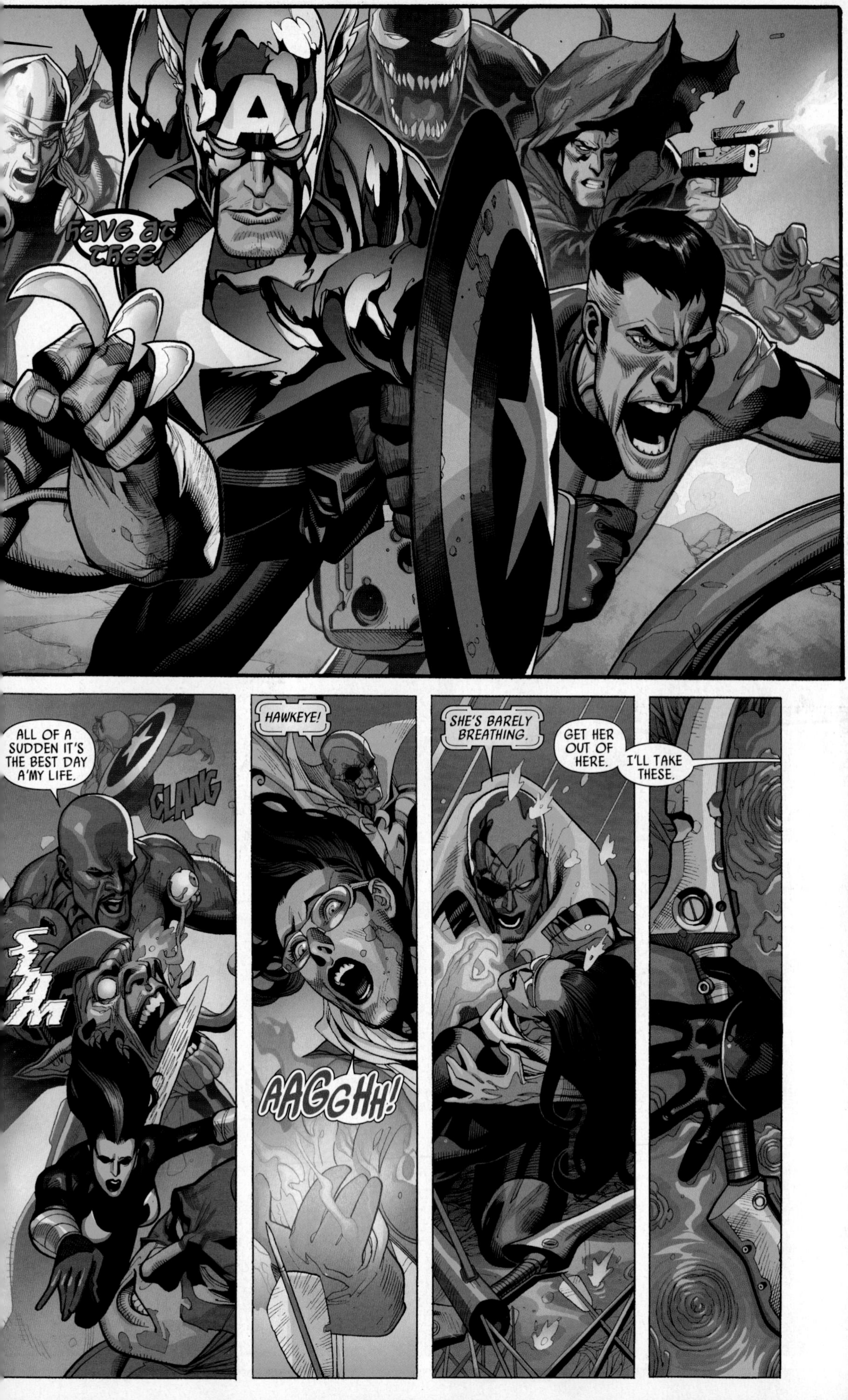
Have at thee!
ALL OF A SUDDEN IT'S THE BEST DAY A'MY LIFE.
CLANG
HAWKEYE!
AAGGHH!
SHE'S BARELY BREATHING.
GET HER OUT OF HERE.
I'LL TAKE THESE.

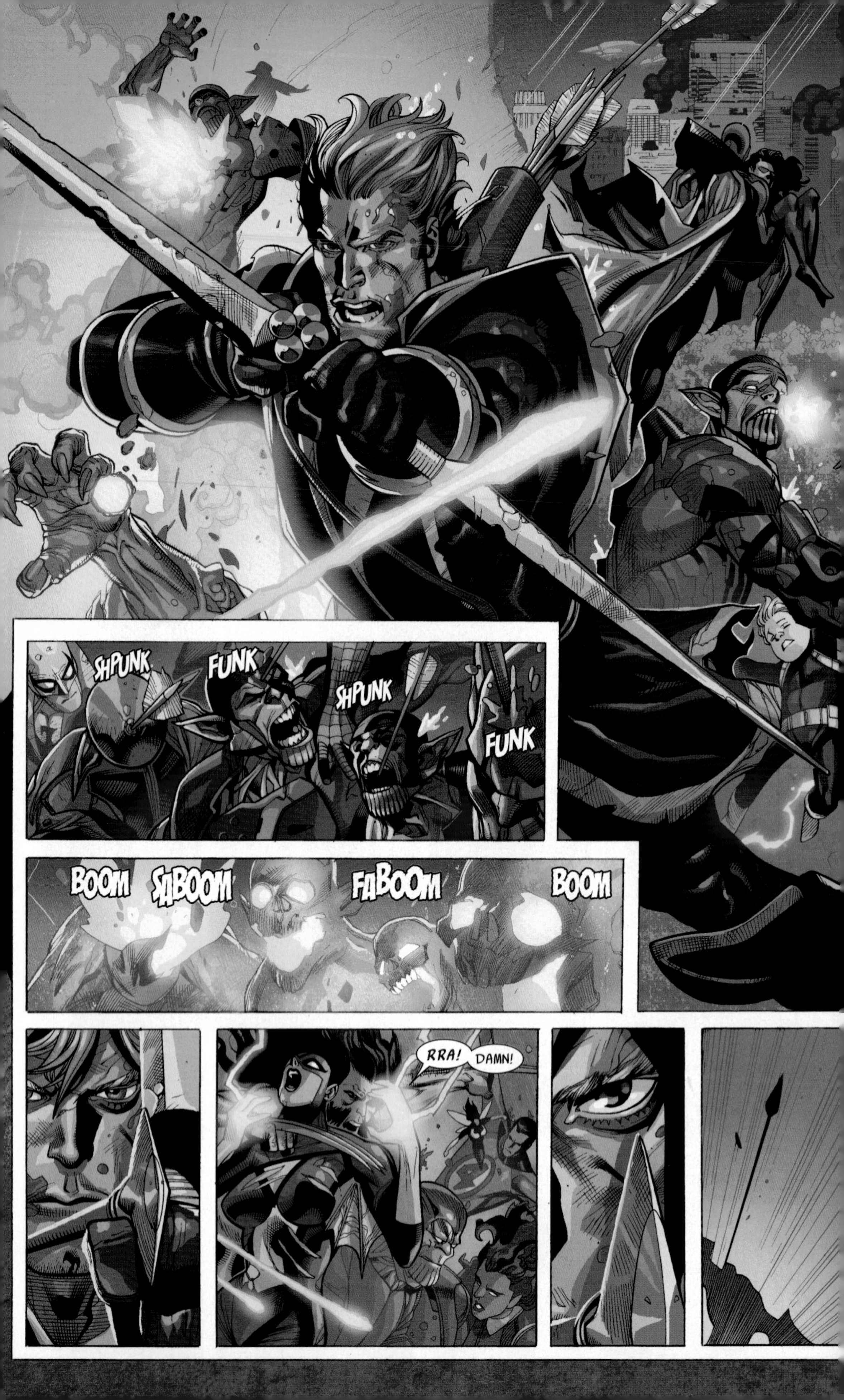
SHPUNK
FUNK
SHPUNK
FUNK
BOOM
SKABOOM
FABOOM
BOOM
RRA!
DAMN!

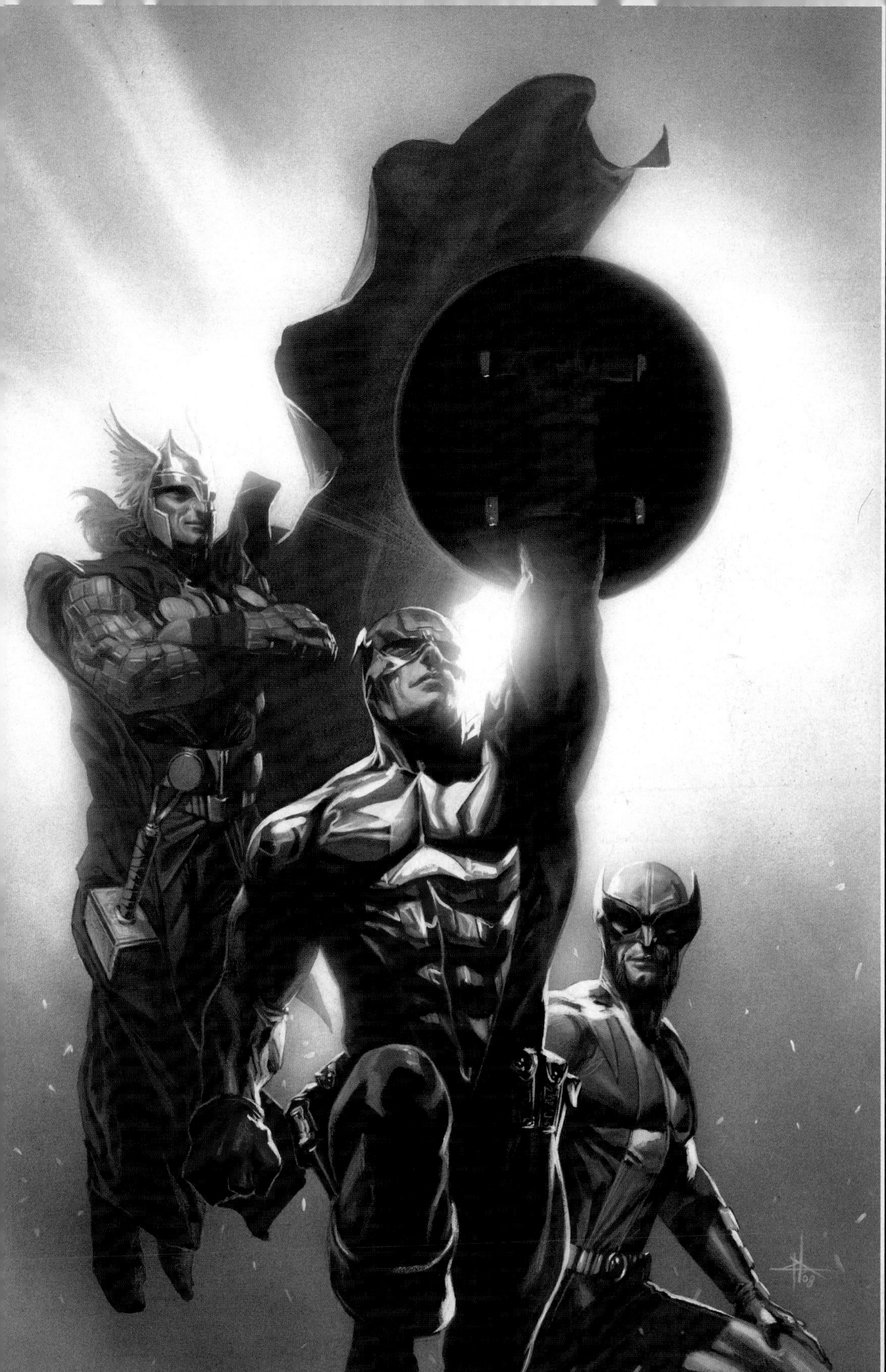

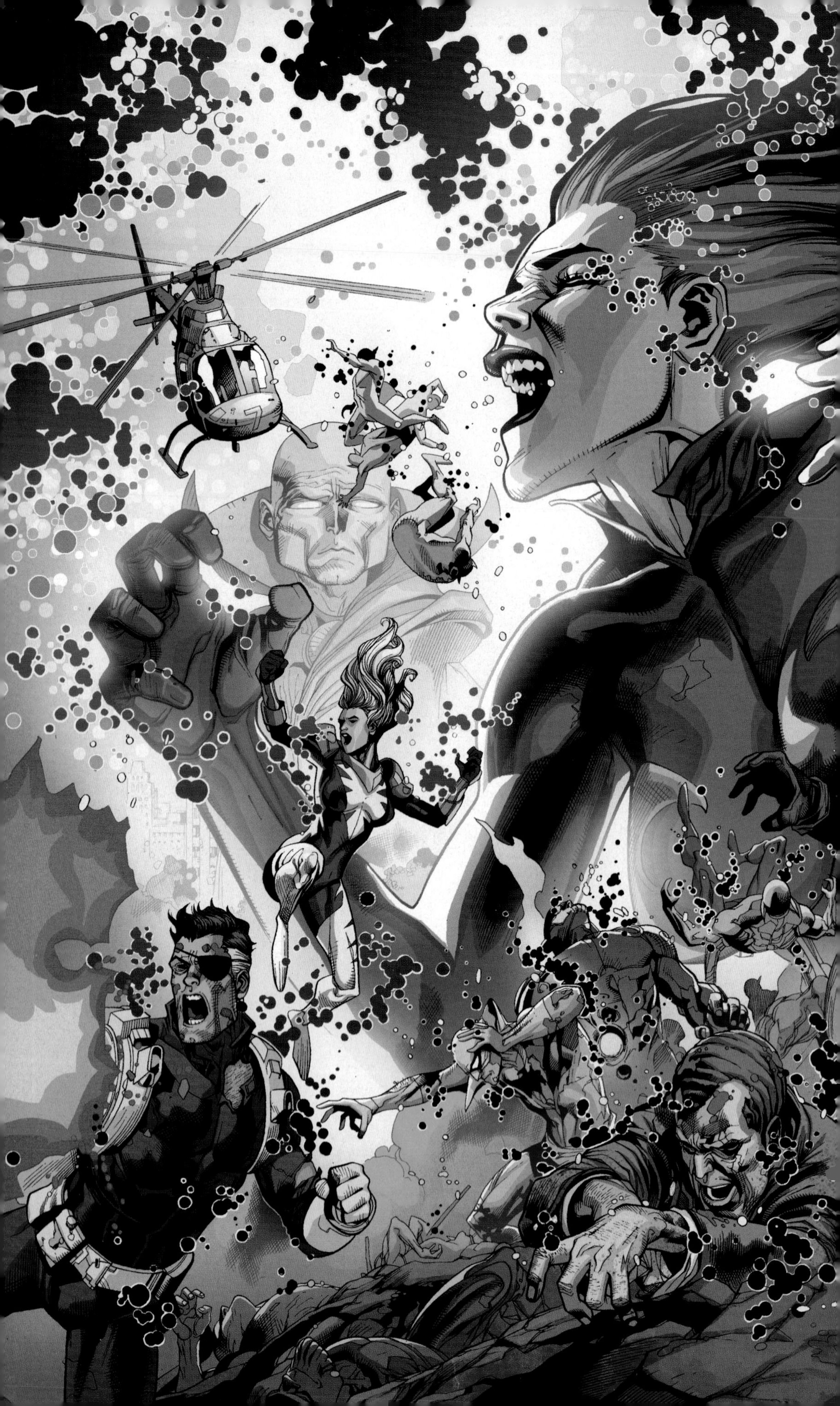

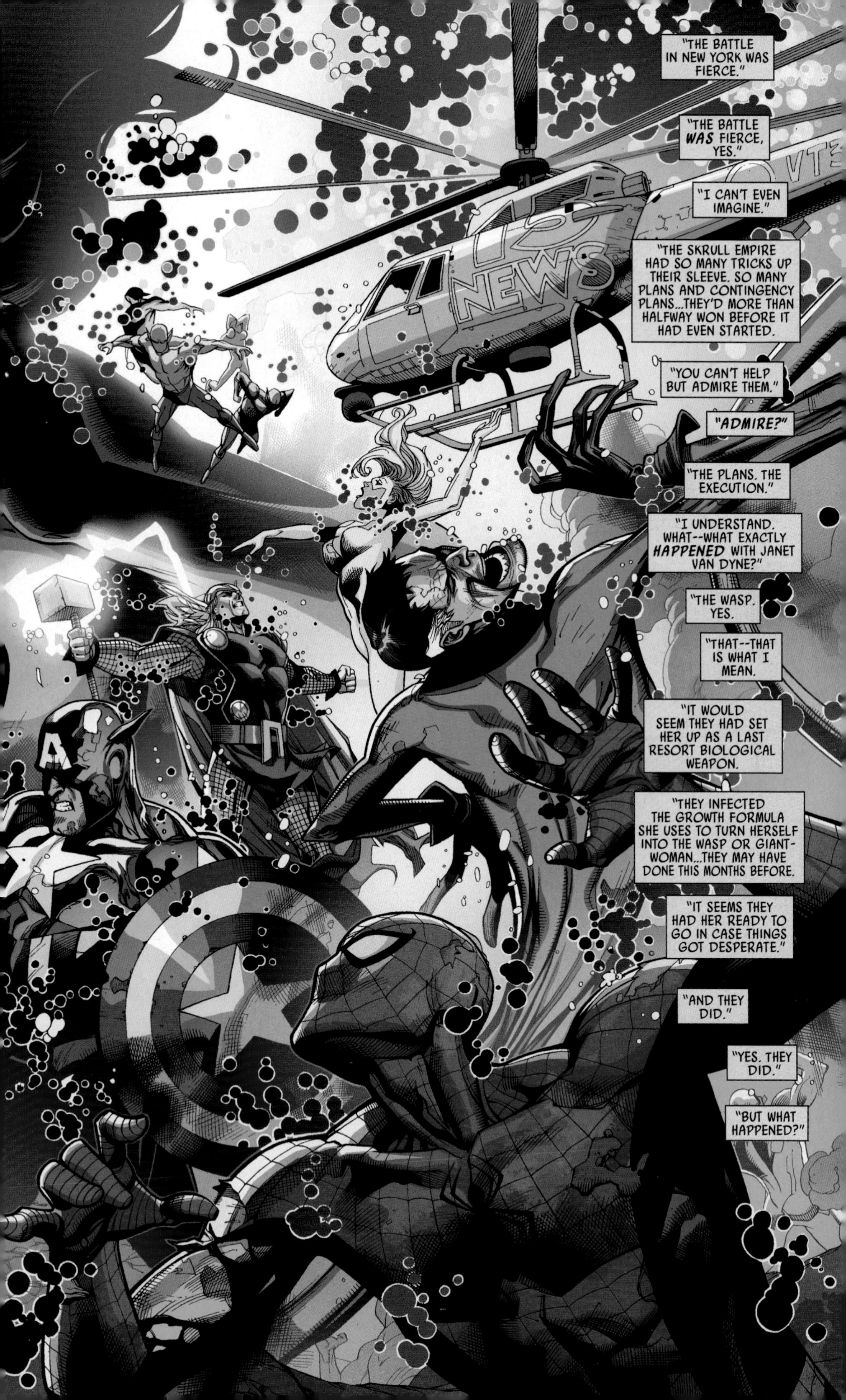
"THE BATTLE IN NEW YORK WAS FIERCE."
"THE BATTLE *WAS* FIERCE, YES."
"I CAN'T EVEN IMAGINE."
"THE SKRULL EMPIRE HAD SO MANY TRICKS UP THEIR SLEEVE. SO MANY PLANS AND CONTINGENCY PLANS...THEY'D MORE THAN HALFWAY WON BEFORE IT HAD EVEN STARTED.
"YOU CAN'T HELP BUT ADMIRE THEM."
"ADMIRE?"
"THE PLANS. THE EXECUTION."
"I UNDERSTAND. WHAT--WHAT EXACTLY *HAPPENED* WITH JANET VAN DYNE?"
"THE WASP. YES.
"THAT--THAT IS WHAT I MEAN.
"IT WOULD SEEM THEY HAD SET HER UP AS A LAST RESORT BIOLOGICAL WEAPON.
"THEY INFECTED THE GROWTH FORMULA SHE USES TO TURN HERSELF INTO THE WASP OR GIANT-WOMAN...THEY MAY HAVE DONE THIS MONTHS BEFORE.
"IT SEEMS THEY HAD HER READY TO GO IN CASE THINGS GOT DESPERATE."
"AND THEY DID."
"YES. THEY DID."
"BUT WHAT HAPPENED?"
NEWS

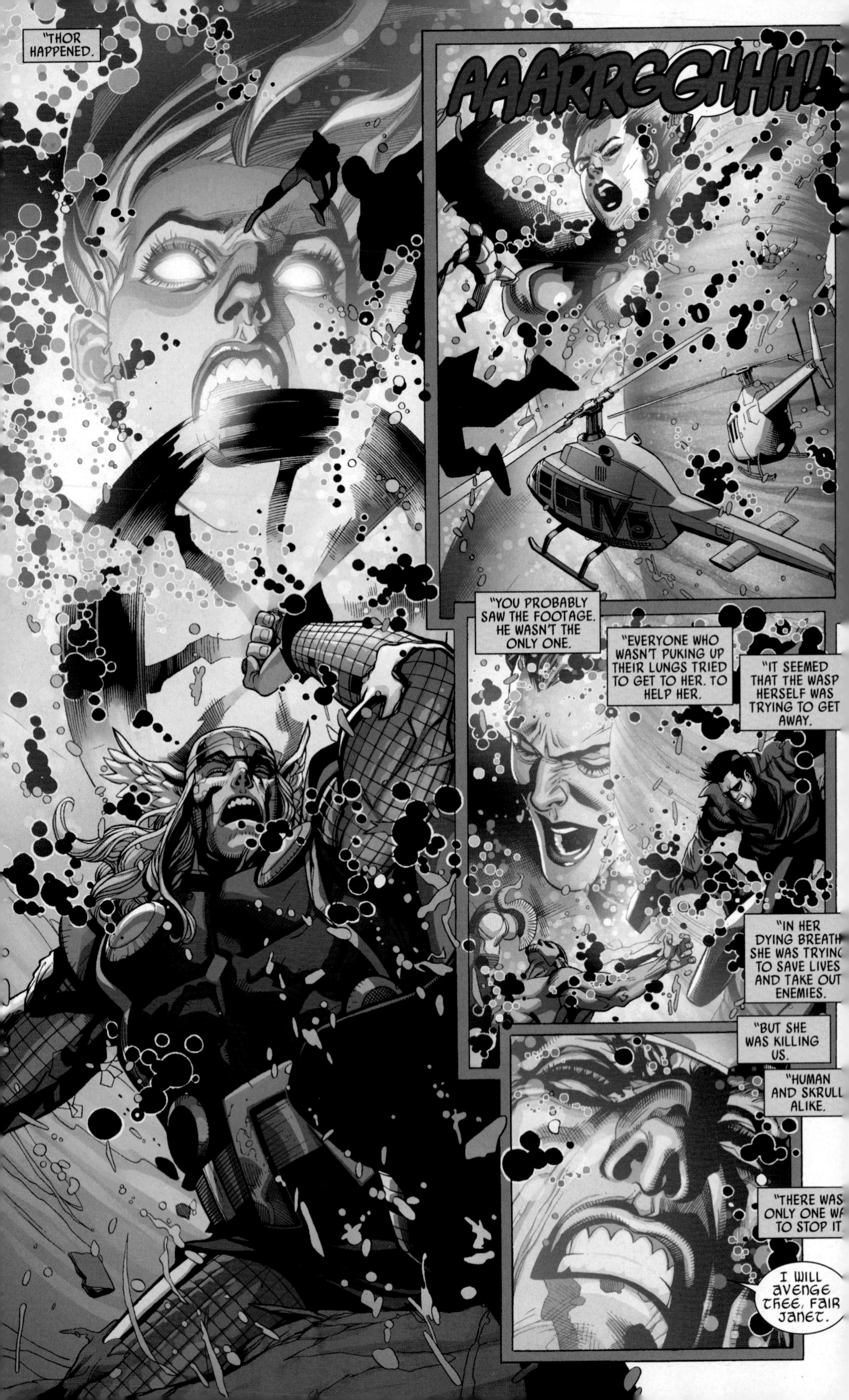

"THOR HAPPENED.
AAARRGGHHH!
TV5
"YOU PROBABLY SAW THE FOOTAGE. HE WASN'T THE ONLY ONE.
"EVERYONE WHO WASN'T PUKING UP THEIR LUNGS TRIED TO GET TO HER. TO HELP HER.
"IT SEEMED THAT THE WASP HERSELF WAS TRYING TO GET AWAY.
"IN HER DYING BREATH SHE WAS TRYING TO SAVE LIVES AND TAKE OUT ENEMIES.
"BUT SHE WAS KILLING US.
"HUMAN AND SKRULL ALIKE.
"THERE WAS ONLY ONE WA TO STOP IT.
I WILL AVENGE THEE, FAIR JANET.

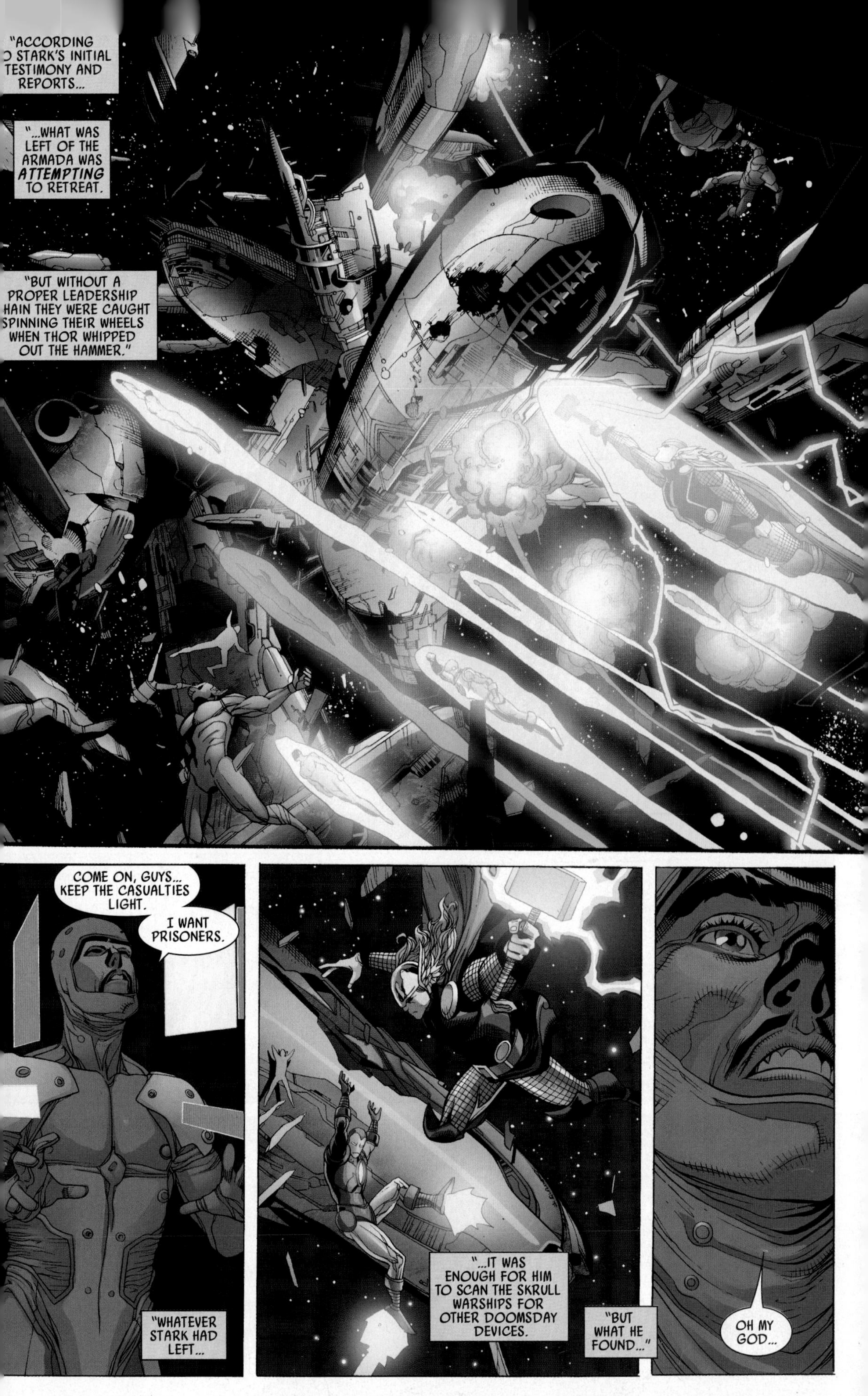
"ACCORDING
O STARK'S INITIAL
TESTIMONY AND
REPORTS...
"...WHAT WAS
LEFT OF THE
ARMADA WAS
ATTEMPTING
TO RETREAT.
"BUT WITHOUT A
PROPER LEADERSHIP
HAIN THEY WERE CAUGHT
SPINNING THEIR WHEELS
WHEN THOR WHIPPED
OUT THE HAMMER."
COME ON, GUYS... KEEP THE CASUALTIES LIGHT.
I WANT PRISONERS.
"WHATEVER STARK HAD LEFT...
"...IT WAS ENOUGH FOR HIM TO SCAN THE SKRULL WARSHIPS FOR OTHER DOOMSDAY DEVICES.
"BUT WHAT HE FOUND..."
OH MY GOD...

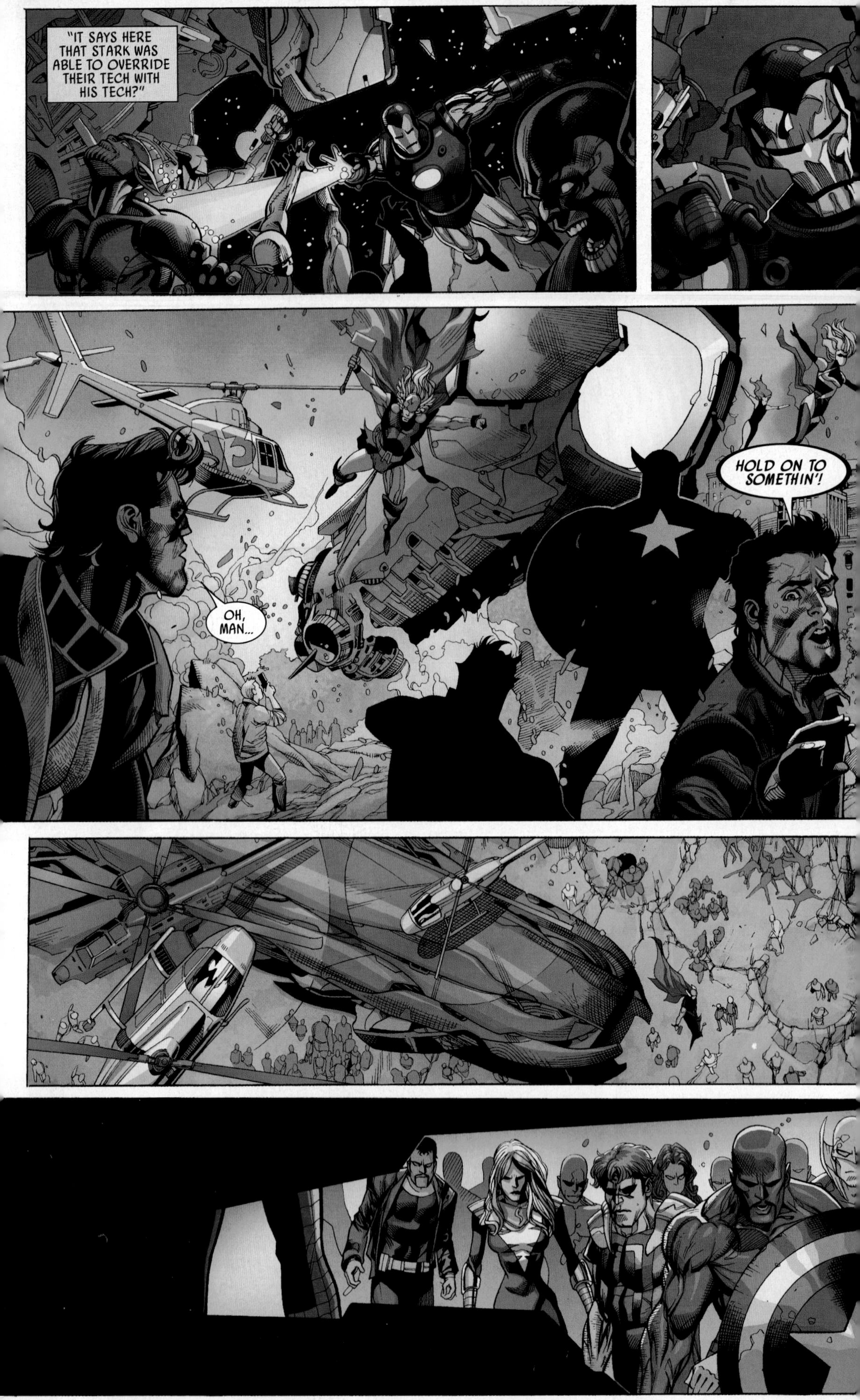
"IT SAYS HERE THAT STARK WAS ABLE TO OVERRIDE THEIR TECH WITH HIS TECH?"
HOLD ON TO SOMETHIN'!
OH, MAN...

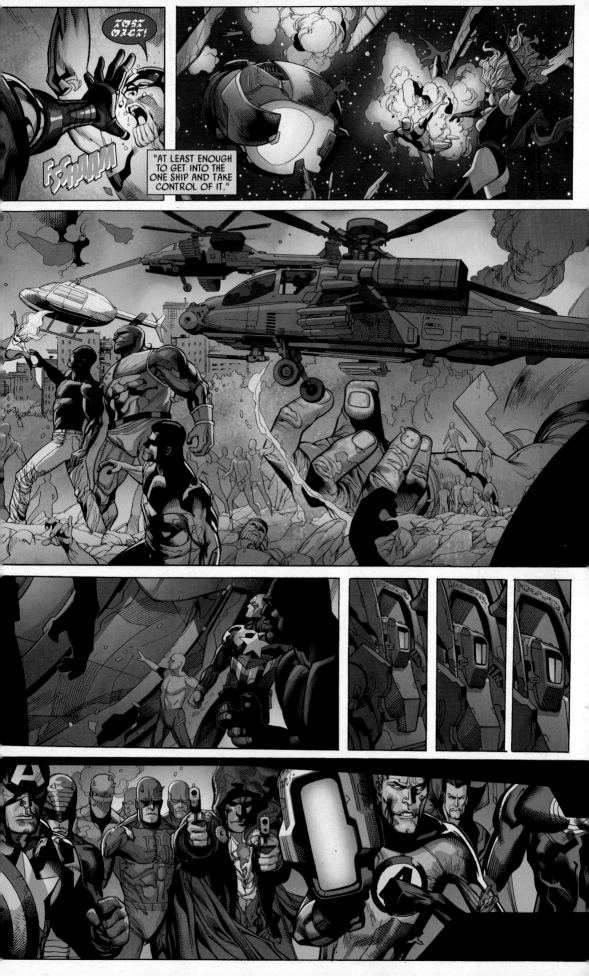

TOSS ME!

FSCHOOM

"AT LEAST ENOUGH TO GET INTO THE ONE SHIP AND TAKE CONTROL OF IT."

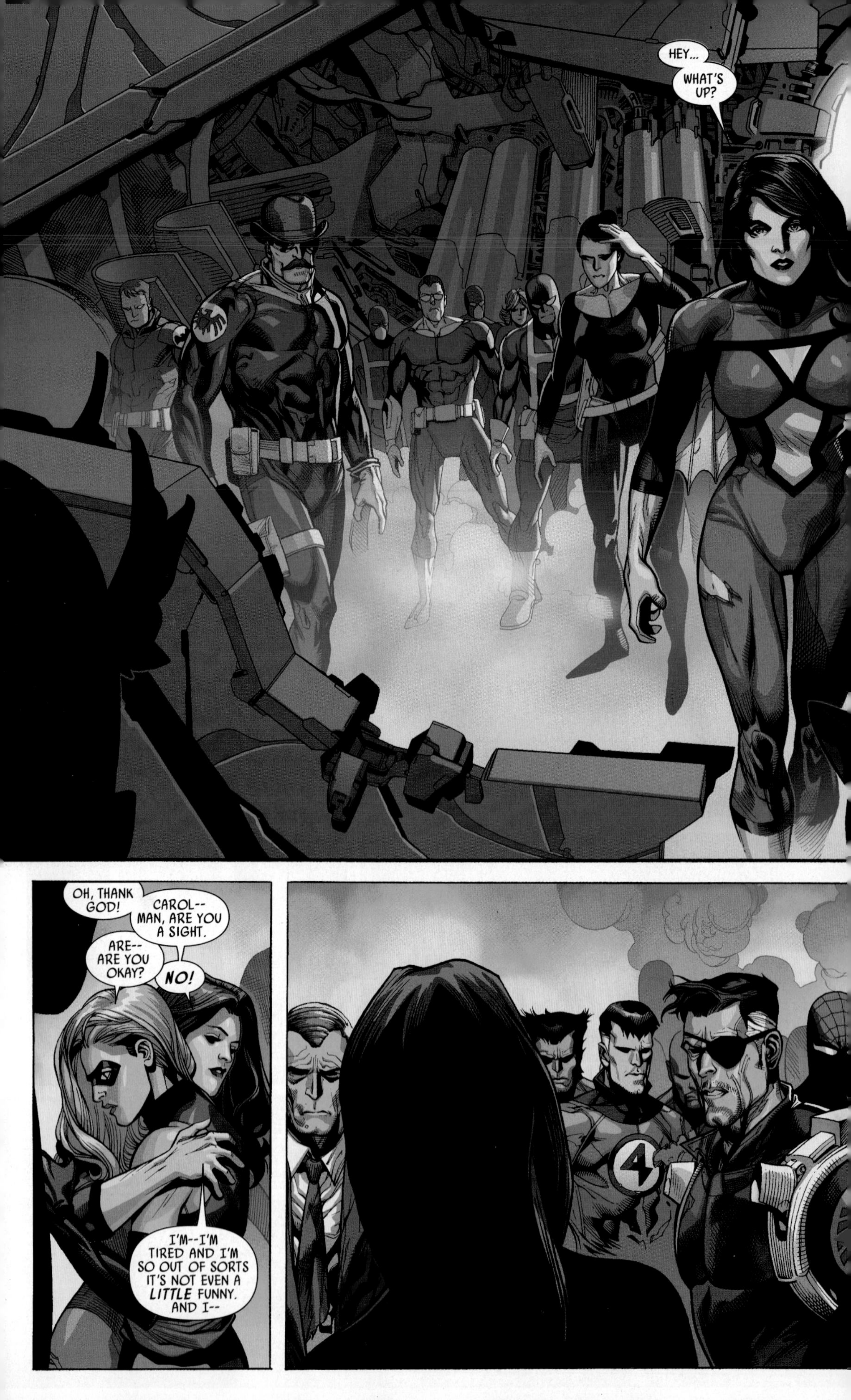
HEY...
WHAT'S UP?
OH, THANK GOD!
CAROL-- MAN, ARE YOU A SIGHT.
ARE-- ARE YOU OKAY?
NO!
I'M--I'M TIRED AND I'M SO OUT OF SORTS IT'S NOT EVEN A LITTLE FUNNY. AND I--

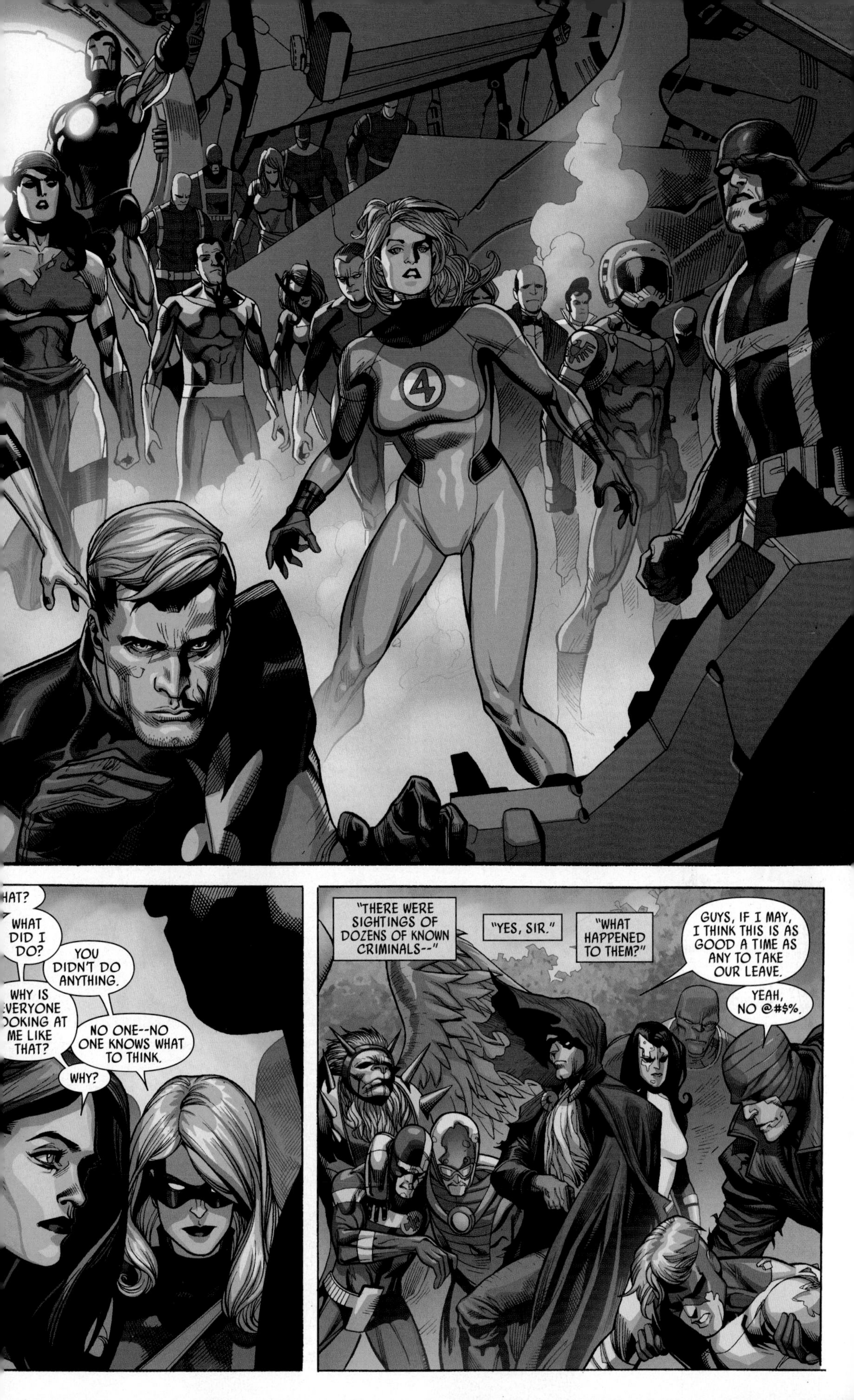
HAT?
WHAT DID I DO?
YOU DIDN'T DO ANYTHING.
WHY IS VERYONE OOKING AT ME LIKE THAT?
NO ONE--NO ONE KNOWS WHAT TO THINK.
WHY?
"THERE WERE SIGHTINGS OF DOZENS OF KNOWN CRIMINALS--"
"YES, SIR."
"WHAT HAPPENED TO THEM?"
GUYS, IF I MAY, I THINK THIS IS AS GOOD A TIME AS ANY TO TAKE OUR LEAVE.
YEAH, NO @#$%.

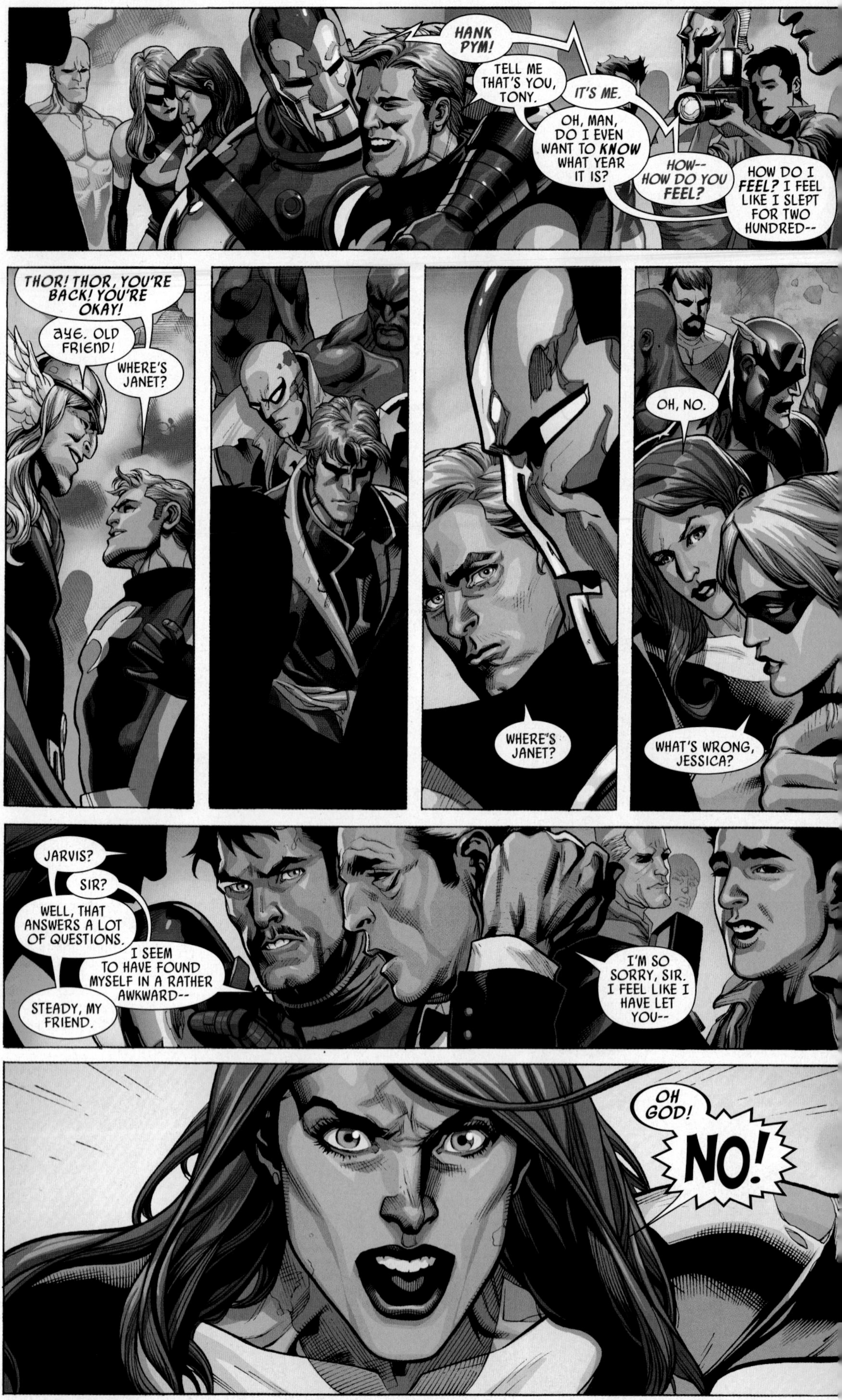
HANK PYM!
TELL ME THAT'S YOU, TONY.
IT'S ME.
OH, MAN, DO I EVEN WANT TO KNOW WHAT YEAR IT IS?
HOW-- HOW DO YOU FEEL?
HOW DO I FEEL? I FEEL LIKE I SLEPT FOR TWO HUNDRED--
THOR! THOR, YOU'RE BACK! YOU'RE OKAY!
AYE. OLD FRIEND!
WHERE'S JANET?
WHERE'S JANET?
OH, NO.
WHAT'S WRONG, JESSICA?
JARVIS?
SIR?
WELL, THAT ANSWERS A LOT OF QUESTIONS.
I SEEM TO HAVE FOUND MYSELF IN A RATHER AWKWARD--
STEADY, MY FRIEND.
I'M SO SORRY, SIR. I FEEL LIKE I HAVE LET YOU--
OH GOD!
NO!

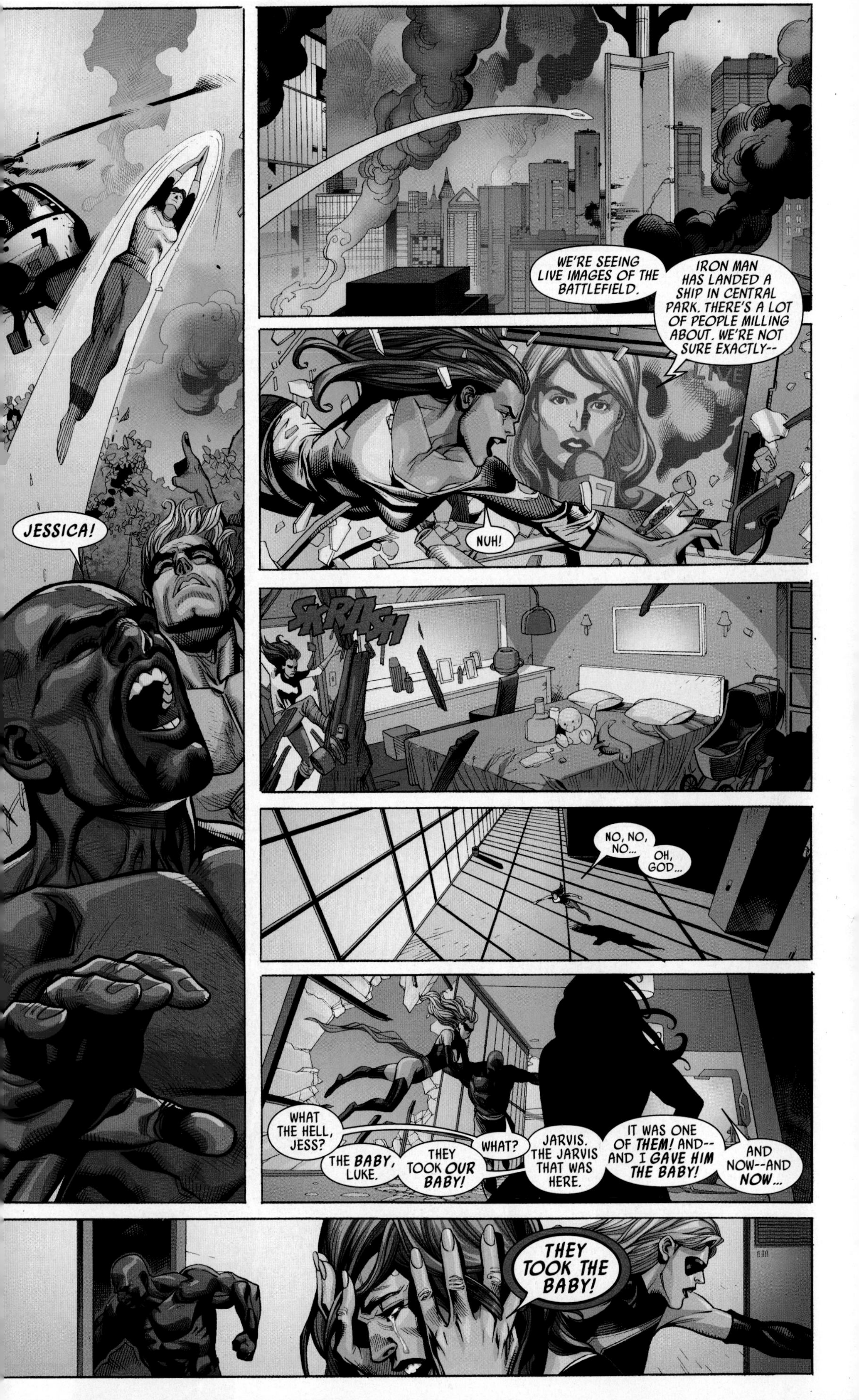
WE'RE SEEING LIVE IMAGES OF THE BATTLEFIELD.
IRON MAN HAS LANDED A SHIP IN CENTRAL PARK. THERE'S A LOT OF PEOPLE MILLING ABOUT. WE'RE NOT SURE EXACTLY--
NUH!
JESSICA!
SKRASH
NO, NO, NO... OH, GOD...
WHAT THE HELL, JESS?
THE BABY, LUKE.
THEY TOOK OUR BABY!
WHAT?
JARVIS. THE JARVIS THAT WAS HERE.
IT WAS ONE OF THEM! AND-- AND I GAVE HIM THE BABY!
AND NOW--AND NOW...
THEY TOOK THE BABY!

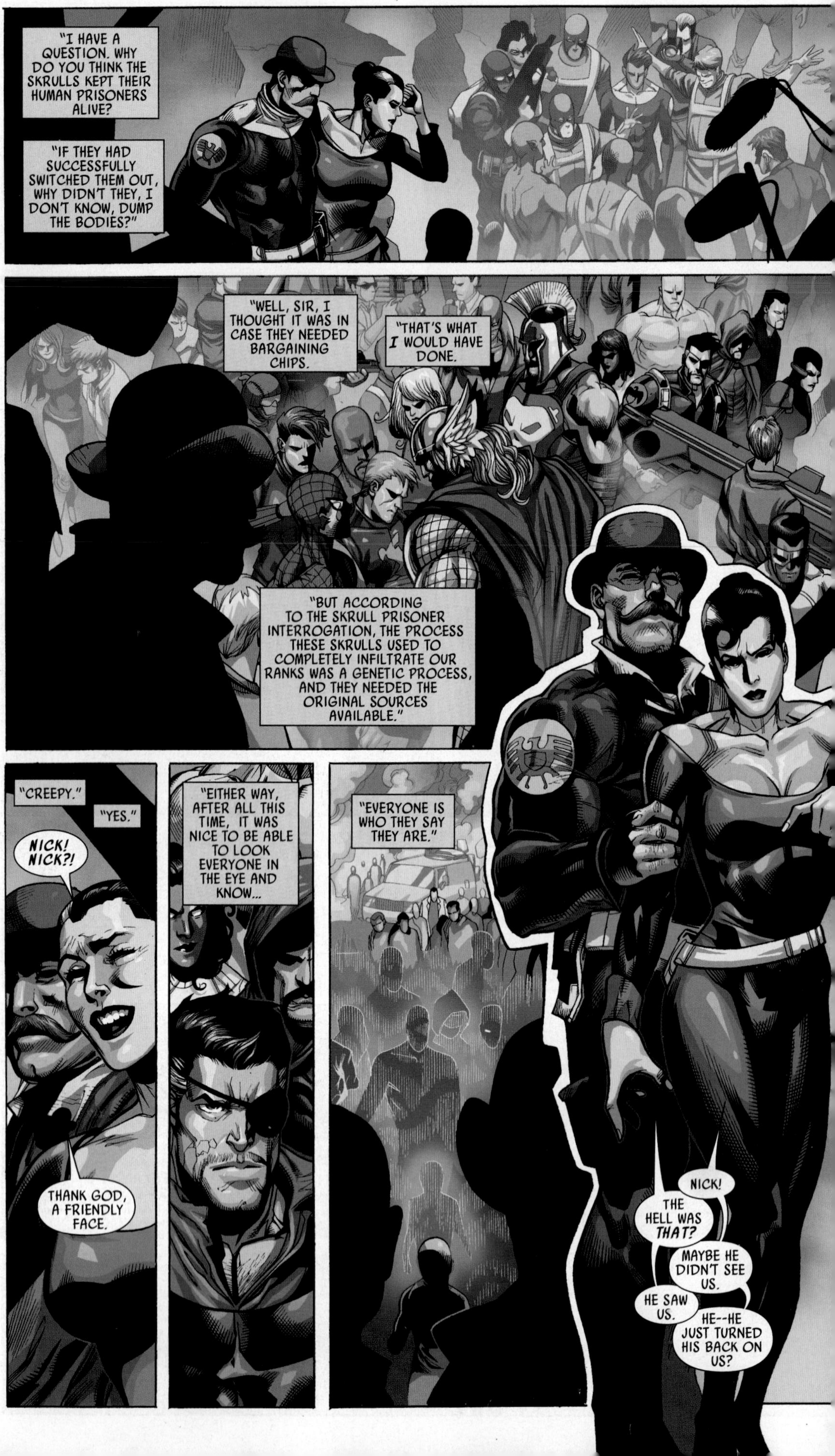
"I HAVE A QUESTION. WHY DO YOU THINK THE SKRULLS KEPT THEIR HUMAN PRISONERS ALIVE?
"IF THEY HAD SUCCESSFULLY SWITCHED THEM OUT, WHY DIDN'T THEY, I DON'T KNOW, DUMP THE BODIES?"
"WELL, SIR, I THOUGHT IT WAS IN CASE THEY NEEDED BARGAINING CHIPS.
"THAT'S WHAT I WOULD HAVE DONE.
"BUT ACCORDING TO THE SKRULL PRISONER INTERROGATION, THE PROCESS THESE SKRULLS USED TO COMPLETELY INFILTRATE OUR RANKS WAS A GENETIC PROCESS, AND THEY NEEDED THE ORIGINAL SOURCES AVAILABLE."
"CREEPY."
"YES."
NICK! NICK?!
THANK GOD, A FRIENDLY FACE.
"EITHER WAY, AFTER ALL THIS TIME, IT WAS NICE TO BE ABLE TO LOOK EVERYONE IN THE EYE AND KNOW...
"EVERYONE IS WHO THEY SAY THEY ARE."
NICK!
THE HELL WAS THAT?
MAYBE HE DIDN'T SEE US.
HE SAW US.
HE--HE JUST TURNED HIS BACK ON US?

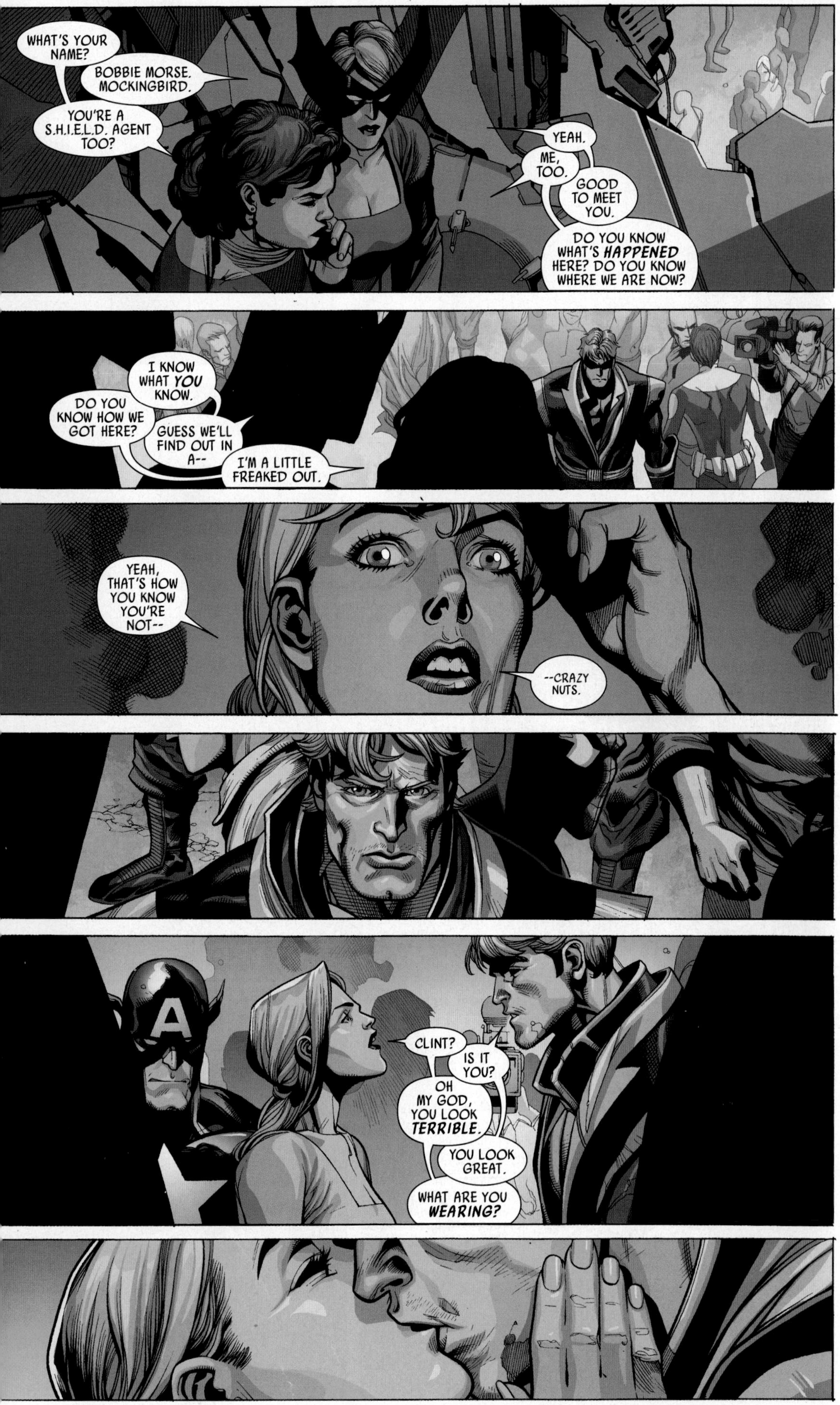
WHAT'S YOUR NAME?
BOBBIE MORSE. MOCKINGBIRD.
YOU'RE A S.H.I.E.L.D. AGENT TOO?
YEAH.
ME, TOO.
GOOD TO MEET YOU.
DO YOU KNOW WHAT'S HAPPENED HERE? DO YOU KNOW WHERE WE ARE NOW?
I KNOW WHAT YOU KNOW.
DO YOU KNOW HOW WE GOT HERE?
GUESS WE'LL FIND OUT IN A--
I'M A LITTLE FREAKED OUT.
YEAH, THAT'S HOW YOU KNOW YOU'RE NOT--
--CRAZY NUTS.
CLINT?
IS IT YOU?
OH MY GOD, YOU LOOK TERRIBLE.
YOU LOOK GREAT.
WHAT ARE YOU WEARING?

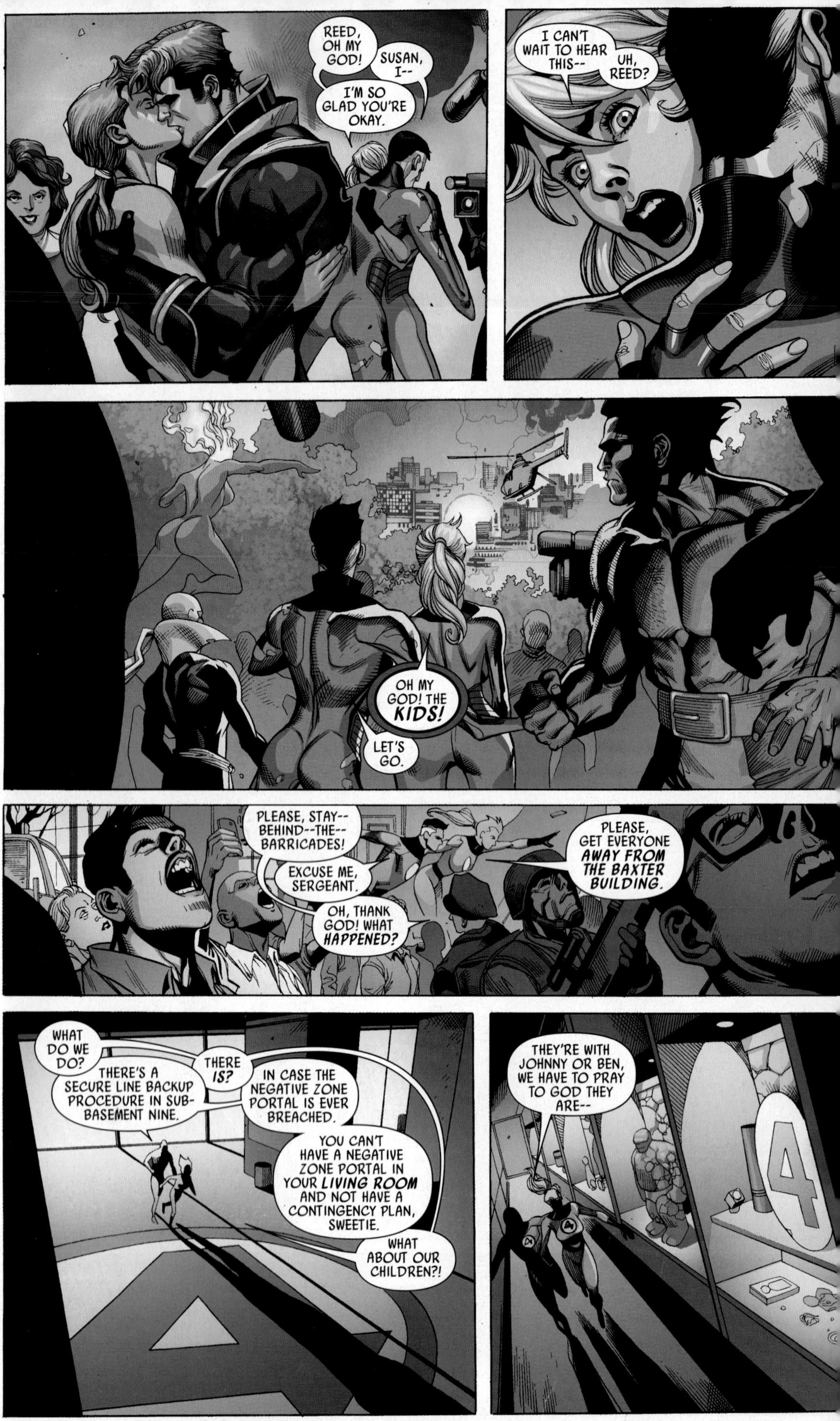
REED, OH MY GOD!
SUSAN, I--
I'M SO GLAD YOU'RE OKAY.
I CAN'T WAIT TO HEAR THIS--
UH, REED?
OH MY GOD! THE KIDS!
LET'S GO.
PLEASE, STAY-- BEHIND--THE-- BARRICADES!
EXCUSE ME, SERGEANT.
OH, THANK GOD! WHAT HAPPENED?
PLEASE, GET EVERYONE AWAY FROM THE BAXTER BUILDING.
WHAT DO WE DO?
THERE'S A SECURE LINE BACKUP PROCEDURE IN SUB-BASEMENT NINE.
THERE IS?
IN CASE THE NEGATIVE ZONE PORTAL IS EVER BREACHED.
YOU CAN'T HAVE A NEGATIVE ZONE PORTAL IN YOUR LIVING ROOM AND NOT HAVE A CONTINGENCY PLAN, SWEETIE.
WHAT ABOUT OUR CHILDREN?!
THEY'RE WITH JOHNNY OR BEN, WE HAVE TO PRAY TO GOD THEY ARE--

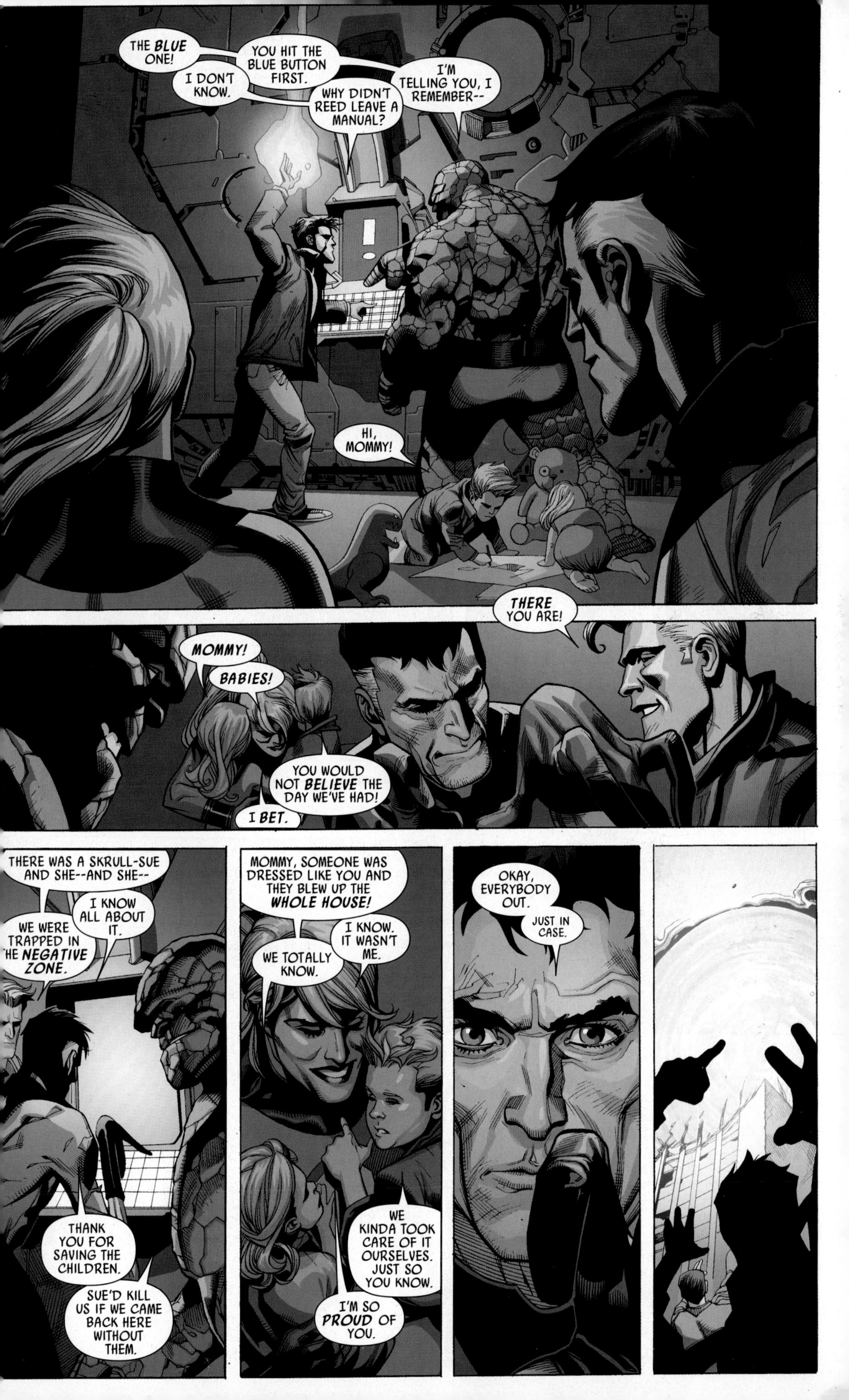
THE BLUE ONE!
I DON'T KNOW.
YOU HIT THE BLUE BUTTON FIRST.
WHY DIDN'T REED LEAVE A MANUAL?
I'M TELLING YOU, I REMEMBER--
HI, MOMMY!
THERE YOU ARE!
MOMMY!
BABIES!
YOU WOULD NOT BELIEVE THE DAY WE'VE HAD!
I BET.
THERE WAS A SKRULL-SUE AND SHE--AND SHE--
WE WERE TRAPPED IN THE NEGATIVE ZONE.
I KNOW ALL ABOUT IT.
THANK YOU FOR SAVING THE CHILDREN.
SUE'D KILL US IF WE CAME BACK HERE WITHOUT THEM.
MOMMY, SOMEONE WAS DRESSED LIKE YOU AND THEY BLEW UP THE WHOLE HOUSE!
WE TOTALLY KNOW.
I KNOW. IT WASN'T ME.
WE KINDA TOOK CARE OF IT OURSELVES. JUST SO YOU KNOW.
I'M SO PROUD OF YOU.
OKAY, EVERYBODY OUT.
JUST IN CASE.

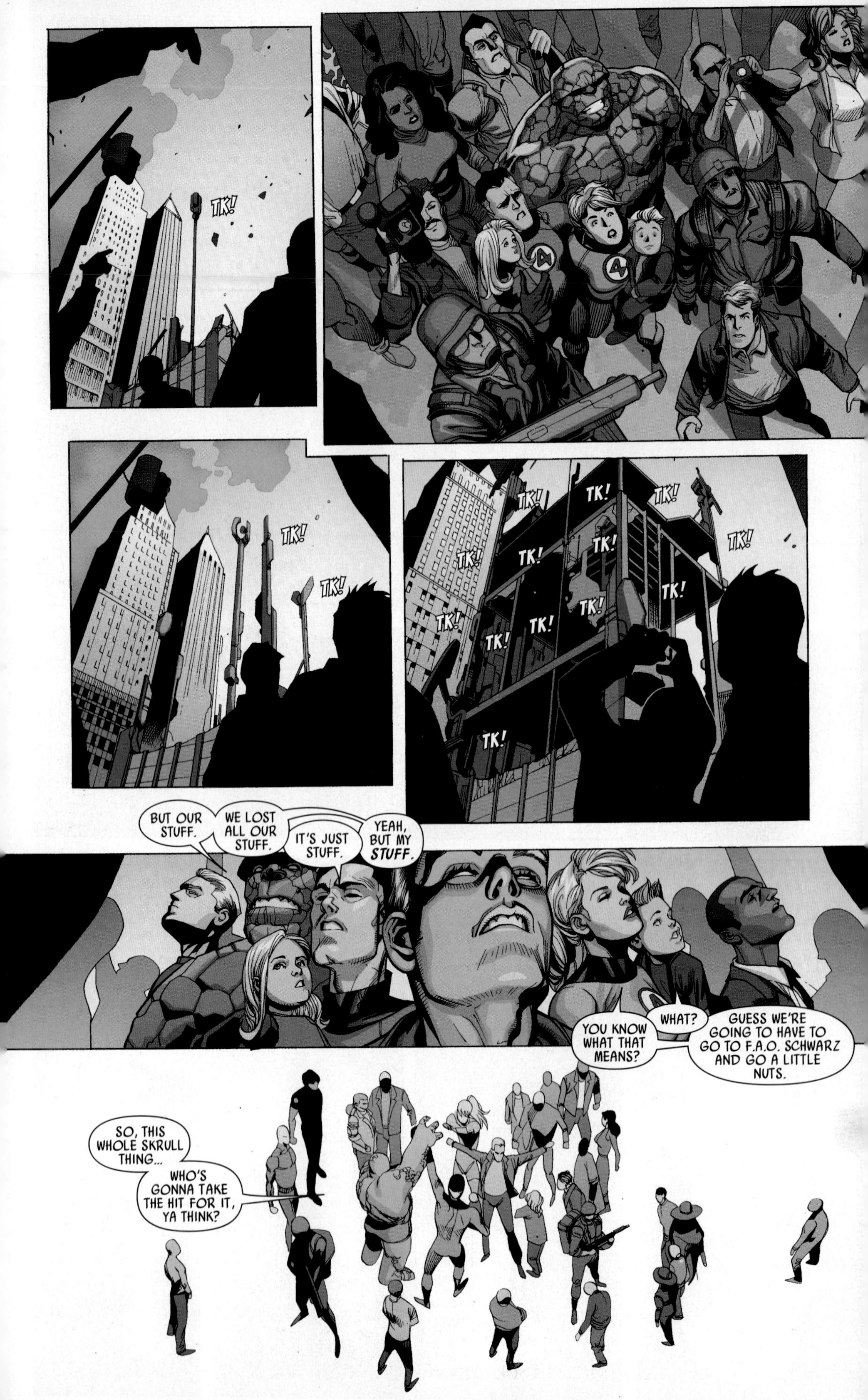
TK!
TK!
TK!
TK!
TK!
TK!
TK!
TK!
TK!
TK!
TK!
TK!
TK!
TK!
TK!
BUT OUR STUFF.
WE LOST ALL OUR STUFF.
IT'S JUST STUFF.
YEAH, BUT MY *STUFF*.
YOU KNOW WHAT THAT MEANS?
WHAT?
GUESS WE'RE GOING TO HAVE TO GO TO F.A.O. SCHWARZ AND GO A LITTLE NUTS.
SO, THIS WHOLE SKRULL THING...
WHO'S GONNA TAKE THE HIT FOR IT, YA THINK?

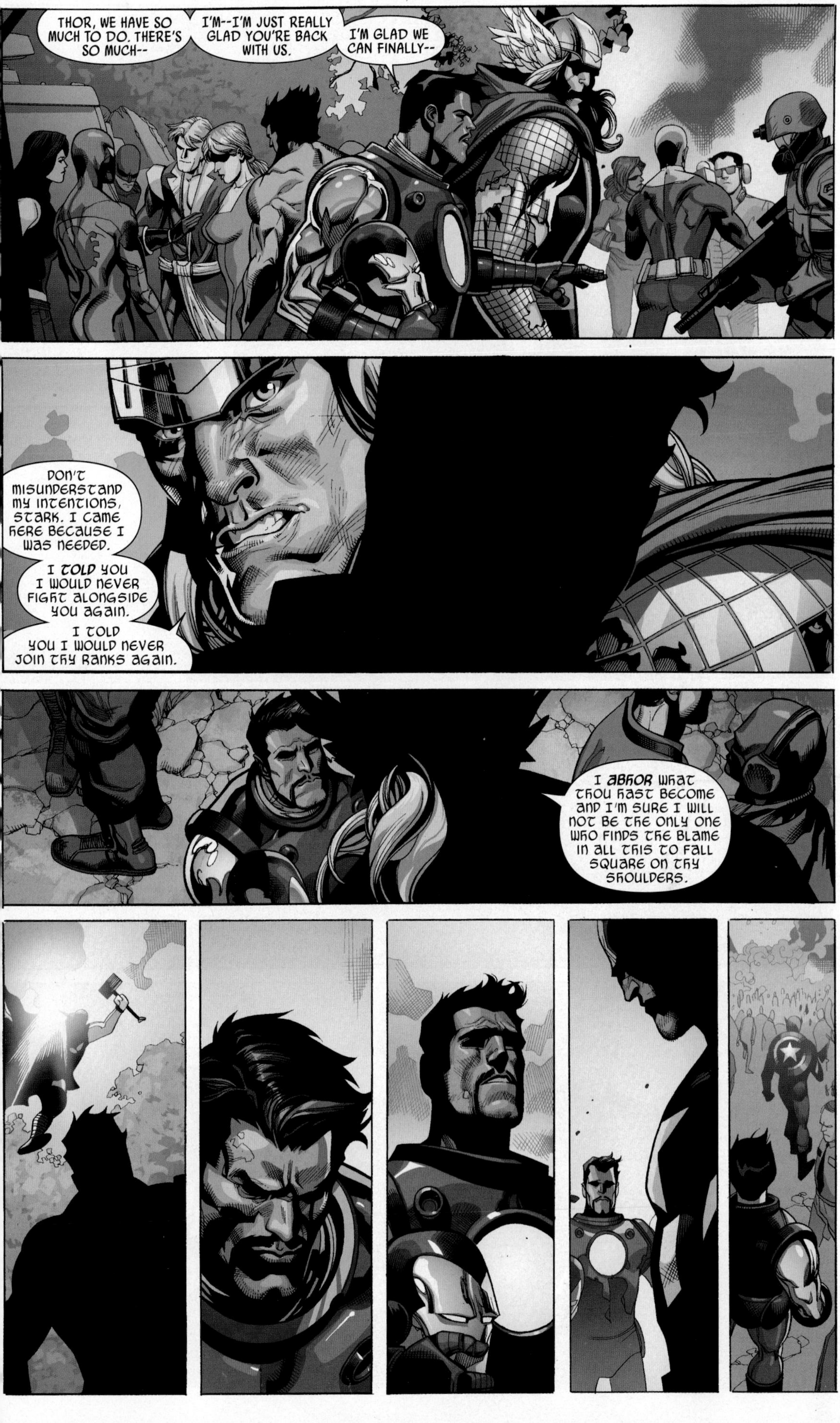
THOR, WE HAVE SO MUCH TO DO. THERE'S SO MUCH--
I'M--I'M JUST REALLY GLAD YOU'RE BACK WITH US.
I'M GLAD WE CAN FINALLY--
DON'T MISUNDERSTAND MY INTENTIONS, STARK. I CAME HERE BECAUSE I WAS NEEDED.
I TOLD YOU I WOULD NEVER FIGHT ALONGSIDE YOU AGAIN.
I TOLD YOU I WOULD NEVER JOIN THY RANKS AGAIN.
I ABHOR WHAT THOU HAST BECOME AND I'M SURE I WILL NOT BE THE ONLY ONE WHO FINDS THE BLAME IN ALL THIS TO FALL SQUARE ON THY SHOULDERS.

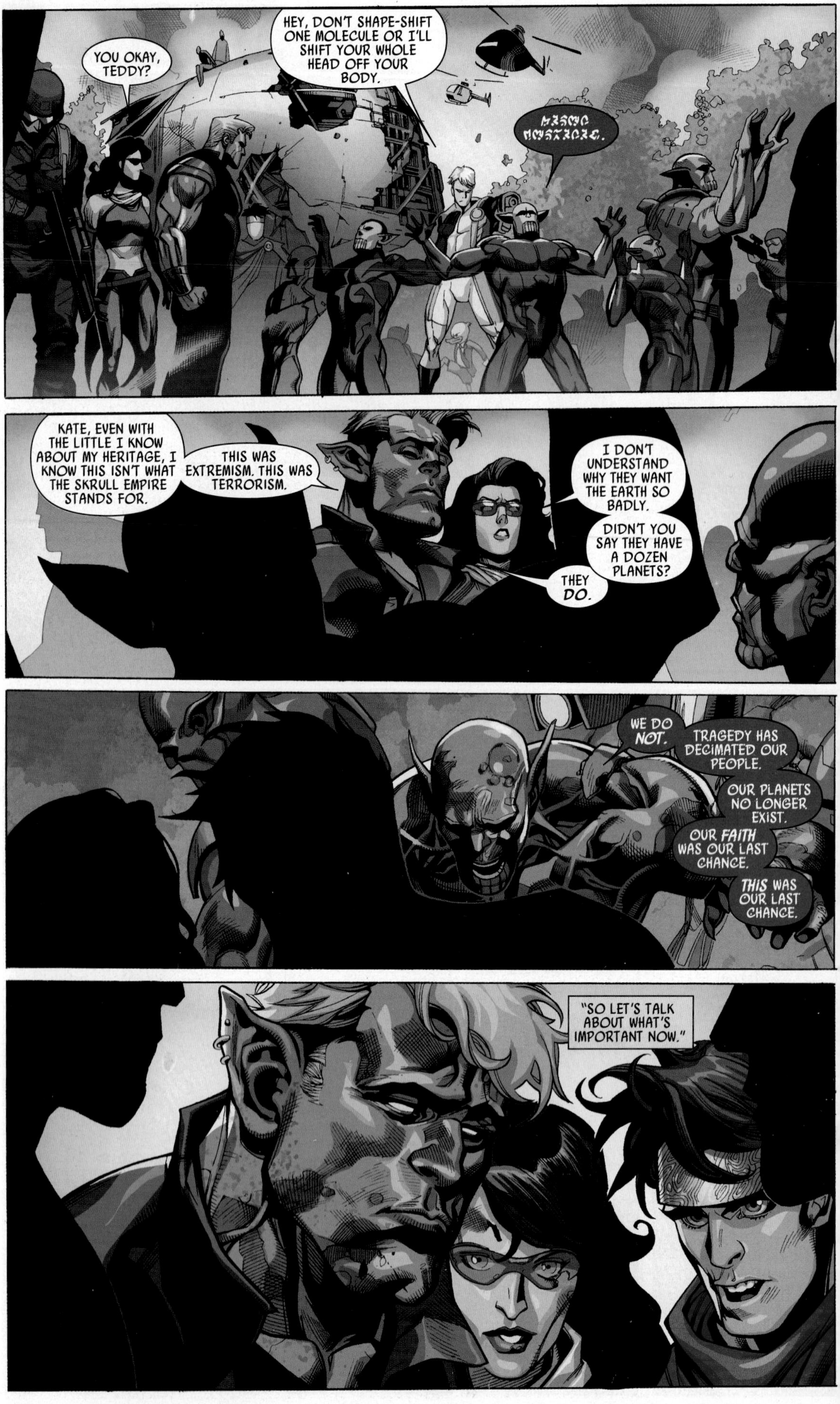

YOU OKAY, TEDDY?
HEY, DON'T SHAPE-SHIFT ONE MOLECULE OR I'LL SHIFT YOUR WHOLE HEAD OFF YOUR BODY.
KATE, EVEN WITH THE LITTLE I KNOW ABOUT MY HERITAGE, I KNOW THIS ISN'T WHAT THE SKRULL EMPIRE STANDS FOR.
THIS WAS EXTREMISM. THIS WAS TERRORISM.
I DON'T UNDERSTAND WHY THEY WANT THE EARTH SO BADLY.
DIDN'T YOU SAY THEY HAVE A DOZEN PLANETS?
THEY DO.
WE DO NOT.
TRAGEDY HAS DECIMATED OUR PEOPLE.
OUR PLANETS NO LONGER EXIST.
OUR FAITH WAS OUR LAST CHANCE.
THIS WAS OUR LAST CHANCE.
"SO LET'S TALK ABOUT WHAT'S IMPORTANT NOW."

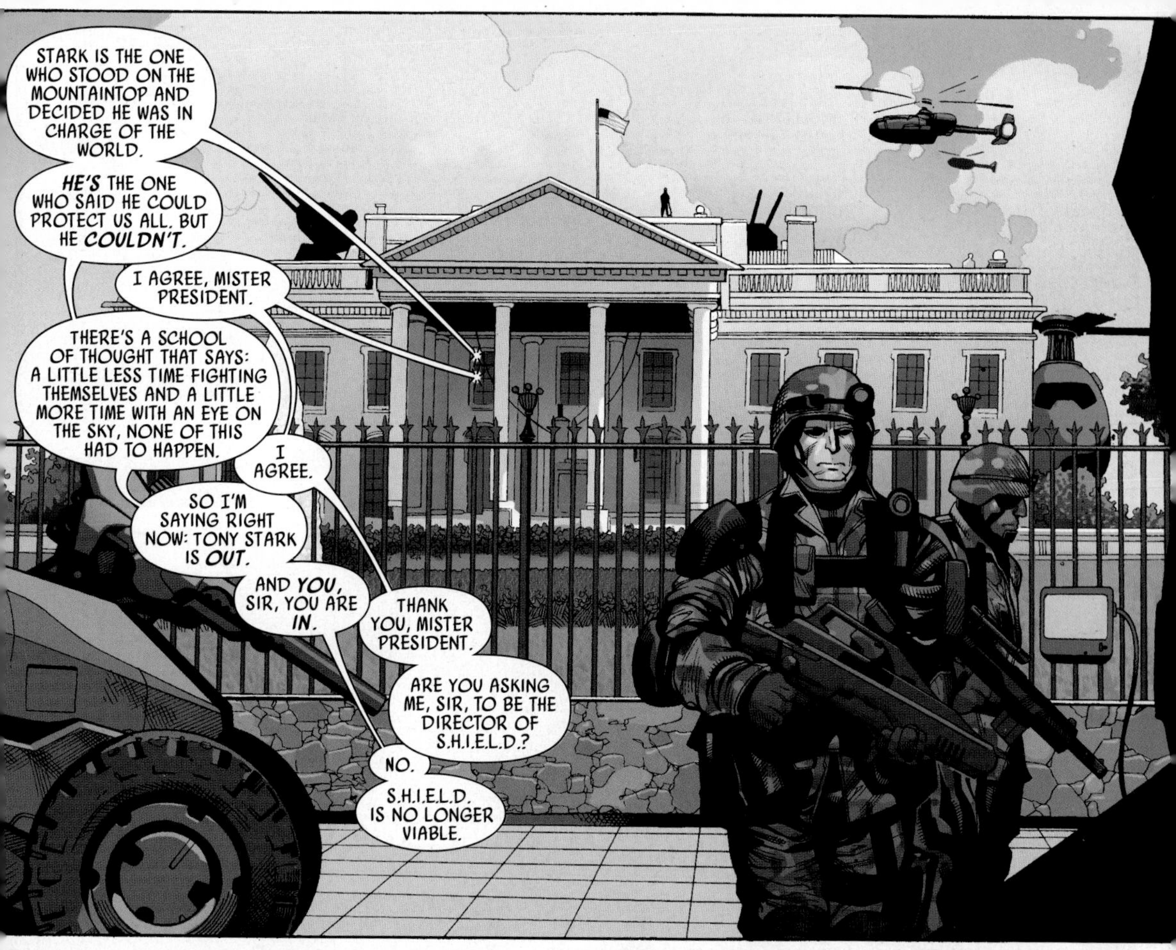
STARK IS THE ONE WHO STOOD ON THE MOUNTAINTOP AND DECIDED HE WAS IN CHARGE OF THE WORLD.
HE'S THE ONE WHO SAID HE COULD PROTECT US ALL. BUT HE COULDN'T.
I AGREE, MISTER PRESIDENT.
THERE'S A SCHOOL OF THOUGHT THAT SAYS: A LITTLE LESS TIME FIGHTING THEMSELVES AND A LITTLE MORE TIME WITH AN EYE ON THE SKY, NONE OF THIS HAD TO HAPPEN.
I AGREE.
SO I'M SAYING RIGHT NOW: TONY STARK IS OUT.
AND YOU, SIR, YOU ARE IN.
THANK YOU, MISTER PRESIDENT.
ARE YOU ASKING ME, SIR, TO BE THE DIRECTOR OF S.H.I.E.L.D.?
NO.
S.H.I.E.L.D. IS NO LONGER VIABLE.

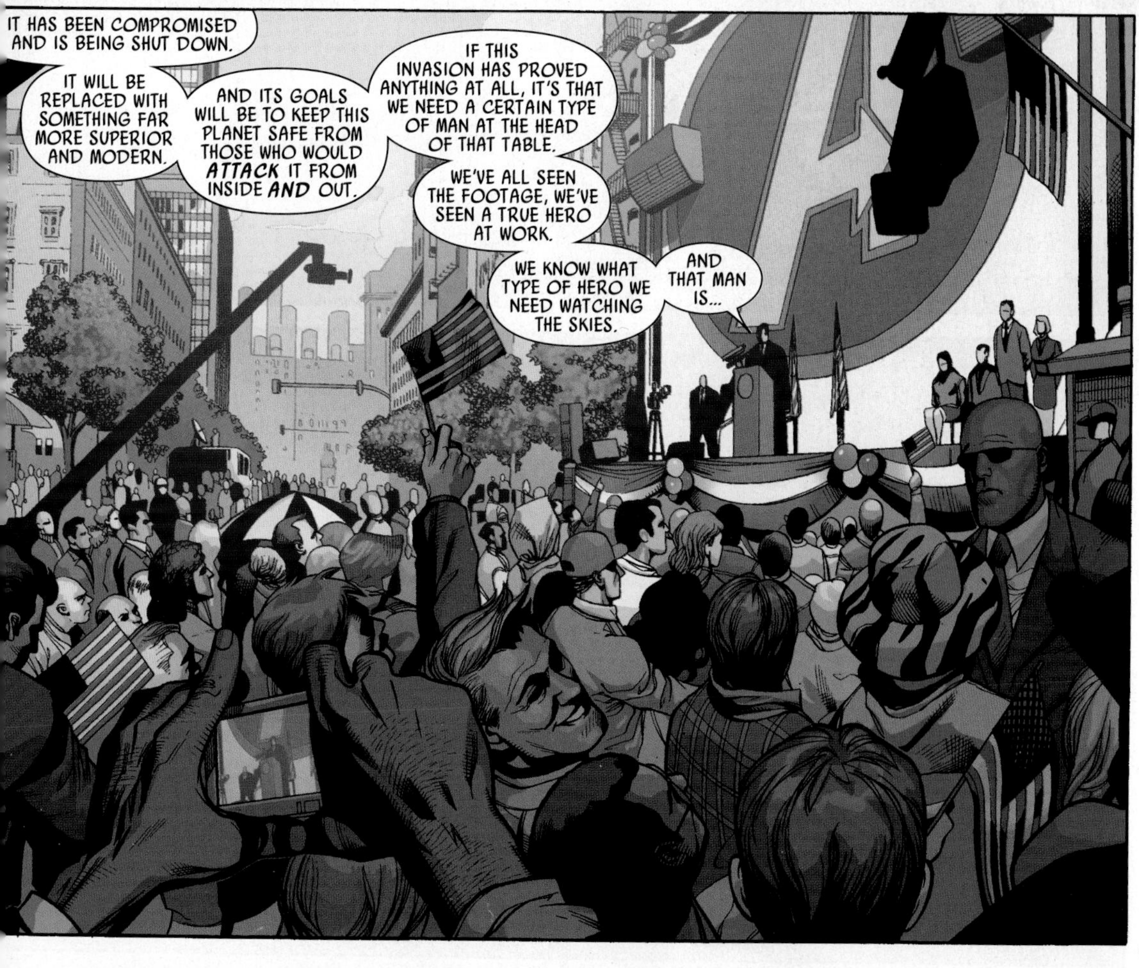
IT HAS BEEN COMPROMISED AND IS BEING SHUT DOWN.
IT WILL BE REPLACED WITH SOMETHING FAR MORE SUPERIOR AND MODERN.
AND ITS GOALS WILL BE TO KEEP THIS PLANET SAFE FROM THOSE WHO WOULD ATTACK IT FROM INSIDE AND OUT.
IF THIS INVASION HAS PROVED ANYTHING AT ALL, IT'S THAT WE NEED A CERTAIN TYPE OF MAN AT THE HEAD OF THAT TABLE.
WE'VE ALL SEEN THE FOOTAGE, WE'VE SEEN A TRUE HERO AT WORK.
WE KNOW WHAT TYPE OF HERO WE NEED WATCHING THE SKIES.
AND THAT MAN IS...

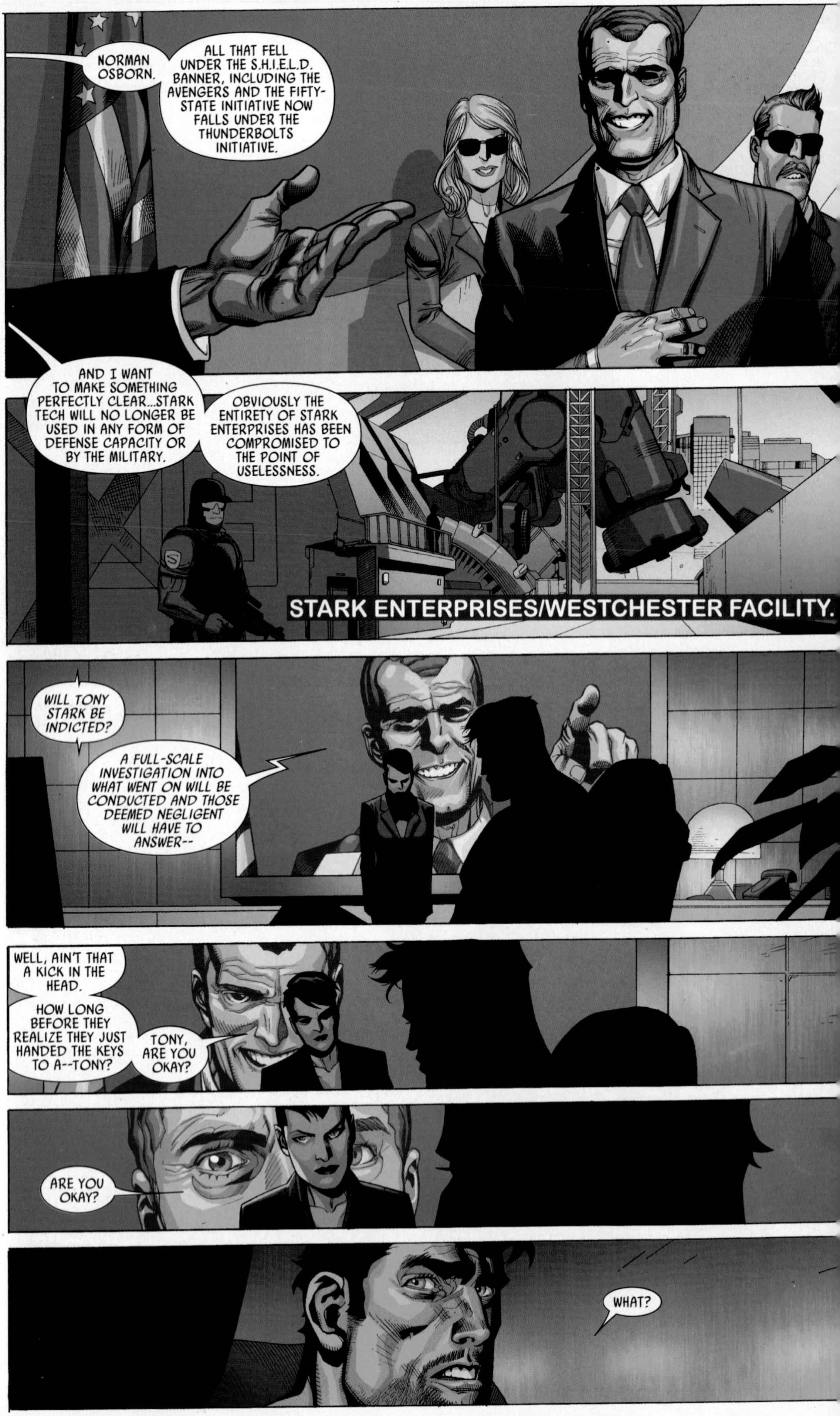
NORMAN OSBORN.
ALL THAT FELL UNDER THE S.H.I.E.L.D. BANNER, INCLUDING THE AVENGERS AND THE FIFTY-STATE INITIATIVE NOW FALLS UNDER THE THUNDERBOLTS INITIATIVE.
AND I WANT TO MAKE SOMETHING PERFECTLY CLEAR...STARK TECH WILL NO LONGER BE USED IN ANY FORM OF DEFENSE CAPACITY OR BY THE MILITARY.
OBVIOUSLY THE ENTIRETY OF STARK ENTERPRISES HAS BEEN COMPROMISED TO THE POINT OF USELESSNESS.
STARK ENTERPRISES/WESTCHESTER FACILITY.
WILL TONY STARK BE INDICTED?
A FULL-SCALE INVESTIGATION INTO WHAT WENT ON WILL BE CONDUCTED AND THOSE DEEMED NEGLIGENT WILL HAVE TO ANSWER--
WELL, AIN'T THAT A KICK IN THE HEAD.
HOW LONG BEFORE THEY REALIZE THEY JUST HANDED THE KEYS TO A--TONY?
TONY, ARE YOU OKAY?
ARE YOU OKAY?
WHAT?

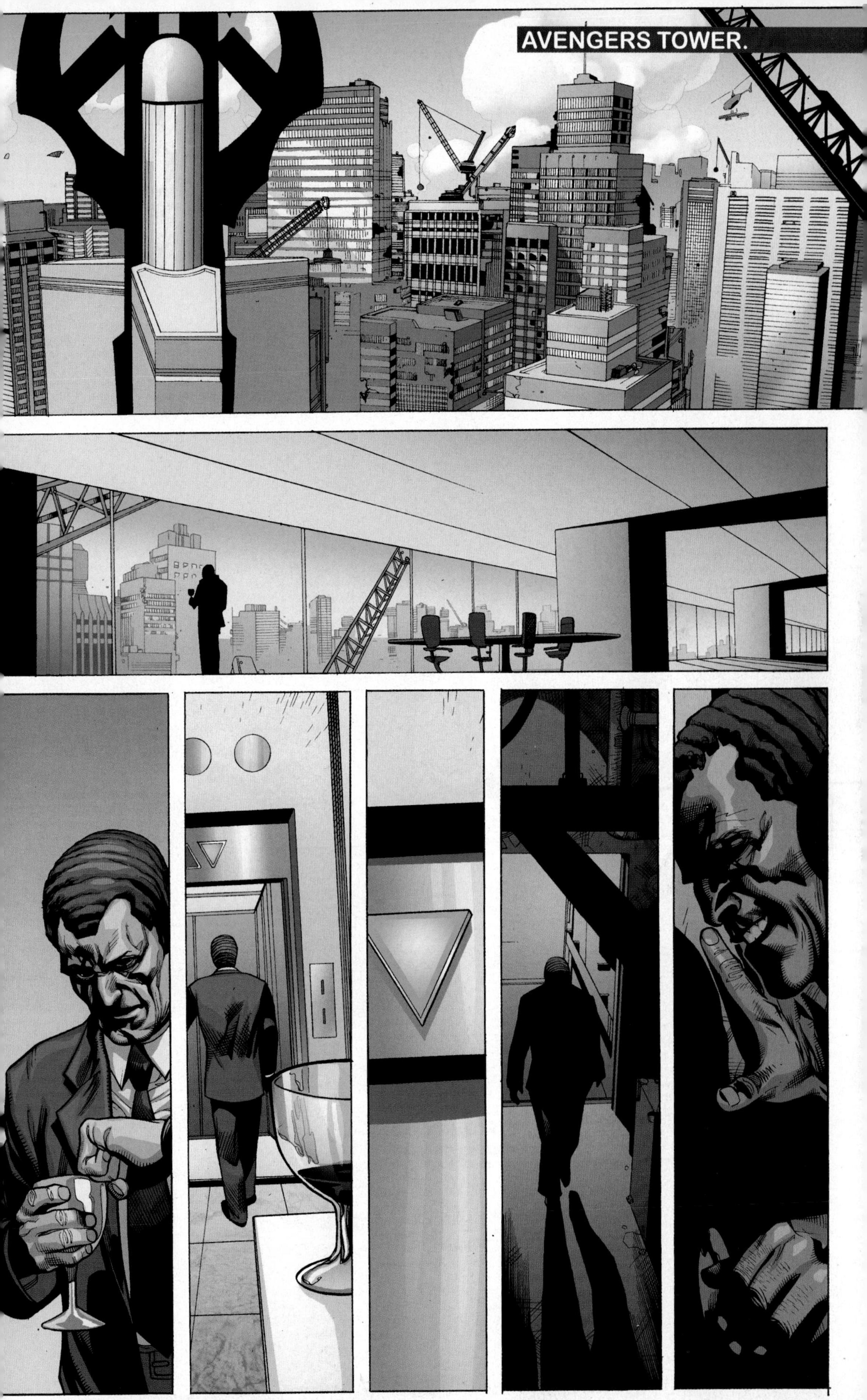
AVENGERS TOWER.

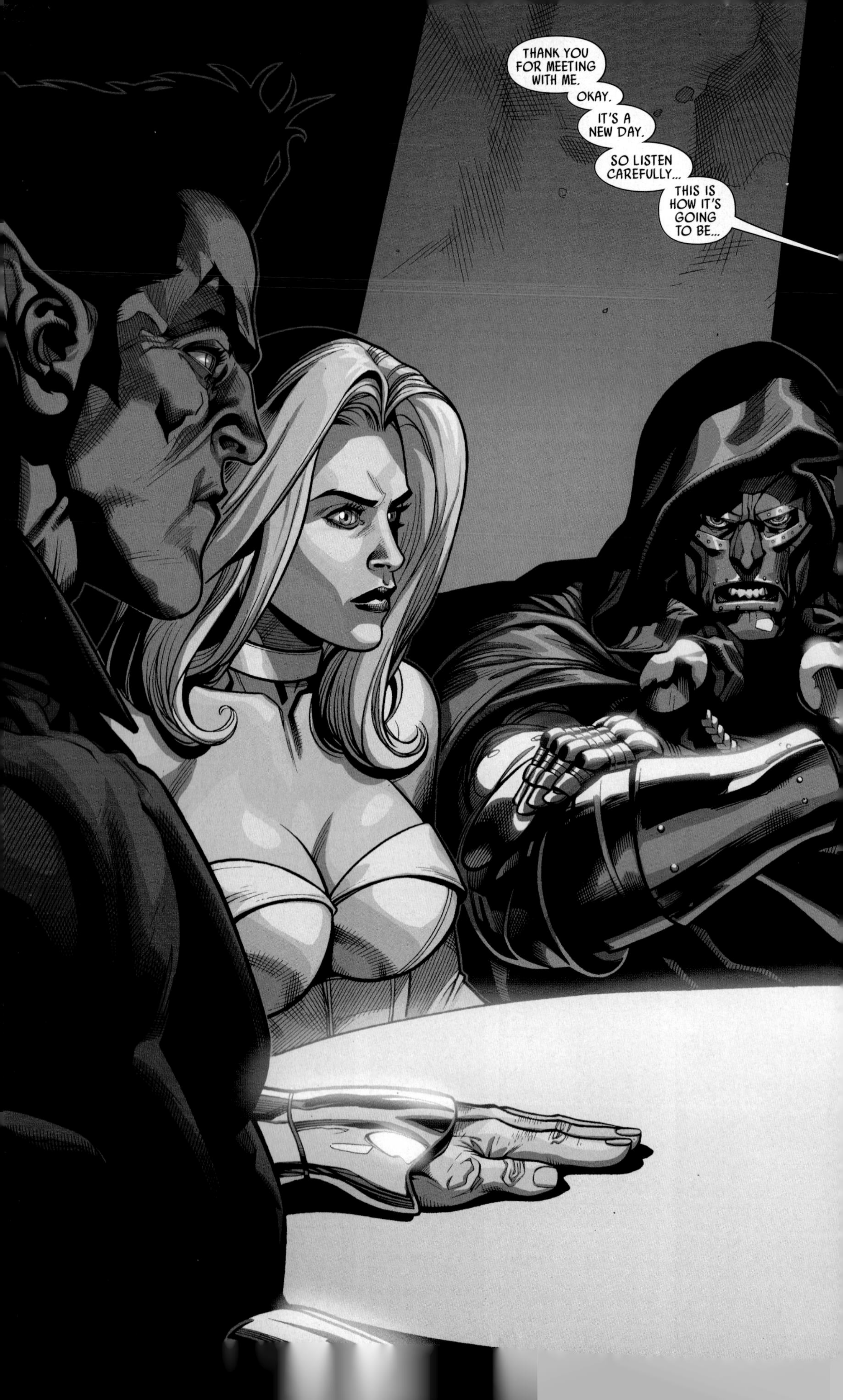
THANK YOU FOR MEETING WITH ME.
OKAY.
IT'S A NEW DAY.
SO LISTEN CAREFULLY...
THIS IS HOW IT'S GOING TO BE...

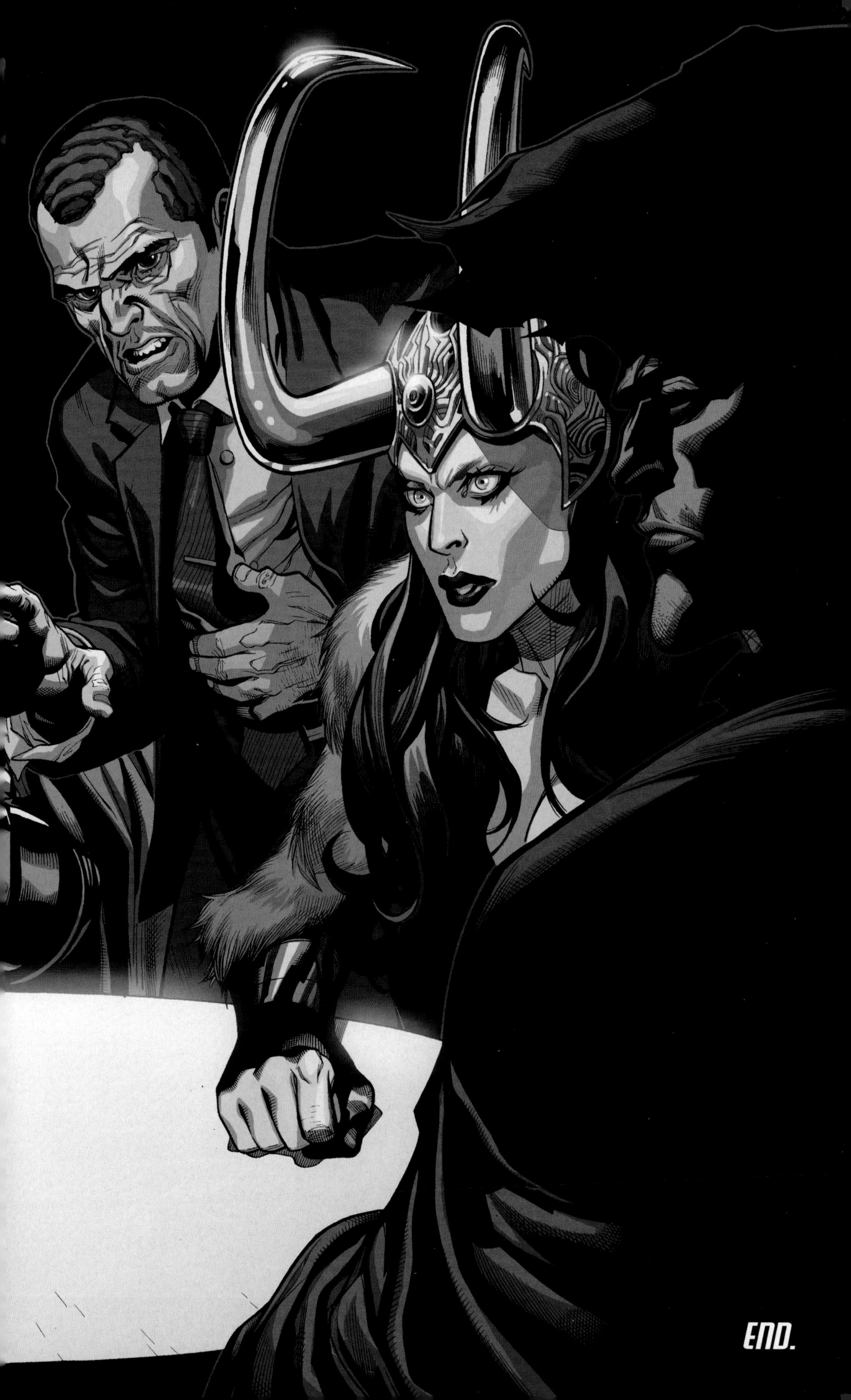
END.

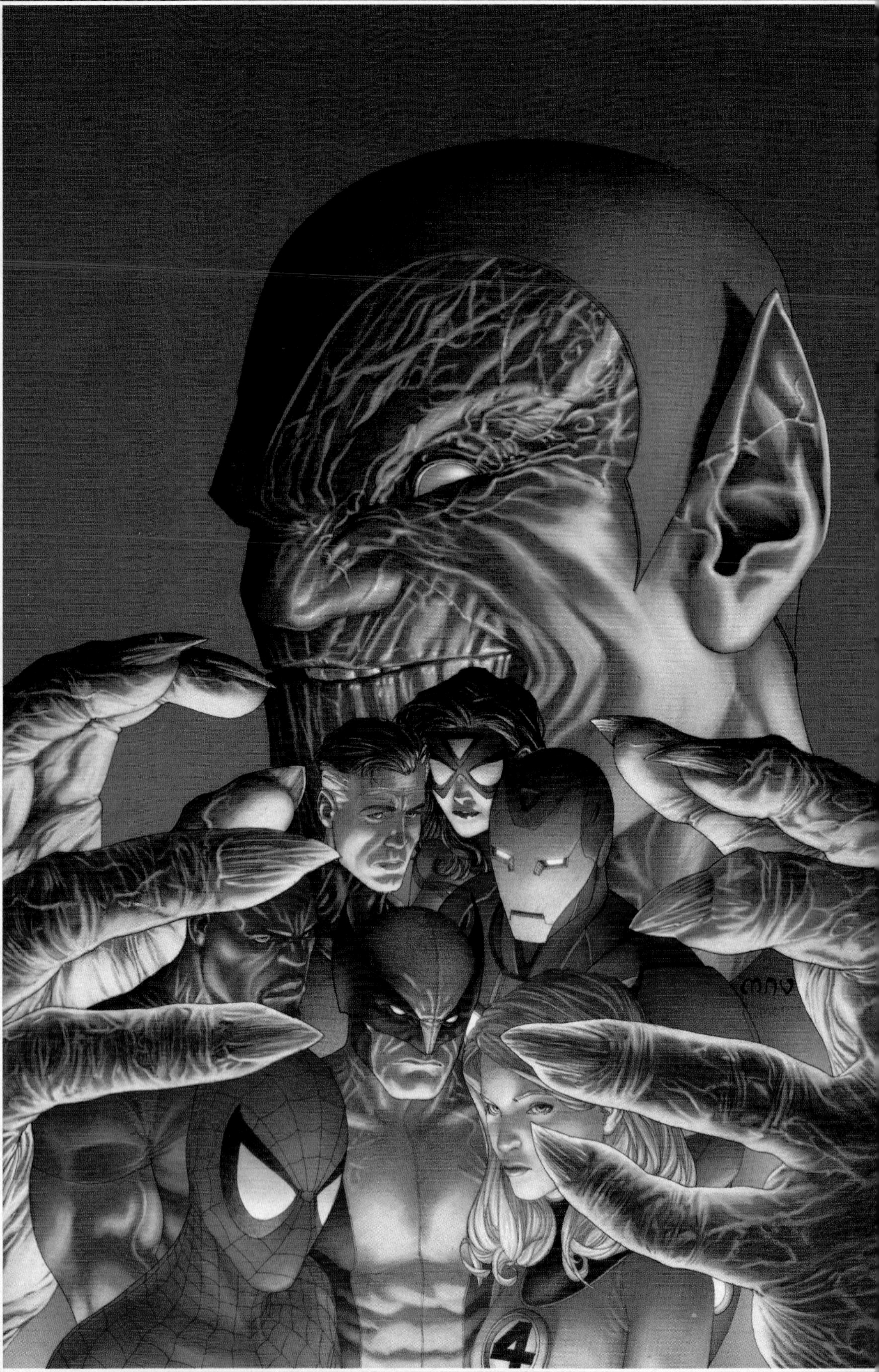
MNV

[1 Variant Cover by Steve McNiven]

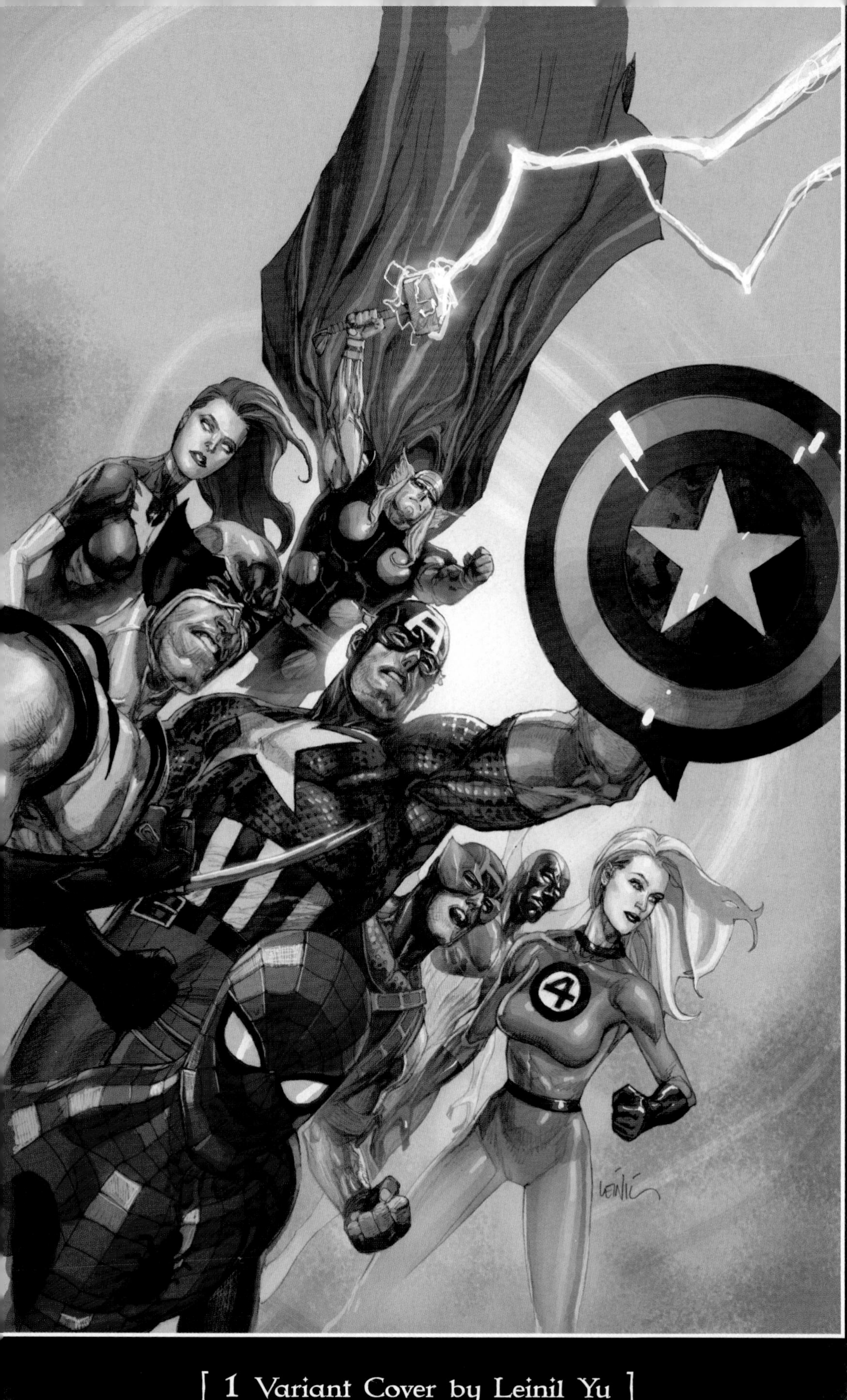

[1 Variant Cover by Leinil Yu]

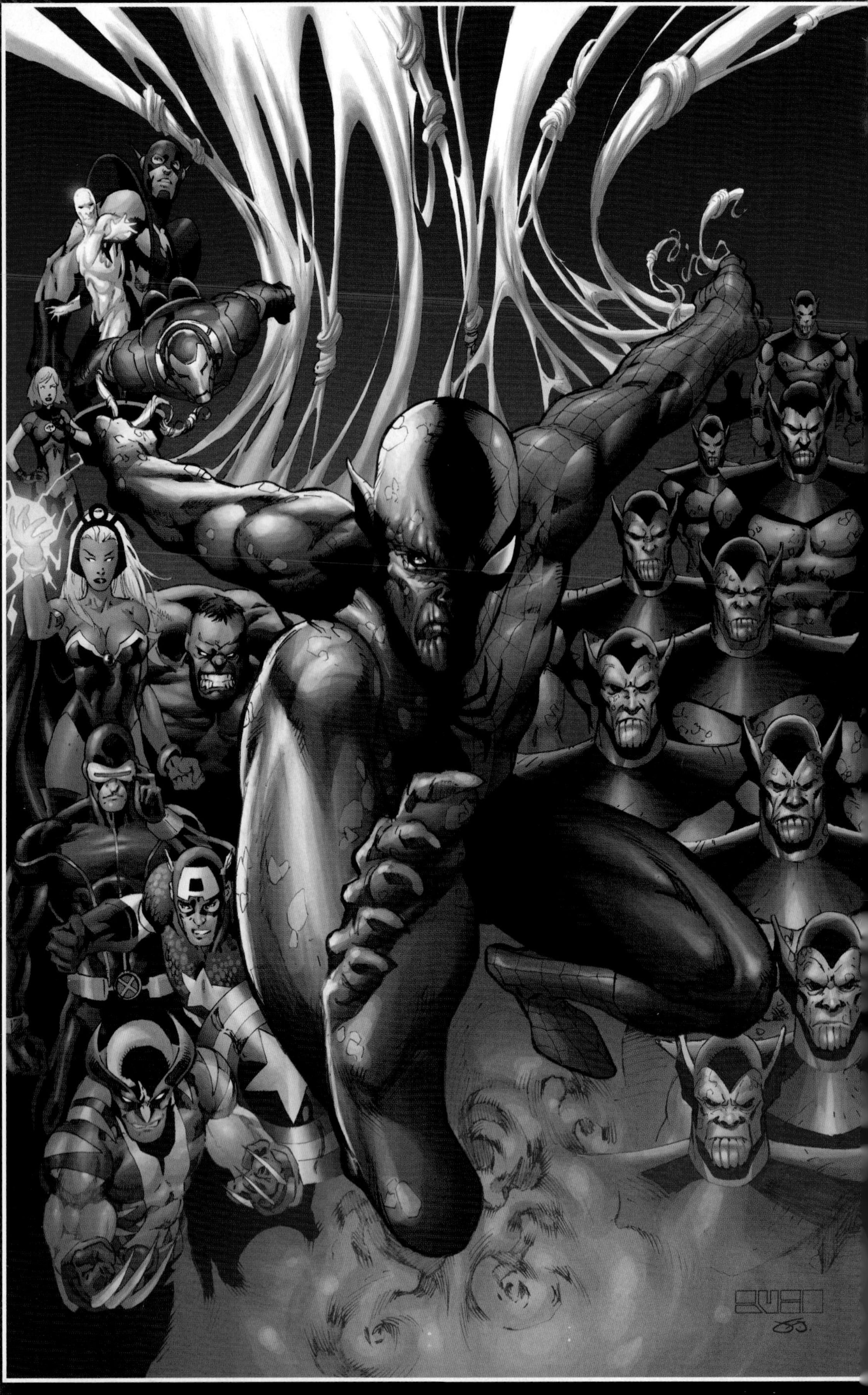

[1 Dynamic Forces Variant Cover by Mel Rubi]

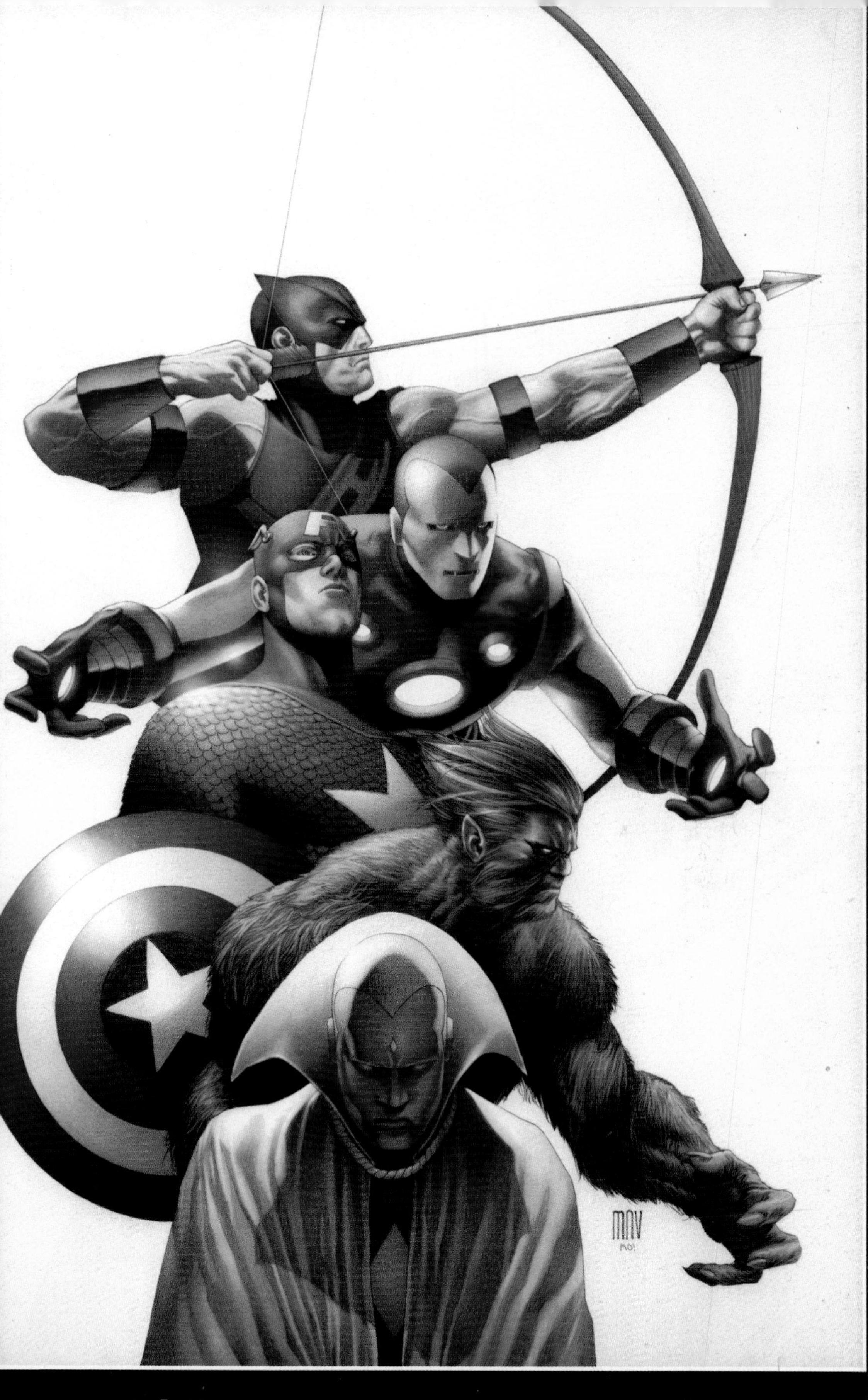
MNV
'05

[2 Variant Cover by Steve McNiven]

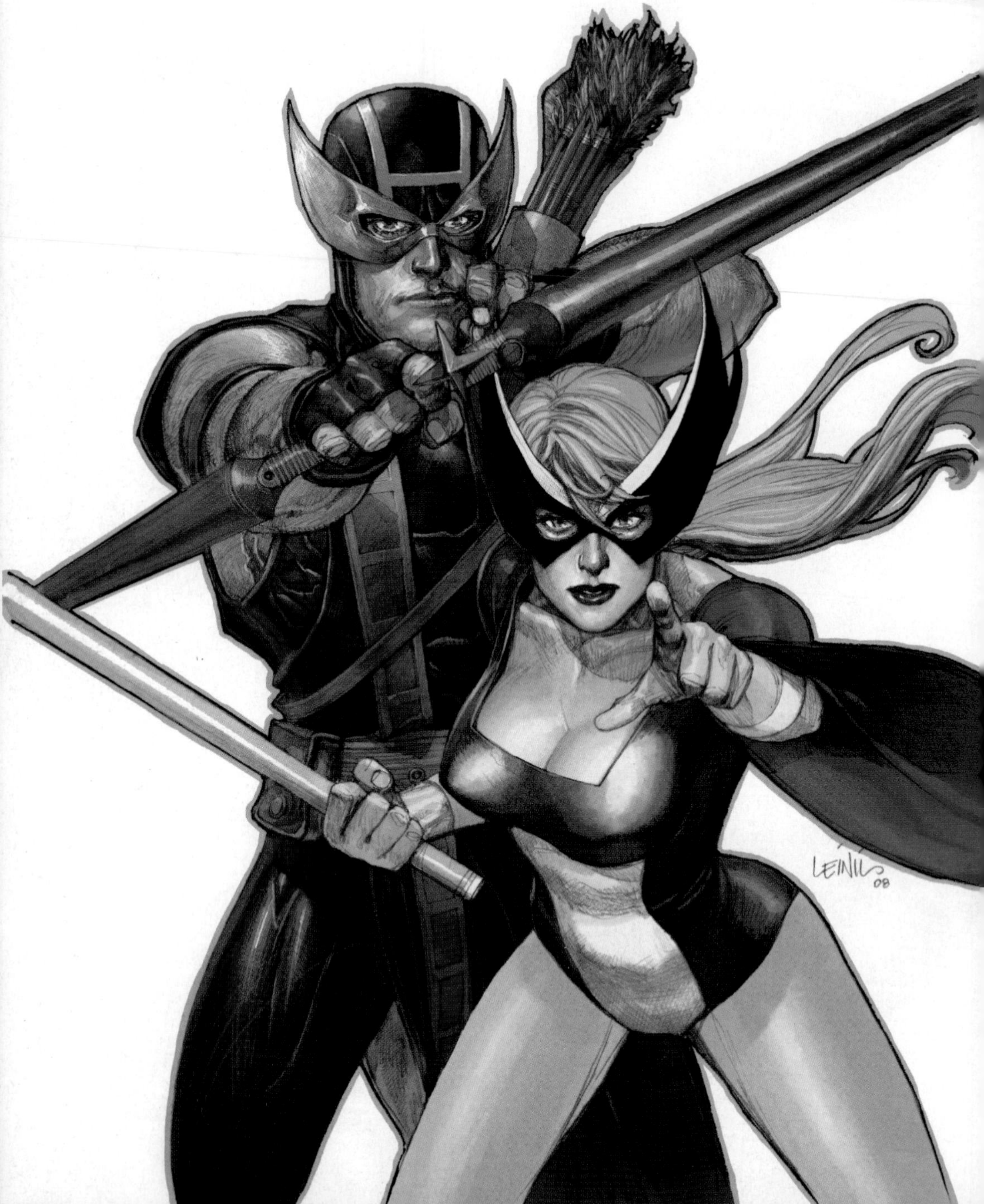
LEINIL 08

[2 Variant Cover by Leinil Yu]

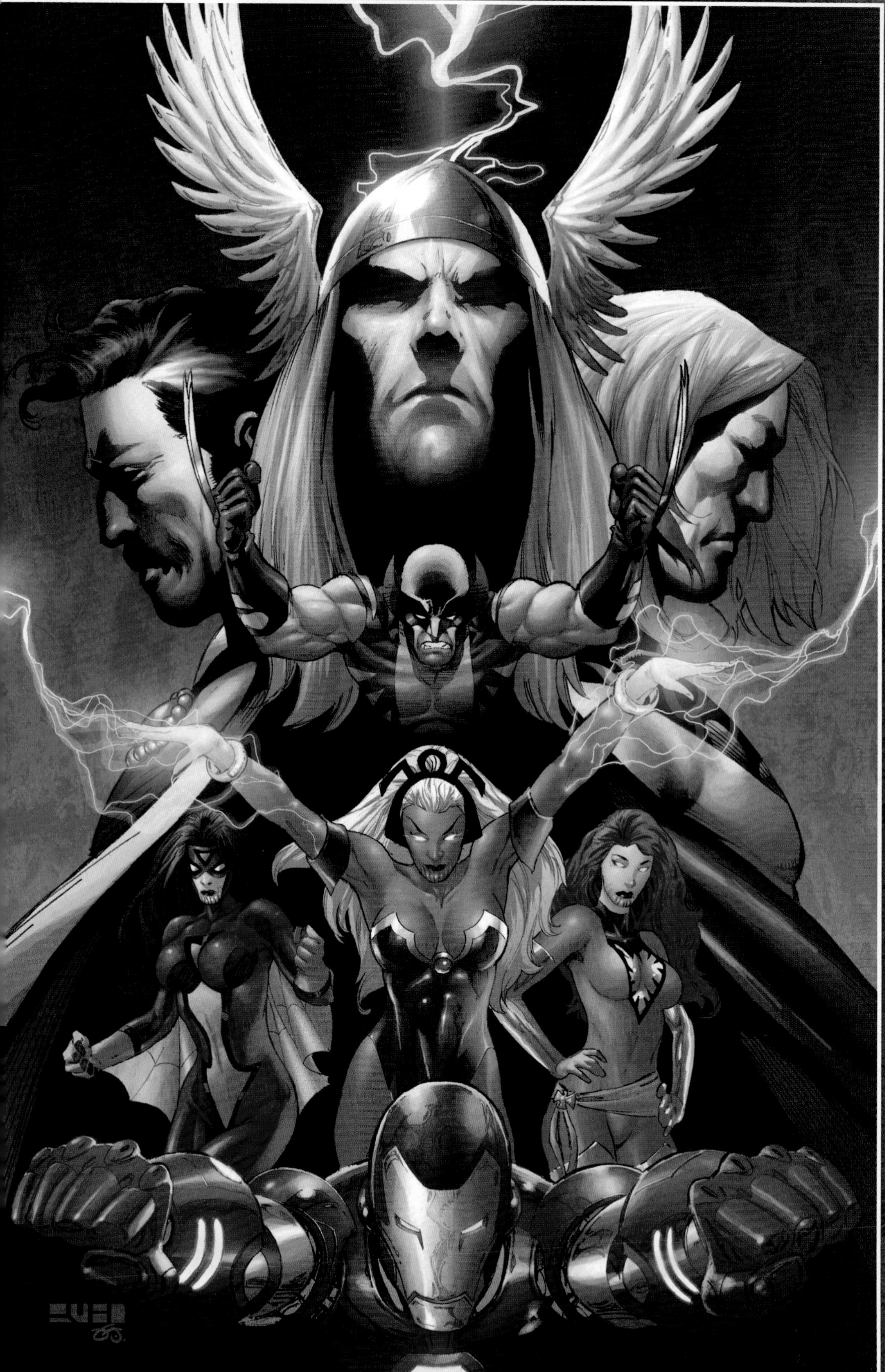

[2 Dynamic Forces Variant Cover by Mel Rubi]

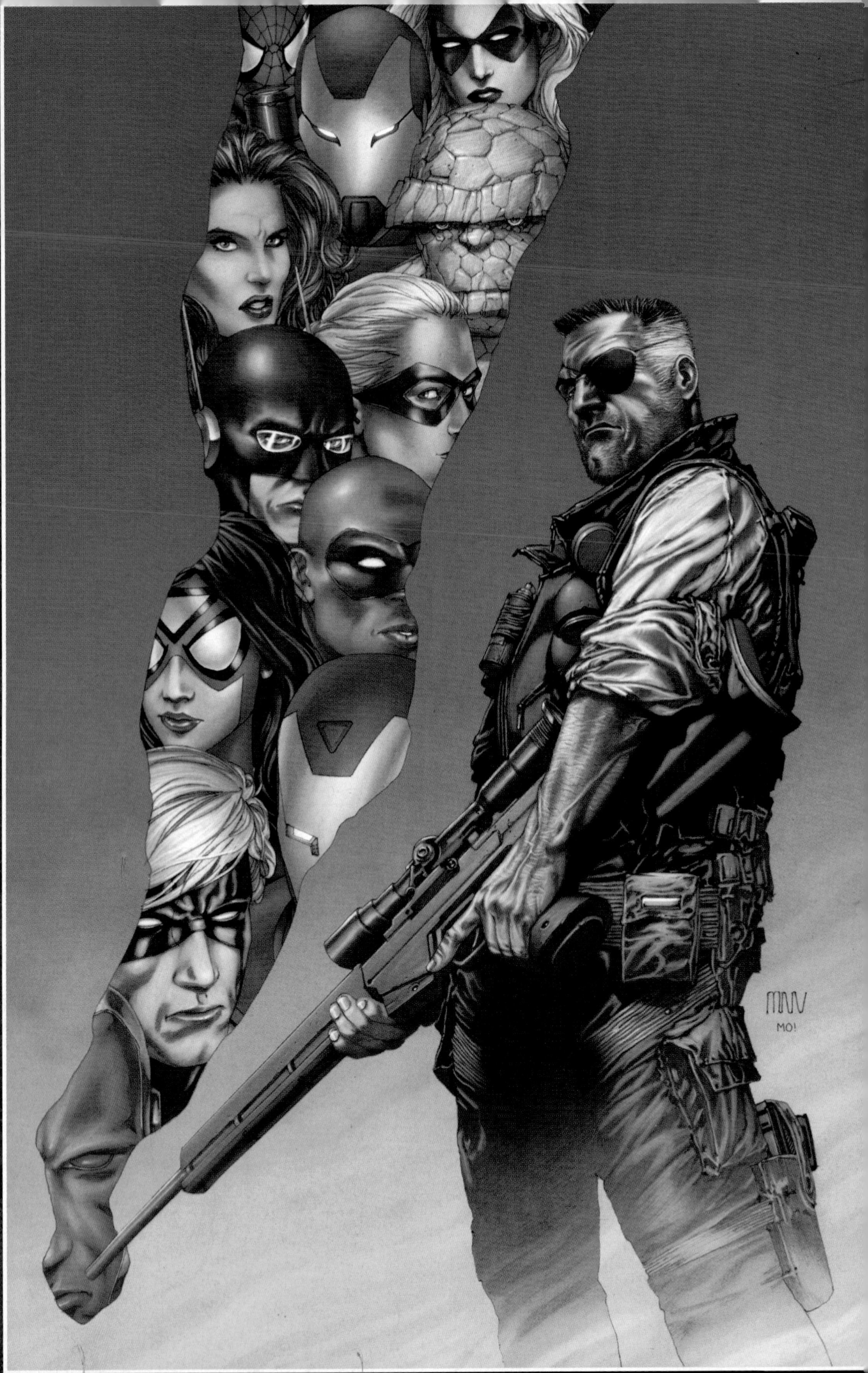
MNV
MO!

[3 Variant Cover by Steve McNiven]

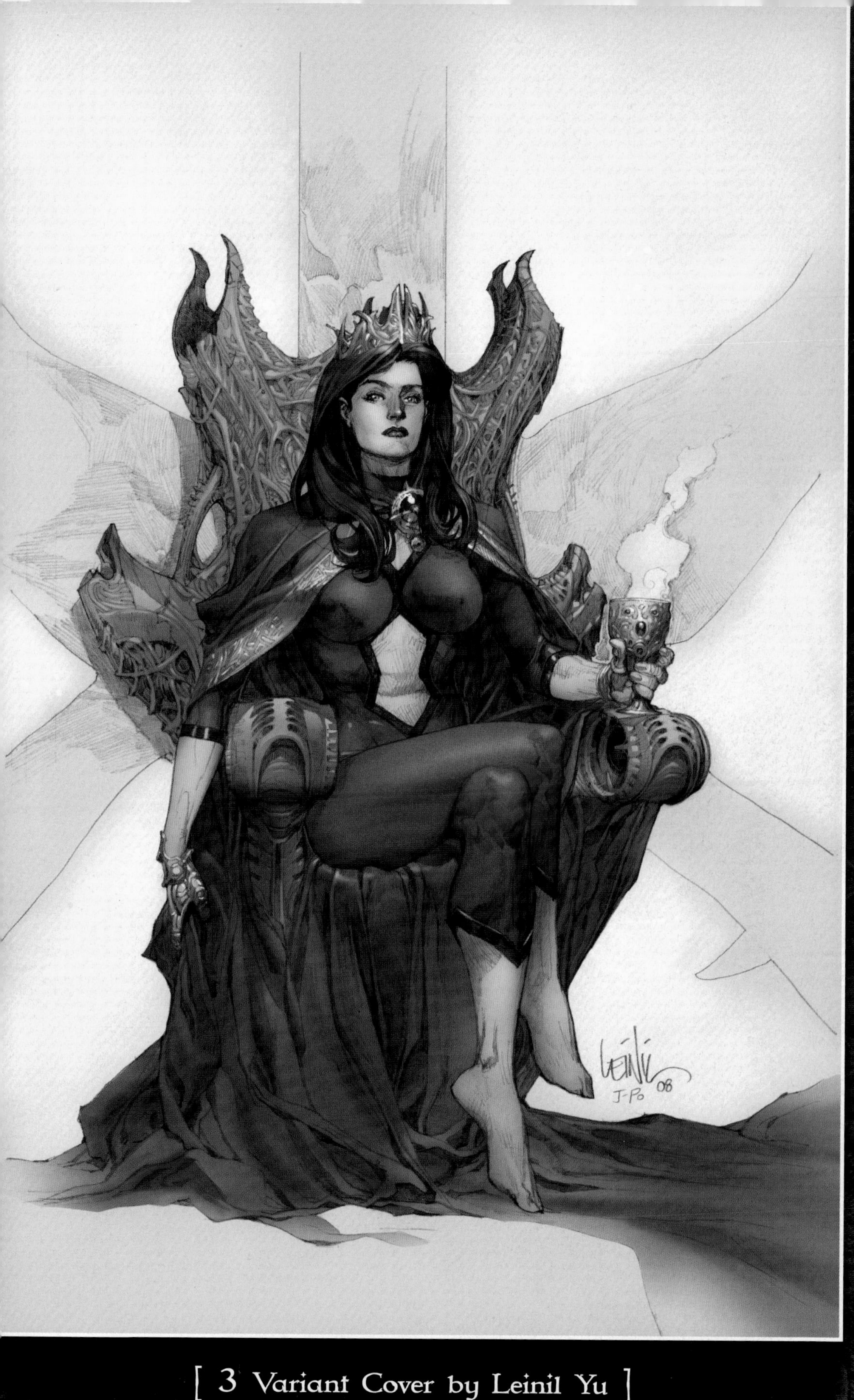
Leinil
J-Po 08

[3 Variant Cover by Leinil Yu]

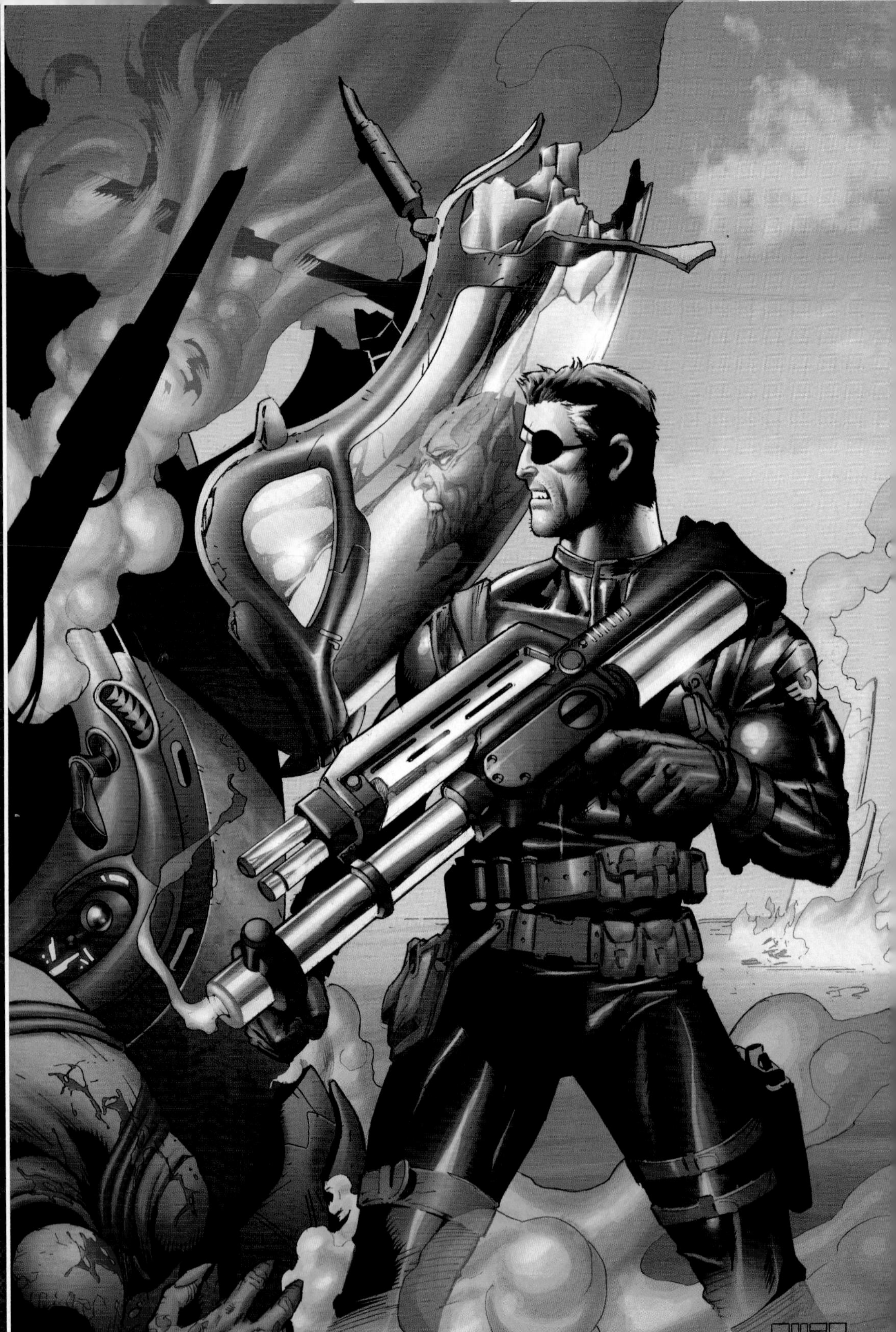

[3 Dynamic Forces Variant Cover by Mel Rubi]

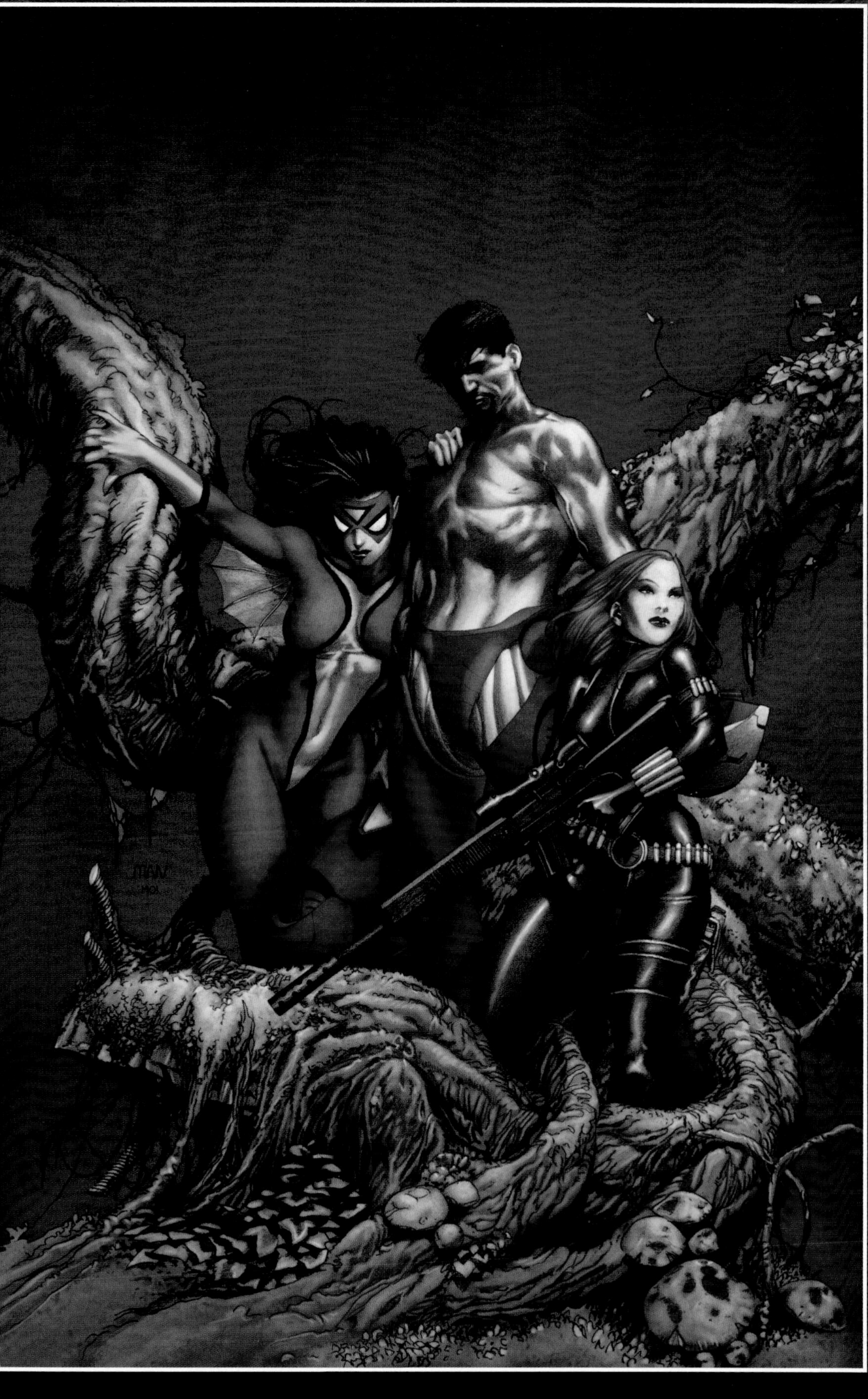

[4 Variant Cover by Steve McNiven]

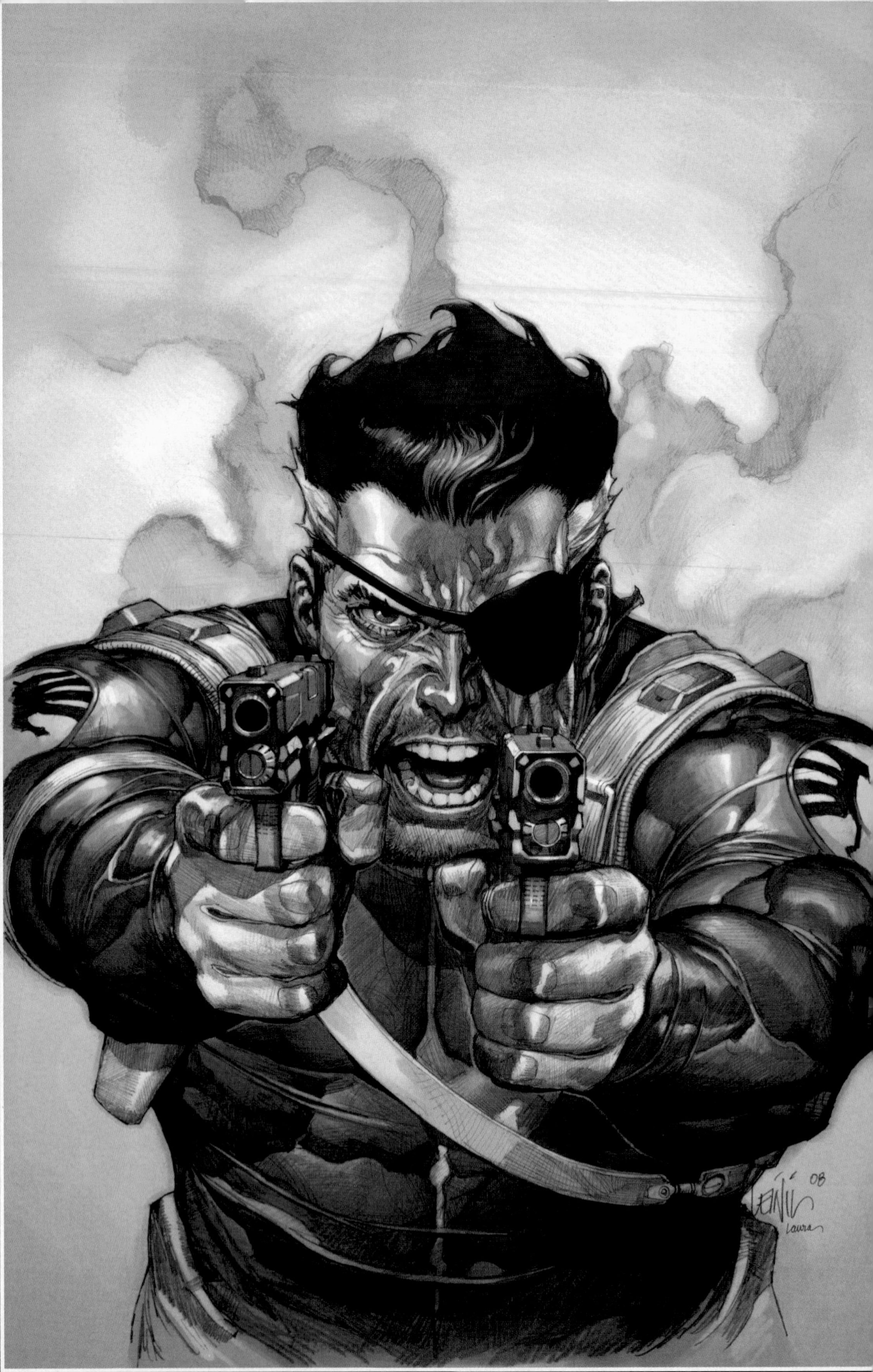

[4 Variant Cover by Leinil Yu]

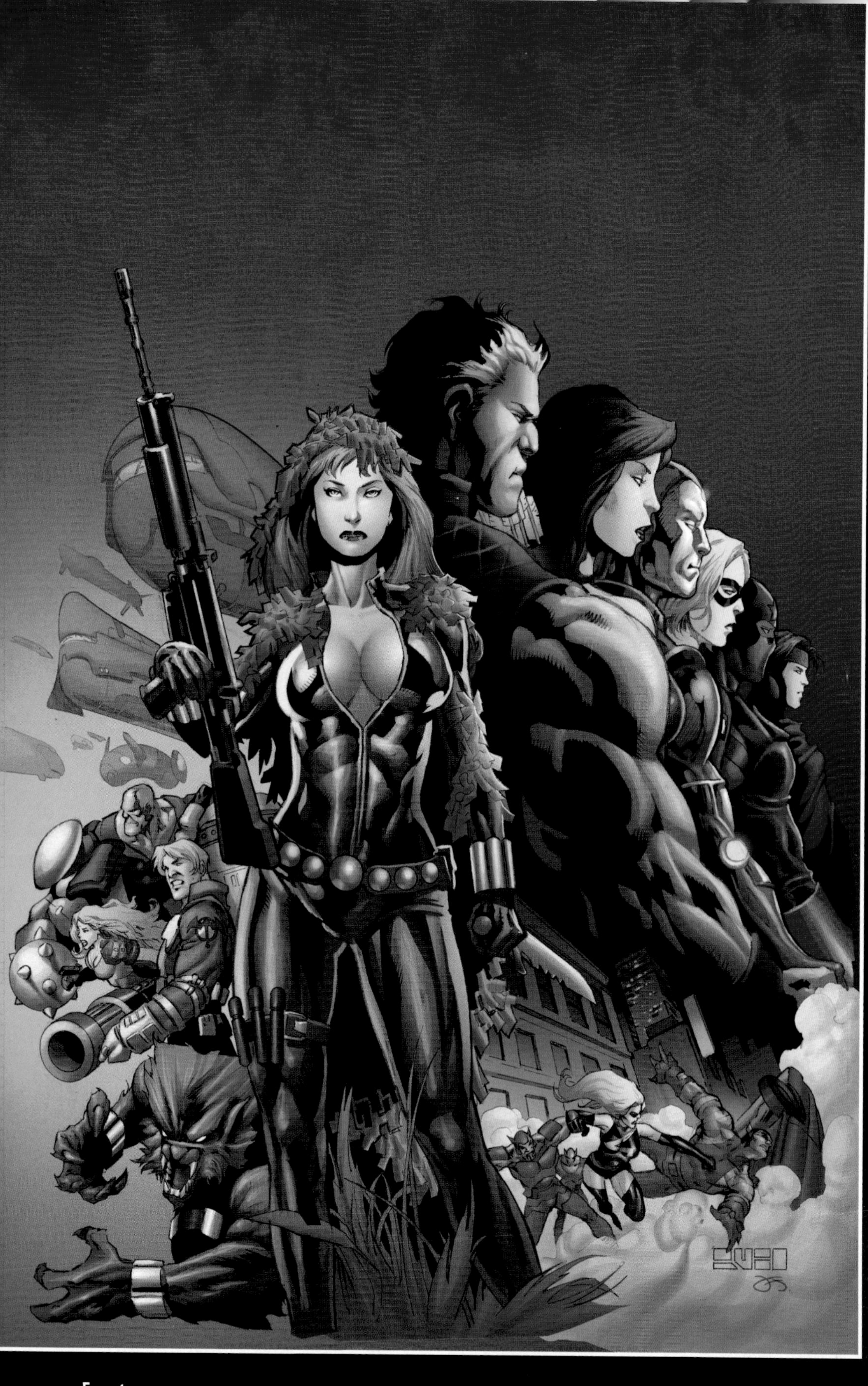

[4 Dynamic Forces Variant Cover by Mel Rubi]

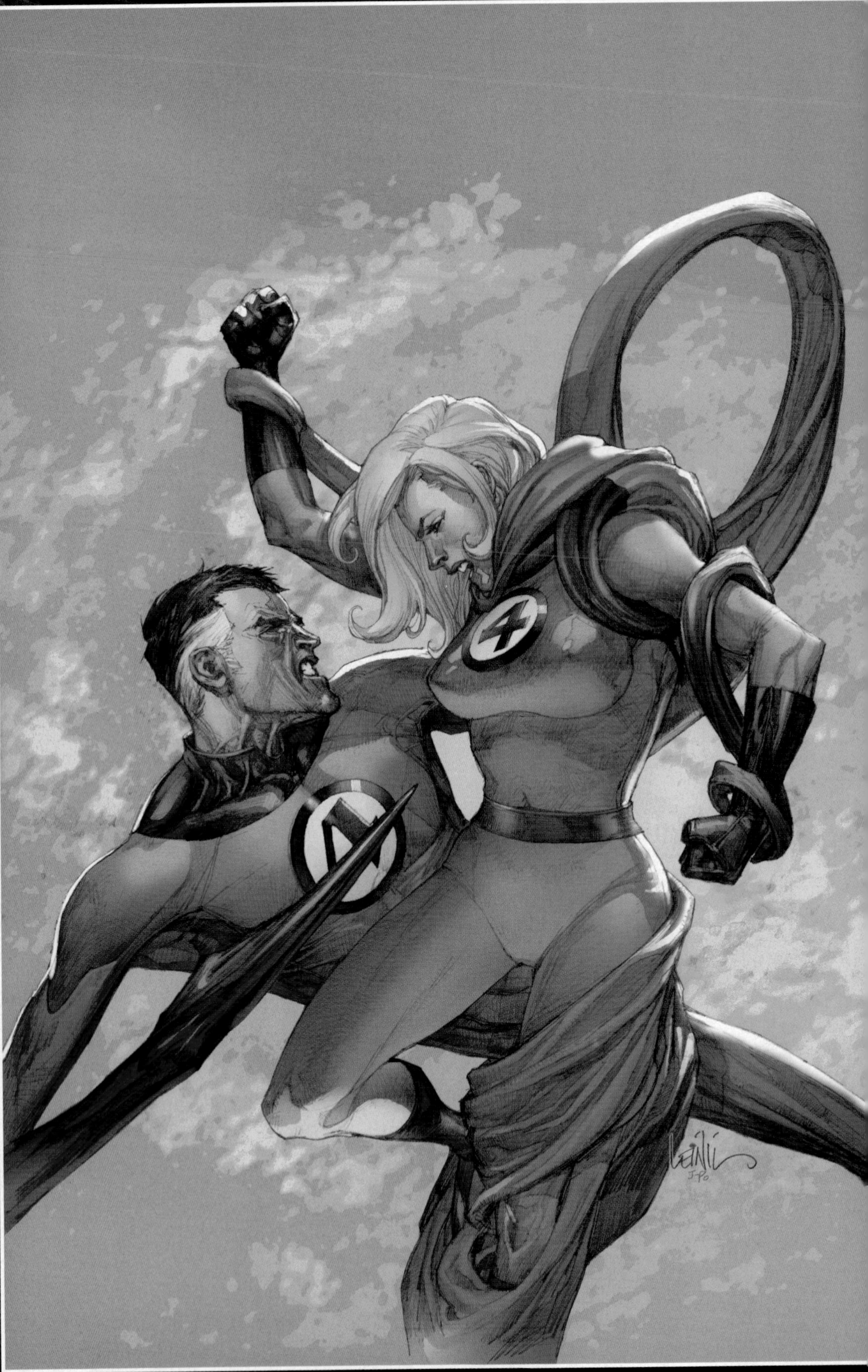

[5 Variant Cover by Leinil Yu]

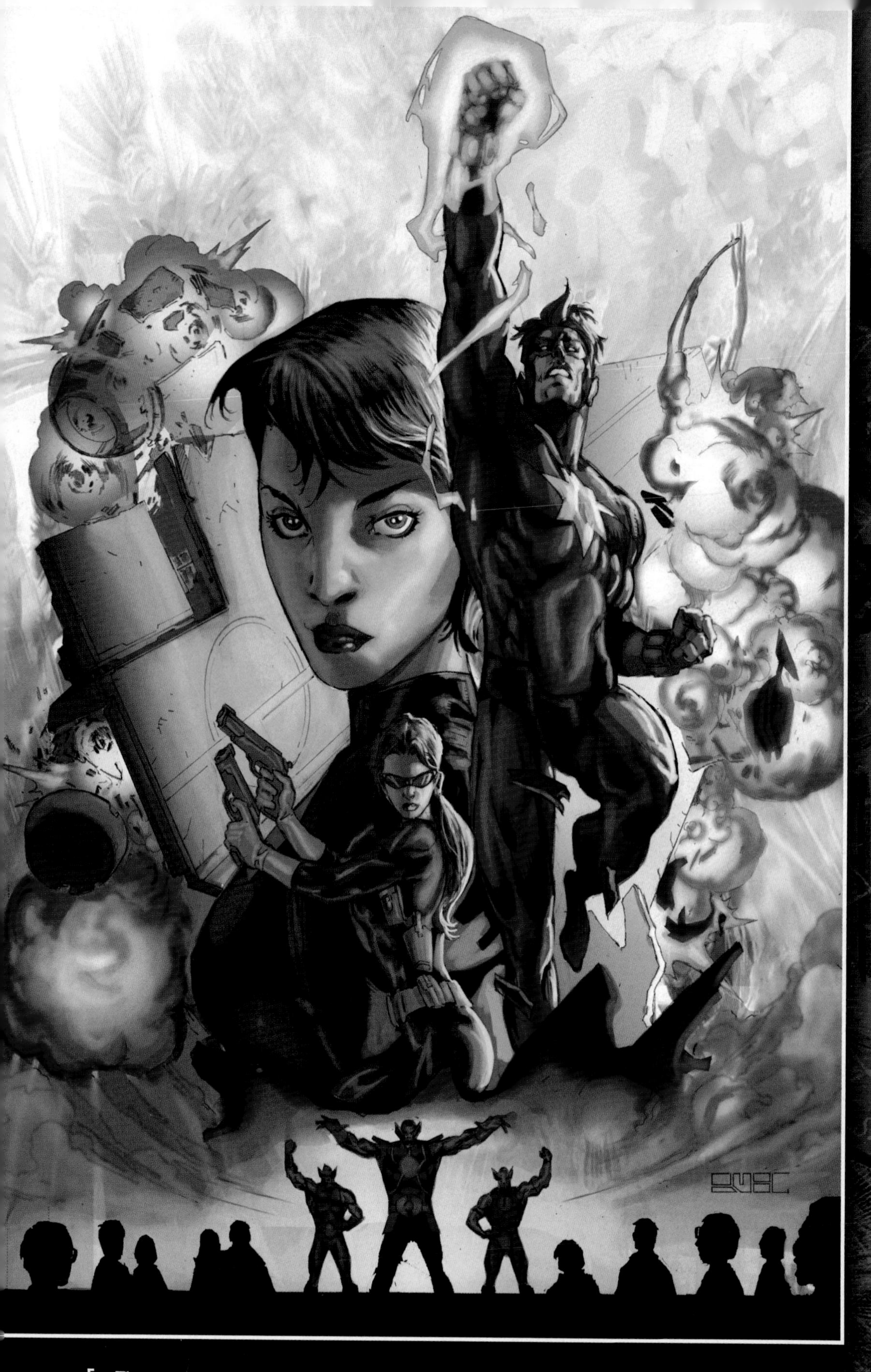

[5 Dynamic Forces Variant Cover by Mel Rubi]

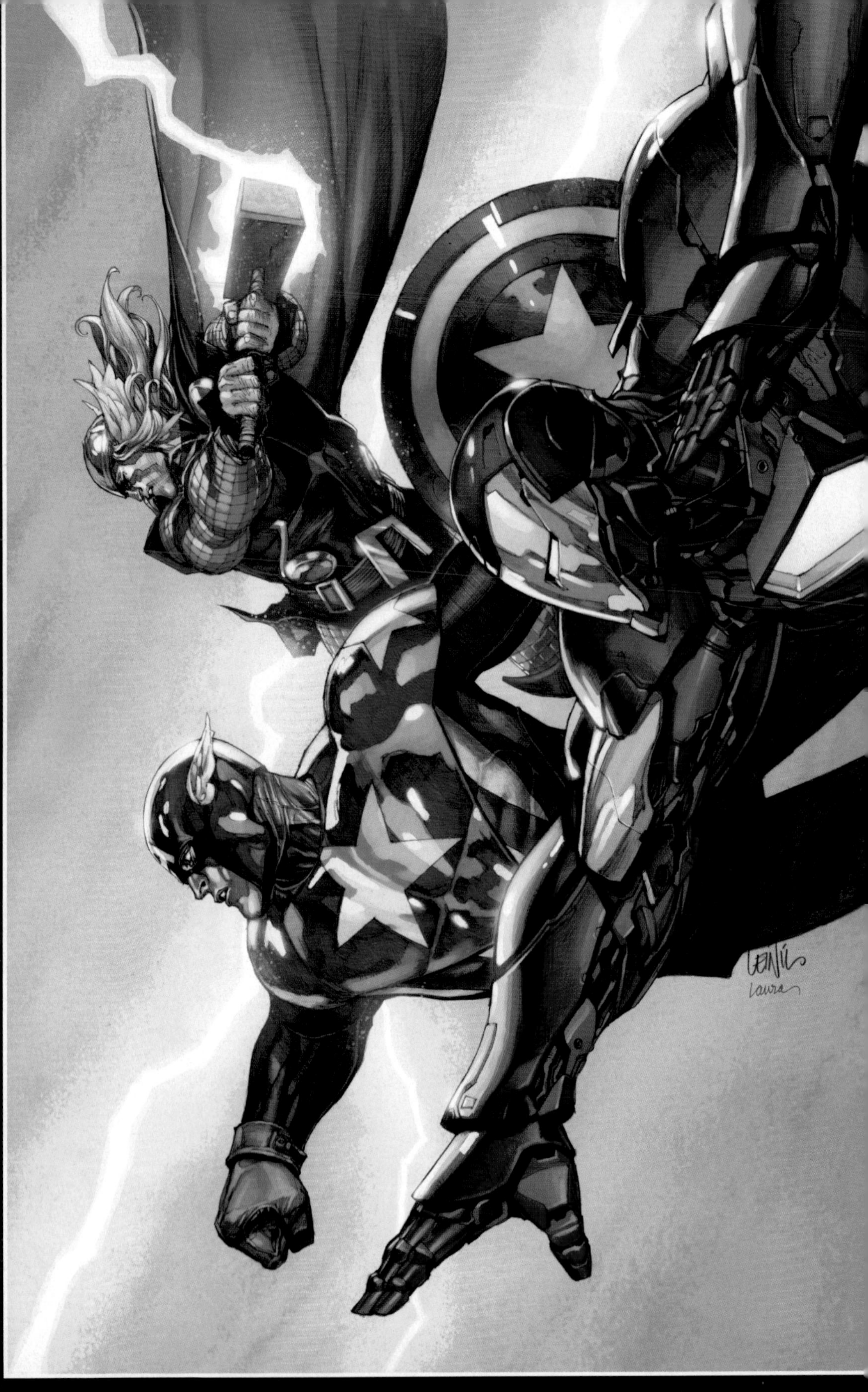

[6 Variant Cover by Leinil Yu]

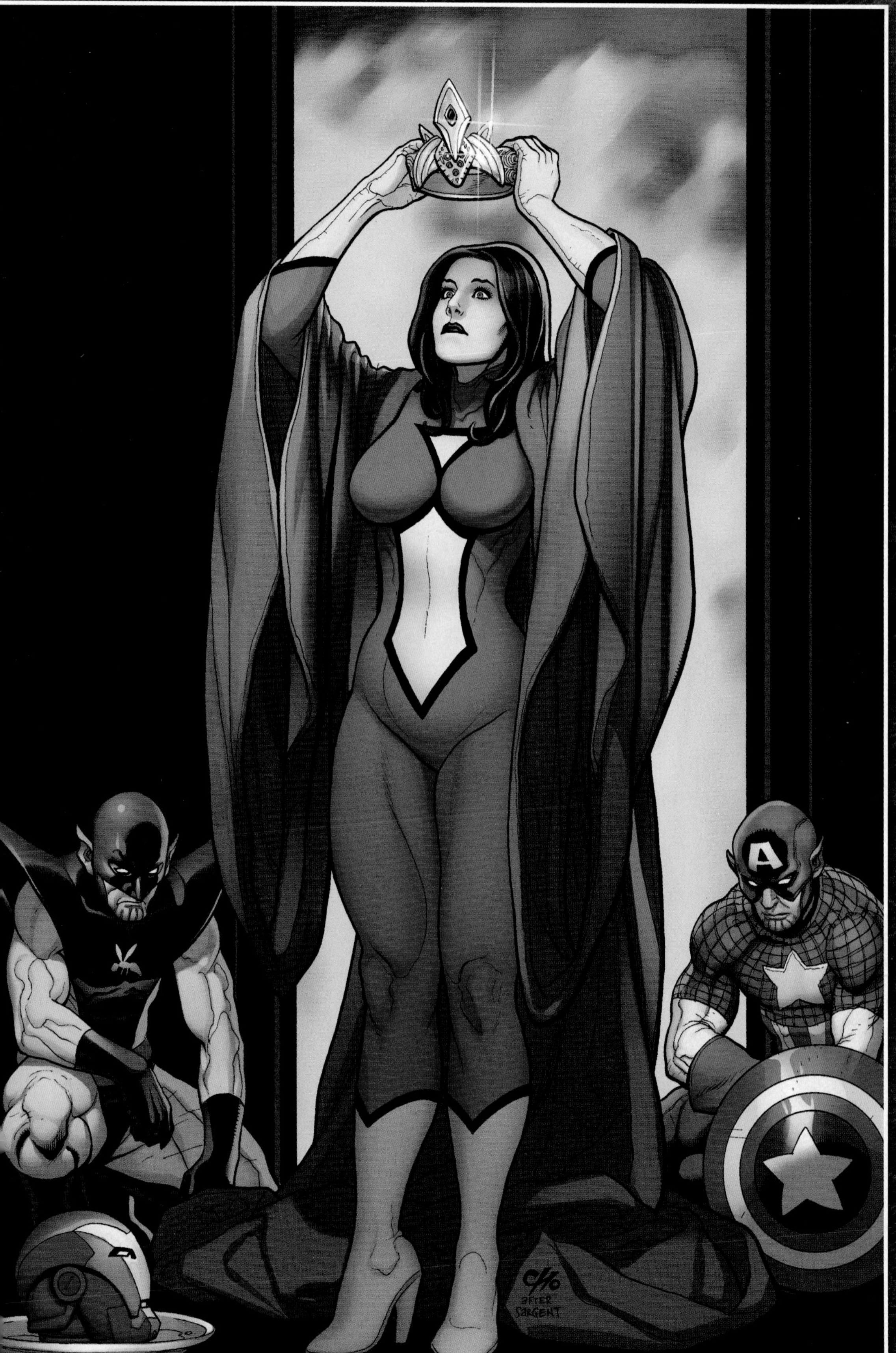
CHO
after
Sargent

[6 Variant Cover by Frank Cho]

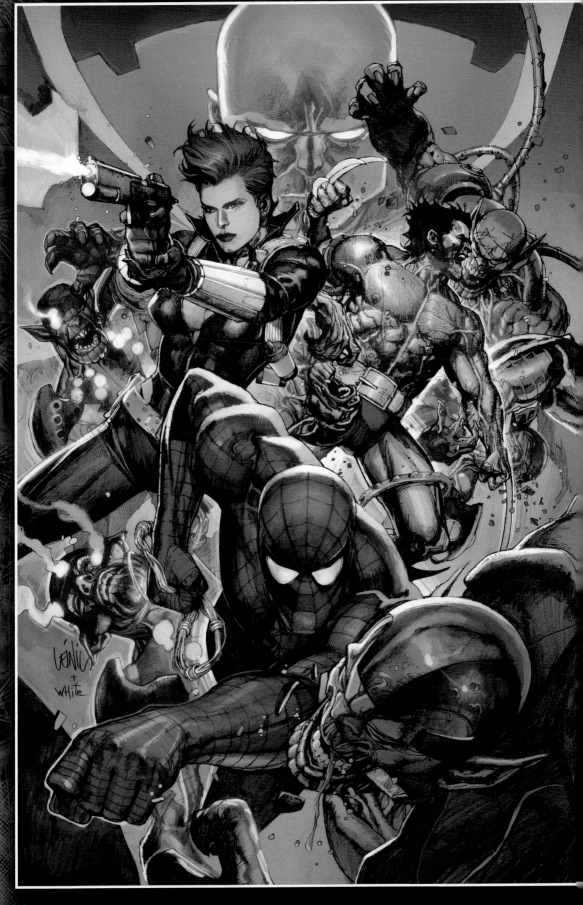

[7 Variant Cover by Leinil Yu]

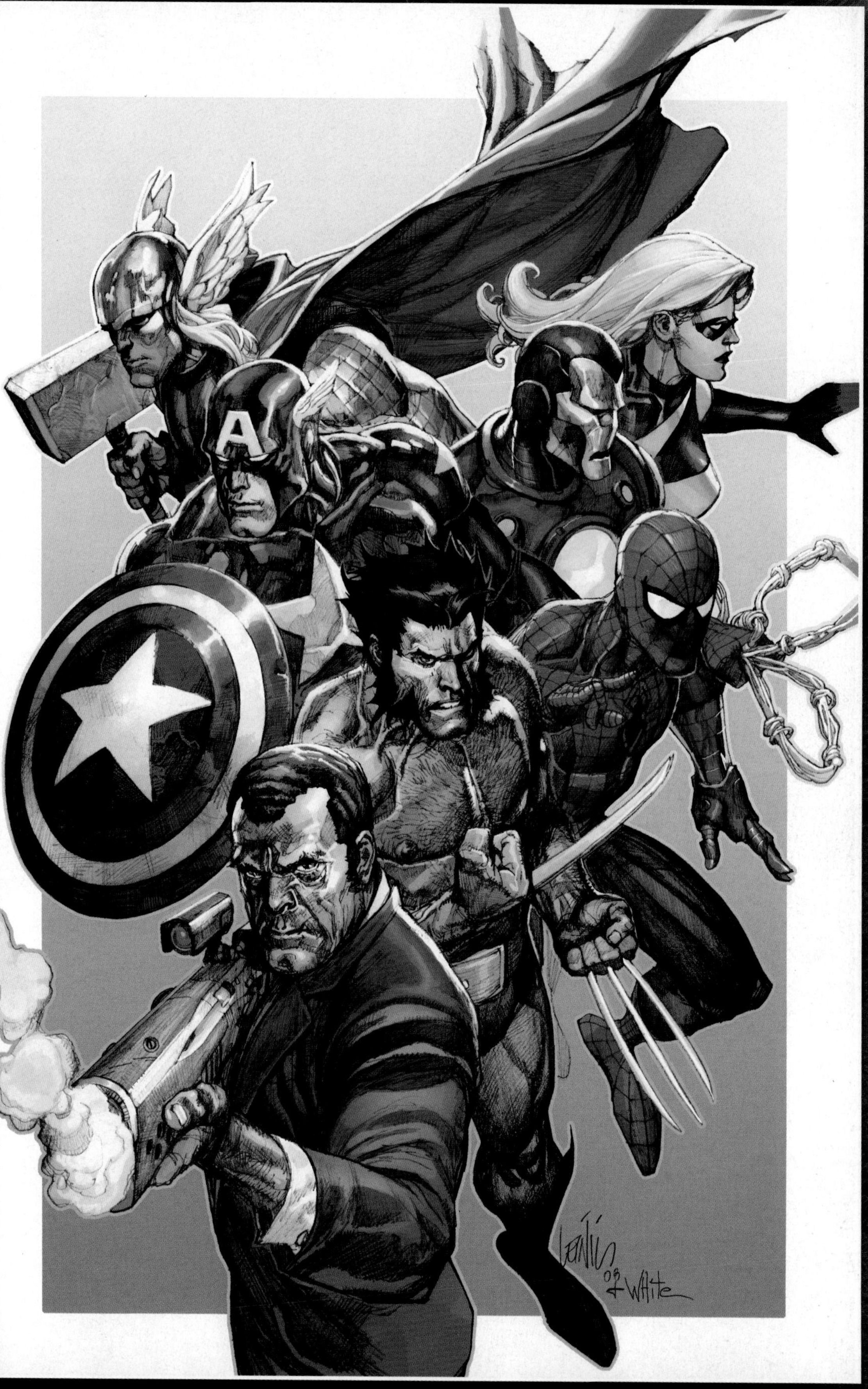

[8 Variant Cover by Leinil Yu]

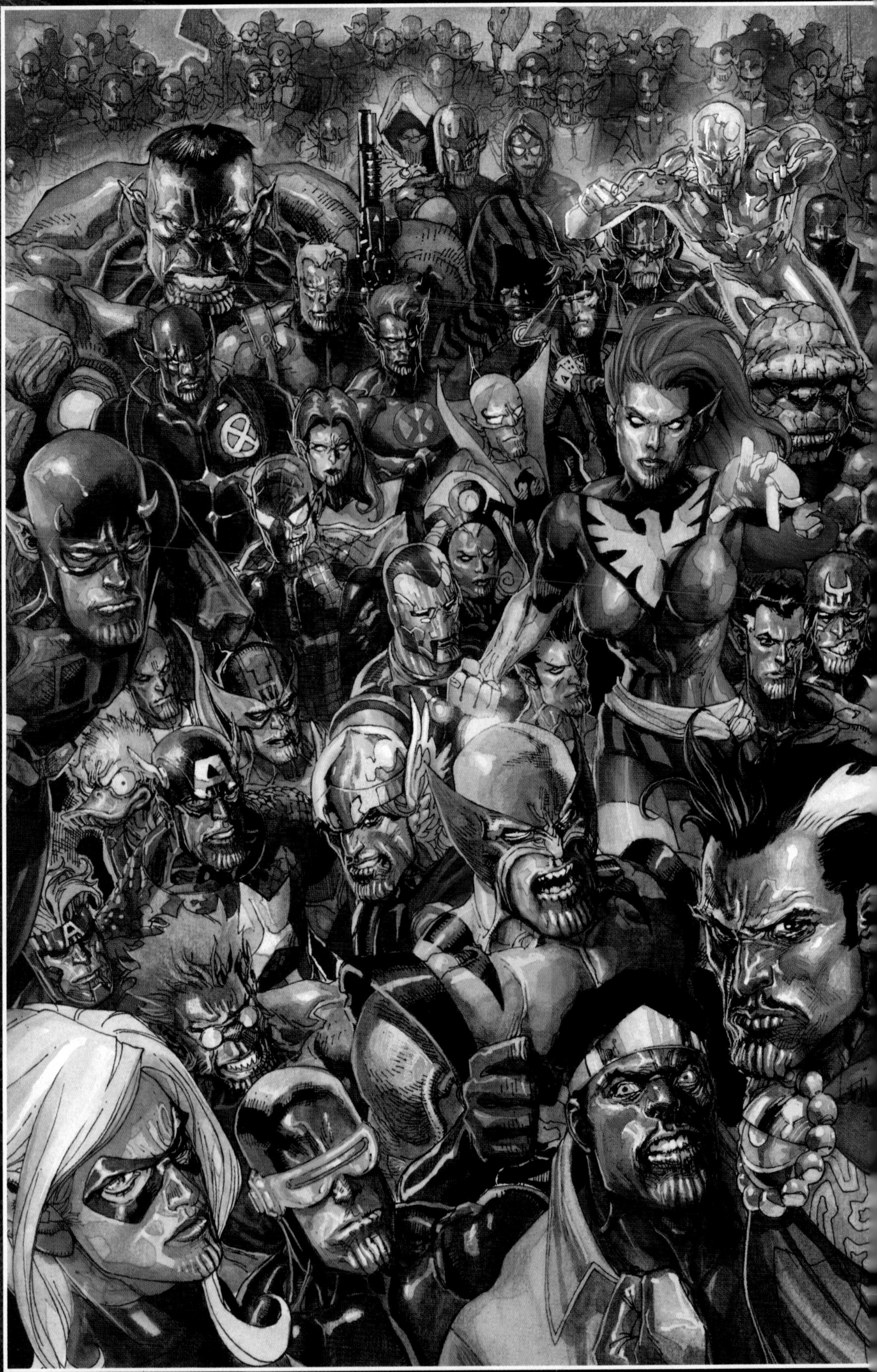

[Promotional Artwork by Leinil Yu]

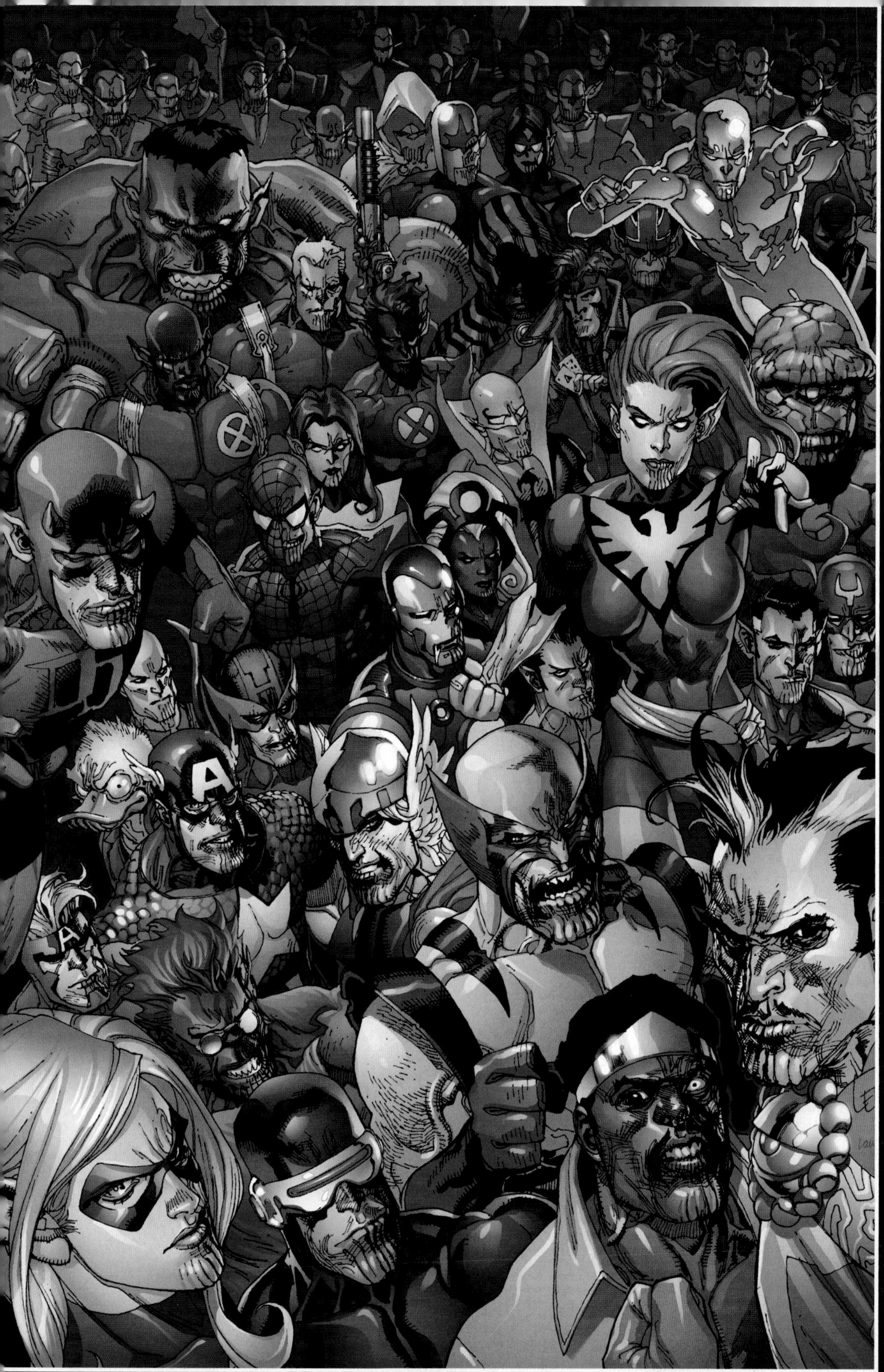

[Promotional Artwork with Colors by Laura Martin]

WHO DO YOU TRUST?

Promotional Images By
Greg Horn

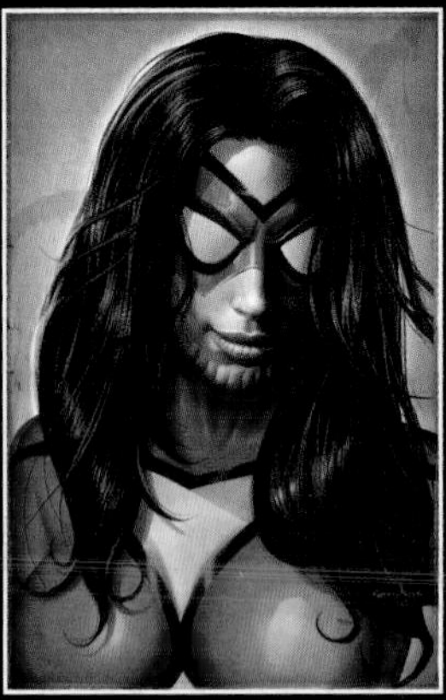
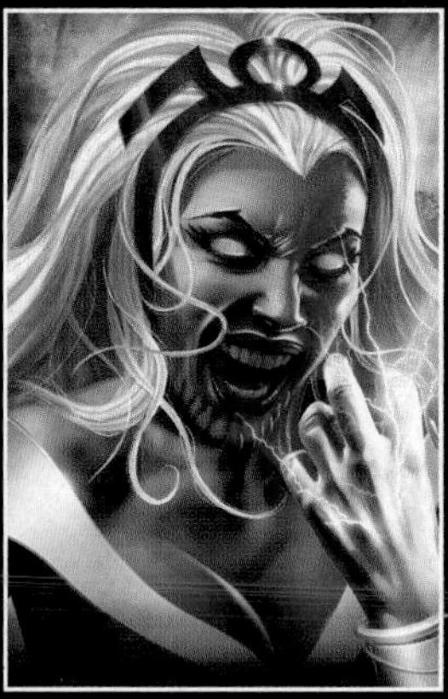
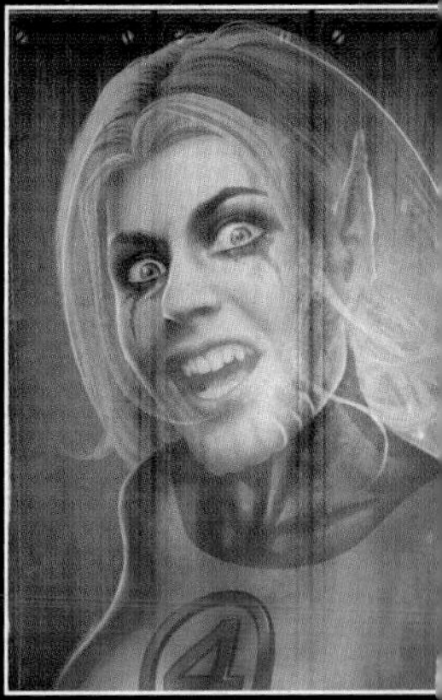
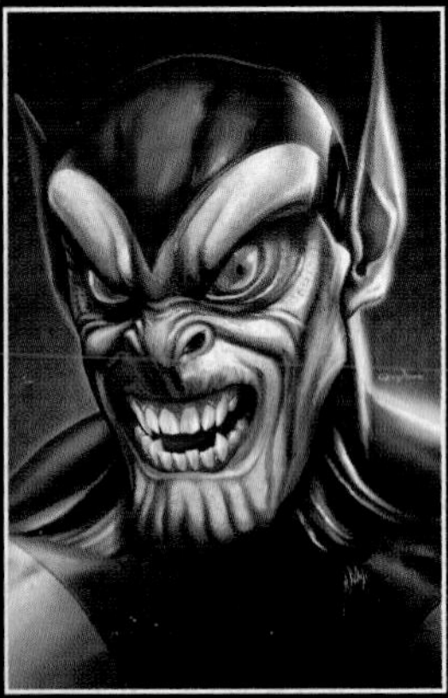
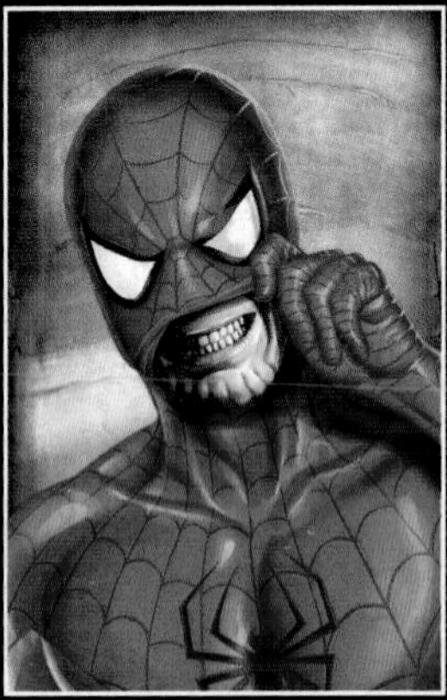
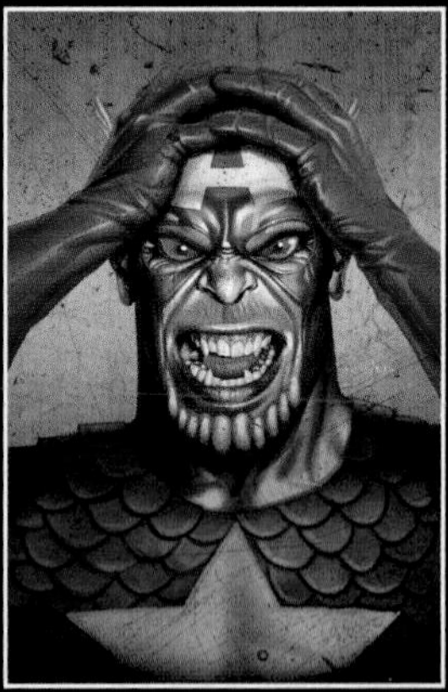
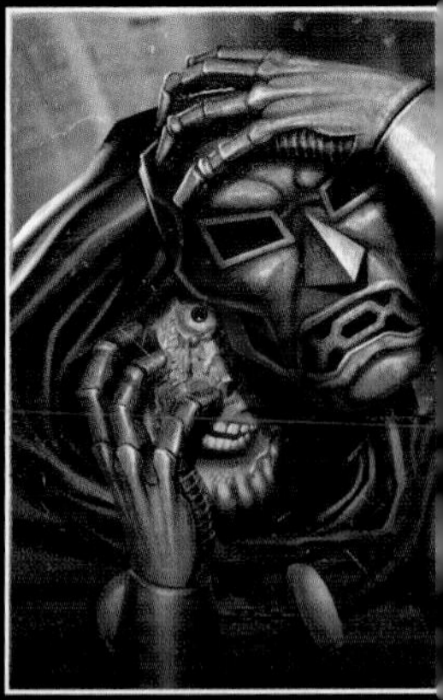
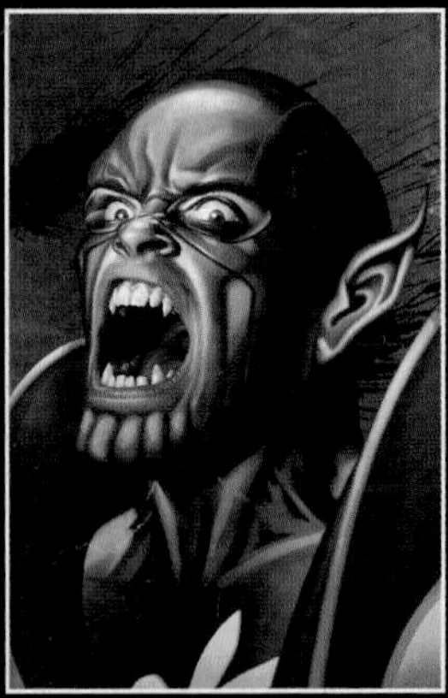
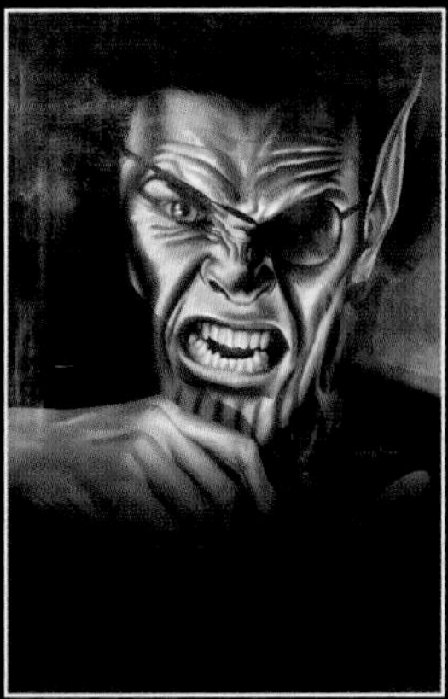
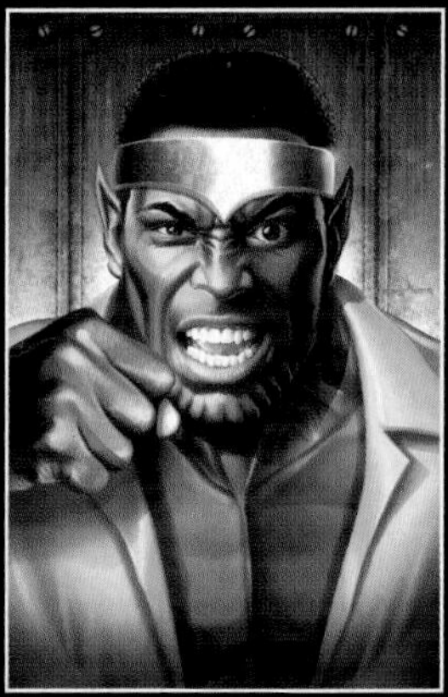
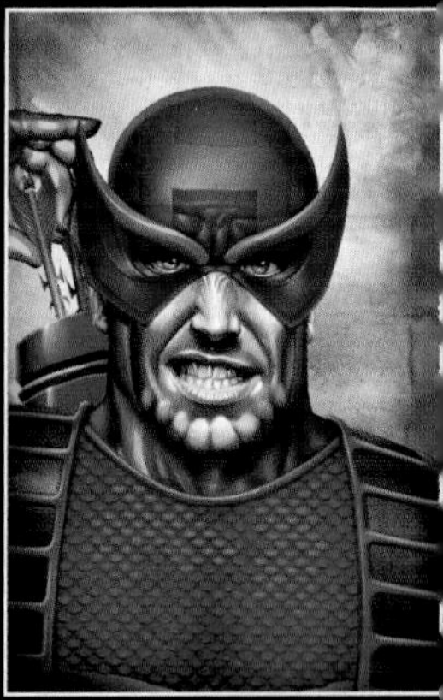
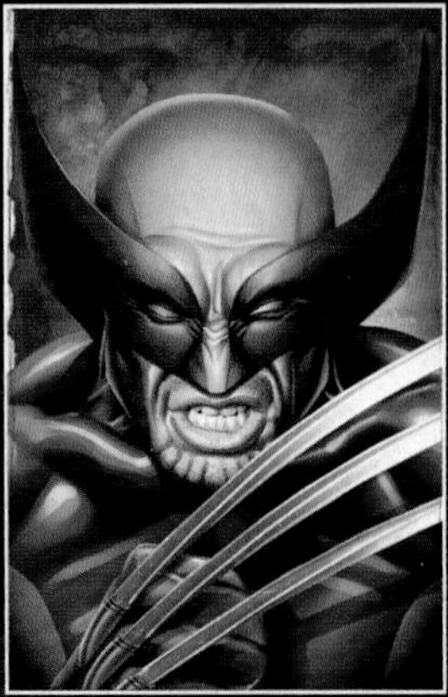
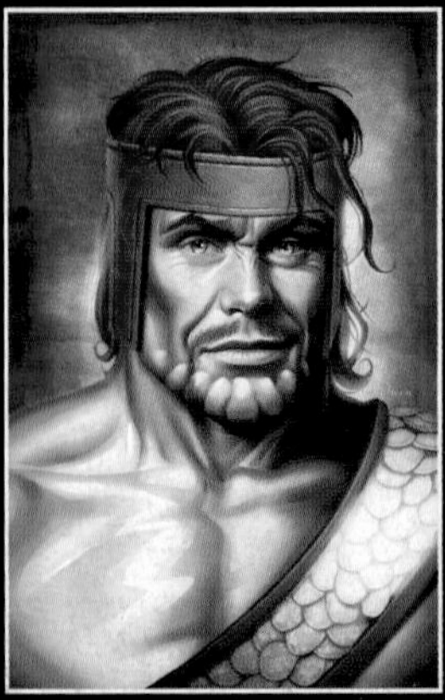
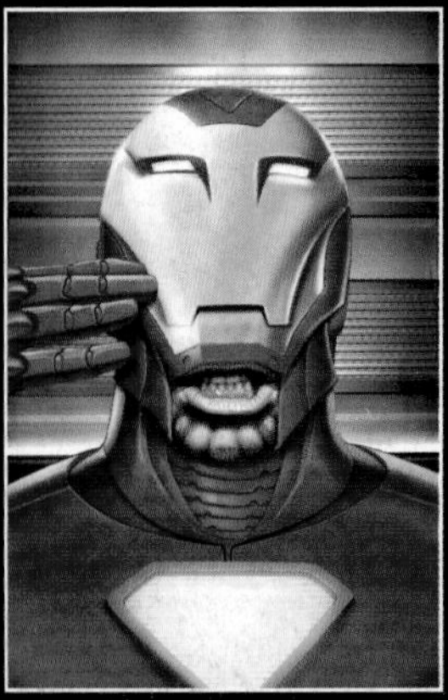
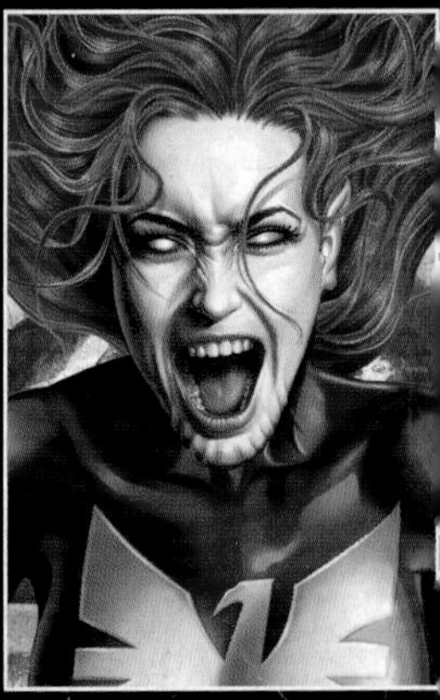

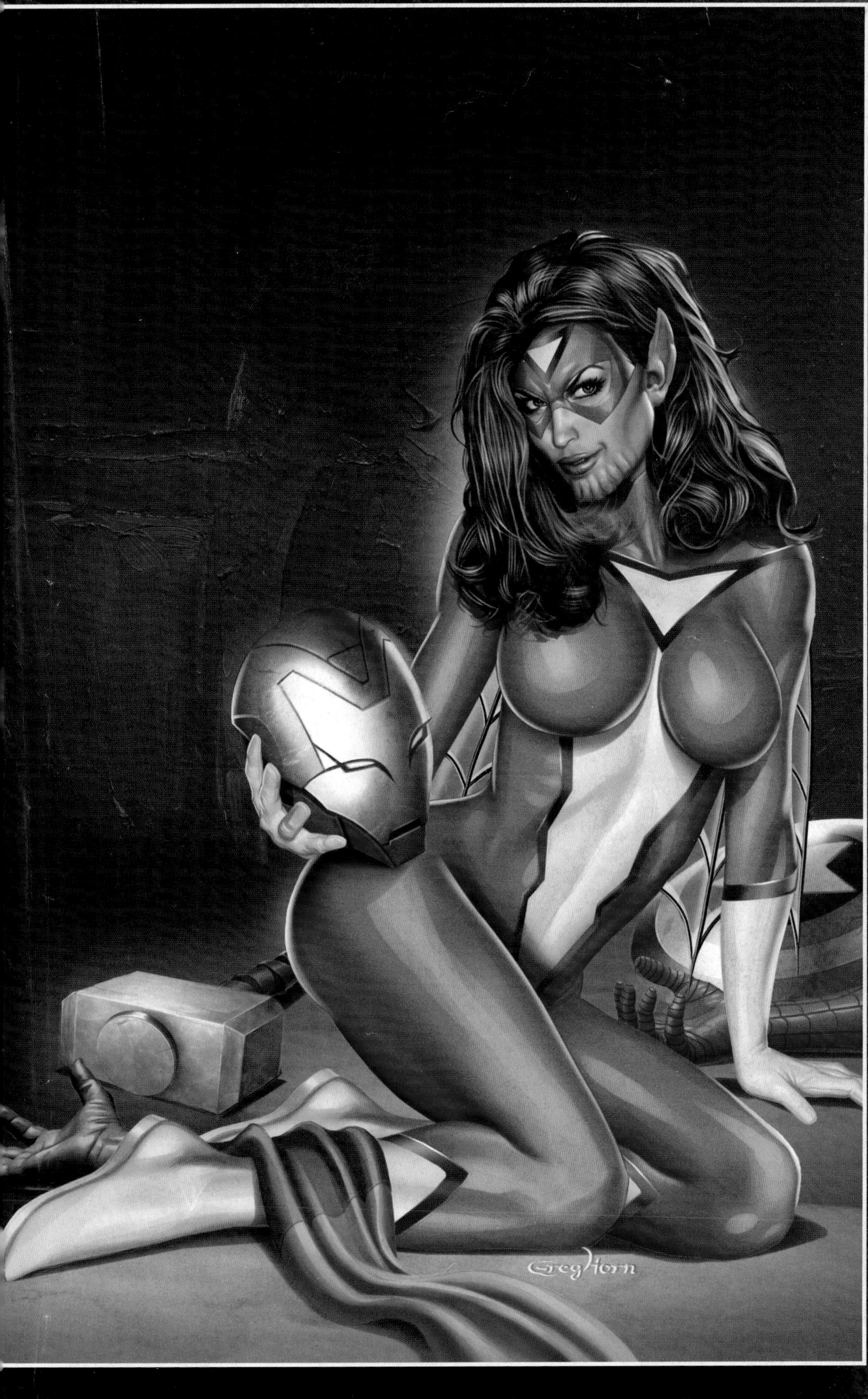
Greg Horn

[Wizard #206 Cover by Greg Horn]

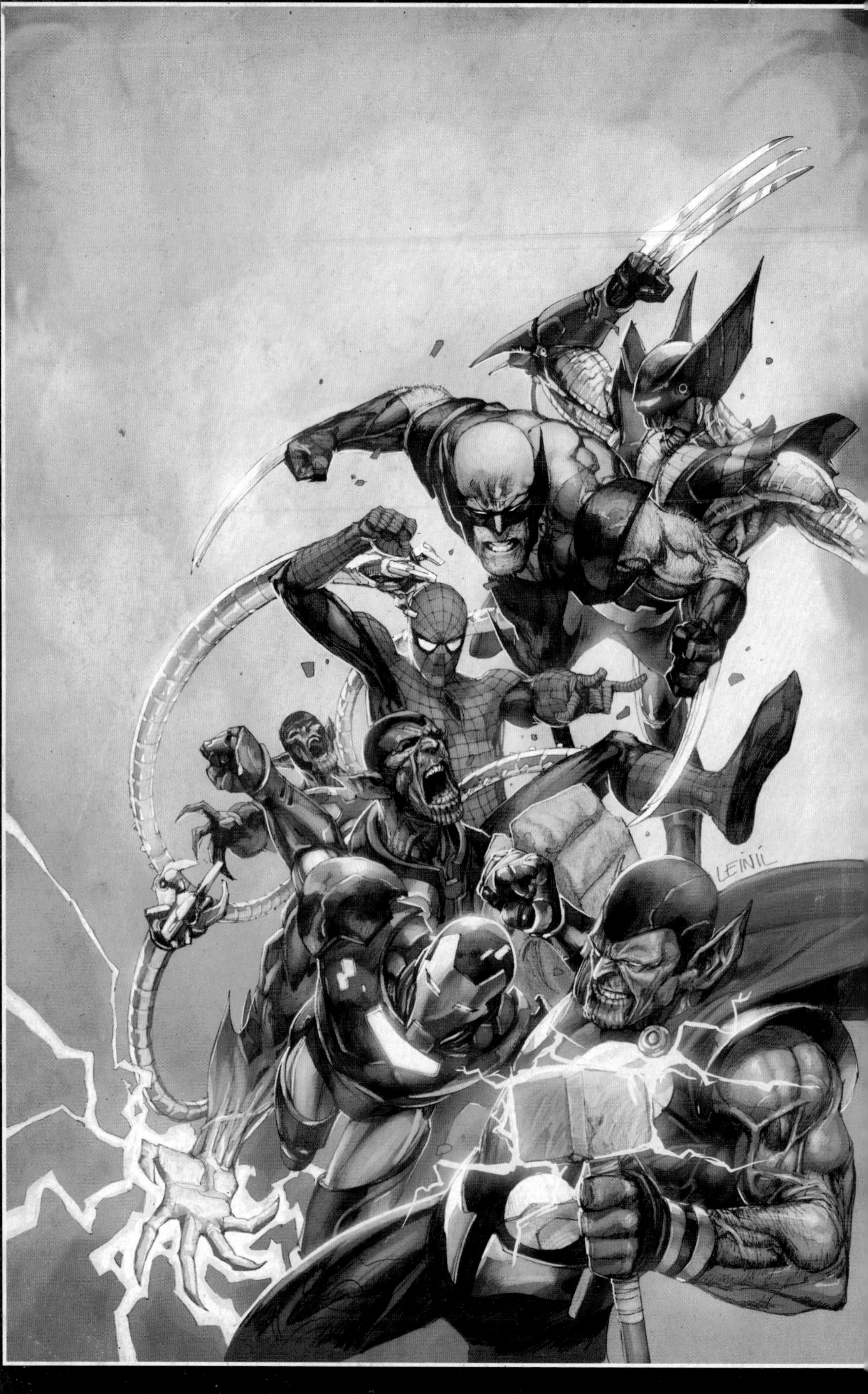
LEINIL

[Comic Buyer's Guide #1642 Cover By Leinil Yu]